S/ASHED DREAMS PART 2

The Nightmare Continues!

RONNIE ANGEL

SLASHED DREAMS PART 2: THE NIGHTMARE CONTINUES
By Ronnie Angel

All text Copyright © 2017 by Ronnie Angel

First published April 2017.

Edited and Published by Ronnie Angel.
Co-edited by Cyrus Wraith Walker
Layout and design by Cyrus Wraith Walker,
Cyrusfiction Productions.

All images are either from the author and/or editor's personal collection unless otherwise noted in the book, or allowed under fair use in reference to the text within the book.

https://www.facebook.com/Slasheddreamsbook

First paperback edition.

ISBN-13: 978-1546401292
ISBN-10: 1546401296

Discoveries Books
C/o Tyler O'Reilly
P.O. box 1512
Marysville, WA 98270

TABLE OF CONTENTS

THANK YOU

There are so many people out there that I want to thank for making my first book a success. The response has been so positive that it's what made this second book possible. First off, I want to thank all of the fans out there who have enjoyed *Slashed Dreams* and for all of the positive feedback. If it weren't for you, I wouldn't be writing this book. To my beautiful fiancé Lucretia, I thank you for all the support through the process and for believing in me. To my friends and family, thank you for always being there for me, especially to my mother Debbie, for getting me first hooked on the horror genre. For James Beach, the man who made my first book possible, an extra big thank you for believing in me and having faith in what I was trying to accomplish. To Cyrus Wraith Walker, the man who made the beautiful designs for both books and made them what they are. To my fellow horror nerds Dan and Hayley Knighten of *The Horror Addicts*, for always being the best friends. To Charity Becker, thank you for all the guidance in the writing process. To Don Sumner and the *Best Horror Movies* staff, for giving me my start in the world of genre writing, where I found my niche. To the folks of Crypticon Seattle for giving me an outlet and a platform to make a name for myself and a place for my voice to be heard. To the good folks at *Scarecrow Video* in Seattle for being so supportive and for giving me more great ideas, every time I thought I had run out of them. Thanks especially to all the wonderful people that lent their time to me for the interviews in these books. Their insights were truly appreciated and I had great experiences with each and every one. Anyone that I missed, just know that you are all special to me. This goes out to all of you. A big thank you to you all. Stay Slashy, my friends!

—*Ronnie Angel*

LISTS-A-PLENTY!

(Author's note: Please note that some of these films would have been and should be ranked much higher on the list, had they been included in the first book.)

MORE OF THE TOP SLASHER FILMS (51~100)

1. Friday the 13th Part 6: Jason Lives (1986)
2. Scream (1996)
3. Identity (2003)
4. SAW (2004)
5. Blood Rage (1987)
6. American Psycho (2000)
7. Hot Fuzz (2006)
8. Inside (2007)
9. Friday the 13th Part 3 (1982)
10. The Texas Chainsaw Massacre Part 2 (1986)
11. Harpoon (2009)
12. May (2002)
13. A Nightmare on Elm Street 3: The Dream Warriors (1987)
14. The Hills Have Eyes (1977)
15. You're Next (2011)
16. Tenebre (1983)
17. Chopping Mall (1986)
18. Who Could Kill a Child? (1976)
19. Sleepaway Camp II (1988)
20. The Final Girls (2015)
21. April Fool's Day (1986)
22. Night School (1981)
23. The Strangers (2008)
24. Cut (2000)
25. The Final Terror (1984)
26. Intruder (1989)
27. Crawlspace (1986)
28. Child's Play 2 (1990)
29. Freddy vs. Jason (2003)
30. Devil Times Five (1974)
31. Opera (1987)

32. Cherry Falls (2000)
33. Wes Craven's New Nightmare (1994)
34. Bad Dreams (1988)
35. Cold Prey (2006)
36. Pieces (1982)
37. Evil Dead Trap (1988)
38. Edge of the Axe (1988)
39. Wrong Turn (2003)
40. Bloody Birthday (1981)
41. Maniac (1980)
42. Madman (1982)
43. The Devil's Rejects (2005)
44. Dr. Giggles (1992)
45. Popcorn (1991)
46. Night Warning (1982)
47. Saint (2010)
48. Death Valley (1982)
49. Amsterdamned (1988)
50. Scarecrows (1988)

TOP TEN SLASHERS IN NON-SLASHER FILMS

1. DR. DECKER -*NIGHTBREED* (1990)

There's a good reason why the good doctor tops this list. In the wide world of slashers, Dr. Decker easily stands tall with the legends as one of the more terrifying. From his creepy lifeless mask with those button eyes and zipper mouth, to his complete disregard for human life, Decker is one scary man. His mask is by far one of the creepiest in movie history and his manipulative character (he frames our hero for his series of sadistic family massacres) just seems to relish in absolute chaos, as seen in the fiery finale. No one is safe from Dr. Decker, be they human or mutant! Plus, he is played by genre legend David Cronenberg! That alone makes this character worthy of the number one spot!

2. THE GOD'S HAND KILLER- *FRAILTY* (2000)

A good friend of mine always used to joke that he could see my dad going bonkers and ending up like Bill Paxton's father character in this movie. *Frailty,* a movie that Paxton also directed, serves as one of the darkest movies I have ever seen. It's one of those psychological movies that is just uncomfortable at times and always leaves a lasting impression on the viewer. Much like The Blues Brothers, Paxton here is on a mission from God. Unlike Jake and Elwood however, Bill makes it his mission to kidnap and slaughter several unsuspecting victims that he believes to be demons, with the help of his two young (and unwilling) sons. Poor kids. It's no wonder they ended up so screwed up later.

3. ADELINA POERIO- *DON'T LOOK NOW* (1973)

Who ever imagined that a midget could be as scary as the one in *Don't Look Now*? As a matter of fact, whoever in their right mind would have imagined that this was the identity of the mysterious killer slashing up the women of Venice and dumping their bodies in the canals? Mind boggling physics aside, the effect was quite the unnerving experience and one of the greatest horror reveals of all time.

4. THE NIGHT SLASHER- *COBRA (1986)*

When it comes down to straight up slashers in non-slasher films, Brian Thompson in *Cobra* is pretty much the poster boy. He and his gang of axe wielding, pantyhose mask wearing psychopaths not only make great, unforgettable villains to oppose our hero Sylvester Stallone, but they also turn out to be some of the creepiest as well. These guys are truly something that nightmares are made of and the type of thing that will make you look over your shoulder the next time you're in that darkened parking garage that's a little too quiet.

5. JOHN DOE- *SEVEN* (1995)

Kevin Spacey is a great actor, in fact one of the all-time greats, but he is still a creepy guy.

Never is this more evident than in the classic thriller *Seven*. Spacey kills his victims as part of his sadistic mission to rid the world of the sinners, using the seven deadly sins as both his motive and the means of dispatch. Some of those means are simply cringe inducing too, such as making an obese man eat himself to death (gluttony), making a lawyer eviscerate himself (greed), and of course the most shocking and disturbing, Sloth. If you don't know what happens there, you're in for one uncomfortable watch! Spacey plays the role with demonic glee and precision and at the end, we get to see not only what his masterpiece was all about, but also what was in that damn box. Yes John, this is something that they will write about and be puzzling over for years to come.

6. PETER SWAN- *THE DEAD POOL* (1988)

No, I'm not talking about the wisecracking superhero here. Instead, I'm talking about one of the most epic films of the entire immortal *Dirty Harry* series. Not only is *The Dead Pool* notable for an early "serious" role from a young Jim Carrey as a heroin addicted Axel Rose type, it also features Liam Neeson as an infamous horror director! Pretty cool, isn't it? Neeson is also the focal point of the investigation surrounding a series of murders based on a dead pool game he plays, focusing on a list of celebrities that end up meeting the reaper. Neeson brings his usual terrifying performance to the movie and it also features several vicious kill scenes. But, there's more to this than meets the eye! A must for slasher fans and *Dirty Harry* fans alike!

7. BOB GOODALL- *SWITCHBACK* (1997)

I must say, Danny Glover can really play a great serial killer! In *Switchback,* Danny joins an all-star cast (Jared Leto, Dennis Quaid, Lee Ermey) as the deadliest drifter (ha! Another movie reference) and someone you would definitely want to avoid a ride from. He drives around in a car adorned with porno pictures and seems like not such a bad guy at first. Why, he even seems downright friendly … that is until he has that knife at your crotch. Yes, his means of dispatch in this movie happens to be an innovative one, severing a victim's femoral artery and letting them bleed out. Ouch! *Switchback* is one of the best forgotten thrillers of the 90s and one that I highly recommend.

8. WARREN STACY- *10 TO MIDNIGHT* (1983)

Here's one I will be going into greater detail on later in the book, but it definitely deserves a mention here. Gene Davis should have won an award for his performance of the psycho-sexual deviant serial killer Warren Stacy in this film. Not only is he a creepy little bastard, but he also holds the distinction of being one of the more unique slashers in film history in that he does he kills naked! That's gotta count for something, right?

9. HENRY MORRISON- *THE STEPFATHER* (1987)

The Stepfather is one of the all-time classic horror films in my book, a suspenseful masterpiece.

Terry O'Quinn delivers the performance of a lifetime here as the title character, a serial killer who has too high of expectations for the perfect family. He drifts from family to family, marrying single mothers and moving in as the stepfather while trying to play up the role to the community as the perfect respectable neighbor. That is, until something sets him off and then he's off on another murderous rampage and then on to the next family under a new identity. A classic.

10. MACHINE- *8MM* (1998)
There's only one thing scarier than a killer like this. Someone who not only gets paid to do it in front of the camera, but someone who also enjoys every minute of it. In 1998's suspenseful and dark *8mm*, Nicholas Cage plays a private investigator hired to find the identity of a girl in what could very well be a snuff film. What he finds is more than he bargained for, as the trail leads back to the psychotic and eccentric porn director Dino Velvet (Peter Stormare), and his leather clad, gimp mask wearing henchman Machine. Machine is one scary individual, seemingly normal behind the mask, but a cold-blooded killer in reality. By far one of the darkest films out there.

TOP FIVE TV SLASHERS

1. SANTA- *TALES FROM THE CRYPT* EPISODE *ALL THROUGH THE HOUSE* (1989)
The late great Larry Drake put on the performance of a lifetime in one of the defining moments of one of the single greatest TV horror shows of all time and left a true legacy with this role. He doesn't have a name, but you'll never forget his face, as Drake plays the creepy killer Santa stalking Mary Ellen Trainor on a snowy Christmas Eve. It's a minimalist horror story that doesn't need much, other than the two main stars' epic performances to get the point across and it earns its spot at the top of the list.

2. TWISTY THE CLOWN- *AMERICAN HORROR STORY: FREAKSHOW*
There's no doubt about it, Twisty is someone straight out of the darkest horror film. A simple clown at first who fell on rough times, Twisty eventually snapped and became the community's worst nightmare. He is by far one of the creepier clowns in the history of killer clowns on screen and that's saying a lot.

3. DANDY- *AMERICAN HORROR STORY: FREAKSHOW*
Twisty may have been the most notable killer on the series, but without a doubt, Dandy was the more unstable and dangerous out of the two. Dandy is a rich boy with some serious mental issues and just needed an outlet to let his inner freak fly. Once he met Twisty and found his muse, it was all downhill from there as he pretty much slaughtered everyone he encountered

in the most horrible ways, including turning a garden party into a literal bloodbath! Dandy, you are one creepy little bastard.

4. KILLER BOB- *TWIN PEAKS*
What if the killer is your very own mirror's reflection? What if that reflection is something a bit more evil and demonic, causing you to do horrible things to others that you would never dream of normally doing? That's Bob, the demonic entity that possesses people in David Lynch's immortal classic TV series *Twin Peaks*. Frank Silva took the role to a truly unnerving level and made Bob one of the creepiest killers in slasher history, one that will haunt your dreams forever.

5. DEXTER MORGAN- *DEXTER*
In the hit TV show *Dexter*, Michael C. Hall brought to life one of the most unique slasher killers of all time. This killer has a certain code of ethics involved in his bloody murders: he only kills other killers, who are proven to have committed their own grisly crimes. A vigilante slasher killing other slashers? Pure genius!

TEN MORE BAD ASS FINAL GIRLS

This list was going to be a natural addition to this book, as a top ten in the last one simply is not enough to spotlight the top girls of this slasher staple. With that in mind, I bring you ten more of my favorite ass kicking femme fatales in the slasher world!

1. ERIN- *YOU'RE NEXT (2011)*
Played by Sharni Vinson, Erin is easily one of the most ass kicking, bad-ass final girls of all time. Despite everyone else in the family getting slaughtered all around her, she proves to be even more dangerous than the killers, and in a great twist, she becomes the hunter! This was an easy choice for the top pick of the list.

2. DANIELLE HARRIS- *HALLOWEEN 4/5, HATCHET II/III*
As if it weren't bad enough having the boogeyman as your uncle, having him return year after year to try and kill you is sure to be something that will scar you for life. Danielle Harris made herself into a horror icon with her portrayal of Jamie Lloyd and she really goes through hell trying to escape Michael's clutches throughout the films. So much so, that you feel bad for the poor girl. She does much of the same on the *Hatchet* series, as well, this time not only surviving attacks from Victor Crowley and escaping, but returning to the swamps to take him out! That's true bad-assery there! Once you're out, I would stay out, but she just goes right back in to fight again. Major props to her.

3. LEZLIE DEANE- *FREDDY'S DEAD* (1991)

It doesn't get much more badass than the ultimate bad-ass bad girl Lezlie Deane in *Freddy's Dead*! She sure doesn't take shit from anyone and proves it. She has a bad attitude and doesn't care about much, but she can really kick some major ass and does so in a big way while fighting Freddy several times. Freddy finally met his match!

4. HELEN LYLE- *CANDYMAN* (1992)

Helen Lyle is living proof that sometimes you shouldn't go chasing urban legends, especially in the world of horror. Oh yes, she does find Candyman. In a big way! Virginia Madsen is great as the inquisitive grad student in *Candyman,* bent on discovering the truth behind the legend of Candyman. She has a certain glow about her and a won't back down attitude, even though that attitude sometimes gets her in predicaments that one would rather not be in.

5. PAM MacDONALD - *THE PROWLER* (1981)

Vicky Dawson brings to life one of the most forgotten slasher heroines of all time in *The Prowler*. Not only does she manage to be the last girl standing at the end, but she also manages to blow the brains out of one of the screen's most vicious killers ever. That's one hell of a thing right there!

6. JESSICA KIMBALL- *JASON GOES TO HELL* (1993)

In *Jason Goes to Hell*, Jessica (Kari Keegan) definitely is put through hell and back. Jessica is not only a new mother, but she is also trying to get over a long relationship with our lead and has just found out that her mother was killed … and that's beside the fact that she has to destroy Jason in the end! Yes, she must have a lot going through her mind at the time, but she manages to use it as incentive to send Jason straight to hell!

7. CASS- *THE HILS HAVE EYES PART 2* (1984)

How amazing is this final girl? How about this, she did the whole freaking thing blind! While all of her friends with perfect vision were getting slaughtered all around her, she was able to use her canine like other senses to outwit the hulking Reaper and kick his ass! That is a major achievement there and it makes her easily one of the most unique and sympathetic final girls in the history of slasher films!

8. JODY- *CHERRY FALLS (2000)*

This was a rather easy choice for inclusion for me. Jody (as played by the late Brittany Murphy) is one of the feistier final girls you're apt to see in a slasher film. Of course, this makes sense as she is the sheriff's daughter and he has taught her many things about hand to hand combat. She unleashes a vicious flurry of attack moves on our killer every time they meet and in the end, gets the best of our killer. Bad ass is this girl's middle name!

9. KAREN BARCLAY- *CHILD'S PLAY* (1988)

There is nothing quite like a mother's love, as Karen proves in the first *Child's Play* film. Played by Catherine Hicks, Karen searches to the end of the earth to find her son Andy the doll he always wanted for his birthday. Unfortunately for both of them, that doll was possessed by a serial killer. It happens to all of us. Once the murders start, she doesn't want to believe her little boy is a nut case and has ways of making Chucky talk (fire always does the trick!). Of course, this leads to some hellacious fights with the killer doll and Karen proves that a mother will do anything to protect her baby. Don't mess with mama!

10. KYLE- *CHILD'S PLAY 2* (1990)

On the same side as the last entry, Kyle (played by Christine Elise- see interviews) will also do anything to protect Andy from Chucky's wrath. She has some rough edges, but really comes through as a very likable sister-like character to Andy and proves that she too will do anything to save him and get rid of that pesky killer doll.

TOP TEN FINAL GUYS

Who says girls get to have all the fun? It's not always a final girl in the slasher world, as many of these final guys will prove.

1. TOMMY JARVIS- *FRIDAY THE 13TH PART IV-VI*

When it comes to Final Guys, Tommy Jarvis of the *Friday the 13th* series is the poster boy of the character. Starting out as your average nerdy pre-teen in Part IV (played by none other than 80s golden boy Corey Feldman) before being pushed to the edge and "killing" Jason in the most brutal of ways. From there, he turns into a near mute shell shocked institution kid in Part V, who also happens to be a total ass kicking bad-ass! After that, he seems to have lightened up a bit after scaring the shit out of the final girl at the end of Part V, and gotten a more laid back approach and sense of humor for Part VI, where he is much more likable than the brooding Part V psycho Tommy. For putting a stop to the king of the slashers twice and an imposter Jason, Tommy deserves the spot at the top of this list.

2. TJ- *MY BLOODY VALENTINE* (1981)

TJ (Paul Kelman) is another quintessential final guy in the slasher world and an easy runner up to Tommy Jarvis. Sure, TJ has his demons and even seems like a red herring at points, but damn it, he cares! He is also the voice of reason in the movie, despite being at constant odds with his rival Axel over the affections of our final girl Sarah.

3. RANDY- *SCREAM 1 & 2*

Let's face it, Randy IS us. He is the all-knowing horror nerd that has seen it all before in the movies and knows the rules and what not to do. Jamie Kennedy is just so damned likable as the dorky Randy, too. That's why it was so sad to see him get killed in part 2, leaving me to yell "why couldn't you just take David Arquette instead??". Ah Randy, you will be missed. Say what you will, but he is what really made the first *Scream* so much fun, honestly.

4. STEVEN- *JASON GOES TO HELL* (1993)

Although he starts out as quite the geek, Steven really comes around in a big way in *Jason Goes to Hell*. Along with our final girl Jessica, Steven ends up kicking some major Jason ass in the end as well as holding off all the possessed versions of the big guy throughout the film. Plus, he makes a daring escape from the police and gets his fingers broken by another would-be final guy, Creighton Duke (who comes off as a sadistic asshole in that scene). Steven really proved to be a great final guy in this entry to the series.

5. HARRY- *RITUALS* (1977)

In *Rituals,* Hal Holbrook takes a completely bad ass turn as the survivalist Harry, one of a group of middle aged doctors who find themselves stranded in the middle of the Canadian wilderness, stalked by a sadistic killer who loves to play fucked up mind games. *Rituals* is one of my all-time favorite slasher films that is sadly overlooked by too many people. One of the reasons for it being so good is Holbrook's almost Rambo like turn here in a fight for survival against the hidden killer. A must see!

6. BOBBY CARTER- *THE HILLS HAVE EYES* (1977)

In *The Hills Have Eyes*, Robert Houston plays the role of Bobby, yet another kid who, like Tommy Jarvis, was forced to grow up way too fast, after his family was killed by the unforgiving cannibal clan. Bobby picks up the role as the protector of the family after their father tries to go for help, but unfortunately, it's too late, as most of the family falls to the crazy clan. Bobby does however get rid of the clan and save the others, with some help of course. The thing that makes Bobby rank so high on the list is the fact that even though he returns for the sequel, he has enough good sense not to join the others and is thus spared. Smart move, Bobby!

7. JIM HALSEY- *THE HITCHER* (1986))

In terms of sheer psychological torture in these films, Jim (played by C. Thomas Howell) is one of the ones who went through the most hell. He basically became the psychotic Ryder's (Rutger Hauer) plaything throughout the film, forced to play along to Ryder's sick mind games, coming close to death himself several times. He was framed for murder, forced to witness murder, lost a love interet in the worst way possible and was mind fucked from frame one until the end. In the end though, he finally took Ryder down and was the last man standing. That's saying a lot, given Ryder's spree of destruction!

8. TOMMY DOLYE- *HALLOWEEN 6* (1995)

Yet another Tommy on our list, Tommy was a pretty insignificant little twerp in the original *Halloween*. Well, at least he was more significant than the lazy little girl. Obviously, like the other Tommy on the list, this one was shell shocked as well by his whole experience of dealing with "The Boogeyman", and it consumed his life from that point on, making him into an obsessive loner in Part 6. He does however know exactly what they are up against and although he fails to save most of the Strode family, he does make a significant save of Jamie's baby and gets to kick some Michael ass as well, so that counts for something.

9. KEVIN SPIRTAS- *FRIDAY THE 13th PART VII/ THE HILLS HAVE EYES PART II*

Kevin Spirtas is one of the few, the proud, the multi-time final guys. In *The Hills Have Eyes Part II*, he gets to race Pluto on his dirt bike and kill the bad guys with the help of the trusty hero dog Beast and his blind girlfriend (see final girls list), despite the fact he spends half of the movie unconscious. I think he really lucked out there, considering what happened to the others. In *Friday the 13th Part VII*, he plays the awkward love interest to our final girl Tina, and gets to participate in the customary Jason fun time game of "find the body", as well as helping fight him in the end. Not a bad resume.

10. ALFRED/TODD- *THE BURNING* (1981)

The creepy, annoying kid Alfred (played by Brian Backer) had all the trademarks of the final kid. He was aware of his surroundings and the danger going on, had a tense chase scene at the end and narrowly escaped the clutches of his would be killer, Cropsy at the end, thanks in large part to the intervention of another final guy Todd (played by Brian Matthews- see interviews). You better thank your lucky stars that Todd showed up when he did Alfred or you would have been shish kabob

TOP TEN WOULD BE FINAL GUYS

The guys in this list could have saved the day. In fact, they came very close to it. However, in a slasher film, "close" can easily mean your own untimely death.

1. ALI- *FRIDAY THE 13th PART III* (1982)

Ali is the classic example of somebody who should have lived. He starts out as an enemy of the kids staying at the cabin, as leader of a local biker gang, but comes through at the end to help save our final girl Chris … well, almost. Instead, he merely provides a distraction for Chris to take down the hulking killer, while Jason is hacking him to pieces. Apparently, the idea of having him live was toyed with in early stages, but the filmmakers had a change of heart. It's too bad, as I would have liked to have seen Ali live.

2. SETH- *HELL NIGHT* (1981)

Seth (Vincent Van Patten) does what anybody else would logically do in his situation- get the fuck out of there! He tries to tell the police what's going on, but the cops chalk it up to a fraternity prank, so Seth has to go rogue and steal a gun from the station and return to the house to take matters into his own hands. Sadly, he probably should have just gone home as it turned out to be a fatal mistake.

3. BILL- *FRIDAY The 13thth* (1980)

Bill, as played by Harry Crosby was by far the most level headed of the victims in *Friday the 13th* and also one who was not afraid to jump in when things got crazy. He is a big help in the movie and is a little too eager to go investigate the strange happenings at old Camp Blood, which proves to be his ultimate downfall. One just has to wonder if things would have gone differently if only Alice had stayed awake.

4. CORBIN- *SCARECROWS* (1988)

Ted Vernon (see interviews) is truly an American original. He is one of the most fascinating people I've had a chance to talk with for the book and in *Scarecrows* he plays the ultimate bad-ass in Corbin. He said it best himself when he said that Corbin is a tough guy with a lot of heart. He seems different from the other militia men in the movie. Sure, he's their muscle and enforcer, but he also comes around at the end and leads our heroine to safety. It seems like he is going to be one to make it out alive, too. Sadly, those pesky Scarecrows made sure that didn't happen.

5. ROB- *FRIDAY THE 13th: THE FINAL CHAPTER* (1984)

You may be noticing a trend on this list when it comes to the first *Friday the 13th* movies. These poor bastards all seem to have sporting chances, but ultimately meet their untimely dooms in the end. In Rob's case, he seemed like he could have been a contender. He was out in the woods on a mission to kill Jason to avenge his sister's death in Part 2 and seemed to be ready for that final battle with Jason. Unfortunately for Rob, he made a stupid move by running back down into the basement where Jason was waiting for him. Damn it Rob, what the hell were you thinking?

6. DETECTIVE TAPP- *SAW* (2004)

It was a very welcome addition to see Danny Glover return to the big screen again in *Saw,* as the on-edge detective with a major vendetta against Jigsaw. You can clearly tell he has lost it a bit, as he spends his hours obsessing over the case and following every move. He even saves Dr. Gordon's family and follows our Jigsaw patsy all the way to the torture dungeon, seeming that he will be the one to save the day. Sadly, he gets a rather undignified sendoff after getting shot in a gun fight. All that hard work for nothing.

7. OTTO- *THE PROWLER* (1981)

This character is one that just had red herring written all over him. That is until he shows up at the end to blast our killer with a shotgun and redeem himself of the creepy vibes he was putting off. You could almost hear the heartfelt music swell as he shares a loving look of relief with our final girl until, BLAM! So long, Otto.

8. PAUL- *FRIDAY THE 13TH PART 2* (1981)

Yet another in the long list of contenders wiped out by Jason Voorhees, Paul was the camp director on Part two. While he helped save Ginny at the end and seemed to have survived at first, his ultimate fate is still up in the air and highly debated to this day. Obviously, the answer is- he's dead, Jim.

9. JULIUS- *FRIDAY THE 13TH PART VIII: JASON TAKES MANHATTAN* (1989)

The last of the would be final guys from the *Friday the 13th* series is one of the most bad-ass characters in the entire series. As Julius, VC Dupree plays the high school tough kid who happens to be an amazing amateur boxer as well. He tries to put these skills to the test against old maggot brains on a New York City rooftop after earlier escaping Jason's clutches, but the second time around he doesn't fare too well. While he does manage to kick Jason's ass very well, Jason ends up getting the upper hand in the boxing match from hell and poor Julius loses his head over the encounter … literally.

10. OFFICER JOE REITZ- *DR. GIGGLES* (1992)

I thought for sure good old Officer Joe was going to make it through this one. He seemed by all means to be a hero in the making. He found out all about the good doctor on the killing spree and managed to track him down to his secret lair under the old Rendell family home and save our final girl from the doctor's clutches in the process. Just when you think it's clear sailing though and he's out of the danger zone, bam! Here comes Dr. Giggles with one final trick up his sleeve. Too bad.

TOP FIFTEEN MEN BEHIND THE MASK

1. KANE HODDER (*FRIDAY THE 13th* SERIES/ *HATCHET*/ *PRISON*)

Let's face it, Kane Hodder is the king of the slashers. He was not only able to be the iconic man to play Jason Voorhees more than any other actor, but he also made Victor Crowley of *Hatchet* a classic slasher villain for the new generation. His performances are the stuff of legend. 'Nuff said.

2. ROBERT ENGLUND- *NIGHTMARE ON ELM STREET* SERIES

Perhaps I spoke too soon. Maybe when I called Kane the king of the slashers, old Freddy might have something to say about it. I would say that both are on equal terms and that both are definitely true icons of the genre. Robert Englund will be forever remembered as the guy who brought Freddy to life and for good reason. He was just so damn good at it! He had equal amounts of comic timing and wit and scare factor, as well, which is quite an accomplishment. He was so good at it, he played Freddy in eight movies to date. That's saying quite a lot!

3. DICK WARLOCK- "MICHAEL MYERS", *HALLOWEEN II/III*

It was quite tough to pick just one of the many people that played Michael Myers as a favorite, but I will go out on a limb here and put Dick Warlock down as my favorite. Why? Well, because Dick took it to the next level with his portrayal of The Shape. He just seemed so much more vicious and terrifying in the sequel and very methodical and deliberate in his performance. In *Halloween III*, he proved he can be just as scary without the mask, with his dead set eyes and his cold, methodical killing methods.

4. TOBIN BELL- "JIGSAW", THE *SAW* SERIES

While Tobin has quite the impressive resume as is, he will always be known as the sadistic Jigsaw from now on. Part of that reason is that he is just so damn creepy and convincing in the series, as a cancer patient who engineers various deadly traps to ensnare people in, who he views as unworthy of life and to teach them a lesson on life ... or kill them in the process.

5. TONY TODD- *CANDYMAN* (1992)

What goes for Tobin Bell goes double for Tony Todd. An accomplished actor with an impressive resume in his own right, Tony will always be known as Candyman. Tony has an otherworldly, unforgettable presence in the films as the vengeful urban legend come to life. His performances in the films are simply amazing, Academy Award material and he quickly became one of the most imposing slasher villains of all time and a true horror legend.

6. NATHAN BAESEL- *BEHIND THE MASK* (2006)

The interesting thing about Nathan Baesel (see Interviews) in *Behind the Mask* is that he does not seem like a killer at all. In fact, he seems like one of the nicest people in the world. He just so happens to have a sick obsession with slasher killers and his life goal is to be one of them. Nathan makes Leslie Vernon into one of the most likable killers in *Behind the Mask* and can also be unflinching and scary, as well, as we see in the finale of the film. It takes a lot to be able to straddle that border as effectively as Nathan does here.

7. DEREK MCKINNON- KENNY, *TERROR TRAIN* (1980)

In terms of creepy killer portrayals, Derek is always one of the top names on my list. Listen to his deep, death-like voice near the end and his dead set delivery. It's reminiscent of Buffalo Bill and very creepy. He also can just be plain soulless and deliberate in the multiple costumes he wears throughout the film. The biggest surprise of all is how he is hidden in plain sight through most of the film in a get-up that will make you want to go back and watch it again. It takes someone truly talented to take on such a demanding role.

8. CJ GRAHAM- JASON, *FRIDAY THE 13th PART VI: JASON LIVES* (1986)

CJ manages to cut one of the more imposing incarnations of Jason in the sixth entry for a few reasons. First off, he is one of the biggest Jasons out there. He also has this very robotic, yet deliberate performance to him, which really makes this Jason stand out. CJ also played the amazing Hell Cop in the horror comedy *Highway to Hell* in 1991, another of my personal favorites.

9. LEATHERFACE, *TEXAS CHAINSAW MASSACRE*

There have been so many great incarnations of the maniacal Leatherface over the years. From Gunnar Hansen's game changing portrayal in the first film, to Bill Johnson/Bob Elmore in part two, to RA Mihailoff in the third installment, up to the modern portrayals, it's hard to pick just one. Well, I can't, so they're all good in my book!

10. PETER COWPER- THE MINER, *MY BLOODY VALENTINE* (1981)

The Miner is one of the best slasher killers in the whole genre and has one of the absolute best costumes ever, as well. Of course, it takes a great actor to play such a great character under that mask and Canadian actor Peter Cowper easily earns a spot on this list for his menacing performance of the rampaging Miner.

11. LARRY DRAKE- *DR. GIGGLES* (1992), THE SCARECROW ON *DARK NIGHT OF THE SCARECROW* (1981)

The late Larry Drake was just a very talented actor in general, and one of the absolute best. Whether playing the intimidating gangster Durant in *Darkman* or playing the simple Bubba in *Dark Night of the Scarecrow*, or playing the maniacal, constantly giggling psycho in *Dr. Giggles*, Larry put 110% into every performance and could play literally any role that was given to him with ease.

12. LOU DAVID- CROPSY, *THE BURNING* (1981)

Now, here's one guy who undoubtedly had to spend a lot of hours in the old make-up chair to achieve his monstrous look as the disfigured killer Cropsy in *The Burning*. Lou's scenes are unforgettable in the movie and when you do finally see the face behind the killer (through most of his screen time, the face is unseen), it's something you won't soon forget!

13. GEORGE WILBUR- MICHAEL MYERS, *HALLOWEEN* 4/6

My second favorite Michael Myers happens to be the man who would later go on to host Quahog's favorite news station. On *Halloween 4*, he was every bit as intimidating and deliberate as Dick Warlock, and then some. Plus, he gets to impale someone with a shotgun!

14. TED WHITE- *FRIDAY THE 13th: THE FINAL CHAPTER* (1984)

Ted White is the man behind another one my favorite Jason portrayals, in what could be my favorite entry in the entire series. Before this, Ted was known as a veteran of Hollywood's stunt industry, having worked with the likes of John Wayne in the day. On this entry, he also proves he has what it takes to play a very convincing and unstoppable monster. From what I understand, he could easily be just as intimidating off screen as on screen!

15. BILL MOSELEY- "CHOP TOP" IN *TEXAS CHAINSAW MASSACRE PART 2* (1986)

Bill Moseley is scary good in his over the top performance as Chop Top in Part Two. It's miles away from his demeanor in person, too. In this film, he just seems to be having way too much fun with the character and seems like a kid on a massive sugar high. Either that, or a crackhead on a bender. The scene in the radio station, where he confronts our heroine Stretch is a truly legendary scene.

TOP TEN FUNNIEST COMIC RELIEF CHARACTERS

1. COCONUT PETE- *CLUB DREAD* (2004)

Bill Paxton hits it out of the ball park with his role here as a washed-up Jimmy Buffet type who apparently had way too much fun in the sixties. His portrayal of the Coconut Pete character is simply legendary. He even sang his own hilarious songs like "Pleasure Island" and "Pina Coladaburgh". They can be pretty damn catchy, too! Probably the funniest part is seeing when he loses his cool several times throughout the film, going on rants and destroying things … especially over his hatred of Jimmy Buffet, ironically.

2. RALPH- *BAD DREAMS* (1988)

From his introduction, when he pretends to be the doctor in the psychotherapy group and attempts to talk our final girl out of her clothes, you can tell that this Ralph guy is gonna be a fun character. Played by Dean Cameron (see interviews), Ralph is a seriously messed up kid with so many crazy antics, I could write a whole page on it. He is one of the best wise-cracking characters in slasher history and just keeps those one-liners coming. Watch for the part when he really loses it near the end and goes on a rampage. It can be hilarious and terrifying at the same time.

3. ETHEL AND JUNIOR- *FRIDAY THE 13TH PART 5* (1985)

These two characters were simply comic gold. Everything out of crazy Ethel's (Carol Locatell) mouth was just saturated in both hilarity and profanity. Calling her simple son Junior (Ron Sloan) a "big dildo" and a "fuckwad", spitting in his stew, and her immortal lines of "Would you shut the fuck up?", "That's the ugliest fuckin' man I ever seen", "I got a bomb on me!" and "Shut up and eat your fuckin slop", make her by far one of the most laugh out loud characters in the series, or more like in slasher history! Junior is just as funny and the back and forth between the two characters is one of the things that really makes this entry in the series so enjoyable.

4. TED- *FRIDAY THE 13TH: THE FINAL CHAPTER* (1984)

"Don't be a dead fuck". So, says Teddy when dispensing friendly advice to his buddy Jimbo after receiving the advice from his non-existent computer. Teddy (Lawrence Monoson) is one of those guys you would love to party with. He's a laugh a minute (especially when drunk or stoned, but he doesn't need that to be funny), as well as someone you can laugh at, watching him strike out with the ladies.

5. KURT/TINA- *THE FINAL GIRLS* (2015)

In a movie like this, it's hard to just pick one character that stands out the most as the funniest. That's why I've picked the best two! Adam Devine steals the show as your typical horn dog jock Kurt, but does the role so over the top, that you can't help but crack up laughing every time he's on screen. The same goes for ditzy airhead Tina, who the rest of the group has to prevent from getting naked by taping oven mitts to her hands and putting her in safety gear. Both characters completely steal the show with their antics.

6. TIMMY- *CHEERLEADER CAMP* (1987)

You can be sure that shenanigans will abound when Timmy (Travis McKenna, interviewed in the first book) is around. He's definitely one of those guys you would want to hang around with and provides endless laughs, from mooning the entire camp on arrival (and getting his ass stuck in the van window), to dressing in drag as an old woman to get a closer peek at some of the bathing beauties. Timmy is always up to something and the results are always hilarious. It was actually sad to see his character get killed off.

7. WILDMAN- *FINAL EXAM* (1981)

I already touched on this character in a list in the previous book. Ralph Brown is just so damn believable as the drunken frat boy Wildman and most certainly lives up to the name. Just watching the guy, you really believe every second that this is him as a character. Really, he is the main reason why *Final Exam* is so memorable in the first place! Sadly, Ralph passed on after filming, so we never got to see more great roles from him.

8. ED- *TERROR TRAIN* (1980)

It's all fun and games until someone gets a sword through the stomach. Ed (Howard Busgang- see interviews) was the definitive life of the party in *Terror Train*. I mean, he basically puts on a stand-up routine for his classmates before boarding the train! It's pretty damn funny, too. Sadly, this funny man was silenced way too early in the film. I, for one, would have liked to have seen more from Ed.

9. SIDNEY- *BODY COUNT* (1987)

Sidney (Andrew Lederer- see interviews) is the essence of that part of the pack that we all know, love and need one of in every group: the drunken fat guy. He's pretty damn hilarious at it, too. Of course, we get the clumsy fat guy pratfalls and stereotypes, but we also get the funniest scenes of the film from him. The best one is when one of the girls convinces him to strip down with her and enter a house because there's an orgy happening inside. Instead, the naked Sidney crashes a nice family dinner. The priceless look on David Hess's face in this scene says it all.

10. HOWARD- *MY BLOODY VALENTINE* (1981)

Howard (Alf Humphreys) is a lot like Shelly from *Friday the 13th Part 3*, an eternal prankster. Both characters share a lot in common in that they both had a morbid sense of humor, involving fake deaths and a love of elaborate and bloody make-up effects. They were also both major pains in the ass. At least they tried to keep the proceedings light around them. Of course, I think that both Jason and The Miner didn't appreciate either one's humor so much.

THE FORGOTTEN SLASHERS

While some of these films may be very well known to horror and slasher film fans, others may be a bit more obscure. When I say that they have been forgotten, by that I don't mean forgotten by the mass majority or overlooked, what I mean is simply the fact that they were omitted from the first book. With many of these new entries, I shall attempt to rectify the situation and truly make my best attempt to cover the films that I missed the first time around.

AMERICAN PSYCHO (2000) ~ (Modern Day Slashers)

AMERICAN PSYCHO

Every now and then, a horror film comes along that completely turns the industry on its head and makes everyone sit up and take notice. Sometimes, they can have a slow build and aren't widely received at first, but quickly gain momentum and become one of the new classics. *American Psycho* is one of these films.

American Psycho is set in the swinging 1980s and follows yuppie banker Patrick Bateman (Christian Bale). By all appearances, he seems like he has it all together. He takes care of himself, he's popular among his co-workers and friends, as well as the ladies and he is a very successful person in general. The only problem is that he's a serial killing psychopath. *American Psycho* proves to be a deep psychological profile of a modern serial killer.

Most of the film, we are in Patrick's head, as we see and hear some of his deepest, most insane thoughts. A good example is his obsession over the hue of his own business cards as opposed to his rival's … another thing that prefaces a brutal and bloody murder later on. He compulsively obsesses over the smallest details and as a testament to Bale's performance, you can see the shakiness in a man about ready to snap. Even if he is normal on the outside, on the inside he has fantasies about killing people in the most horrific ways and even gets to live out some of those fantasies on some unlucky few.

This movie is by far one of the more interesting out there and can be a tense psychological thriller at times. At times, you can see the psychotic glee in Bale as Bateman as he tortures hookers or chases them down a hallway, while naked and wielding a chainsaw (one of the stand out scenes of the film). Another scene has him joyfully splitting the skull of his rival (Jared Leto) with an axe as Huey Lewis plays in the background, another standout scene. There are many insane scenes throughout the film that really stand out and make American Psycho truly memorable. Even with all of the good in the film though, there is still one thing that has always bothered me about it. Honestly, I'm still not quite sure what to make of the ending of the movie and that's one of the things that has prevented me from liking it as much as some of the other slasher heavyweights. Did it really happen? Was it all in his head? Did he really kill all of these people and the other people around him just didn't care? Who is Kaizer Soze? I really can't say. I know that there are many theories out there on it and it's a hotly debated subject in the horror world, but I just think that the film went off track a bit towards the end. This is sad too, because I was really enjoying the madness of it all up until then.

All in all, *American Psycho* is still one of the better modern slasher films out there and serves as a tense psychological portrait of the Ted Bundy like killer who is perfect by all outward appearances, but a bubbling cauldron of a psychotic killer underneath. Christian Bale does an impressive job as the man on edge and makes Patrick Bateman into one of the most realistic and highly unstable killers of recent memory. I give *American Psycho* three and a half out of five stars. Sure, it can be confusing at times, but it's still one hell of a fun ride! Just take my advice and stay away from the horrible 2002 sequel, starring Mila Kunis.

BLOOD FRENZY (1987)

Blood Frenzy is an obscure and often overlooked desert survival slasher, similar in many ways to films like *The Hills Have Eyes*. Oddly enough, this is director Hal Freeman's only foray into the world of slasher films, although he has a long history of delivering such award-winning films as *Naughty Cheerleaders* and the *Caught from Behind* series. I'll give you three guesses what those are and the first two don't count. Indeed, ol' Hal dove right back into pornland after *Blood Frenzy* and never did a horror film again.

The movie begins in a similar fashion to many other films of the era (*Pieces, Boogeyman,* etc.) with good old fashioned childhood murder as an unseen child slashes their drunk, abusive father's throat in rather gory fashion, with a spade. Flash forward years later where we meet our gang. Despite what IMDB says, this is not a teen slasher film, by any means! Rather, it's about a psychologist who takes a group of troubled patients out for a retreat in the desert. This group of social misfits includes an old drunk, your standard blonde nymphomaniac, a troubled Vietnam vet with severe flashbacks, a girl who hates being touched, and a man with anger issues. Naturally, Mr. Angry and the vet are always fighting. Rounding out the cast is none other than former Wednesday Addams Lisa Loring, in yet another slasher film in the Eighties, aside from *Iced*! She is much more animated here than in *Iced*, as a man hating, horny lesbian with severe anger issues herself. Not bad! In true slasher fashion, one of our misfits is found with his throat slashed and the group find their bus on the fritz. Well, before you can say Michael

Berryman, our group decides to split up to find out help and start to drop like flies. Naturally, there's a lot of speculation as to who the unseen killer is, but our group soon starts to dwindle and narrow down the suspects.

Sadly, the ending of *Blood Frenzy* is one of those crazy, convoluted, overly explained reveals that one would see in a TV drama, but it's still fun before we get to that point. The kills throughout are extremely gory and more extreme than your average slasher flick of the time. Most of these involve slashings of some sort and tons of the red stuff. The thing that really sticks out here is the diversity amongst the characters though. They are fun to watch and it's fun to see them interact with each other and bicker.

One thing that keeps *Blood Frenzy* an interesting title is that it's different than your average slasher film. However, it's still pretty average. Overall, *Blood Frenzy* is a passable effort and worth a watch, yet still ultimately forgettable. I seriously doubt it's on anyone's top ten list and there's little doubt that the film, which still has not had a proper DVD or Blu-Ray release, will remain in obscurity. I give it two and a half stars out of five.

BLOOD VOYAGE (1976) - (Pre-slashers)

After watching *Blood Voyage*, I have to say that without a doubt, the original Dos Equis guy (Jonathan Goldsmith, here as Jonathan Lippe) really is "The Most Interesting Man in the World." Who knew, that before he was that marketing icon, that he was also a crazed slasher? I sure as hell didn't know that! Well, that's what we get here in this pre-slasher boom slasher film set almost entirely on a yacht in the Pacific Ocean. And the sea will Tell, indeed!

Blood Voyage is one of the earlier slasher films that came to us in 1976 from director Frank Mitchell. While Mitchell was a veteran actor, with credits dating back to the 1920s, this was sadly his only directing credit. Sad, because it was a pretty damn good effort in my opinion! *Blood Voyage* starts off on the right path, with gratuitous nudity, and goes from there. We soon meet our cast and boy, are they an unlikable bunch. There's a middle-aged doctor (John Hart) on his way to Hawaii to get married to his young bride to be Jill (Laurie Rose) who is half his age; his scheming daughter Carol (Mara Modair) who wants to kill him and get all the money, his patient (Hawaiian bombshell Midori, who did things such as *Gilligan's Island* in the 70s, but sadly, very little is known about her), who has a bad addiction to drugs and mental problems, plus our captain and three crew members. There is also a nice turn from Goldsmith as a crazy Vietnam veteran on board the boat. Gee, I wonder who the killer will be? It doesn't help that the daughter keeps asking him questions about killing folks in 'Nam and wants him to kill her dad. Well, soon enough, a killer does start knocking off the folks on the Hawaii bound yacht one by one. It's easy to tell who the killer is, but there's some nice additions. For one, he shoots up our young Midori with heroin in one very sleazy scene and covers her in blood, to make the others think that she is the killer. Of course, the kills continue until there is only one girl left on board alone with the killer, and as you can probably guess, when you're on a boat in the middle of the ocean, there's really nowhere you can run!

Blood Voyage is definitely not your average slasher film. Reading some of the reviews online after watching it, I feel that many were quite unfair and didn't see the big picture. I felt that it is definitely one of the more unique slasher films out there, very different from the rest. There's some blood, but not much and plenty of sex, drugs and nudity as well from our lovely ladies, but this is not one of those films to revel in the excess. It works better on a suspenseful level. While many of the characters are of the unlikable sort, the actors still turn in good performances, especially Goldsmith as our off-balance killer (of course, would we expect anything less from "The Most Interesting Man in the world"?) The fact that the entire film is set on a yacht gives it a unique, nowhere to run feel. I also like the surprising choice of our final girl. She was not the one I was expecting, given her character development, but it made perfect sense and there are some fun final girl chases and showdowns. While the killer reveal itself is one that even a blind man could have seen coming a mile away, I must say that the aftermath and the climax are what make the film really special and it does have a bit of a surprise at the end. I give *Blood Voyage* three stars out of five, easily, and highly recommend giving it a watch. That is, if you can find a copy. It wasn't easy to come by.

BLOODBEAT (1982)

Stop me if you've heard this one: a seven-foot-tall, glowing samurai starts slashing rednecks in Northern Wisconsin … sadly, that's not a joke. Instead, it's the basic plot of our oddball title *Bloodbeat*, and the whole movie is the punchline. This is definitely one of the oddest slasher films in the history of slasher films.

Ted and his girlfriend Sarah head to his mom's place in the rural Wisconsin countryside to spend Christmas with the family. The only problem is, Sarah is one weird chick. She spends most of the film staring and has weird, psychic visions. Apparently, Ted's mom is just as weird and has the same problem. Jesus, it's like everyone is psychic in this stupid movie. So, who's weirder, Mom or Sarah? The film is filled with a lot of annoying close-ups of random objects for extended periods, random color flashes and frantic violin playing, all for no reason. It soon takes on a weird supernatural turn, ala *Boogeyman,* with laughable effects (lights flashing, color flashes, doors opening and closing, pantry attacks, etc.) This is about the time that the kills start. Oddly, every time that we see a kill happen, thanks to our ghostly glowing samurai, who seems to hate hunters, Sarah is seen miles away getting herself off to the visions! You read that correctly. Why, in one kill scene, it's actually interspersed with scenes of Sarah getting herself off from the visions! Um, okay. Yes, this is a very sexual film. I guess that just may be to make up for the fact that the kills are pretty horribly done, hard to follow and random.

Bloodbeat is very slow moving and very random. It spends way too much time on the drama surrounding the family, especially the fact that Sarah and Ted's mother don't like each other. I guess there's only room for one psychic in that house! There's not much of interest here. About the only part that was mildly interesting is a scene with our glowing samurai slashing up a redneck bonfire party in the woods, and even that is so badly done, it's not even worth the watch.

My final thoughts on Bloodbeat are this … what the fuck did I just watch? Bloodbeat is just one pointless, confusing mess of a movie with terrible effects, acting and one of the most nonsensical plots in existence. How this even got made is beyond me. I actually hated myself just for sitting through the whole thing. I give Bloodbeat just one star out of five, and that's just for it being so incredibly Fubar. Heed my words, avoid this or ye shall perish!

BOARDINGHOUSE (1982) ~ (Shot on Video/ The Worst)

Before Blood Cult, before Sledgehammer, before the Woodchipper Massacre, there was another film that paved the way for these other Shot on Video, or SOV disasterpieces, and that was Boardinghouse. Keep in mind, that particular distinction is not necessarily a good thing.

I'll try to keep this review as brief as possible, as I don't want to spend too much time on it. Boardinghouse centers around a "spooky old murder house" with a local reputation for being haunted, like as seen in so many other films. Unfortunately, the house is not spooky. It just looks like the director's house in California, surrounded by palm trees and with a nice pool out back. Spooky? Hardly. Years after a few murders, a man decides to turn the place into a boardinghouse. By "boarding house", I mean that he only rents out to Playboy bunny types, who spend most of the film running around in various stages of undress, splashing each other in the pool and acting rather dumb and slutty. It's kind of like watching an in-depth video of the Feldmansion, minus the cultish Corey Feldman. In this case, that role is played by the director himself, as he plays a pimpdaddy sort to all the girls at the house and spends nearly the entire movie in a speedo. Ugh. I wonder how he got that part? Of course, there's lots of nudity, bad acting and truly inane dialogue before the murders start up. It's a supernatural killer, so of course, there's going to be a lot of bad creature and ghost effects. Then, there's the murders, all of which are advertised at the start of the film as being in the groundbreaking "Murder Vision", which

26

is basically an infra-red looking filter over the camera. Yee-Haw. There you have the time-wasting *Boardinghouse,* in a nutshell.

I tried to like *Boardinghouse.* I truly, honestly did. I just found myself drinking heavily and screaming into a pillow at times because it just would not get any better, even though I stupidly held out hope that it would. At least a movie like the similar *Nightmare Weekend* was so bad it was good. Sadly, *Boardinghouse* is just the bad kind of bad. I give it half a star out of five. Even that's being generous and just for the fact that it is recognized as the first SOV slasher film, which is not necessarily a good thing, but still notable nonetheless.

CARDS OF DEATH (1985) ~ (Shot on Video)

To quote James Karen from *Return of the Living Dead*, "Kid, I have seen weird things come and I have seen weird things go, but the weirdest..." ... just may happen to be the little shot of video oddity *Cards of Death.* Not only is this one of the weirdest slasher films I had ever seen, it's also one of the rarest. Perhaps there's a good reason for that.

I had never even heard of *Cards of Death* before until I interviewed Ron Kologie from *Iced* for this book. I immediately had to make it a new quest to find this movie and watch it. What I found out about the background of the movie, just may be an even stranger story than the movie itself, proving that sometimes reality can be stranger than fiction. *Cards of Death* is one delightfully sleazy little cheapie from 1985 that is not your average slasher film. In fact, it seems quite innovative at times. The plot focuses on an underground fight club type of place where participants gather in a poorly lit room, surrounded by half naked S&M chicks and lots of cocaine. The participants all have to wear cheap Halloween masks and partake in the deadliest game ... a card game involving Tarot cards, where whoever draws the death card gets to kill the rest. It's meant to set up a stalk and kill spree and at times, the film is just that. In one other innovative scene, the winner simply stands up and brutally kills the other participants at the table, before snorting a line of coke, saying "I'm a busy man." Priceless!

Naturally, all of the dismembered bodies that start to turn up in back alleys give the local police a cause for alarm, especially when the Chief of Police turns up missing after getting too deep into the case and his body parts start getting mailed back to the department. The son of the Chief (Ron Kologie) teams up with the others to do their own investigation and it leads him right into the seedy world of the underground game of death.

Cards of Death can easily be looked at as one of the first torture porn films ever. I would say that it could have been very influential, but honestly, who the fuck could have seen it? That's where the back story comes in. The film had a hard time finding distribution in the States and it was only able to find a very limited release in Japan. While it never saw an American release, it soon became one of the most sought after slasher films of all time, the holy grail, if you will. Well, apparently, a fan of the film managed to find a bad copy in the land of the rising sun and brought it back to the states. He ended up getting the rights somehow and had it re-released in 2014 on VHS, of all things. Yes, in the digital age, they thought it was fitting to have it released on VHS of all things. Yeah, I don't know, either. That does not by any means mean that it's readily available now on the market, though. On the contrary. It's still a tough movie to find and I myself had to search high and low for my copy. Was it worth it? I would say yes, actually!

Cards of Death is an unapologetically sleazy and perverted film for sure. The deaths (and there's a lot of them, in vivid, gory detail) and back alley realism are taken to sickeningly realistic heights here and at times it seems like it could be some lost snuff film you've stumbled on. There's an overabundance of nudity in the movie too, as nearly every woman gets naked, topless or some form of it. The man playing the ringmaster behind the game really stands out here as one of the sleazier villains of all time, even mustache twirling at times … literally. He just seems like a complete sleaze ball, which fits perfectly with the tone of the film. The movie can be dark at times, has bad dialogue and acting, and has shaky camera work, but hey, we're not exactly expecting Oscar material here, right?

I give *Cards of Death* two and a half stars out of five. It really is what it is and if you can appreciate it for what it is, it can be quite enjoyable, even if it is very dark and bordering on a snuff film. In fact, it may actually be. Maybe that's why distribution was so tough.

CARPENTER, THE (1987) - (Just plain Weird)

Here's another cinematic oddity that I can't seem to make heads or tails out of. The 1987 slasher film *The Carpenter* comes across like a really fucked up version of *The Money Pit* at times and is one of those films that can just be very confusing. I still don't quite know what to think of it.

The Carpenter comes to us from Canadian director David Wellington, who has gone on to quite the illustrious directing career in Hollywood. The plot centers around a married couple who move into their dream home in the countryside and live happily ever after. Okay, not exactly. Perfect is not exactly the word to describe this couple by any means. The wife is recovering from a nervous breakdown and has some real mental instability, while the husband is a professor in the midst of an affair with a student, who he just so happened to knock up. After moving into the house, they hire a crew to do some much-needed extensive repairs and start to realize that the crew is pretty unreliable … well, all except for the good-natured handyman (Wings Hauser) with a strong work ethic, who only works alone at night in the house and who only the wife sees. Soon, our handyman buddies up with wifey and the two form quite a friendship. He seems to be willing to do anything to protect her … including viciously killing folks with various tools. Eventually, we come to find out that he is the spirit of a man who was building his wife a dream house, only to have her leave him. Devastated, he kept working on the house, trying to achieve perfection, and killing several people in the process before getting sentenced to have a seat in old sparky, and now he's back. But, is he really back or is it all in the wife's head?

The Carpenter is definitely a weird one. Parts of it seem like a dream and at times you think it has to go in some clever route and it would be dumb to just leave the happenings at surface level (i.e., a twist ending). For that, I must say that many people will be disappointed. There are some great, gory kills throughout the film though, all involving power tools. One shady contractor gets his arms amputated with a power saw, and others include a power drill kill, a head in a vice and death by nail gun. It's about what you'd expect from a movie with that title. While it borders on the slasher category, I fail to classify it as an official slasher film. At times, it's actually more like an awkward black comedy.

Wings Hauser does put in a great performance as the title character, but I expected a little bit more nuttiness from him as opposed to the calm and cool killer we see. *The Carpenter* does have its moments, but overall, it's a pretty forgettable experience. I give it two stars out of five.

CHERRY FALLS (2000) - (Teen Slashers)

Cherry Falls is sadly one of the more forgotten films of the teen slasher cycle in the late 90s. It starts off in a classic slasher way, with the slaughter of two horny teens on a dark lover's lane by a mysterious killer dressed like a woman. It soon leads into *Scream-like* territory as we are introduced to our young cast at the local high school dealing with the aftermath of the murders and trying to understand them. Our lead Jody (played by the late Brittany Murphy) is the daughter of the sheriff (Michael Biehn), and soon finds herself thrust right into the middle of the investigation, finding herself a target of our crazy mascara wearing psycho, as he bumps off her classmates one by one. It is soon revealed that our killer is actually targeting the young virgins at the high school, as he stalks and stabs them, seemingly at random. This of course leads the teens at the school (all of the teens, that is) to try to save themselves from the killer the only way that they can … by losing their virginity. It soon takes on a hypersexual feel (and gives a whole new meaning to the title *Cherry Falls*. This is not lost on the filmmakers either, as they mention it themselves) as the teens stage a massive orgy party at an abandoned house. Seems like a pretty legit idea. Is it going to save them from our Buffalo Bill like killer though? Hell no! The movie takes some interesting twists and turns towards a surprising end and gives us one hell of a reveal before our final killer climax.

Cherry Falls is not your average cookie cutter teen slasher flick. It's not as cutesy and it doesn't play it safe like many others of the genre. Instead, this one is refreshingly balls to the wall. I really appreciated the throwback settings, such as lover's lane, the darkened corridors of the school, etc. It was nice to see that there was a genuine love of the old-school slashers happening and I appreciated that. Many of the kills are cut, but that doesn't really matter. What matters is the great story and the action. The actors all do great jobs here. Murphy is one of the feistier final girls I've ever seen and Biehn is always nice to see in a film. Jay Mohr is the real surprise here as the lead teacher at the school. I've always known Jay as a comedian and from *SNL*, so it was refreshing to see him in a straight role like this. He's really the one who makes the film stand out and gives a top-notch performance here. I just wish he did more films, as he was so damn good here. The other characters, such as the students seem cliché as usual, but also a bit more fleshed out than usual, as well. The final reveal itself is surprisingly clever and one that's quite fun and involved and it leads into one of the better chase scenes and climaxes around, going bat shit crazy at times, as the killer chases our final girl right through the middle of the orgy party. Yeesh, nothing breaks up a party faster than a crazy transvestite killer crashing the party and slashing everyone.

I must admit that I did not have the highest expectations for *Cherry Falls*. Let's face it, the whole direct to video craze after the teen slasher slasher cycle got a little out of hand and many of the films kind of jumbled together. Surprisingly, I thoroughly enjoyed it. In fact, I found it to be one of the most entertaining films out of that teen slasher cycle and one of the best modern slasher films, in general. I give it three and a half stars out of five. Sadly, forgotten and overlooked by many, I highly recommend it.

CITY OF BLOOD (1983) - (Foreign slashers)

City of Blood comes to us from the land down under. No, not that land down under, the other land down under, South Africa. The land is steeped in history, as well as centuries of mysterious rituals and ancient rites, giving it an eerie feeling. Add in the years of political turmoil and animosity of the last century, and it's the perfect setting for a horror film.

City of Blood opens with a very stylish bang back in ancient times, as a tribesman kills two others with a spiked club. It's a great start to the film. We soon fast forward to the present in Johannesburg and meet our lead, a depressed medical examiner. He soon gets thrust into investigating a serious of prostitute murders. The girls are all killed in a rather unique way, via spiked club. Sound familiar? It's as if the ghosts of the pasts have returned … to kill hookers? Okay. It seems like a promising start to a slasher film. Unfortunately, the rest is not as interesting as it leads down the road of political conspiracies and more. Sometimes, I even forgot it was supposed to be a slasher film.

I actually found *City of Blood* to be quite the boring film, honestly. There's not a whole lot that happens over the course of its runtime and there are only a few deaths that happen. The ghost warrior aspect does make for some interesting watching, I'll give it that. I think that maybe *City of Blood* might be a better film if you're not expecting a slasher film. It really isn't much of a slasher by any stretch of the imagination, and the whole slasher aspect really takes a backseat to the political aspect. I loved the African scenery and some of the stylish visuals in the film, but the fact that it leads into such a politically centered plot leads it down a different road than what you would expect out of it and it spends the majority of the film dwelling on that, which gets boring. I don't blame the filmmakers at all though, as that was what was happening there at the time. *City of Blood* is not a total waste though, as it has its good moments and some nice scares and a few thrilling sequences. It just doesn't have enough of that and focuses too much on the other end of the spectrum.

I give *City of Blood* one star out of five. It's not one of the worst movies I've ever seen and it does have some interesting points and a great killer disguise, plus I can appreciate the local lore on display here. I am just hard pressed to call it a slasher film, no matter what they try to sell me on it. You can give me a hot dog and call it a sandwich, but it's still a hot dog, damn it.

COLD PREY (2009) ~ (Foreign slashers)

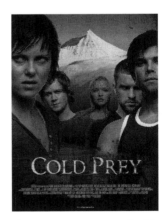

Time and time again, it's been proven that slasher films can come from anywhere in the world. In 2006, Norway decided to throw their entry into the slasher market with *Cold Prey* (No, not Coldplay!). They delivered the goods too, with an effective and chilling (no pun intended) snowcapped slasher film.

Cold Prey starts out in quite the bone chilling way, as we see a young boy being chased in the snowbound countryside by an unseen killer, before being buried in the snow. We then get to see that apparently, our killer has been a busy, busy boy over the years, as various news reports cover what amounts to hundreds of disappearances of skiers and hikers in the harsh Norwegian back country over the years. We enter our characters, a group of five twenty somethings on their way to a weekend of snowboarding in that very same isolated back country. Uh oh, that can't be good (wink, wink). After a long hike and a great snowboarding scene, our lovable loser Marten Tobias crashes and burns hard, breaking his leg. They're miles from civilization, but luckily the group spots an old abandoned lodge in the hills and takes their friend there for shelter from the storm. Only, it's not so abandoned. The friends break in and make themselves at home, which had to piss off our already pissed off killer residing in the basement. Soon,

31

while our group is getting cozy in the building, our killer comes out to play and brings his pick to the party.

Cold Prey is highly reminiscent of other such snowbound slasher flicks as *Iced, Blood Tracks, Shredder* and several others, but on a larger scale. It proves that the stark white stillness of the snowy landscape are the perfect grounds for a stalk and slash picture. Speaking of the landscape, the scenery in the film is beautiful and eerie at the same time. The hotel itself provides a great spooky setting with plenty of dark spaces, and dimly lit hallways. The place actually reminded me a bit of the setting of the 1983 Canadian thriller *Ghostkeeper.* It really conveys a trapped, isolated feel perfectly. The actors all do well and the characters are quite identifiable and even likable. Our final girl Jannicke is one tough and smart cookie and a new favorite for me in the category. The character that really sticks out is our slacker comic relief character Marten Tobias, who is genuinely funny and likable, reminding one of that lovable fuckup drinking buddy we all had in college. Plus, he spends most of the film on a broken leg, which gives us that extra feel for the helpless character. The character of Mikal makes some of the biggest bonehead decisions in slasher history, on the other hand. You know that's gonna be his downfall.

There's not a lot of blood or nudity in the film, but it's not needed. What *Cold Prey* relies on instead are good, old fashioned scares and tension, and it works very well. It can be a bit slow at times before the killer comes in to play, but it's realistic given the situation and the mood built is tremendous. The killer has an interesting backstory that keeps you interested and the fact that his weapon of choice happens to be a pick is a nice little nod to *My Bloody Valentine*. There's only a few kills, but they're all done very well and are very tense moments. The first one is the best, as the girl is killed literally feet from her friends and no one notices until later.

If you happened to like *Cold Prey*, as I did, then you may want to check out the two sequels. Part Two is a direct sequel, while Part Three is a prequel. Both are good additions. I give *Cold Prey* a solid three and a half out of five stars.

CUT (2000) ~ (Teen Slashers/International)

Here's another international entry into the slasher market. *Cut* comes to us from the land down under and has been called by many over the years, "The Australian *Scream*", and for good reason.

Taking on two meanings in its title, (to cut someone and the term, as it relates to filming. Clever, eh?), *Cut* starts out in a very *Scream-like* fashion. The start is very cliché, featuring our teen girl alone at home, a shower scene, a mysterious call, and even a cat named Freddy, by God! But wait, it's a trap! It turns out that this is just a generic slasher film being filmed, called Hot Blooded. Well, behind the scenes it's anything but generic. The man playing the killer goes bonkers on the bitchy director (Kylie Minogue) and kills her. He is stopped by several others and thus begins our story. Years later, a group of film students, led by Rafferty (Jessica Napier), hear about the unfinished film and set out to finish it themselves as a class project. The only problem is, the film is cursed, as we hear from their teacher/our prophet of doom, who tells them how anyone who has tried to finish the film over the years has been murdered horribly. Sure enough, that does not dissuade our plucky crew!

The crew soon sets off to complete the cursed film and convene at the old country estate where the original filming took place. They even manage to get the lead actress from the original film (Molly Ringwald) to fly in from Hollywood to play the lead again, and boy is she a handful! Soon enough, someone gets a hold of one of the killer's masks and sets out, stalking and slashing the cast and crew. Naturally, when they see the man in the killer's mask, the victims assume it's the actor playing the killer (who takes method acting very seriously), but is it?

Cut reminded me of several other "horror on the film set" slasher films such as Return to Horror High, Scream 3, The Hills Run Red, and Urban Legends, only better than all of those combined. Throw in some of the tongue in cheek, self-referential humor of the teen slashers and Scream, and you have Cut. The effects and kill scenes are bloody enough, and the weapon of choice is an interesting one, like shears modified by a Rabbi, almost. There are a lot of fun scenes that stick out, such as a scene where the cameraman keeps filming the killer, thinking it's part of the film, and my favorite scene, where the actor playing the killer meets up with the real killer, both in masks, and the two have a bit of a stand-off. It's a very clever scene! The end reveal is one that caught me off guard and a very interesting, yet odd angle, but it works. The effects in the final showdown are simply phenomenal, as well!

While I wasn't expecting much from the start, Cut has quickly become a new favorite of mine. I think maybe the stigma of being direct to video may have had something to do with the low expectations. Funnily enough, Cut actually was released theatrically in the international market and was a hit overseas. Why we got shafted in America is a mystery, but I digress. Cut is just a fun, entertaining slasher film all around and it works very well. The cast is very competent and it's great to see Molly Ringwald at it again. She plays a great bitch in the movie, as the high maintenance lead actress (art imitating life, perhaps?). The comedy in the film actually works and can be quite laugh out loud funny at points, and the film is self-aware and realizes exactly what it is, which is nice, but expected (thus, some of the Scream comparisons).

I give Cut a score of four out of five stars. It has easily earned a place on my shelf of favorite slasher films. If you haven't seen it, I highly recommend checking it out.

DEATH BY DIALOGUE (1988) ~ (Just Plain Weird)

I just want to touch on this one briefly. *Death by Dialogue* is one odd duck, for sure. It revolves around a group of young actors who start to get killed off one by one by demonic forces released by an evil, possessed, killer script. Yep, I just said that. One of the things that stands out here is the fact that *Nightmare on Elm Street* survivor Ken Sagoes plays our final guy. The film also serves as proof why Ken was never a lead character again. *Death by Dialogue* features one of the worst opening scenes ever, an incredibly weird scene where one character ends up in an atrocious hair metal video in the woods. It also features one of the most annoying characters in film history, and one of the weirdest sex scenes ever that turns unintentionally hilarious as a girl is literally blown off a guy and through a second-floor wall!

The film gets a bit better when we finally get to see our ghoulish demonic killer and his unholy minions towards the end and their appearance is a highlight, leading to a fiery finale, which saves the film from complete destruction. Still, this is by far one of the goofiest slashers of the 80s and can only be recommended for fans of those "Good-bad films". I give *Death by Dialogue* two stars out of five. Nuff said!

DEVIL TIMES FIVE (1974) ~ (Killer Kids)

Let's face it, kids can be creepy little bastards. Sometimes they say or do the creepiest things. It makes sense then that the killer kid category is such a big thing in the horror movie world. From *The Omen* to *The Bad Seed*, to *The Brood*, to *Village of the Damned*, killer kid movies will always have a place in Hollywood because it is a real fear that is out there. One of my favorite examples of the genre is one that is sadly forgotten by many, and it just so happens to be one of the best examples of the genre, *The Devil Times Five*.

The Devil Times Five (also known as *Peopletoys*. Seriously, how fucking terrifying is that name? That other title really says it all) starts out with a bus full of homicidal children on their way to a new facility, traveling down a snowy mountain road. You know that can't be good. After the bus wrecks and the children crawl out of the wreckage, they make their way to a ski lodge nearby, where a group of adults (including Boss Hogg himself, Sorrell Booke!) are staying for the weekend. The kids come to the group for help and are taken in, but what the adults don't know is that the kids are psychotic little killing machines. The kids include an older girl who takes on the guise of a nun named Sister Hannah, a girl who is obsessed with fire, a black kid who fancies himself a soldier and talks in military lingo (the leader of the group), and a young, mop topped Leif

34

Garret. Before the kids arrive, we get a little taste of what's to come in a very long, drawn out, slow motion scene that's borderline sadistic as the kids all take turns beating their psychiatrist to death in a shed with hammers, chains and more! It's vicious to say the least and it doesn't stop there. They soon take to killing the adults in the house one by one in very vicious ways including stabbing, hanging and shooting. In one scene, the children even drown the heavily endowed Carolyn Stellar (who also happens to be the real-life mom of two of the killer kids here, Leif Garrett and Dawn Lyn … and is in a nude scene in front of them … um, okay. Times were different then, I guess) and drop killer piranhas in the tub! They then drag her naked corpse around. Geez! These kids are just cold, unflinching killers. Prepare to be shocked folks.

One of the things that I really appreciated about *The Devil Times Five* is the meanness of it all. It's just one of those films that does not hold back and takes no prisoners. The adults give okay performances, but the kids are the real stars of the show here. The kids are vicious killing machines and like a ravenous pack of vultures when it comes to the killing. They're also very manipulative and fun to watch. If you're expecting a happy ending, you better look elsewhere because there is none to be found here. Those are the types of horror movies I love to watch too, the ones with a bleak ending where there are no heroes, nothing is resolved and the chaos will presumably continue. The final scene of the killer kids marching around the dead adults in the snow is unnerving to say the least.

I must mention that there is a lot of controversy surrounding the film, mostly surrounding the director Sean MacGregor. The actress Gail Smale, who plays the character of "Sister Hannah" was allegedly Sean's very underage girlfriend, which caused several issues. The shooting was difficult and ultimately the director was fired from the film and his footage was deemed unusable. Director David Sheldon stepped in to re-shoot the scenes and finish the project, while MacGregor allegedly ended up in a mental institution. It wouldn't be his last film, but he has rarely worked since. It's quite the story, isn't it?

The Devil Times Five is truly one of the best of the killer kid films and definitely a product of its time. It's vicious and unflinching and there is a major sense of dread throughout. This, coupled with a snowbound, desolate setting just makes for the perfect combination for a horror film. If you want one that will keep you up for a while afterward, go with *The Devil Times Five*. It's a classic, in my opinion. I give it four stars out of five.

HAUNTEDWEEN (1991)~ (Holiday Slashers)

Ah, the good old walkthrough haunted house. For many of us, this was a tradition growing up and no Halloween could be complete without at least one visit to one of the local haunts. Now, imagine if you will, if a masked killer were to set upon one of these haunts and kill the actors providing the scares, all while the patrons are oblivious to the fact, thinking it's all part of the show. That's the premise for *Hauntedween,* an innovative little indie film straight from Bowling Green, Kentucky.

The film begins with a little girl getting brutally murdered in a local haunted house around Halloween. Flash forward years later and we meet the boys from a nearby local fraternity. They decide to hold a haunted house for a fundraiser this witching season and decide to use the infamous site of the girl's murder years before. Soon enough, our masked killer shows up and starts to take out the college kids one by one, placing them in his own "Kill room" in the haunt and making a public spectacle out of their gruesome deaths, for all of the patrons to enjoy. If only they knew that it wasn't part of the show, right?

Hauntedween is one wickedly fun college slasher film with an interesting concept. Despite it obviously being super low budget and indie, it's something you have to take in stride to enjoy the film. The concept is great and there's enough gore, laughs and fun ideas to keep many genre fans happy, along with a competent cast who make the proceedings watchable. One of the only drawbacks is the abrupt, lazy ending and I would have ranked it much higher if not for that. Also, the Halloween theme itself was quite light throughout the film, and I would have liked to have seen more in depth use of the holiday.

Other than these minor details, *Hauntedween* is fun and very watchable for a sadly much forgotten and obscure slasher film from the early nineties. I give it three stars out of five. For more information on the film and a place to order it from the filmmakers themselves, check out their website, www.hauntedweenmovie.com. You can find out tons of information on the film. Also, the DVD is full of interesting extras, as well as behind the scenes footage and stories. Happy haunting!

HOLLYWOOD'S NEW BLOOD (1988)

Here's a film where the entire title happens to be a lie. Let's break it down, shall we? First off, we have Hollywood. No, the film is actually set in the woods and nowhere near the bright lights of Hollywood. New: well no, there's really nothing new to be seen here. Blood? Sorry, but there's not much of that to be seen in *Hollywood's New Blood*, either.

Directed by James Shyman (see interviews), the director of another notoriously bad 80s slasher film, *Slashdance* (so bad it's good in that case), this is a film that even the director has gone on record as saying he's not too proud of. The plot centers around a film crew (by film crew I mean a director and a group of horny young actors) that is ready to shoot a movie in the woods outside of LA at the sight of a disaster years before while a crew filmed another movie there. Apparently, that crew ended up blowing up a house with a family of hillbillies living in it and now they're back, and they're pissed! What follows is your standard run of the mill slasher fare as the incredibly slow moving killers return to take out all of the young

SLASHED DREAMS PART 2

Hollywood hopefuls in some of the most standard ways, i.e. stabbing, slashing, strangling, etc. There are a few good moments here and there, such as few interesting death scenes, some nice visuals and such, but they are few and far between. One of the best things that the film boasts is an innovative way to take out the killer, as one of our survivors end up jabbing the skull of the mother of the family right in the face of the killer, who runs screaming off into the woods with the skull stuck to his face. I, for one, would have liked to have seen a sequel with that killer on the loose!

While not one of the worst films out there (and I'm not putting it on that list because it does have its moments), *Hollywood's New Blood* still suffers from a lack of originality and just seems so by the numbers at times. The killers don't seem too original or intimidating, but they still work for the film, even if they are a bit slow. The deaths themselves are all very tame and sadly heavily edited for the most part, as well. Personally, I was a bit disappointed and had very high hopes for it, due to the great title and the awesome cover art. I was expecting something a bit more out of it, like a masked killer stalking the streets of Hollywood itself and killing victims in dark film lots and back alleys, maybe something like the real-life Skid Row Slasher. Instead, I got this movie that really failed to live up to my high hopes. That doesn't make it completely unbearable, mind you, just disappointing. Perhaps a re-imagining should be in order? I give *Hollywood's New Blood* one and a half out of five stars.

HOME FOR THE HOLIDAYS (1972) - (Pre-slashers)

When it comes to the early influences of the slasher film genre, there are many films to look at as true pioneers along the way. Of course, there's the Giallo films, the exploitation films of the Seventies, the films of the late Herschell Gordon Lewis, Agatha Christie, *Psycho, Black Christmas, Texas Chainsaw Massacre* and many more. Many of these were covered in my previous book, but one of the films that slipped by me is just as important of a piece of the slasher puzzle as any of the others, and that's the Sally Field starring TV thriller *Home for the Holidays*. Without a doubt, this one has slasher written all over it!

Not to be confused with the awful family drama from the nineties with the same name, this *Home for the Holidays* is a spooky, atmospheric, dark film that is simplicity at its best. The plot centers around an old man (Walter Brennan) on his death bed. He is convinced that his wife (Julie Harris) is trying to kill him and summons his four daughters (the talented ensemble of Eleanor Parker, Sally Field, Jessica Harper and Jill Haworth) to his sprawling countryside manor for Christmas weekend. Sure enough, once they get there, the plot starts to thicken as the girls start to get killed one by one by a mysterious shrouded ghoul wearing a yellow rain slicker and carrying a pitchfork. It's quite the decent murder mystery with a few twists and turns, plenty of intrigue and multiple red herrings.

There is no doubt in my mind that this often forgotten made for TV film was an early influence on the slasher genre. It has all of the trappings of a slasher film and can also be an intense thriller. It's very dark and gritty, especially surprising given that it's a TV film. It rains nearly the entire film (just like my area, The Pacific Northwest!) and it adds a real dreary sense of foreboding and doom to the proceedings. There are many effective scares and a spooky atmosphere to be found throughout *Home for the Holidays*. While it may be low on the body count, it really doesn't need it. Instead, this is just an example of good old fashioned horror and terror that doesn't need a lot of blood or bodies to be effective. The killer here is one of my personal favorites and has always stood out to me. It's a very creepy guise, with the killer clad in a dark rain slicker, with their face hidden.

Home for the Holidays easily gets a score of three and a half stars out of five from me. It may not be the scariest or bloodiest, but I'm sure most slasher fans will appreciate the history lesson.

HORROR HOUSE ON HIGHWAY 5 (1985) ~ (The worst)

Here's another film that I only want to briefly touch upon, for the sake of my own sanity. As many readers have probably already gathered, I am not the biggest fan of the SOV videos of the eighties. They are by far the schlockiest, worst films of the era, with bad lighting, horrible acting, cheesy effects and some of the worst storylines and writing this side of Ed Wood. While there are a few out there that do happen to stand out and gain some kind of sick pleasure out of the viewing experience, being so bad that they're good, there are others, like *Horror House on Highway 5* that make for just a truly horrendous viewing experience.

Horror House on Highway 5 is just a mess of a film. It could also be one of the strangest films I have ever covered, at times feeling like a bad acid trip. There are several stories going on at the same time throughout the mercifully short run-time, many of which don't fit together. One plot revolves around two bickering redneck brothers living in what looks like Cherry Forever's house from *Porky's*, who are apparently neo Nazis (though they don't look it, they just look like dumb inbred hicks). The two like to kidnap and sacrifice girls for some unknown reason. One of them is quite the special idiot, too, seemingly falling in love with some of the victims, while his brother is the brains of the operation (if you can call him that). At the same time, there is a killer hanging around the backroads, wearing a Nixon mask and killing teenagers. Now, while some of this may sound intriguing on paper (which it did to me), it fails to be anywhere near as good or interesting as you would hope. It looks as if it were shot on a camcorder and there are several moments of inane dialogue between the characters that drag on forever, plus nothing is ever really explained. The actors seem to

---

physically struggle at times to even complete the nonsensical dialogue and it's clear that the film was probably just made by some college kids with a camera after a few too many Miller High Life's one night. There you have the film, in a nutshell. Beyond that, there's so many weird visuals and elements that come into play for no reason throughout, that you'll swear someone may have spiked your drink. Weird does not even begin to describe some of these scenes. I would try to list them, but I'm not even sure I could do it justice. Besides, why would anyone want to watch this? Take it from me, while a killer in a Nixon mask is a neat idea, the end result is not worth your time. You've been warned.

Horror House on Highway 5 is easily one of, if not the worst, slasher films I have ever seen. It's just a jumbled, incoherent mess of a movie that was thrown together with no rhyme or reason. It's confusing at times and can even physically hurt to watch. It's amateur hour all the way and a very good example of what not to do when making a film. I give it half a star out of five and that's just for the interesting idea of having a killer in a Nixon mask, which isn't even the focal point of the film.

HOT FUZZ (2005) ~ (Intentionally Funny)

I have been a fan of the British comedy team of Simon Pegg and Nick Frost since I first happened upon their clever cult classic take on the zombie genre (or Zomedy, as some have come to call it) *Shaun of the Dead*. They managed to do something very unique with it and ended up basically making the slacker's guide to the zombie apocalypse, something that has really stood the test of time. It also launched the careers of these two talented Brits on a worldwide stage. Naturally, they had to follow it up with something big and they did so with their own take on the slasher genre in *Hot Fuzz*, one of my personal favorites.

Sergeant Nick Angel (or Angle, as the local newspaper constantly misprints his name) is the best officer on the police force in London. In fact, he's too good. He is actually making the rest of the force look bad, so they give him a new assignment and he is sent to work in the sleepy village of Sandford. Upon arrival in the quiet hamlet, he soon makes himself known ... on his first night in town (a night not on the clock, by the way), as he arrests several juveniles, drunks and more. He soon finds out the next day, his first official day on the job, that the drunk he arrested the night before is in fact his new partner Danny Butterman (Nick Frost), a slovenly, yet lovable fuck-up of a drunken man child. Danny takes an immediate shine to Nicholas, who he sees as some kind of supercop and wants to learn everything he can from him, along with showing the uptight Angel how to loosen up a bit. It sounds like your average buddy cop comedy, right? Just wait, there's more! The town is very quiet, with calls varying from having to chase a lost goose to catching shoplifters, so there's not a lot happening ... that is until local townspeople start getting murdered soon after Angel's arrival by a hooded killer. The two officers soon discover that the town has one hell of dark secret behind it's squeaky clean veneer and the conspiracy reaches deep to some of the most prominent citizens in town.

Let's just put it bluntly, *Hot Fuzz* is a God damn masterpiece of a movie! It is one of the most fun takes on the genre in quite some time. It manages to walk that thin line of being funny and serious at the same time, which is something that the Frost/Pegg team is quite adept at. The setting is perfect and the type of town where you feel like nothing could go wrong, and the cast of characters in town (red herrings, and some ... not so red?) make it all the more enjoyable, including the giant Michael Armstrong, who can only utter the phrase "Yarp". Supermarket manager Simon Skinner is by far the most prominent of these red herrings and sticks out like your average mustache twirling old timey villain here. Hell, his name is Skinner! Add in the fact that on his first meeting of Angel, he tells him, "Lock me up. I'm a slasher ... of prices!" All of the jokes in *Hot Fuzz* hit the nail right on the head and it's one that never loses its charm, no matter how many times you watch it. The killer(s?) makes quite the impression and appear as your classic dark cloaked, hooded reaper type who uses an array of weapons. Speaking of which, the deaths in *Hot Fuzz* are surprisingly bloody and well done, including a woman getting garden shears in the throat, a man getting the axe in the head, and a nosy reporter getting his head smashed by a church spire in a surprisingly splattery scene! The climax of the film throws in one of the most hilariously over the top reasons for murder ever seen on screen and leads to another hilariously over the top old west type shootout in the center of the village. It has to be seen to be believed!

Hot Fuzz is simply a work of pure genius. It's one of the most enjoyable films in the book (both books, in fact), and is pure fun all around. Like its predecessor, it doesn't take itself too seriously, but also takes itself just seriously enough at the same time. I give *Hot Fuzz* four and a half stars out of five. It is probably the best slasher inspired comedy out there today. In fact, I would have ranked it much higher on my list, if I only had included it in the previous book.

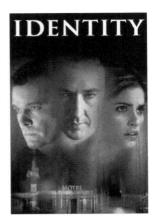

IDENTITY (2003) ~ (Modern Day Slashers)

Is *Identity* considered a slasher film? You bet your ass it is! Maybe not by many in the horror community, but I sure as hell can see all of the slasher movie influences here. *Identity* has a very heavy slasher influence and an old-school horror feel to it, along the lines of Agatha Christie, while at the same time being a very clever psychological horror film.

Identity is a classic old school horror film all the way with a very clever new twist to it. At the start, we see clippings of a series of grisly killings and see several doctors gathered around a table at a hospital for a review, including veteran actor Alfred Molina. They are there to decide whether or not a serial killer should face the death penalty or be found insane. They then produce the killer's diary which recounts him being left at a motel by his prostitute mother as a child and his later killing spree.

From there, we go out to the middle of the desert during a fierce storm. We get to meet our cast, who are all brought to the same lonely place to meet their fate, a lonely out of the way motel on a dark desert highway. The cast includes a limo driver/ former cop (John Cusack) and his actress client (Rebecca De Mornay), a prostitute looking to start a new life (Amanda Peet), a cop (Ray Liotta) and his prisoner transport (Jake Busey), two young newlyweds and a family of three, including the oddball father (John C. McGinley), the mother who was just in a horrible car accident and their shell shocked young boy. The ten strangers all meet at the hotel and soon start to be killed off one by one by a mysterious killer. All of them soon learn that they are connected in some way. They all have states in their names and have the same birthday, as well as several other strange coincidences. There are many red herrings that switch from one to the next at a rapid pace such as Jake Busey (the first obvious suspect), and the hotel manager with a terrible secret in his freezer. Even Ray Liotta has his own terrible secret that makes him a prime suspect. Cusack does his best to play detective and try to find the identity of the killer before everyone is dead, and he soon finds out that it might be a futile effort.

Featuring stellar performances from an all-star cast, *Identity* starts out big and manages to keep the suspense up for the entire duration of the film. It's one of those films that will keep you guessing until the very end. What does the serial killer at the start of the film have to do with everything? Is he recounting his killing spree, or is it something else? The twist at the end is a very clever one and it makes *Identity* an even more intriguing film. The makers of the movie really keep the suspense at an all-time high and the dark, stormy, secluded setting is a perfect place for a twisted murder spree and whodunit like this to take place.

I give *Identity* four and a half stars out of five. I saw it when it first arrived in theaters in 2003 and I have been a fan ever since. It's very clever and one of those fun films that just keeps you guessing until the end. Very well done with an incredibly talented cast, *Identity* is a must for any horror fan.

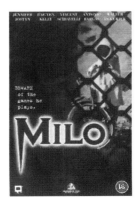

MILO (1998)- (Killer Kids)

Milo just so happens to be one of the few films that has ever legitimately creeped me out. There's something about it that is very creepy and sinister. Maybe it's the creepy kid with the voice of the puppet from *Dead Silence*, maybe it's the hidden menace of the killer kid, maybe it's just the unnerving music of the film, I'm not really sure. What I am sure about, is the *Milo* really got under my skin, despite not being the greatest slasher film out there.

Milo is one bad, bad boy. Our film starts out years ago in small Anytown, America. The young girls in town all convene together to take up the creepy local kid, Milo's offer to come to his father's home gynecologist office and see some real aborted fetuses. That's a creepy start. Even creepier is the fact that part of the deal is that Milo gets to give one of the girls an exam! Well, things go bad fast as Milo ends up killing the girl. Fast forward years later and the girls are all grown up now. One of the girls, Claire (Jennifer Jostyn) is now a substitute teacher and returns to her hometown for her friend's wedding. After arriving though, she finds out the friend died under mysterious circumstances. Claire decides to stay in town and take a job at the local school and reconnect with her friends, but that damn past always comes back to haunt the folks in these movies. Claire soon starts to see what looks like that creepy Milo kid around town, but he still looks just like a kid. Supposedly, Milo was killed shortly after the incident years before, so it couldn't be him, right? Soon, Claire's friends start to get killed by the demonic little boy in the yellow rain slicker and soon, it's up to Claire and the wise old black janitor (Antonio Fargas! Always a welcome addition to any film) to stop the killer kid.

I must say that I was very surprised by *Milo*. It has a unique story to it and manages to keep a creepy, unnerving edge to the film. It's a very dark movie and manages to keep the suspense and scares coming along at a fairly even pace. The music is downright unnerving and the appearance of Milo, with his face covered up by his slicker, like a demonic Kenny from *South Park*, is just a creepy sight to behold. The kid is just downright creepy and his voice is even creepier, when you hear it. Seeing some of the notable names such as Fargas (who happens to steal every scene that he's in, naturally) and Vincent Schiavelli, as Milo's father, add a lot to *Milo*. Another notable name in the cast to watch out for is a very young Mila Kunis in one of her first roles as a student at the school. The kills and the scenes leading up to them are full of suspense and will leave you on the edge of your seat. One drawback to *Milo* is the fact that the whole thing is never explained clearly. What exactly is Milo? Apparently, he's some aborted fetus zombie clone of the doctor's son or something along those lines. Okay, sure. The ending still leaves several questions unanswered, but I suppose I can let that slide, as the movie is just so damn effective, as it is.

Milo is one of those movies that I am ashamed I wasn't aware of before. I have to admit that I really didn't expect a whole lot from it, being a late 90s direct to video horror film, but I was quite surprised. It's one that I'm sure I'll watch again. I give *Milo* a score of three and a half stars out of five.

NATIONAL LAMPOON'S CLASS REUNION (1982) - (Intentionally Funny)

It has been said before that parody is the true way to know that you have truly made it in the entertainment world. In the early 1980s, the slasher film was king and it was ripe for parody. Why, just in that time period alone, we had a slew of slasher parodies come out,

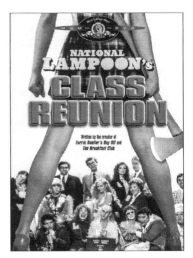

such as *Wacko, Pandemonium, Student Bodies, The Private Eyes* and this one, one of the more forgotten of the bunch. Perhaps it has to do with the National Lampoon's affiliation. That could be the reason why it wasn't as lumped in with the others. Well, let me tell you, *Class Reunion* is a slasher parody through and through, just as much as the others!

Class Reunion follows the exploits of the graduates of Lizzie Borden High School (if the National Lampoon's affiliation wasn't a dead giveaway as to what to expect, the name of the school sure as hell should be!) as they attend their class reunion. Many familiar faces are in the group such as genre favorite Gerrit Graham as the snooty Bob Spinnaker and Flounder himself, Stephen Furst as the sleazy loser of the bunch Hubert Downs. What our gang does not know is that the kid that they pulled a horrible prank on years before (played by Blackie Dammett from *The American Scream*. Who is Blackie Dammett? Trivia time! He is the dad of Red Hot Chili Peppers lead singer Anthony Kiedis!) has escaped from the mental hospital and is planning on a surprise appearance at the reunion with one thing on his mind ... REVENGE! He soon sets out to kill those that made him make out with his twin sister, leaving him emotionally scarred and a bit homicidal. The class alum has all kinds of goofy characters such as a Hare Krishna, a girl who is possessed by Satan and breathes fire, a horny blind girl with a chipmunk voice and more. We also get to see several other notables like Anne Ramsey of *The Goonies* as the lunchlady (perfect casting!), Michael Lerner and Art Evans (*Fright Night*).

Naturally, you can expect this one to be jam packed with goofy one-liners and shenanigans, as any *Airplane* style spoof will have to the max. For the most part, the jokes work too, which is nice. Some are dated, naturally, but most are well done. Graham and Furst are the real winners of the cast here, especially Graham who reaches the heights of snobby obnoxiousness in the most hilarious of ways. One thing you should not be looking for here however, is a big body count. Really, there's only a couple of victims throughout the film and those are (naturally) goofy as hell. Don't be disappointed though, it is a National Lampoon's comedy, after all and not a full-blown slasher film.

Although it can be quite the funny film at many times, it just lacks a certain something that the other slasher parodies of the time had. Maybe it is a lack of body count that the other slasher parodies had. I can't quite put my finger on it. Still, that doesn't make it a total waste of time. *National Lampoon's Class Reunion* is what it is, a campy *Airplane* style take on the slasher genre that cannot be taken seriously and shouldn't be. Just enjoy it for what it is. It's not the best of the subgenre, but can still be an entertaining watch and some of the well-known names add a lot to it. I give *Class Reunion* a score of two stars out of five.

PAPERBOY, THE (1994) - (Killer Kids)

Imagine if you will, if they decided to make a full-length horror movie based on the psychotic paperboy from *Better Off Dead*. Well folks, that film would be very similar to *The Paperboy*, a fun little Canadian killer kid film brought to us by director Douglas Jackson.

Johnny seems like the perfect kid, except for the fact that he is highly obsessive over his new neighbor and also homicidal. The target of his affection happens to be Melissa, played by Alexandra Paul, who previously survived a run-in with a killer car in *Christine*, only to now have to deal with the killer pre-teen boy living next door to her. The movie doesn't pull any punches, starting with Johnny killing an old woman with a bag over the head and just progresses from there. The woman's daughter moves back home after the funeral, with her own young daughter and tries to get back to a normal life, even reconnecting with an old high school flame (William Katt). Very soon, the boy next door starts coming around and making himself at home in the creepiest ways. He hits it off with Melissa's daughter and starts doing things for the family, like making them presents and cooking them meals. Plus, he always seems to be around, even when he's not wanted around. He also breaks into the home several times, sometimes taking personal belongings and pictures to make his own creepy, obsessive collages. Soon, Melissa becomes concerned with Johnny's obsessive behavior, jealousy, and his ability to snap and break things when told to stop. Before you know it, little Johnny is back to his killing ways, murdering anyone that stands in his way of creating the perfect family with his neighbors.

The Paperboy is one of those great throwback films that has a timeless quality. It can be pretty much any time frame and never really shows its age. The cast all does a decent job, but the best performance by far is from Marc Marut as the obsessive Johnny. He is just phenomenal in the role, especially when he gets his violent anger outbursts. Watching him violently break things and scream or beat his bed with a baseball bat or bash his head against the wall is a truly intriguing experience. Marc truly goes above and beyond in the role and it's a shame he didn't do more. There are some good kills in the film, such as the opening one and Johnny killing his dad with a golf club and keeping the body in the freezer (there's even a scene where he casually grabs a Popsicle from above his dad's frozen corpse). The best scene is when he captures an old woman's dog in a pillowcase and beats it with a bat until the old woman dies of shock. Of course, Johnny's not a total monster as he just replaced the dog in the bag with a rack of ribs and beat that instead. See, maybe he's not all bad ... okay, maybe not. There's also several attempted murders throughout the film as well and an explosive finale. All in all, *The Paperboy* really does a great job at keeping the suspense up and getting your attention the whole movie.

I give *The Paperboy* a score of three and a half out of five stars. It's just a fun, suspenseful thriller all around with some mild slasher undertones and is heavily reminiscent of other obsessive suspense films like *The Stepfather, The Hand That Rocks the Cradle* and others. Highly recommended.

PRIVATE EYES, THE (1980) ~ (Intentionally Funny)

Don Knotts and Tim Conway in an old Agatha Christie type mansion murder mystery/ slasher film? You just know going into this one that it's going to be goofy as hell!

In *The Private Eyes*, we start out at the stately mansion of Lord and Lady Morley in the English countryside. The couple are murdered in the opening moments by a mysterious hooded figure dressed all in black. Never fear though! Scotland Yard's two worst American detectives are on the case, in Don Knotts and Tim Conway. They arrive at the mansion to investigate the murders (and engage in lots of comical banter about things such as "Wookalars"), and soon meet the oddball group of employees at the mansion. Our duo tries to question the residents of the manor and investigate the case, but wouldn't you know it, the killer is still there and starts bumping off all of the Lord's faithful servants, one by one. Naturally, the goofy characters get killed in goofy ways and the killer loves to leave around the worst poems ever at each murder scene. Every time you think they're going to rhyme, it's a swing and a miss! Soon, the population of the mansion dwindles down and it's up to our fearful duo to solve the mystery of who's on first, I mean, who's the killer.

The Private Eyes is a rather tame film by anyone's standards. It's relatively bloodless, has no bad language, nudity or anything like that. Of course, there's plenty of suggested things like that, such as scenes with the bouncy, top heavy French maid, but this is pretty much a family movie ... with a hooded killer lurking around a dark castle. Some of the jokes are quite dated, but others still manage to hold up to this day. The comedy is purely old school with lots of funny banter between the two leads, plenty of double takes and loads of physical comedy. Obviously, Conway and Knotts are a great comedic duo and do another great job here. The setting is pretty much on par for the type of movie that it is and there can be some spookiness to it, at times. Plus, it's fun to see our bumbling nitwit detectives stumble around the dark mansion, finding bodies and having some major freak out moments. It really reminds one of the old Abbott and Costello monster movies. The best thing here, in my opinion, is the unique characters in the cast. You have the hunchback with a missing tongue (played by the late Irwin Keyes, no less!), the samurai chef, the busty maid, a drunk gypsy caretaker (who loves digging for worms at night in the yard), and an insane former Nazi butler, who goes on manic rants and has serious anger issues. All of them seem like carnies or cartoon characters and are the real fun ones to watch in the movie. Seeing our leads interact with them is the real fun part. The only disappointment is the ending, which kind of would feel like a cheat for many other films, but I guess I'll let it slide here, this being a "family" film. No, it still feels like a cheat, actually. Damn it, I really do hate endings like the one here. That's the only real downside to the movie.

Don't get your hopes up about this one being a bloody, proper slasher film. It was marketed as a family film, after all. It's just a fun, old school comedy film with a slasher story to it, while being heavily influenced by both Sherlock Holmes and Agatha Christie. It's always been a favorite of mine, and still is to this day. It's just a harmless, stupidly fun film. I give it three and a half stars out of five.

RUSH WEEK (1989)~ (School Slasher)

Quickly after finishing my first book, it came to my attention that there were quite a few slasher films that slipped by me for one reason or another. Naturally, I made it my duty to try and rectify the situation as soon as possible! One of these films happens to be *Rush Week*, an often-forgotten relic from the year that the slasher film went into remission for the first time.

In *Rush Week*, our plot involves a number of nubile female students who take to doing late night nude film shoots in one of the buildings for the sleazy college cook. Soon, these same girls start getting stalked and murdered by a mysterious masked killer with a real axe to grind (tee hee). Enter Toni (Pamela Ludwig), a young reporter who goes undercover at the college to cover the rush week shenanigans. Toni soon finds herself in a much bigger news story, as she tries to get to the bottom of the recent co-ed killings, while trying not to end up as a victim of the masked slasher herself.

Fans of the slasher kingdom will no doubt notice two notable names in the cast, Dominic Brascia (Joey from *Friday the 13th Part V*) and Kathleen Kinmont (*Halloween 4*). Dominic just has a small supporting role as one of the frat boys, while Kathleen gets to play victim again here. Yay! Also, keep an eye out for another odd cameo from rocker Greg Allman as a hippie professor. *Rush Week* is pretty much your average, by the numbers college slasher flick. There's little deviation from the formula and the killer is one that is easy to spot a mile away. Does that make it bad? Hell no. It's still a fun little slasher flick, albeit one we have all seen before. The killer's disguise is a rather effective one, too. I appreciate the look, with the old man mask and black cape, as well as the weapon choice of a double-sided axe. Nifty. Some of the kill and chase scenes are well done enough. The killer's demise is another bloody highlight of the film, as well and fans of multiple kills will be happy with the film's body count. However, there is a decided lack of gore to the film and many of the kills happen off screen. Maybe the filmmakers were just hoping that adding in tons of boobs and young college cuties in the buff would help even things out. Oh, and there is a lot of that to go around in *Rush Week*!

In summary, *Rush Week* is just your average school slasher. It has its moments and there are some definite highlights throughout, but it's easy to see how it gets lost in the shuffle and remains forgotten by many. This is why I wasn't even aware it existed until after the last book was published. I'm glad I saw it though, and I wouldn't mind watching it again, but I'm also not rushing out to do so. I give *Rush Week* two and a half out of five stars.

SAVAGE LUST (1990)

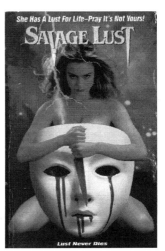

Upon the first glance, *Savage Lust* (aka *Deadly Manor,* a much more fitting title) doesn't even look like a slasher film at all. In fact, it looks more like your standard late night Showtime softcore porn fare. The cover features a beautiful naked woman behind a giant creepy mask. Yes, the cover art is indeed confusing in many cases, but especially so here in the case of *Savage Lust*. When I first heard that this was a slasher film, I was shocked to say the least. I had seen it many times before in the old video shops of my youth, but obviously never drew the connection. I wasn't expecting much when I found a copy, but as can happen, I was very surprised.

Savage Lust was brought to us in 1990 during the slasher film doldrums, by director Jose Ramon Larraz, who also brought us the criminally underrated slasher film *Edge of the Axe* in 1988. Actually, it's a film that would have fit perfectly in the slasher filled eighties, but just barely missed the boat by a few months, so maybe it could be considered either one of the last of the cycle or part of the doldrums. Either way, *Savage Lust* centers on a group of twenty-somethings on their way to a lake for some sun and fun. They pick up one of those perpetual bad boys on the way that's obviously way too cool for school, and (whispers) he's dangerous. You know, because he has a leather jacket, bad attitude and a knife. The group end up doing what any dumb kids in a film like this would do and take a detour onto some private property, ending up at a mansion deep in the woods that is obviously still inhabited. What would you do? Turn around and leave? Nah, just kick in the door and make yourselves at home! Well, it's been nice knowing you. Soon inside, the group starts to uncover a mystery surrounding a mysterious woman seen in pictures around the house and strange goings on, like the old car on display whose horn keeps going off, one character's dark sexual fantasies about a mystery woman in a white mask (hence the cover art) or the walls leaking. Soon enough, our group begins to dwindle, getting killed one by one. The funniest thing is the one you would peg for a final girl, who is smart enough to leave the property and her friends … only to get killed first. I guess the smartest one doesn't always live. Soon enough, while dealing with both a killer on the loose and the bad boy trying to hide his criminal past (big shocker, right?) by resorting to assaultive/ homicidal ways, we finally find out who our real killer is after a *Scooby Doo* like mystery plot unfolds. It's convoluted for sure, and an odd reveal, but not bad, either.

While not the greatest slasher film and featuring an overabundance of cliché dumb victims, *Savage Lust* is also not a complete waste of time. It can be quite the fun watch and manages to keep your attention and keeps things interesting, while moving along at a decent pace. There are some good kills here and an interesting killer reveal, but the real star here is the location, the Deadly Manor. The film manages to have one of the better locations around and some great atmosphere. For that, I say that *Savage Lust* is definitely worth seeking out. I give it two and a half out of five stars.

SAVAGE WATER (1979) ~ (The Worst)

In my time reviewing these films, there have been some tough ones to track down a copy of. Sometimes I feel like the Indiana Jones of exploring slasher films, going to the ends of the earth to find some of these ... okay, not far from my computer, in reality, but I digress. *Savage Water* is one of the rarest of the rare, and perhaps with good reason. It was never officially released in the US back in the day and only got a release on DVD thanks to Vinegar Syndrome a few years back, but even that was pulled from shelves due to legal issues. Thankfully, I found a copy of that DVD release so I could review it for you good folks. I hope you're happy what you put me through.

Savage Water centers around a mismatched group of yokel tourists on a rafting trip down the Colorado River that start getting bumped off one by one by a mysterious killer. That's the Cliff Notes version of it, anyways. What lies just beneath the surface is a mountain of steaming crap. This is one of those goofy seventies films with goofy slapstick montages with weird parade music over the scenes, goofy sound effects, and some of the most annoying characters in film history. Those things don't even compare to all of the filler material, either. Who wants to listen to long drawn out lectures on why we shouldn't litter or what plants not to eat, or how to use the portable toilets? One good thing it does have is scenery, and there's some good rafting scenes, even if it is some of the most disgusting looking brown water around. As a straight up rafting film, it would have still been bad, but could have worked. As a slasher film, it just fails horribly. When the kills do happen, most are very weak. In fact, in some cases I wondered what even happened to the character, as it was so weak looking. One guy is gently pushed into the river and dies, a woman is poisoned, the annoying kid gets a snake in the tent, the one good looking woman in the cast is stabbed under a waterfall (the one good kill in the film) and a few others.

Most are pretty forgettable, but not as forgettable as the random, annoying characters. You have the elderly "German" couple (who apparently packed only beer and sausages on the trip. Way to go, stereotypes!), a Saudi prince (who is very horny for any American woman apparently), and many others who don't really stand out. One funny one though, is the annoying kid of one couple. There's a humorous scene where one guide is telling them not to litter and the boy throws a bottle in the river. In response to this, the dad picks him up and chucks him overboard telling him to go get it. You can tell it didn't go the way they planned though, as it damn near looks like the kid is drowning and struggling to swim in reality! Ah, the Seventies. Good times. There are many flaws like this throughout the film that were kept in rather than being cut out, such as the actors stumbling over lines and many bad edits. It's just a disaster all around!

Without a doubt, *Savage Water* is easily one of the worst slasher films I have ever had the displeasure to sit through. It's just painfully slow. To even get to the kills, you have to sit through so much pointless filler that's it's almost unbearable. It was so bad that it physically hurt to watch it. Hearing the horrible actors stumble over their lines or hearing the sappy warbly tunes playing over scenes of playful shenanigans without dialogue reminds one why The Seventies really wasn't the greatest decade in film. I have to wonder what was going through the filmmaker's minds as they shot this crap, honestly. Well, I think I may know what was: cocaine is a hell of a drug. I can honestly understand why this one is such a hard film to come by, as I could not in good conscience recommend it to anyone. I give it one star out of five and even that's being generous.

SHADOWS RUN BLACK (1984)

Shadows Run Black is one of those rare slasher flicks that happened to slip by me in the first book and that I was informed about after the printing. Thankfully, I have round two to rectify the situation. So, is *Shadows Run Black* a significant piece of the 80s-slasher puzzle? Well, not really, other than the fact that it happens to be one of the slasher films that boasts a big-name star early in their career. With this film, we come to find out that even Kevin Costner has a certain slashy background.

The plot of *Shadows Run Black* centers around the hunt for a killer dubbed by the press "The Black Angel". Detective Rydell is on the case and spends the majority of the movie hunting down our ski masked killer, as he happily slashes away the young cast. There you have it for the film. It moves at a snail's pace for most of the film and the action is few and far between.

As I said before, *Shadows Run Black* happens to be an early work of megastar Kevin Costner. It's not his first film and he happens to have a small, but significant role as an asshole boyfriend as one of the victims and is also the prime suspect for the murders. Other than that, there isn't too much of significance here. It does boast more nudity than your average slasher film. Funnily enough, most of the girls are not even given names in the film. *Shadows Run Black* also features such highlights as the good old head smash in the car hood, an extended magic scene, one of the most racist and volatile cops ever seen on screen, interracial dating (which was rare for the time, believe it or not), and a substantial body count. Unfortunately, our ski mask wearing killer is not very original and the final reveal is just flat out horrible. There's a few high points to be found here, but not many.

    Shadows Run Black does not bring anything new or anything that interesting to the table. It's about as standard as they come in the world of slasher films, where it really takes something special to set you apart from the pack. In that sense, it's easy to see why it gets lost in the crowd. The only real thing going for it is the addition of Kevin Costner in a small role and that's about it. I've seen worse and it's not unwatchable, but it is easily forgettable. I give *Shadows Run Black* two stars out of five.

SLASHDANCE (1989) ~ (Killer Workouts)

Clever title, isn't it? Or, is it just cheesy? The answer is yes. As if the title weren't already a dead giveaway on what to expect. Goofiness abounds in this movie from director James Shyman (see interviews), the same director who brought us the disappointing *Hollywood's New Blood* around the same time period.

This is another one of those dance centered slasher films that were popular for a time, and is more in line with the similar (yet also horrible) *Stripped to Kill*. Several young spandex and legwarmer wearing dancers that are auditioning for a musical start to get whacked one by one. Who do you call? Why, one of the 'rasslin ladies of *GLOW*, of course! Cindy Ferda, aka Americana of *GLOW* (Gorgeous Ladies of Wrestling) stars as one badass policewoman, who goes undercover into the dance filled world to catch the cloaked killer before he strikes again. Of course, in the meantime we get to see a few stabby kills, a bit of expected nudity and tons and tons and tons of choreographed dance sequences. Actually, that takes up the majority of our film, making it quite the chore to get through at times. It all leads up to one of those crazy reveals with a motive steeped in jealousy and another convoluted explanation. We've seen this all many times before.

    Slashdance is a movie I dare you … no, I triple dog dare you to try and take seriously. I guess that's the best way to view this film, by knowing what it is before you watch it. It's just a goofy movie all around with way too many dance sequences, slapsticky comedy, oddball characters and little gore. It's about on the level of a Troma film. I guess in that sense, it does have a certain charm to it. You just need to view it as a bad movie from the start. There are some funny parts, such as a hilariously over the top scene with a flasher on the beach and the addition of some burly, beastly looking *GLOW* girls as steroid smugglers (well, one of them is named Beastie, after all). *Slashdance* can be looked at as one of those perfect flicks for a beer soaked bad movie night, but never a good movie for a good movie night. With a name like that, would you expect anything less? I give *Slashdance* one star out of five.

SLEDGEHAMMER (1983)~ (Shot on Video Horror)

When I first popped in my DVD copy of this film, one thing was running through my head constantly. Of course, it was the Peter Gabriel classic song *Sledgehammer* playing on repeat in my head. Sadly, that has nothing to do with this review and it makes no appearance in the 1983 debut of director David Prior *(Aerobicide), Sledgehammer*. Along with *Boardinghouse, Sledgehammer* holds a true place in slasher history as one of the first of the SOV (shot on video) slasher films. But, is it any good or is it trash like the rest?

Sledgehammer starts out with a lesson for all parents out there: don't lock your kid in the closet to go have sex with your lover ... you will get killed. Naturally, the kid bashes both mom and her boyfriend with a sledgehammer. I'm just impressed that a little kid was able to wield such a heavy object with such precision. Anyways, we fast forward years later as we meet a group of muscle head jocks and their girlfriends as they come to party at the murder house. Funnily enough, a few of them look like pro wrestlers (one actually looks like Lionel Richie, as well) and includes onetime Playgirl centerfold Ted Prior (brother of the director, naturally) as our lead, who spends half the film with his shirt off. Watching them all party and interact is like seeing the guys from Alpha Beta take over. There's a lot of drinking and shenanigans to start out with. Hell, there's even a massive food fight scene (which looked like they had a lot of fun filming)! There's also quite a bit of overbearing slo-mo shots and sappy scenes with sappy music, which is a major drawback.

Soon, the real slasher fun starts after our gang partakes in a spooky and nicely done seance scene and invokes the spirit of our murderous boy. Only now, he's not a boy, but a giant hulking killer with a clear grinning mask and carrying a sledgehammer. How did that happen? Soon, he is stalking the halls of the house killing the partiers left and right. The killer does make an imposing figure, too, and is shot to look like a giant. The guy can also appear and disappear at will (with the cheapest transitions you could imagine from the time), which adds an interesting touch to our killer. He kills with knives and his hands, but mostly with the title weapon. The kills are bloody, but cheap looking and there's quite a few. Despite the slow start and some scenes that really drag down the film, it does reach a good stride and has some fun final girl chase scenes. The ending is a bit lacking too, but overall, I was somewhat impressed by it and entertained, in the end.

I must admit that due to my rocky relationship with most other SOV slasher films, I was not expecting much out of *Sledgehammer*. I was quite shocked to find that it was quite enjoyable and most of the time, I didn't even notice the dreaded SOV effect. It's obviously of the lowest budget and uses one house as all of the locations, but it works. It's a true exercise in minimalist horror at its best. Many of the kills are different and innovative from the rest of the time. It's cheap, but it is what it is. It's not the best by far and has its expected flaws, but it stands above the rest of the category and fits in well with the mainstream slasher films of the time, being a fun and effective effort. I give *Sledgehammer* a score of two and a half stars out of five.

WITCH STORY (1989) ~ (Supernatural Slashers)

Witch Story starts things out on a light note in the 1930s … with a good old fashioned all American witch burning! Naturally, the witch curses the town and all that jazz. Fast forward to the Eighties where we meet a group of college kids on their way up to the old witch house. Apparently, our lead brother and sister have inherited the property from their deceased father. Among our merry gang are your usual stereotypes (slutty blonde, nerd, jock, etc.), but the one that sticks out is Paul, our comic relief fat guy. Boy, they really go out of the way to let you know he's fat too (although he really isn't. He does resemble Ron Howard, though), turning him into a slovenly, food obsessed pig who burps, farts, chews with his mouth open and complains and screams at people for no reason. Yep, they wrote a real winner with him. I found him to be quite funny, honestly. There's also a black girl, who in a meet and greet moment has to say, "I'm 21, and I'm black". Another character conveys my thoughts with his response of "No shit". We also meet Simona, the sibling's cousin who seems to have quite the incestuous thing for one of her cousins, oddly. Along the way, the gang runs into our prophet of doom on the bus, a ghost priest (now there's a movie I'd pay to see!) who warns them to stay away from the house.

Soon, they arrive at the house and settle in, meeting a little ghost girl on the property (who no one thinks oddly of). Danger! We also get to see the slutty blonde perform a striptease on the kitchen table for no reason. Soon, the girls decide to have a seance, become possessed by the witch and go on a killing spree. Some of the kills are quite brutal and bloody, too, including one man getting his head bashed against a car hood, our fat guy getting fed by our black beauty, clad in lingerie, then stabbed repeatedly while squealing in horror (did I just write that? Well, she even says "You're such a pig ... and all pigs should be slaughtered!" Subtle). The true stand-out moment of wackiness though, is one of the girls coming out of the pool with a running chainsaw and sawing up one helpless guy. It's one of the more bonkers things you're apt to see. The movie soon takes an *Exorcist* style turn after the killings as our brother and sister duo hunt down the old priests to do away with the bad old witch. What follows in the last act is more all-out weirdness, leading up to the witch and the priest fighting over the little girl's soul, shouting religious diatribes at each other as the girl unleashes an ear-piercing scream. By the time it's all done, you'll be asking yourself, "What in the hell did I just watch?"

While there is no doubt in my mind that *Witch Story* is a slasher film during many times (and a balls-out crazy one, at that!), it definitely does have more in common with other such possession films as *Night of the Demons* and *Superstition.* In fact, this is one of those Italian films that were so rampant in the Eighties that tacked on a sequel tag to it that had nothing to do with another film, as in some places it's actually known as *Superstition 2*! All in all, even though it's your typical cheesy 80s B movie and can be very weird, this one has a lot going for it. Despite some horrible acting and incoherent plot points (another staple of 80s Italian films), *Witch Story* still manages to be an interesting display of the old ultraviolence and offers something away from the norm. I give it two and a half stars out of five.

ZOMBIE ISLAND MASSACRE (1984) ~ (Weird)

Ah, good old zombie island. Sounds like a nice relaxing place for a getaway, right? It's gotta be better than ape island. Now, I know what you're already thinking. A zombie film in a book on slasher films? What gives, Ronnie? Well, let me tell you, *Zombie Island Massacre* is about as far removed from a zombie flick as you can possibly imagine.

As I'm sure you've already gathered, *Zombie Island Massacre* is a tropical island set slasher film. Things start off sleazy with a busty blonde in a shower scene, complete with porno music in the background, followed by a sex scene between her and a balding, middle aged guy twice her age. That's Hollywood for ya, folks! We soon meet our cast of sun baked tourists, as they embark on a cruise to various islands. Among the crew is our hero Paul (played by David Broadnix, also the writer! Sadly, he did not do much else, despite his potential), who is reminiscent of *Dawn of the Dead*'s Ken Foree in his calm, cool demeanor and ass kicking ability. The group of tourists stop on an island and get to take in a local voodoo ritual, but when it's all over is when the real terror starts. The group find their bus broken down, their driver dead and the guide missing, so they have to walk through the jungle in the dark to reach civilization. Soon, a killer in an awesome massive native mask starts to kill off our group one by one. But, there's a huge twist waiting at the end, one that's a bit convoluted and more complex than your average slasher film.

Zombie Island Massacre comes off like a mix of *Friday the 13th* and *The Serpent and the Rainbow* at times, making for quite the interesting combination. Even the music is almost an identical ripoff of *Friday the 13th*! There's plenty of sun soaked scenery, voodoo mysticism and rituals, plus a hefty amount of deaths in the film. My favorite scenes are: one involving a spike pit trap, a hanging and one with a machete decapitation that would make Tom Savini proud. It also has one of the most interesting reveals ever, involving a drug cartel, voodooo and more.

While there are no actual zombies to be seen on this zombie island, there is an intriguing whodunit murder plot and some nice surprises. The name itself stems from the old-time zombie tradition, mixed with a healthy dose of voodoo. The film mixes in the voodoo element and a subplot of drug trafficking that ties everything together in the end and makes *Zombie Island Massacre* quite the unique and innovative little film. The subplot makes for an intriguing watch and there's also one of the more bad-ass final guys in slasher history, plus a nicely done reveal at the end that I have to applaud.

It's still not a great film, but some of the unique elements involved make the film stand out from your usual slasher fare. I actually feel that it's very underrated and gets a bad rap because of the zombie expectation. It's worth a watch, now that we are clear on what exactly the film is. I give *Zombie Island Massacre* three stars out of five.

THE NEW BLOOD

31 (2016)

After the disappointing Lords of Salem, many fans were skeptical of Rob Zombie's next effort 31, which had been shrouded in mystery since it was first announced. Many wondered what it was and if it would put his career back on track. We knew it involved clowns, but that was about it. Needless to say, I had no expectations going into it. I already knew to expect the usual trashy dialogue and trailer trash characters, so I was prepared.

Rob Zombie's *31* focuses on our usual group of trashy dialogue spewing redneck carnies and carries on in the spirit of his earlier films, being set on Halloween night in 1976. Our group (including Sheri Moon Zombie, of course, and the always fantastic Meg Foster) is traveling across the South when they run into a scarecrow roadblock on a dark back road (similar to *House of 1,000 Corpses*). Before you know it, half of our group is dead and the others wake up chained up in a warehouse. They are released into a giant funhouse like maze and have twelve hours to survive the night against various nasty clowns with various weapons, at the behest of their powdered wig wearing ringleader Malcolm McDowell, for the pure amusement of he and his friends. What follows is a chaotic game of life and death, as the group try to survive against the group of killer clowns.

31 is exactly what you would expect from a Rob Zombie film. I equate it to Rob Zombie's grease paint and monkey brains version of *The Running Man*, and it's very similar to the indie slasher film *Slashers*, just on a smaller scale. There's some good performances to be found throughout the film. Richard Brake does an excellent job as the most dangerous of the clowns Doom Head and gives us some seriously disturbed scenes, like one where he beats himself bloody to work himself up for the game. Pancho Moler is our tiny Hitler loving, sai packing, Spanish speaking first clown Sick Head and probably the best of the bunch. He's not much of a threat, but fun to watch. Watching his scenes just leaves you with a dirty feeling and he is very effectively creepy and weird in the part. The second batch of clowns is just completely garbage, with Psycho Head and Schitzo Head, two foul mouthed redneck clowns with chainsaws. Their dialogue, like many others in Robs film, took me completely out of the film and was just too trashy. Note to Rob, people don't have to be loud and trashy to be scary! I noticed many times when characters could have easily taken them out and did not. The end result was ripped off from another film, *Smokin' Aces*. The audience gasped at the scene, but I just groaned, as I've seen it before. That's how I felt with most of the film. We also get the oddball couple of Sex and Death, played respectively by Dottie herself, EG Daily, in a role that blatantly rips off Harley Quinn, and everyone's favorite nihilist (well, behind Peter Stormare and Flea anyways) Torsten Voges, who wears a tutu and carries a spiked bat. Um, okay. Malcolm McDowell is fun to watch as the aristocratic overlord of the chaos, although his part leaves more questions than answers. How do he and his friends see the action? There is never a camera to be seen in the maze of chaos and there isn't a single scene of the villains watching the action. The things that make you go hmm.

On the hero/victim side, Meg Foster does a stellar job as the dirty fortune teller turned vigilante. David Phillips (known to many as the Geico caveman) is one of the best in the cast as our final guy, and the always present Sheri Moon Zombie (It is a Rob Zombie movie, remember) is decent here as a final girl, once you get past her usual introductory banter. All in all, after some awkward opening scenes and once the game starts, *31* can be a fun film, even if we've seen many of the elements before. It's gory at times, but not overly so, and it makes an enjoyable enough watch. It's actually one of Rob's better films and was better than I expected. There is a missed opportunity at the end, which I felt could have tied the film to some of his earlier films, which would have been epic, yet it doesn't go that route. Instead, the closing scene is an open-ended showdown between Brake and Sheri Moon, while *Dream On* plays in the background. I felt that it was nicely done, even if it could have been better. I give *31* a score of three stars out of five. It's not the greatest, but is definitely a good popcorn slasher film and worth a watch.

ALL THROUGH THE HOUSE (2016)

Ah, the good old Christmas slasher film. It's an interesting little subgenre of the slasher world that surprisingly brought us a slew of films, both good and bad. *Black Christmas*, the *Silent Night Deadly Night* series, *Christmas Evil*, *Santa's Slay* and many more similar jolly yuletide slashers have all contributed to the genre over the years. Newcomer to the genre, director Todd Nunes sought to bring back this sometimes loved, sometimes hated subgenre with this little indie film. Although it did get some notice on the festival circuit, the results are less than satisfying to those who wanted a true throwback.

Our story begins fast, as we see a psycho decked out in a creepy metallic mask and Santa outfit make short work of a horny young couple in gory fashion, with some overly sexual murders. We then meet Rachel Kimmell (Ashley Mary Nunes ... hey, wait a minute, that name sounds familiar. Hmmm), a student who has returned home for the holidays to spend with her foul mouthed, wheelchair bound grandmother. She soon runs into her old neighbor Ms. Garrett, who is obviously a few beers short of a six pack. Actually, that's stating it lightly. She has a very dark, angry side and spends most of her time obsessing over the holidays and sleeping with/talking to/dining with mannequins. Yup, you better believe she has something to do with the masked psycho offing horny young Abercrombie models in our small town. Soon, Rachel finds out the truth of the local murders and it all has something to do with the mysterious disappearance of Ms. Garrett's shut-in daughter (who was afflicted with a skin disease) years earlier. Prepare yourself for gallons of the red stuff and some very messed up twists.

All in all, *All Through the House* was a rather unspectacular addition to the new generation of slasher films. It wasn't really a throwback like the rest from the time period, and was way more influenced by the latest generation, like Rob Zombie films. That means that you can expect several foul-mouthed characters and almost all seem to be hypersexual, as well. There's more than one scantily clad sex scene in the film and it seems like that's the only real pastime in the old neighborhood. As far as the acting goes, it can be easily equated to reality star/pornstar level. Most of the dialogue is painful and the majority of the actresses seem to come from the valley girl pornstar variety. As far as gore goes, this is one department in which the film truly excels, sometimes to an extreme, sickening level. Expect blood to fly, spurt, spew and many gushing geysers of it throughout the film. The deaths are all very gory and gruesome and many border on the sadistic side. I mean, this Santa slasher has a penchant for lopping off ding-dongs, for Christ sake! This is not subtle at all, either, as these scenes are shown in the most sickening detail. The killer has a reason for this hatred though, as the ending reveals. The big reveal is along the lines of *Sleepaway Camp* or *Texas Chainsaw Massacre 4* and a very twisted one. This is the one saving grace of the film, as the rest is just passable and forgettable tripe. As we all know, gory does not necessarily make a good horror film.

The one thing that sets the film apart is that little twist at the end and how the film plays out in the finale. It's not great, but it makes for an interesting watch. I liked the disguise of the killer in his metallic looking, blank mask. It's a creepy and effective part of the film. The enjoyable part is when our silent killer starts to get a bit more animated towards the end, and it makes for some fun scenes. The mom character is also fun to watch as she goes batshit crazy, and the ending brings to mind the song Mommy's Little Monster. That pretty much sums it up, right there.

I put *All Through the House* in the same boat as the similar recent slasher film, *Silent Night*. It's lacking in several areas and seems too polished, like way too many other recent films. The cast all seem to be models and it gets annoying. It's hard to bring it to reality in that sense and you never find yourself in the film too deeply. It's more like reality TV. It does have some of those aforementioned plusses, though, so it is a bit better than the awful *Silent Night*, but it sure as hell ain't no *Black Christmas*, either! It's nothing spectacular. I give it two stars out of five.

FINAL GIRLS, THE (2015)

Just when we thought we have seen it all in the slasher genre, another film comes out of left field that is so clever that it completely changes how the whole genre is viewed. It happened with other tongue in cheek takes on the genre such as *Scream, Behind the Mask,* and *Tucker and Dale vs. Evil.* Now, there's another film that can proudly take a stand on the podium next to these others as one of the cleverest, most self-aware slasher-comedies of all time. *The Final Girls*!

The Final Girls follows our lead girl Max Cartwright (Taissa Farmiga). She is still grieving the loss of her mother Amanda, a famous scream queen and star of many slashers in the 80s, who lost her life in a car accident. Max and her friends decide to go to a special screening of her late mother's famous film, *Camp Bloodbath,* but a fire breaks out during the screening. Our group find the exits blocked and decide to go through the screen, which transports them right into the freaking film! See, it's one of those film within a film films! They find themselves right in the middle of the slasher flick, interacting with the oblivious cast, including the ditzy and horny Tina (Angela Trimbur) and the equally horny douchebag of the bunch Kurt (Adam Devine), as well as Max's mother's character of nice girl Nancy. Our group finds things odd at first as they decide to stay in one spot and realize that everything starts over every ninety minutes, like a movie. They realize the only way to change things is by moving and make their way to the camp, where they pose as new camp counselors and try to fit in, despite being obviously out of place in the 80s time warp. Max and her friends decide to put their knowledge of the genre to good use, to prevent the deaths of the cast. Thus, they spend a good deal of time trying to keep the characters from having sex, doing drugs, etc. It's pretty hilarious. The best part is when they put oven mitts on the horny Tina, to prevent her from taking off her clothes. Of course, the killer is still out there and ready to hack and slash both the cast and the new additions, so the group needs to come together for a plan. That is, whoever is left anyways. All the while, Max finds herself bonding heavily with her late mother's character, proving that the film has a lot of heartfelt emotion in it.

I have to give director Todd Strause and crew a lot of credit here. With *The Final Girls,* they managed to create one of the most clever and most unique takes on the slasher genre since ... well, ever! It's a perfect throwback to the old days when the slasher was king, with a modern twist and a heavy dose of self-deprecating humor thrown in. It knows exactly what it is. They know the usual trappings of the slasher film and all of the cliché characters and play those factors up to a tee here. While there is little blood or gore and no nudity (often a killer of the slasher film genre), it just does not matter here. The humor and story is much more important and it works, by God, it works! The characters are all engaging and fun, especially so with the performances of Adam Devine as the ultra-jock douchebag Kurt, and Angela Trimbur as the slutty airhead Tina. Both of their performances are hysterical and you can't take your eyes off of them. They really steal the show. That's not to say the rest of the cast is bad, as they're all competent enough in their roles. The whole experience as a whole is pretty damn fun and enjoyable, plus there's a lot of new ideas here in a genre where we thought we've seen it all.

One of the most surprising aspects of *The Final Girls* is that it's really not all fun and games all around. It has a surprising amount of heart to it and some heartfelt scenes between mother and daughter Max and Nancy. Some of these scenes, coupled with the fact that Max lost her mother at such a young age, make some of these scenes truly overpowering and emotional. Therein lies the true success of *The Final Girls*. It manages to bridge that gap between laugh out loud comedy, slasher film and heartfelt drama, something that not many others have been able to pull off quite as seamlessly as seen here. For that, the film is truly special and it makes it even more of an intriguing entry into the genre. I give *The Final Girls* four stars out of five. A new classic!

GIRL HOUSE (2015)

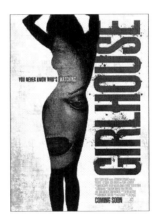

When I first discovered the indie gem known as *Girl House*, it was described as "a *Halloween* style slasher for the digital age" (Hmm, wasn't that *Halloween: Resurrection*? Never mind). Uh oh, I thought. That can't be good. Needless to say, I wasn't expecting much from the film. However, sometimes low expectations can deliver great results!

Girl House starts things out with a quote from Ted Bundy plastered across the screen, blaming his actions on the effects of "evil" porn. With a start like that, you can tell what you're in for. We then meet our little killer in training, as a young, pudgy child years ago and find out what makes him tick. He is chased and ridiculed by two local girls and decides to get his revenge on one of the girls in the most brutal way. The start is surely one that you won't forget in its brutality and sets the pace for the rest of the film perfectly. We then flash forward years later and meet Kylie (Ali Cobrin), a young college co-ed looking for ways to pay her tuition. She soon finds *Girl House*, a *Big Brother* style house full of cam girls for a porn website. She gets an audition and wows the producers and the other girls with a strip tease and immediately gets the job, thus beginning her new double life. Kylie immediately gets the (ahem) "lay of the land" at the house and quickly becomes a hit with her cam show, with all kinds of horny guys from around the world tuning in to watch her. Unfortunately, she also attracts the attention of our little psycho all grown up, now calling himself Loverboy (rapper-actor Slaine). He develops an unhealthy fixation on Kylie and spends his time in his basement putting her picture over other pictures to show the two as a couple, and making out with a mannequin. Seems normal, right? He also happens to be a computer genius, so when shit hits the fan and the creepy Loverboy, initially thought of as "sweet" by the house girls, ends up being ridiculed and ostracized by the girls, he goes nuts. He dons a wig and a creepy, lifeless, girl mask and hacks into the system, finding the address of the house, hacking into the high-tech security system and then sets out on a vicious killing spree of all the girls in the house (shades of *Slumber Party Massacre*). Things get very brutal very fast once Loverboy gets to the house.

Girl House can at times be lacking in many departments that you would expect from such a title and genre, namely nudity, which there's a bit of, but I expected much more from the premise. This can be seen as either kind of a cheat and akin to watered down teen slashers, or it can be seen as a bit of a classy way to present the material (if there is such a thing), without having to resort to tons of nudity. Your call. The other thing is that while the kills can be very brutal and bloody at times, many happen off screen. Again, it can be viewed from either perspective. One of the best aspects to the film, however, is the killer himself. He is actually one of the scariest and best slasher killers in recent memory! Loverboy, clad in his woman mask and dark wig, is insanely creepy and comes off like Buffalo Bill crossed with Michael Myers. He also has one of the more innovative aspects of a slasher villain, in that he is able to see what is happening in the house at all times via his I-phone and know where the girls are hiding. It's pretty hard to hide from that!

Loverboy also has an interesting attack style, which is fast and brutal. It's like a blitz attack, really. There's some very effective scare scenes that involve the killer hiding and reappearing in the house and some very inventive and interesting kills. There's of course your usual stabs and strangling, but watch for a scene when one girl gets a dildo rammed down her throat and chokes to death! You read that right. I had to rewatch it just to make sure I had really seen that. It was that freaking insane! There's also a very cruel and effective one where our killer carves up a girl's face and hacks off her fingers, then leaves her in the room where she can't type for help on the computer or even open the door. Can you say yikes? It's one of the more brutal kills in slasher history and very cruel, too. Other than that, there is also a very well done and tense scene with one girl locked in a sauna and a pool kill. Overall, *Girl House* definitely hits the mark when it comes to kill scenes, scares and tension. It also has one of the most innovative final girls of all time as Kylie cuts the power and brings Loverboy down to her level. Some of the final chase scenes in *Girl House* are very exciting and I was quite impressed.

Although lacking in a few departments, *Girl House* definitely makes up for it in others. There is a great back story to the killer, good kills and scare scenes, a great final girl and chase and an amazing killer, which all make this one a winner in my book. I was very impressed and consider *Girl House* one of the best of the new generation of slasher films. I give it three and a half stars out of five.

LOST AFTER DARK (2015)

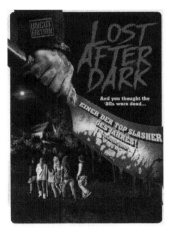

2015 seems to be a slasher fans wet dream. There have been so many fun slasher throwbacks released in this year, that it's unreal. Yet another one of these modern slashers happens to be *Lost After Dark*. *Lost After Dark* is a nice little throwback to the slashers of the 80s, with a modern twist. It also continues the rich tradition of Canadian slasher films from the great white north of Canada.

Lost After Dark starts on the right path, setting itself in the height of the slasher boom (and the year that yours truly entered the world), 1984. A group of teens decide to ditch the high school dance and hotwire a school bus to take up to our main girls cabin in the wood for a weekend of partying. The usual gang of slasher teen cliché victims is here. We have: the good final girl, her handsome love interest, the bad girl with a heart of gold, the token black guy, the lovable fat comic relief, the bitchy princess, her asshole boyfriend and the final girl's nondescript best friend. It's really by the numbers. Of course, in true slasher fashion, the bus breaks down in the middle of nowhere leaving our teens (gasp!) … lost after dark! Soon, our gang stumbles upon an abandoned farmhouse in the woods. It's your usual dark, creepy slasher house complete with many farming implements of mass destruction. It seems nice … except of course for the crazed slasher killer who lives on the property and offs anyone who trespasses. Soon, our gang start to drop like flies, in a battle to the death with our killer. Sure, it's standard, but it's a fun ride!

For the true slasher enthusiasts like myself who long for the good old days, *Lost After Dark* is a true blessing. It's a modern slasher set back in the good old days, which means no annoying modern technology. That's right, you won't be seeing any I-phones here! Instead, get ready to jump back to a time full of side ponytails, Trans-Ams, spandex and good old fashioned slasher fun! I thoroughly enjoyed the film. The characters are all likable enough and played competently, making it quite watchable. The most likable are our chubby comic relief guy Tobe (Jesse Camacho) and bad girl Marilyn (Eve Harlow). The relationship between the two is sweet and fun to watch, but sadly short lived. The jokes work, but thankfully it doesn't get too jokey and plays it with a straight face, which is nice to see. A fun factor that really caught my attention was the fact that the final girl keeps changing. As soon as you think you have her pegged, it's so long! In the end, it turns out that the last one anyone would have guessed is that final girl set to go toe to toe with our killer. Speaking of the killer, I thought that department was a bit lacking. There's a nice back story to him, but he just looks like Rob Zombie. Nothing special. The kills are all well done and bloody, including kills via pick, hand drill, a blood spewing impalement and car crushing, plus a gory homage to the most uncomfortable scene in horror history, the eye scene from Fulci's *Zombie.* You know the one I mean! All in all, there was not a whole lot for me to complain about when it came to *Lost After Dark.*

Lost After Dark turns out to be quite an enjoyable little throwback to the golden days of the slasher film. Sure, it has its flaws, but it manages to be fun and entertaining, which is what really matters. Overall, it's a nice melding of today's modern horror films and the slashers we all grew up loving. I say it's definitely worth a watch and most slasher fans will get a kick out of it. I give Lost After Dark three and a half stars out of five.

SLASHENING, THE (2015)

The Troma endorsement on the cover of The Slashening should be enough to tell you just what to expect from the film. We all know what to expect from really any movie that has any affiliation with that particular company and one thing you know you're in for is one goofy ass film that can't be taken seriously, by design. Some of these titles are hit and miss. While all are goofy as hell, some actually hit the mark and manage to be quite funny and clever, while other ones miss that mark by a mile. So, what can we expect from Troma's latest slasher parody?

There's not a whole lot to be said about the plot of The Slashening. In many ways, it's similar to Slumber Party Massacre and about as mindless, as well, only this film revels in how bad it is and takes a heavy-handed swing at the genre in general. The plot basically is just about a high school house party being held by our lead Lucy (Anna Callegari … is that a real name?) that gets crashed by our burlap sack mask wearing killer (nice nod to a couple of my favorites), who starts to hack and slash through our cast, as well as a slew of random pizza guys. That's our plot. Sure, there's your standard farfetched reveal and motivation scene at the end and it has all of the trappings and clichés you'd expect to see in any slasher film along these lines, but the big difference here is that this one is poking fun at it all, but in the most loving way possible. It's clear to tell that the director, Brandon Bassham (also of the other slasher parody Fear Town, USA. As a matter of fact, many of the cast of this film were in that one, as well) is a fan of the genre.

Before I rate The Slashening, I must take into account the Troma affiliation. We know it's not going to be Gone with the Wind exactly and that Troma has released its fair share of crap over the years. What I found with The Slashening is that while it was nowhere near the level of cleverness from other recent tongue in cheek slashers of late (The Final Girls, Tucker and Dale vs. Evil), it still manages to entertain and be funny enough when it needs to. Sure, many of the characters are cliché and some of the acting is quite sub-par, but given what it is, that's something I can roll with and it's to be expected. After all, it is made that way by design and I don't think the filmmakers were trying to make a masterpiece.

What did stand out to me is that there were actually some rather clever moments in the film and even a few laugh out loud moments that really stood out. The fact that the pizza guy is killed and the partiers keep calling about their missing pizza, which causes the company to send more pizza delivery guys to get slaughtered, is hilarious! It's like deja-vu in these scenes and soon, the entire yard is littered with dead pizza boys! (Jesus, how many employees does that company have??) The coked-out girl is another funny addition, from her inability to get her lady parts working for a guy (such a ridiculous, laugh out loud scene!) to her inability to feel her own face being bashed bloody by the killer. Another hilarious part occurs when another girl is getting slaughtered outside and writes a help me note in blood on the sliding glass door and the guy inside can't read it because it's backwards and he disregards her! Those are some insanely clever takes on some of the oldest slasher clichés! Plus, some of the deaths actually do turn out pretty violent and horrifying. There's plenty of slashing and bloodletting to be the seen, and our killer racks up a huge body count (well, there are like twenty pizza delivery guys killed, as well as our main cast). We also get to see what could be one of the most horrifying deaths EVER in the film when we see our cliché "nice guy" try to reason with the killer and "talk it out". This of course leads to a very violent death as our guy gets his head bashed back and forth on everything in sight, then stabbed, then has boiling water poured on him, then gets his eye taken out! Even our victim has to say (tongue in cheek, of course), "Well, at least it can't get any worse" … oh, it does though as the killer unzips the guy's pants and proceeds to cut off his manhood. I didn't know whether to laugh or cry at that scene! I think I was just horrified beyond speech.

For such a low budget, under the radar, Troma sponsored slasher parody, I must say that *The Slashening* actually does manage to be an entertaining and funny time waster. There's enough laugh out loud funny parts and clever jabs at the genre to keep it entertaining enough. It's not one that I will necessarily go out of my way to watch again and again, but I enjoyed my viewing of it enough. I give *The Slashening* two and a half stars out of five. It's worth a watch just for the sake of insanity.

NON-SLASHER SLASHERS

10 TO MIDNIGHT (1983)

Charlie Bronson don't take no shit from anyone, least of all a psycho serial killer, especially one that messes with his family!

10 to Midnight is one of a long line of crime films featuring a bad-ass cop dealing with a psychotic serial killer on the loose (see *Dirty Harry*). Bronson plays Detective Kessler, who, along with his partner Detective McAnn (Andrew Stevens), is on the trail of a serial killer who has the department at a loss, in that not much evidence is left behind. We soon meet our killer (Gene Davis) Warren Stacy, a creepy and awkward office equipment repairman who does not do too well with the ladies. In fact, he takes rejection very personally after he comes across too creepy and he viciously kills the girls. What sets Stacy apart from other killers is how he does it. He happens to strip down completely naked before making his kills, wherever that may be (a park, an apartment, etc.). This makes Stacy one of the oddest killers ever seen on screen. He racks up quite the body count too, and dispatches of all the woman via knife. Of course, the cops are hot on his trail as they discover many things tying him to the victims, such as the aforementioned bad dates and creepy behavior. He doesn't do much to change their opinion either when questioned, bringing even more doubt on him. Yes, he is indeed a creepy guy. He then targets Kessler's daughter, sending her various dirty phone calls, stalking her and killing her friends. You can bet your ass old Charlie is not going to take that one lightly and he goes to war with our killer, who thinks he is too smart to be taken down. He's got another thing coming, for sure.

Davis puts in an amazing (and highly demanding) and convincing performance as our creepy killer Stacy on *10 to Midnight*. He just comes across as a very unlikable guy, who is on the edge. His manic mood swings are a sight to behold and some great acting. Bronson is his usual bad-ass self here and is just as good here as in any of the *Death Wish* films for which he is famous for. The film can be quite perverse at times, as can be expected from a film with a naked serial killer. The calls he makes are very sleazy and can be downright wrong, as well. There are quite a few bloody kills throughout the duration, including one massacre scene that is obviously highly influenced by the real-life murders of Richard Speck. Our two leads are fun to watch in their cat and mouse game as they get under each other's skin and it really makes for a film that keeps your attention throughout.

As far as slasher killers and serial killers go, it doesn't get creepier than Warren Stacy, which is what really makes *10 to Midnight* stand out. There are plenty of kills to keep any horror and slasher film fan happy throughout the film. I give *10 to Midnight* a score of three and a half out of five stars.

CREEPSHOW 2 (1987)

In the world of cinema, there are very few sequels out there that surpass the original film in the series. Usually, it's something that was so good, that it's hard to top. However, in some situations, the sequels can actually be much better than the original film. Just look at *Lord of the Rings, Star Wars* (I know what you're thinking, so stop with your "trilogy" semantics!), *The Godfather* and more. Another one that I put up on this list, where the sequel turns out to be a far better film is none other than *Creepshow 2*! I'll admit that I loved the first movie and that *The Crate* is one of my all-time favorite short stories, but side by side, I definitely enjoy the sequel more. Now, you may ask, what is it doing in a book on slasher films? Well my fellow creeps, *Creepshow 2* just happens to have one of the best slasher stories of all time in it, in *Old Chief Woodinhead* and the other stories stand out as well, so why not include one of my favorite films in the book?

Creepshow 2 follows suit with the original film from the team of George Romero and Stephen King, this time bringing us three more short horror stories inspired by the old EC comics. We start out with another wraparound story, as a young boy waits to pick up the latest issue of his favorite comic, Creepshow. He soon gets it from a heavily made-up and almost unrecognizable Tom Savini as the Creeper (boy, he does seem like a creeper here, too!). It then goes to animation for the rest of the wraparound story throughout the film … really bad, almost annoying animation. But, that's okay, as the segments more than make up for it!

Our first segment is a slasher personified with *Old Chief Woodinhead*. George Kennedy and Dorothy Lamour play a kindly old couple trying to keep their shop afloat in a dusty, dying ghost town on the rez. The couple happen to have a big wooden Indian on the front steps of the store that George seems to enjoy spending time around. One night, three hoodlums break into the store and rob the couple at gunpoint. Things get out of control fast and the psychotic and narcissistic leader Sam Whitemoon (son of the tribal leader, played by veteran actor Holt McAllany) ends up killing the couple in cold blood. The gang decide to leave that night for Hollywood, but the old chief has other plans, as he come alive looking for revenge and he's pissed! He ends up killing the kids brutally and exacting his bloody revenge before the night is over.

This is by far one of my favorite slasher inspired stories. The couple is very likable and the gang is very unlikable. It's prefect casting and you can really feel for the characters. The effects for the chief are simply amazing and he is played with expert precision by Dan Kamin (see interviews). The chief makes for one of the best slashers out there and his justification is very strong and one you cannot argue with. It makes for a strong morality tale, as all of these stories are.

The next segment is *The Raft*, and it's a classic. Four college students venture out to an isolated lake for a swim on one of the last days of the season. What they don't know is that there is a monstrous creature lurking on the surface of the water that has a taste for human blood. One of the teens, Randy, (Daniel Beer, see interview) notices it first, but the others don't listen until it's too late and they're soon stuck on the raft in the middle of the lake. Soon, our teens get eaten by the blob one by one. Can Randy beat the blob and swim to the shore and live?

I absolutely love *The Raft* and it may be my favorite segment here (I know, the chief is tough to beat and I keep going back and forth on it). The effects are amazing and they can be very gruesome at times, as the blob looks like it almost melts the screaming teens, as the blob reducing them into gooey, bloody masses, in some truly horrific and painful looking scenes. The teens are all likable in their roles and there is a real sense of dread and isolation conveyed by the setting. It's not hokey and it's not comical, which is an easy trap to fall into on a story like this, but it manages to play the segment with a straight face, which is nice to see. The ending itself is an incredible twist and one of the all-time great shocks of 80s horror. Like I said, this segment is a classic.

Our third and final segment is *The Hitchhiker*. It's a take on a classic tale from as long back as there have been cross country highways in America, of a vengeful spirit of a murdered hitchhiker. Our story follows the story of Annie Lansing (played marvelously sleazy and unlikable by Lois Chiles), a woman who is cheating on her husband. She has to rush back home in the middle of the night before her husband gets home, and ends up accidentally running over a hitchhiker (Tom Wright, see interviews) en route. Rather than stop and help, she takes off. Soon, she finds that the vengeful spirit of the dead hitchhiker is following her, with his trademark "Thanks for the ride, lady" line. She fights him off over miles of dark road, but the zombified hitchhiker just won't stay down, no matter what she does.

The Hitchhiker is another classic tale on *Creepshow 2*. It's pretty much a one woman show and Chiles is fun to watch, as she constantly talks to herself and comes up with excuses for when she gets home. Tom Wright is incredibly creepy in the part (something he went back to years later on *Tales from the Hood*, another horror anthology) and plays it well. The effects are simply phenomenal, as we get to see Wright's ghoul get bloodier and more messed up with every hit he takes. It's a long, drawn-out cat and mouse game, but every second has you glued to the screen. It's another winner.

When it comes to anthology horror, *Creepshow 2* is near the top of the list for me. Every segment works and it's one of those fun films that never seems to get old. I've seen it so many times, I can't even count. It's definitely a must have for any horror fan and slasher

SLASHED DREAMS PART 2

fans will no doubt love the first segment with the chief. I give *Creepshow 2* a score of four and a half out of five stars.

CRUISING (1980)

Sometimes a movie comes along that is so unique and beyond the norm, that many people sadly miss out on it during its initial run. Either that, or it runs into a fair amount of controversy and public outcry over its controversial subject matter. Such is the case with director William Friedkin's 1980 thriller *Cruising,* a film that was met with a great deal of controversy from many communities upon its initial release.

Based upon a real-life string of murders in the homosexual community of New York City in the 1970s, *Cruising* takes us deep into the heart of the underground gay S&M subculture of the time, where a mysterious stranger in a leather jacket is slashing away many of the men involved in the scene. Enter Officer Burns (Al Pacino), a rookie cop willing to do anything to make it to Detective. He agrees to go deep undercover into the underground gay S&M scene in order to catch the killer. Obviously, this is not an easy task, as he comes to find out. He runs into many red herrings and crooked cops (one of whom is genre legend himself, Joe Spinell of *Maniac* fame) along the way and also begins to feel the strain at home with his girlfriend Nancy (the always phenomenal Karen Allen), due to his involvement in the scene. Burns befriends his gay neighbor Ted (Don Scardino) and soon finds himself developing feelings for him. As all of this is going on, Burns is fully immersing himself into this foreign subculture and getting closer to the killer than he ever thought.

Directed by legendary director William Friedkin, who brought us the classic *The Exorcist,* *Cruising* takes up deep into the seedy underbelly of New York's homosexual S&M scene of the late 1970s. Friedkin does a great job capturing the griminess and grit of the inner city and takes us deep into the heart of a scene that most people didn't even know existed. The whole film is a very ballsy effort and one of the ballsiest players in it all is Pacino, already a well-respected actor at this time. For taking on such a controversial role in such a controversial film, you have to give the man credit. It's a role that could have easily broken a career in those more conservative times and he did an excellent job in it. You can really feel for his character and the confusion that takes over him, as he delves deeper into the scene. It's obvious that what he sees and experiences while leading this double life in two distinctly different worlds will forever change him and make his home life much different afterward. Is there any getting over it? The film leaves us on a very ambiguous note, where we don't exactly know the answer to that. Obviously, he is forever changed, but to what extent? That's the other beautiful part of *Cruising* is the fact that the ending leaves us with more questions than answers. In that sense, *Cruising*

67

was well ahead of its time. While many films these days love to use that ambiguous ending, it was almost unheard of at the time. Did the real killer get caught? Is he still out there, stalking the clubs? Did officer Burns' home life ever return to normalcy? We may never know. I suppose it's on the viewer to figure that out.

When it comes to mainstream films that are heavily slasher influenced, *Cruising* is at the top of the list. It manages to keep your attention throughout the duration and can be very tense at times. There's several times when Burns crosses paths with the killer and doesn't even realize it. The final confrontation in the park has to be one of the tensest sequences ever caught on film and you can cut the tension with a knife (no pun intended). Our "killer", played by Richard Cox, is very effective in the role and downright creepy at times. All of the death scenes are tensely built up and really pile the suspense level high right until the bloody acts themselves. There's a decent body count and there's quite a few bloody kills as well. Given that and the intense subject matter and loads of nudity, this is one that is definitely not a family film.

I give *Cruising* my full endorsement as one of the best and most suspenseful films in this sub-category. It earns a score of four and a half stars out of five from me and I highly recommend it for anyone looking for a suspenseful pseudo-slasher film that is different from your usual fare. Despite being such a highly controversial film upon its initial release, it has gained a wider cult following over the years and definitely deserves a look.

DEAD POOL, THE (1988)

Clint Eastwood's legendary *Dirty Harry* character is no stranger to dealing with his share of psychos and scumbags. In the first film, he fought against the cunning Scorpio killer (a direct take-off on the real-life Zodiac killer that plagued San Francisco at the time), terrorists in *The Equalizer*, crooked cops with a vendetta in *Magnum Force* and a woman scorned who goes on a killing spree against her attackers in *Sudden Impact* (All classics!). So, what was next for our favorite super cop who doesn't take shit from anyone? How about him squaring off against a slasher? I'm sold!

In 1988's *The Dead Pool* (No, it has nothing to do with the smart-ass superhero), Harry's next case has him trying to get to the bottom of who is knocking off celebrities tied to a list of the famous notables of the same name, a game played by an infamous horror director in the area, Peter Swan (Liam Neeson), which bets on the next celebrity that will bite the big one. Soon, the celebrities on the list start getting bumped off one by one (including Jim Carrey in an early role as a drug addicted Axl Rose type rockstar!) by a mysterious black gloved killer. It's up to Harry and his new partner Al Quan (Evan Kim), as well as plucky reporter Samantha Watson (Patricia Clarkson) to solve the mystery of who is killing the celebrities before the list is done. There's a good reason to, as well, as Harry himself is on that list!

The Dead Pool is as exciting of a film as we have come to expect from the *Dirty Harry* series. I will actually go out of my way and say that it's one of my favorites in the series. The excitement is at an all-time high here and the suspense is top notch. We get several deaths, such as by explosion, by forced overdose, by several brutal knife attacks and even a death via harpoon. All of the players involved here do a tremendous job, but the real star (well, besides Eastwood) here is Liam Neeson as Swan, himself playing a bit of an iconic horror director, who is working on his next big slasher film, *Hotel Satan*, when the murders start. Naturally, that factor as well as the fact he came up with the morbid list, puts him at the top of the suspect list. Neeson is amazing as the smarmy director with a real fascination with the dark side and the macabre. There's plenty of bloody kills and slashings to keep slasher fans satisfied enough in this side trip into pseudo-slasher territory, as well as several of the ass kicking action scenes we have all come to expect from the series. You know what that means ... guns and explosions! It's a perfect combination! The tensest scene by far is a scene in which Harry and his partner are chased in their car across San Francisco by an explosive remote control car. It's quite intense and one that is sure to keep you on the edge of your seat. Whoever would have thought that a remote-controlled toy car could be terrifying? Well, here it is, and it works very well! Keep your eyes peeled for a cameo by the guys from *Guns N' Roses* themselves, as well as Jim Carrey lip synching to *Welcome to the Jungle* (with his typical wild flailing and wacky mannerisms) for an *Exorcist* inspired music video, in one of the most entertaining scenes in the entire series. That right there should be enough to pique the interest of many horror fans.

The Dead Pool is an exciting and fun film all around, that is sure to keep fans of many genres happy. The Dirty Harry fans will be satisfied, as it follows suit with the other films. Action fans will definitely be happy, as this one is loaded with it, and slasher and horror fans will no doubt be happy at the genre influenced points and brutal kills. It's a winner all around. If you haven't seen it, go ahead ... make your day, punk. I give *The Dead Pool* four and a half stars out of five.

NIGHTMARE CITY (1980)

Hey, you got zombies in my slasher film! Hey, you got slashers in my zombie film! (Sorry, I had to go there). A zombie slasher film? How is this possible? Well, director Umberto Lenzi found a way and the results are quite intriguing.

Nightmare City follows the story of a reporter who shows up at an airfield to interview a scientist, who was just involved with a major chemical spill. Once at the airport, it becomes apparent that something is very wrong as there is no communication coming from the plane as it makes an emergency landing. As the reporter films and the police and National Guard gather around the plane, the doors open and out spills a horde of seemingly unstoppable zombie-like psychos, who start to slaughter everyone in sight. The chaos continues into the cities, then the countryside, until soon the madness has spread across the land. The zombie-like killers not only kill and drink the blood of their victims, but they turn them into the undead as well. We follow several different characters through the mayhem as they try to survive the ordeal. Some make it and some don't. What you can count on is one hell of a bloodbath in the meantime!

Nightmare City is quite similar to other plague films like *The Crazies*, but with a little bit more of a slasher edge to it. The infected don't just bite and drink the blood of their victims. Oh no, rather they will use any kind of weapon at their disposal such as knifes, axes, machetes, guns and more. The results are quite gory and make the movie on par with its zombie film brothers in terms of the amount of sheer visceral gore. There is pure chaos throughout the movie and there's dozens of gruesome deaths to be seen. There's also some decent zombie makeup jobs and tons of great action scenes and scare scenes. My favorites are the massive hospital massacre scene, a great scare involving people trapped in an elevator, and a rather nasty scene involving a zombie and a girl in a basement. What is it with Italians and those damn eyeball impalement scenes anyways? Those sick bastards! Top it all off with a funky late 70s soundtrack, a finale atop a roller coaster and one of those "uh-oh" endings, and we have ourselves a winner here.

Whether you're a fan of slasher films or a fan of zombie films, either way, you'll no doubt love *Nightmare City*. It's got something for everyone and it's a fun, exciting thrill ride of a film done with the usual Italian flare, style and gory effects that we've all come to expect from them. I give *Nightmare City* a score of four stars out of five.

SILENT RAGE (1982)

This one could easily be billed as "Walker vs. The Stalker!". I could just see that on the marquee now, as if it were a fight at Madison Square Garden being promoted by Don King. So, the question is, how tough really is Chuck Norris? Well, apparently, he's tough enough to take down a superhuman Michael Myers clone who can't be hurt by bullets, fire, and explosions! What we have here is truly a fight for the ages.

Silent Rage starts out in a very big way, with a double axe murder from a man who is clearly on the edge. I'm not a doctor, but when a patient says that he is losing it (honestly, if I lived in a house this noisy, I'd probably lose it, too!), you should probably listen. Well, his doctor is a bit too late to stop the carnage. What do you do when there's an axe wielding psychopath on the loose? Send in Chuck Norris, of course, the man so bad-ass, he doesn't need back-up to deal with the situation. Not that his pudgy, inept deputy (Stephen Furst, better known to many as Kent Dorfman aka Flounder from *Animal House*) is much help anyways. Well, Chuck gets his man, but he soon breaks free and is mowed down by a barrage of bullets. Somehow, the man survives and is just barely hanging on for life in ICU. Well, just leave it to the sinister looking doctor to fuck things up as he injects our killer with a new experimental drug that causes him to not only recover quickly, but gives him the ability to heal wounds very fast (ala *Absurd*). Naturally, this causes our madman to turn into an indestructible killing machine, as he first targets his psychiatrist (who tried to warn the doctor that this could possibly be a really bad idea. Sigh, nobody listens) and then sets out on a killing spree. So, what do you do when you have a now superhuman killing machine on the loose? Why, send in Chuck Norris, of course!

Sadly, the ending of *Silent Rage* is a bit lacking. I for one, was glued to the screen trying to figure out the solution to this twisted puzzle. If the killer heals quickly and cannot be hurt by conventional methods, how can you kill him? My theory would have been just to blow him up, but then again, maybe our killer would have miraculously come back together ala the T-1000. Of course, the solution presented here was the one I joked about at the start of the article. Sadly, it's no joke, the way that our indestructible killing machine is finally put down is via a Chuck Norris ass kicking. Seems a bit anti-climactic, doesn't it? Therein lies the one true flaw of the film ... well, besides Deputy Flounder, in that the ending is quite lame and it's a shame given that there was such a build-up. Oh well, I guess you can't win them all.

Still, *Silent Rage* does make a fun watch, even with these minor setbacks. It's a fun story and a nice tribute to the shape himself. At about the halfway point, the film takes on a decidedly slasher route and it obviously owes a lot to *Halloween*. There's the similar music, the similar dress of the killer and silent mannerisms (just imagine Michael without the mask and you have our killer here). Some of the similar POV shots are lifted right out of *Halloween*, in fact! There are quite a few deaths in the film, mostly involving brute strength and breaking bones, so it's not the bloodiest film, but makes up for it with some great suspense, intense chase scenes and of course (c'mon, this is a Chuck Norris film!) kick ass fight scenes! Sure, there's a lot of filler scenes throughout, like Chuck and his nurse love interest (and apparently for Chuck Norris, no means yes, I gathered) and scenes of Chuck taking on an entire biker gang in a bar, in a bad-ass fight scene. These don't really detract from the film at hand, but don't offer a lot either, other than building up old Chuckie in the bad-assery department. It's not a bad thing, I suppose. Fans of action films and slasher fans alike should get a kick out of *Silent Rage*. Ha! Get it? Kick! Okay, I'll stop now. I give *Silent Rage* three and a half out of five stars.

INTERVIEWS

ADAM MARCUS
(Director- JASON GOES TO HELL)

RA: I noticed while reading your bio, that you started at a very young age. How did you get involved in the film industry?

AM: I really got involved in film because of Sean Cunningham. His son Noel and I were actually best friends when we were kids. Sean made a lot of movies when I was a kid, growing up in Conneticut. I was born in New York, but raised half of the time in Conneticut. Noel and I spent a lot of time together and that got me to work with, and under Sean. In fact, he was instrumental in helping me put together my first theater company. He donated money to the first theater company that I created when I was fifteen. But, I had already worked in the industry for them as an apprentice editor and as a PA (Production Assistant), in the summertime. Susan Cunningham was his editor and Noel and I worked with her for a little bit, helping edit a movie called *Spring Break* that they made. I was always there. I did a lot of table reads with them and a ton of film activity from the time I was about ten or eleven. I went to NYU after high school and was doing really well there. It's a great school. While I was doing that, I was running two theater companies in Conneticut, which were helping to pay my tuition and pay for my student films. I ended up doing about eighty productions from the time I was 15 to when I was 21. We made quite a bit of money, so I paid off my student loans and paid for my thesis film at NYU. We swept the awards and got best picture there. They even came up with an award for it, for best ensemble cast. It's a pretty cool movie, a romantic comedy, funny enough, sort of like David Mammet meets John Hughes. So, it was teenage kids, but kind of foulmouthed (laughs). It had a great cast. Thomas Lennon, from *Reno 911* and David Letruglio from *Brooklyn 99*, were my two leads. The movie did great and swept the awards, so I thought "great, they'll have it at the festival, they'll bring it to LA, and we'll get the notice we deserve. That would be awesome!" Then, NYU informed me that while it was awarded all these awards by the faculty, the dean didn't deem it "NYU enough". (Me: Oh No!) Well, it was shot in color and it was funny. It wasn't people sitting in cafes, sipping coffe in black and white and crying about the girl that got away.

RA: Not "artsy" enough for them?

AM: Not NYU enough. So, they didn't bring it to LA. The people that had seen it at the festival in New York were with David Lynch and Mark Frost's company, and they offered me a job on *Twin Peaks* season two, which was amazing. Then, I got an offer from Sean, who told me that it's awesome and that he would like me to come work for him. He called me up and basically said, if you could be my bitch for a year and I'll give you a shot. (laughs) So, that's how it happened. I was Sean's bitch for about six months. So, I went to LA. Sean had moved from the Northeast by that time and was officially in LA. I moved to Los Angeles with about three hundred bucks in my pocket, which was about all that was left after paying everything off, and I had no driver's license because I had been living in New York and didn't need one. I bought a car with my three hundred dollars. It was a '63 VW Bug, yellow, the exact same thing that Kevin Bacon had in Footloose. That was about the only cool thing about the car. (laughs) I literally had to live in it, since I had no place to stay.

RA: Oh wow. Sean didn't put you up?

AM: No, what happened was, Noel actually put me up at first, but Noel's place was really roach infested. This was back when Venice was a really scary place, not like it is now. In the early Nineties, Venice was a pretty dicey spot. This was pre-Julia Roberts moving into the area. She kind of turned the tide on Venice. So, his place was so roach infested that I was like, "Yeah, I'm not gonna stay here", so I lived in my car, showered at a nearby car wash and I was a runner for Sean Cunningham. But, I couldn't drive the car, so I had a 10-speed bike that I borrowed from Noel that I could do the runs on. Being a bike messenger in LA is crazy different than in New York. Things are a crazy number of miles apart, and in the heat and uphill many times. While I was doing that, I had this script that I had been working on with my best friend Dean Lorey from college. He had given me this script and it was what I wanted my debut to be. It was this romantic horror comedy, that was also a musical, called *Johnny Zombie*.

RA: Aha! *My Boyfriend's Back.*

AM: Exactly. I loved this movie. Dean Lorey and I worked on it for three years together, and I was really excited to go get this thing made. So, while I was in LA, I crashed a lot of charity events and would try to schmooze with people that I thought I might be able to get to make the movie. I talked to the Cormans and they were interested. I pitched it to them at this gala event. They asked if they could read the script and I said absolutely. I told Noel the good news immediately, knowing that if I told him, that it would go right back to Sean. I didn't want to tell Sean directly. The next morning I was in the offcie making a copy of the script to send to the Cormans, when Sean came in. Sean asked what it was and I told him. He then grabbed the script, didn't say a word, walked into his office and slammed the door shut. About ninety minutes later, Sean asked me to come into his office. He said "I hate the script, but I love the title. I'm going to give you a million and a half to go shoot this in Conneticut". I was like, "Say what now?" (laughs) At this point, I was twenty-one and I just couldn't believe it. But, he said he wanted to bring in a different writer to work on the script. I then told him, "Then I won't sell it to you." Those are the words that could only come out of the mouth of a dumbass twenty-one-year-old kid. I told him all about my friend that I trusted, and how we wrote it together and I suggested that Sean fly him out and just put us up in a hotel for six weeks and we would re-write it. I told him we would write whatever he wanted, and if it doesn't work out, then he could just fire us both and he could just have the script. It was awesome, because he went for it. I got to get the hell out of my car and into a hotel room, which was amazing. We were living up in the Sunset Holiday Inn and we re-wrote for about five weeks or so. Dean and I did a brilliant job and Sean just loved the script. So, we would set up readings for executives, to try to sell the picture, which is something that I did a lot back in New York and have these great actors come in and read for it. Adam Sandler, who actually lived next door to Dean and I at NYU, actually read for Johnny at the first reading of *Johnny Zombie*.

RA: I had no idea. That's amazing.

AM: Yep, true story. New Line and Disney had both heard readings of it and they both really loved it. There was a little bit of a bidding situation, which was terrific, and Disney ended up buying the film. I found out very quickly that Disney wanted to make it into a PG-13 film and get rid of the zombies. I said, "Well, the name is *Johnny Zombie*". The they said, "Well, we can change that. Can we make him less dead … and more tired, possibly?" That was when I said I'm out and I wasn't directing it anymore, so I became the associate producer of the film. I went to Sean and picthed it to him to direct, telling him that he could make a boatload of money on it. Sean then told me that Paramount was selling the rights to the *Friday the 13th* franchise to New Line and told me, "If you can find a way to get that God damn hockey mask out of the movie, you can write and direct it."

RA: Wow, that's a big thing to get!

AM: Huge! But, let's remember, there had been diminishing returns for some time by that point. Part eight had really hit a low point for Paramount, which is why Paramount was okay with selling it. Nowadays, they talk about the series differently, but back in the eighties, it was Paramount's dirty little secret. It was like the ugly stepchild. They treated *Friday the 13th* the way that Jason was treated. Like here's this deformed kid who makes us a lot of money, so we keep him in the basement and keep him around, but we don't really talk about it, even though movies like that and *Halloween* and *Texas Chainsaw Massacre* are the movies that keep our business afloat. These are the ones that pay for disastrous one hundred-million-dollar loss movies. In horror, we are the only group that never loses money, we have an unbelievable fanbase who sees everything, buys everything, and they're such an army of positive consumerism for our industry. Even with that, it's always been the dirty little secret, which drives me crazy.

RA: Especially back then. I think a lot of the mainstream back then viewed horror as something beneath them.

AM: Yep, it's true. So, like I was saying, the series was in a downturn at that point and they wanted new blood. I was part of that new blood. They wanted someone to come in, that was gutsy and didn't really care what anybody thought. I was a huge fan of these movies. I was even involved in the first one, as a young kid.

RA: Really? What did you do on that one?

AM: (laughs) It's a long story, really. I was at the first table reading for *A Nightmare on Elm Street*. Wes Craven was "Uncle Wes". (laughs) Those movies really were my lifeblood, so when I got into this thing, my feeling was that as a fan, I was so tired of watching what had basically become, in a sense, wrestling pictures. It was like, there's Jason, there's the mask, he's going to kill about fourteen people in the movie, it will happen every few minutes, each one will get gorier, blah, blah, blah.

RA: Yep ... final girl, chase scene ...

AM: Right, it's almost the same damn movie over and over again. The one exception for me in the later films is Part 6, because that movie has a sense of humor and it basically says, we have got to stop acting like this creature is human because he's not. I love when people say that up until that one, he wasn't zombie Jason. Stop. No human body can take what he went through in those first four movies. It's sort of like when people say that *Jaws* isn't a horror movie. Here's the deal, there are no sharks that fly in the air, jump onto boats and sink the boat while eating everyone on deck. It doesn't happen. It's a monster movie, and it's a horror film.

RA: Well, with *Jaws,* I always put that on people that now, because of the film, whenever you go in the water, be it the ocean or a lake or a river, what do you think of? That is the true meaning of horror and terror, right there.

AM: Yep. It's a boogeyman movie. It's the thing that's under the bed. It just happens to be under the water.

RA: Exactly. With *Friday the 13th*, people always argue that point that he became a zombie on Part 6, where I say, if he apparently drowned as a kid, isn't he a zombie technically from the start?

AM: Exactly, and in the first one, he is still a boy, jumping out of the lake. In Part 2, which happens only a short time after, he's a full-grown man with a sack over his head, doing an Elephant Man impression in the woods. There are so many leaps of logic that the fans are willing to make. I took away the big visage of this creature and said, well, what if it's more? What if this thing is more evil, and meaner and crazier, and what if its abilities are more than just walking around the woods with a machete? Honestly, Sean hated that hockey mask and wanted nothing to do with that hockey mask. It showed up in Part 3. By the way, God bless the hockey mask. I love it and don't have a problem with it, but Sean really did not like it and did not like that these films seemed to have no mythology. The mythology that Victor Miller created was that the mom lost her kid, she went nuts and she's the one that's killing everybody. Jason didn't do a damn thing, and really, the end of the movie was simply a rip off of *Carrie*. They thought, "how do we have a great final scare? I know! We talked about that kid who drowned. Let's do the Carrie White moment." Again, God bless them all for that ending. It's one of the best endings ever! So good! The problem is, that the fans don't want to see any changes. It's kind of a crazy thing. For some reason, the Freddy franchise was allowed to change more in his persona and he was allowed to become quippier. I still think that the first *Nightmare on Elm Street* is the best out of all of those films. It's just flat out scary. Sure, he has a sense of humor, which is why we love Freddy, but it is evil personified. So, for me, I got Sean's wanting to get rid of the mask and my feeling was that I would bookend the movie with the mask. But, Jason is in the whole movie. His presence is always there. That's why we did the reflective surface gag where every time he walks by a reflective surface, we see Jason, so that the fans are reminded that it's the same guy, he's just wearing a different mask. The funny thing about *Jason Goes to Hell* is that it was originally called *Heart of Darkness.* It was a totally pretentious thing. I did that because the title made sense to the movie, and I'm a huge Orson Welles fan. At the time when I was doing this movie, Orson wanted to do an adaptation of Joseph Campbell's *Heart of Darkness*. I love Welles, so I thought I would call my movie *Friday the 13th: Heart of Darkness*. Sean loved it, but eventually they wanted the hell thing and New Line wanted an ad campaign that would really freak people out, something that could get banned in several states, which it did, which is awesome. They knew exactly what they were doing.

RA: It was right in your face, too and didn't pull any punches with that campaign.

AM: You mean like the angry penis demon coming out of the mask? (laughs) To this day, Bob Kurtzman is still a good friend of mine. Bob was so upset by the poster. He was like, "You didn't even ask us to make this stupid penis demon. What the hell?" Again, when you're getting giant censored bars across your poster and USA Today is running a cover story, you can't buy better publicity. My original story was far, far darker, by a country mile, way more brutal. It was more about Jason's brother and you find out that Jason has a brother, Elias, who is so much worse than Jason, but the brother is debilitated by all these diseases, like skin disorders. He pulls Jason's body out of the lake. What I was told by Sean is to make like Part 8 didn't even happen and start off where Part 7 ends, where he is in the lake. So, he dredges him out of the lake and drags him into one of the cabins where he built this makeshift, hideous operating theater. He then cuts open Jason to get his heart and as he starts to pull at the heart, the chest cavity starts to fill up with this black fluid and suddenly, Jason's eyes open. Jason grabs Elias's head and starts to crush his head while Elias is trying to pull the heart out of Jason's chest. So, you have this hideous tug of war between these two siblings. At the last moment, he yanks the heart out of Jason's body and Jason falls to the ground in a heap. Elias then eats Jason's heart and that's how the evil moves. What Elias doesn't plan for is that by consuming Jason's heart, he has now become partially Jason, so you've got these two evil characters inside one guy, which gives him all of these abilities, like being able to survive death. It was a much darker movie. A lot of the characters were the same, but the meanings were different behind many of them. We ended up going this different route where it was purely body hopping and it became a little more comedic, which is my sensibility anyways, trying to keep a bit of a sense of humor. So, then that's pretty much how *Jason Goes to Hell* came about, through those means. I was 22 when I wrote it and 23 when I directed it.

RA: Being so young, did you ever run into the problem of people kind of going, "Well, who the hell is this kid?" or anything like that?

AM: Yep, and I will tell you, it did not bother me at all. My whole family is in the industry. Most of my family is actors. My uncle Joe wrote, produced and directed *Don't Go in The House* in 1980. So, I've always been in and around the business. I started working professionally when I was eleven years old and by the time I was thirteen, I was editing, and running two theatrical companies. So, when people looked at me because of how many years I had been on the planet Earth and said, "Well, who the hell does this guy think he is?", I had been working since I was eleven, so I was actually in the business for twelve years before I directed my first film. Also, I had won best picture at NYU and there's not a lot of us. There's one a year and it's a giant honor. So, I cut my teeth to some degree. That being said, I didn't know what the hell I was doing. I got upset my very first day. My shot list was like forty-seven shots and my DP (Director of Photography) said, "Yeah, you're going to have to cut that in half". By the third day, my shot list was twenty-five shots, so I learned my lesson quickly, but I got my crew doing pretty much forty set-ups a day, because I move really quickly and I rehearse my actors before they come to set. By the way, *Jason Goes to Hell* may have been the first *Friday the 13th* up to that point to have the full rehearsal schedule. I rehearsed with my actors for weeks before we shot anything. Even if people hate the movie, I would challenge them to find bad performances in the film. The movie is a collection of really talented actors and a lot of actors who went on to really wonderful careers. They wanted desperately to be better than what their perception of a horror movie was, which is something that I've always found a little insulting from the outside world. I mean, Tom Hanks came out of a horror movie. Kevin Bacon, Meg Ryan, Demi Moore, Alec Baldwin, these are all people who have done horror films. Sigourney Weaver, Jamie Lee Curtis, we're talking about a really rich genre that a lot of people denigrate. A lot of people do, but we still make more money than anyone else. For me, the exercise of *Jason Goes to Hell* was about giving great performances and moving like lightning, so that you couldn't see how low budget the picture was. The other thing that people tend to forget about *Jason Goes to Hell* is that we had less money than any of the other *Friday the 13th* films, besides the first one. We had two and a half million dollars. Again, I dare anybody to tell me that it looks like a two and a half million-dollar film. A big part of the reason why that is, is because of Sean Cunningham. He's a brilliant producer, always has been. The guy knows how to make a movie look great, even though there's no money.

RA: That really surprises me, because I always thought that it had a bigger budget than all of the other ones.

AM: Nope. This is one of the things that's really funny. I was on the phone with the producer, at a studio I was doing a picture for, about six months ago. She told me that they would probably only be able to have about five million for the budget. I told her that five is luxurious. She said, "Well Adam, I'm sure that you're used to much bigger budgets. I mean, you make studio pictures. For *Jason Goes to Hell*, what did you have, like twenty million for it?" I said, "No, I had about two and a half." She wouldn't believe me! She went to Studio Report Tracker, which is the place where you can see exactly how much money a movie was made for, and she gasped as she was on the phone with me. I said, "You know, I took a lot of crap when I was twenty-three years old and I was able to deliver that movie at two and a half million dollars." There's also this misconception that somehow, Sean Cunningham was directing the movie behind me, which I love hearing (sarcastically). Sean was nowhere to be found on a day to day basis. He did have to come in and direct Kari Keegan for one day of re-shoots, though. Kari and I disliked each other so intensely that we wouldn't work together, so Sean had to direct two shots of her on one day.

RA: One of the things that I always liked about *Jason Goes to Hell* is that I think it just may be the goriest one in the entire franchise. I know that there are two cuts of the film out there, the theatrical version and the director's cut. Was there a lot of controversy when people saw the original version?

AM: Well, here's what happened. When we shot the film, New Line had asked me, very deliberately, to have some scenes that we would have to cut. They said, "You go as gory as you want to. It's your movie." The executives there put their full trust in me. There was never any of that "Good going, kid!", there was none of that. It was, "You go make the goriest, coolest movie you can come up with." The reason behind that, was that they knew that the whole world would want the gory version and that America would be the only place with a controversy. They also knew, and it was the first time that this had ever been done up to that point, that they were going to release the movie in two versions. It was the very first VHS that was released at the time in both a rated and an unrated cut.

RA: That's right. I don't remember seeing that before *Jason Goes to Hell*. Now, you see that sort of thing all the time.

AM: Exactly, my movie was the very first one. It was, at that point, the highest grossing video release that New Line had ever put out, because everybody had to buy two. It doubled the orders from everyone. Then, Blockbuster did such a sleazy thing. Blockbuster back then was sort of a Christian run company. They ordered the unrated boxes, but the rated VHS.

RA: Oh no! That's low, man.

AM: Oh yeah, so the people were renting what they thought was the unrated version and wondering what was supposed to be different about it. Then, they would finally see the unrated version and say, "Oh my God! It's a completely different movie", which it really is. When we were at the ratings board with the MPAA, they turned the movie off two reels in. It was when they hit the camping scene.

RA: (laughs) That's what I was going to say, probably at the tent scene!

AM: (laughs) Oh yeah, they called Sean Cunningham and said that they wouldn't even give this movie an NC-17 rating, so it needs some sharp cuts. They said that they wouldn't even look at it again until we made the cuts. So, we did and we knew that we were going to in the first place. It ended up making a lot more money and the cool thing about it, was that it gave the film a little bit of mystique, that there was this other version that you had to see. I just wish that people were able to see the uncut version in the theater. That part sucks. Now, you can actually get 35mm copies of the film in the full, unrated cut. By the way, because Paramount put together that box set of all of the *Friday the 13th* films, they didn't bother to put in the unrated cut of *Jason Goes to Hell*. It's the one Blu-Ray that did not have the same treatment that it had on DVD. It really sucks for the fans.

RA: It's funny, I actually remember watching the uncut version with my buddies as a kid. It was like a big taboo thing we had to be sneaky about. I remember when we got to the tent scene, I was like, "Holy shit, am I really seeing this? It's like a porno, then … holy shit!"

AM: (laughs) That's great! That was the idea. I was like, if we're gonna go for it, let's go big. The interesting thing is that scene is from the re-shoots that were done about six months after we wrapped the film. All of the stuff with the campers, we added to the movie. The reason why, was that we had done test screenings of the film, and while it had tested very well, New Line said that they wanted a "campers getting slaughtered/sex equals death" scene in the movie. I told them that I would figure it out, even though I was against the whole sex equals death thing. So, Dean Lorey, Bob Kurtzman and myself got together and started brainstorming. I was always in the mindset that I hated how in these movies, you do anything fun and you get murdered for it. It's like this weird, Christian Right, Puritanical version of the world, which I don't buy into. So, I came up with the idea that if these kids decide not to use the condom and get killed, then I'm okay with that. I'm okay with unsafe sex equals death. Especially, being the early 90s, that was about as huge as you could get. When they decide to throw the condom out of the tent and Richard Gant steps on it on his way to killing them, the audience went nuts! In fact, The Washington Post gave us a great review because of that scene. I have a real fondness for that scene. I liked the actors and

I'm still friendly with them. I still think the first movie was the most overtly sexual of them all, until *Jason Goes to Hell*. Sean was not afraid of going there, and I wanted to do what Sean did, but I kind of wanted to go the extra mile. I was thinking that half of the audience or more is women for these movies. So, I was thinking, why just have all of the naked girls? Why not give them something to look at? So, there's another cut scene from the movie with Vicki and her boyfriend, when she is taking care of the baby. It's floating around on the internet. This great guy named Jonathan Penner came in to play Vicki's boyfriend and he was naked too. It's like the table scene where Josh is tied to the table being shaved.

RA: I was actually going to ask you about that! What was up with that? I want to know. (laughs)

AM: I know, everybody does. (laughs) I did another interview where that was the first question that they asked me.

RA: (laughs) Well, yeah. My question has always been, why the hell does he have to shave him? And why does he have to be naked?

AM: Here's why. Because people are still talking about that scene. I know my audience, because I'm part of that audience and I knew that putting in that weird, homoerotic scene with a middle aged naked guy strapped to a table and having some guy come in with a straight razor to shave him. I knew that people were going to lose their minds, and sure enough everyone lost their minds. It was like with the Jason thing. I knew that people were tired of seeing the same thing over and over again.

RA: You wanted to do something different

AM: Yes. By having some of these scenes and some of the quick jolts of fear in the film, I wanted the people to think that they're in the hands of a filmmaker who may be a bit out of his mind. And that's scary. When people watch this scene, they're like, "what the fuck is going on in this?" It just throws people off enough. It doesn't make any sense. I know it's ridiculous. It was ridiculous back then, but I also knew that I had just put the first homoerotic scene into a *Friday the 13th* movie and I also made a scene that would get people's attention, because it's so weird. That was truly the purpose.

RA: While we're on the subject, there's something else I wanted to ask you about that bugs me. It has to do with the character of Creighton Duke. By the way, that's one of my favorite characters in the series and Steven Williams really knocked it out of the park there.

AM: He's a phenomenal actor. Watching him act is like taking a master's class in what an actor can truly do.

RA: Definitely. There's actually two things that I wanted to ask about him. How exactly does he know so much about the family history of the Voorhees family? I actually brought this up at a convention once, and had a theory on it.

AM: Great! Let's hear it

RA: My theory is that maybe Ms. Voorhees liked black guys. Maybe Creighton was actually Jason's real dad and at the time, in the fifties, that was unacceptable by most of society, so it was hidden from the public.

AM: That's actually a really cool theory. I like that! It's not the actual story, but it's awesome. I love that theory. Plus, it goes a bit into *Candyman* territory. By the way, had we all been a little bit braver back then, that might have been the story. What the real story is, and there was a scene that we shot that was cut from the film and I hate that it was cut, when Jessica comes to the house to get her baby back, Creighton tells her how long he has been after Jason. What he tells her is that in the '60s, he was out with his first girlfriend on Crystal Lake, they were capsized in their boat and Jason dragged her to her death. Ever since then, he's been tracking Jason. Because his knowledge of the subject is so rich, he starts to become the expert bounty hunter on serial killers. I wanted that in there so badly. The problem is that the studios think that nobody gives a crap about this stuff, which is totally not the case. We really built this full mythology and I wanted the fans to be able to see that.

RA: The other question that I wanted to ask you about is another one that I have often joked about. The scene where Creighton breaks Steven's fingers in the jail cell. It really makes Creighton come off like a sadistic asshole. What does he really get out of that, other than some kind of sick joy? It just seems sadistic.

AM: (laughs) Well, it's sadistic and it's not. That scene is actually one of my favorite scenes in the movie. Originally for that scene, we had this eight page Van Helsing scene. A lot of that expositional dialogue had to come out. The problem was, it was just two guys talking in jail and it was really boring. Dean and I agreed that Creighton has to have a reason why he is giving this kid this information. What Creighton is doing, is kind of like putting this kid through the tasks of Hercules. He has to earn the information through pain, much like Daniel does in *The Karate Kid* through getting his ass kicked so many times. The idea was that Creighton had to turn this sort of nothing of a small-town guy into a hero that can go up against the monster. It's preparing him. The turning point is after the second finger is broken and for the next bit of information, Steven puts his hand through without being asked, then Creighton tells him it's on the house. It's really a warrior scene, it's turning this kid into a warrior, but in eight pages of dialogue. By the way, the whole setup to that part, with Creighton stroking the kid's hand is meant to make the audience nervous, like they don't know what the hell is going to happen there. The whole idea was to make the jump to hero status. With some of the final girls, they're just in that role because they're spunky. Don't get me wrong, I love all of them, though. My favorite was Tommy Jarvis in Part 6. He has just been through the ringer. He has been put through the nine circles of hell and is being put to the test.

RA: Very cool. I have always thought that in terms of deaths in the series, there's been some pretty horrible ones over the years, but by far one of the worst happens in your film to poor little Leslie Jordan.

AM: (laughs) Yeah, it's a pretty awful death. Poor Leslie. I love Leslie. With him, we knew how he had to die and we knew what the gag was. The fryer that he was shoved into was just a metal container with a hose that pushes bubbles into a liquid. I wanted a liquid that would look like fryer grease and be pleasant for him, as well, so I asked him what his favorite kind of soda was. I think it was birch beer. So, we filled it with that and ran the airline into it and then had to literally shove his head into it. I feel terrible to this day about doing that to him, because I adore him, but it's brutal and it works. That whole diner scene works. I wanted to do kind of a Sam Peckinpah scene in the movie and the diner became that scene. It's a fun scene and completely brutal. I mean, how many guns are in that scene? It's insane! When it came out, Mike Deluca compared that, very sweetly in my opinion, to *Terminator 2*. By that, it means that we didn't want to make just another *Friday the 13th* film. We made something with more action. Sean Cunningham taught me something very valuable before I made this when he said, "the same audience that will pay to see *Terminator* will see your movie."

RA: That's another thing. I think that your movie may have one of, if not the highest body counts in the entire series.

AM: Yeah, it is. We had the highest body count.

RA: I think people often forget about that. I mean, how many people that were unnamed were killed in the diner scene or in the police station? It's a lot.

AM: Yeah it is. It's a ton of carnage (laughs) In fact, I'm in the police station scene and I think I'm the only character that gets away. Creighton just knocks me out. I think that I'm the only cop left standing in Crystal Lake at the end of the movie.

RA: (laughs) I've always wondered what became of him

AM: I actually did a joke take for the scene where John Lemay and Kari Keegan are walking into the sunrise at the end. There was one take where I put on the police uniform and I'm running out of town as they're walking into town. It was really funny. Sean was furious and told me I was wasting the day. I just said, "Ah dude, relax. It was funny."

RA: I actually would have liked to see that!

AM: Yeah, it was a fun bit, but again it would have been fun for the movie, but it was wrong for the emotional ending. I wanted it as an extra, though.

RA: By the way, speaking of the officers in the film, your brother Kipp did an amazing job in the movie, as well.

AM: Thank you. My brother Kipp was a child star. They did a sequel to *Leave It Beaver* that was on TV for years and my brother played Beaver's son Chip Cleaver on the show for five and a half years. He went to NYU with me as well, and won best actor there and the Circle in the Square award. He did very well, but he really wanted to break the image of that squeaky clean, cute kid thing and I offered him the part on *Jason Goes to Hell*. He was all for it, so we wrote Officer Randy for him.

RA: One of my favorite parts was the two of them squaring off outside of the cop car.

AM: Funny thing, I actually had to shoot a version of that scene with different actors as my director's test for New Line. They loved it and that's one of the things that got me the job. I mean, they loved my script, but they just wanted to be sure.

RA: Of course, I remember the ending was the part that everyone will always remember. It was so shocking and so cool that the two of them were finally coming together. It took about ten years before we saw *Freddy Vs. Jason* though. I just have to ask, were you a part of any stages of that in the beginning?

AM: We were at the very beginning. When New Line made, *Jason Goes to Hell*, Bob Shaye was running the show. Bob was awesome. Soon after *Jason Goes to Hell* came out, Ted Turner bought New Line. I had a deal with them and I was originally supposed to make

SLASHED DREAMS PART 2

three movies with New Line. When Ted came in, he said no more horror movies, so that was the first thing that derailed any plans for *Freddy vs. Jason*. So, suddenly New Line was making all of these movies like *Gods and Generals*, and I was like, "Wait, this was the house that Freddy built." They were the Lions Gate of the time. There were some amazing things that came out of that though, like *Lord of the Rings*, but horror kind of went to the back of the bus. Dean and I had a couple of pitches for *Freddy vs. Jason*, but the term uphill road doesn't even come close to describing it. We had one version of the story where Creighton Duke was the lead. It was him going after these two guys. The basic concept was that they were hell's assassins, and kind of along the lines of that hell was too small for the both of them, so they're sent back here to duke it out and then Creighton comes in and complicates things. We wanted to make it a more heroic, epic thing. So yeah, we were involved initially, but it became one those "life is too short" things and quite frankly, I didn't want to be the guy that only made movies that were sequels. I got offered a ton of those movies right after Jason, but I was like "You know, I really don't want to do the next *Leprechaun* or *Pumpkinhead*." God bless those movies though. I think they're awesome and I'm a fan. I just wanted to make original content.

RA: Well, maybe if you were involved, the *Pumpkinhead* sequel could have been good (laughs)

AM: *Pumpkinhead* was actually the one movie that I was interested in. The problem was, that the whole movie was set in the bayou and there were no black people in it, and they wouldn't let me cast the movie black. I was like, "Wait a second, you're asking me to make a movie in the Bayou with witches and voodoo, yet everyone is white?" They told me that black actors don't sell to the foreign market. I told them if that's the case, I don't want to make it. That's why I ended up not doing that film.

RA: Let's talk about another film that you were involved with, *Texas Chainsaw 3-D*. How did you get involved on that one?

AM: It was being produced by a producer at our management company and Lion's Gate. They really didn't like the first draft of the script and they wanted to go a completely different way. There were seventeen different writers or teams going in to pitch for that movie. Debra and I went in and really wanted the job. We spent two weeks prepping for that and wrote a fifteen-page treatment, and the first eleven pages of the script, knowing that they would have to move quickly on it. We came in and hit it out of the park and beat a lot of huge writers for that job, mostly because we just love the genre and the characters and knew what kind of movie we wanted to make. We had a great time with Lion's Gate. The problem is, they didn't end up making the movie. They only did the distribution on the film. The producer went off to make a movie that was half of the budget that we were initially told we were shooting at. We originally had this scene near the end where Leatherface was trying to find his cousin, who was hiding amongst a thousand head of steer. He starts to walk through them with his chainsaw and they start to stampede, all around him. For me, that was the 3-D moment of the movie. That was the kind of stuff we had in there that they just couldn't afford when they made it.

RA: In my mind, the one thing that really hindered the movie was the casting itself.

AM: Oh my God, thank you! You're so right!

RA: I think if they got someone older to play the lead, maybe it would have matched up better, but they had this girl who was born in the seventies played by a college age girl now. It just didn't add up to me.

AM: Well, here was the problem, we really wanted to attach the film to the original and be a direct sequel. By the way, one of the nicest calls I ever received was from Tobe Hooper, to tell us that he loved our script. That was amazing. The problem was that they threw out the timeline, thinking that "the kids won't get it if it happened twenty-five years ago." How is it the early seventies and now it's 2014 and this girl is nineteen years old? Trust me, that wasn't us. That was purely a producer's decision, because they wanted to get cell phones in the movie.

RA: That's what I said in the theatre. If they just got rid of the modern technology, it would have worked.

AM: Yep, that's exactly what the screenplay was. That was something that got added later. The other thing that I found insulting was that in our script there was no hitchhiker. There was no guy they pick up, then leave alone in the Grandmother's house to rip them off. What? That was so dumb. Plus, there was no sassy latina girlfriend. They completely jacked around the characters and made them unlikable. Also, I was thinking, why is everyone in this movie outside of the lead girl and Abercrombie and Fitch model?

RA: Exactly. Thank you.

AM: It was like, have they seen the original film? That cast of characters are people that look like your friends. You bought it. You looked at them and said, "Those are the people that I would go on a road trip with." I hate that kind of "everybody is beautiful" casting. I don't think that it shows the world as it is. For me, if you don't have the world as it is in a horror movie, you're saying it doesn't happen in this world. If it doesn't happen in this world, then why are we afraid of it?

RA: That's one of the gripes I have with so many modern films, those casting decisions.

AM: Ugh, it's terrible. But again, the movie did really well and made a lot of money. We all strive to do artistic work, but business is business and they have to make money. There's a responsibility you have to uphold to those who put up the money. For me, I think there is a way you can do that, while remaining true to the fans.

RA: Where do you think that slasher films are headed?

AM: I think we have to redefine what the slasher movie is. I hated the idea of a *Friday the 13th* series. I think it would get pretty boring by week four. These are like specialty items that you wait a couple of years for. For me, making them ordinary is boring. Do I think there can be a rich, fertile ground for new killers? Yes, but I think people have to not be so in love with the slashers we've had and be willing to embrace something new and different, and get excited about new characters. I loved the first *Sinister*. That killer was interesting and scary, too! A guy that can get kids to be that vicious? That's cool! I think that there's a great opportunity for some great, new horror icons to emerge, but I think that we have to put away the old ones for that to happen. It's almost too much nostalgia. I think what Adam Green did with *Hatchet* was awesome. I think that the first couple of *Saw* movies were awesome and inventive. The thing about slasher movies is that you love the people that are getting slashed, and I think that a lot of people have forgotten that and that's a shame. You have to create great characters that are going to die and you have to care about those characters. Then, when bad things happen, you're really scared because you care about those characters. I also think we need to stop making horror movies about horror movies. I loved *Scream,* but I'm really tired of the jokey "I'm in on it and know what happens" thing in horror movies. Don't get me wrong, I love all of the characters like Freddy and Jason and Leatherface, but the fact that they would make a *Nightmare on Elm Street* film without Robert Englund is beyond me. He is Freddy! I love Jackie Earle Haley, but that wasn't the role for him.

RA: Oh yeah, I loved him in *The Watchmen*, but not so much as Freddy.

AM: It would be like somebody else playing Ash. Why would anyone want to watch that? They're saying that the character is somehow different than the actor, but that's not true. The character is the actor.

RA: It reminds me of those bad made for TV movies from the nineties, like *Problem Child 3*. Oh, we can't get anyone from the original cast, so we're just going to fill it in with random people.

AM: I totally agree. I still think that if they're going to make another *Friday the 13th*, that Kane Hodder should come back as Jason. He totally understood the mechanics of the movement for that character so well, and he cared. It wasn't just a job. It was something that he had such a connection to as an actor. You have to respect that. I have to say to all the fans out there, love Jason, love Freddy, love Leatherface. Keep them true to you, but also open up to all of the other stuff that's out there. There's so much good horror going on. If fans can jump onto this new stuff, they're going to end up getting more of that stuff.

ALEC GILLIS- HOLLYWOOD SPECIAL EFFECTS LEGEND
(ALIENS, HOLLOW MAN, AVP, ALIEN 3, MONSTER SQUAD, ETC.)

RA: Now, I know that you have a massive resume in the film business under your belt and have worked on hundreds of huge projects over the years. The one film that I specifically wanted to focus on for this subject though is one of my all-time favorite slasher films, *Friday the 13th: The Final Chapter*.

AG: If only it was the final chapter, right? (laughs)

RA: (laughs) True that! So, tell me, how did you get on board with that project?

AG: I had done some work for Greg Cannon on *Radioactive Dreams*, I think it was. He got the show, originally. I believe that Rick Baker recommended him for it, at first. So, he got a hold of me and had me come over and go over it with him. He said that there's this kid named Tommy with a room full of alien masks, and Greg knew that I loved aliens and designing that stuff, so he told me to come over. It was a dream come true. I thought, "This is great, I'll get to go over and do a bunch of masks and sculpt them. It should be fun!" So, I went and we worked together for maybe a month or so, but then Greg left the show. Then, Tom Savini came on board and that shifted the dynamic there. In fact, on his first day, Tom came up with a box full of rubber masks and started pulling them out and said, (excitedly) "Look at these, I bought these off some kid. Aren't they great?" But I was like, (sadly) "But, all my drawings … " He was all excited and said that we could save money and don't have to use those ideas. I was like (lets out a loud Argh sound), "How can I turn this ship around?" But I never could. I think I did get to sculpt Tommy's alien mask that he is wearing while he's playing video games, though. I got to do that one and one other.

RA: How was working with Tom on the effects anyways?

AG: He was great. I really had a great time working with him. Being that he was a guy from Philly and not from Los Angeles, we were kind of skeptical. I mean, he was already a name and had done tons of great gory stuff, but we were kind of like selling him short, honestly. I like to tell this story. When he called up, he was very soft spoken and timid. He asked if I could get silicone in Los Angeles, and here I was looking at these five gallon buckets of it. When he showed up, he had these little pint containers of silicone that he bought at a craft store. I looked at that and said "Well, this is what we have", and I pointed to the big buckets. It was like his eyes popped out of his head. He had never seen that much silicone in a container. I kind of started feeling like maybe this guy is okay. He really wears his heart on his sleeve. He explained to me that he always wanted to go to Hollywood to work, but then Hollywood came to him in the form of George Romero and his movies, so he got to stay in his hometown where he wanted to be. But, he had to invent all of his technology on his own. He's a guy who is self-taught and learned on the job, which means that he comes up with ways of doing things that are really very clever and impressive. When he was showing me this stuff, I was thinking I had been a real jerk because Tom is very clever and very talented and I learned a lot from him.

RA: Did you get to help create a lot of the gore effects and death scenes?

AG: Yeah, we were there for a lot of them, like the guy who gets his throat slit and his head turned around. I worked on all of the aspects of that. Also, the kid who gets his face crushed in the shower and that effect. I did the under structure for that. We did a head cast and had a foam latex head. Everything was foam latex back then. Basically, I sectioned up the core in that area underneath there, and made a skull so when you applied pressure, it would collapse the front of the face. I always thought that it needed to be a little more extreme than it actually was. I think we contained it too much to one area, when we should have had Jason's hand disappear up to the wrist. I think it was too subtle of an effect.

RA: Subtle? I thought it was a pretty brutal effect! (laughs)

AG: (laughs) Yeah, I guess so. I just wish we could have done more. I also did the scene with the meat cleaver with Crispin Glover. Crispin Glover was awesome. He was such a strange dude.

RA: Definitely, I met him last year and talked with him a bit. I found him very fascinating and very articulate, too.

AG: Oh yeah, he's a very unique guy. We made a head cast of him and then we made a prop cleaver. Then we cut it along his silhouette. Then he asked to let him know when we had it done and we gave him a call. When he came in, he sat there with it, holding it to his face and looking in the mirror making all these faces. He was there for like three hours and we were like, "Who is this guy? He's so weird that it's awesome." I've been a fan of his ever since. Then, when Jason gets the machete to the face and slides down it and everything, I came up with that with Tom, and mechanized the head. Jim Kagel sculpted the head and I think that Kevin Yagher painted it, and then I mechanized it.

RA: Do you have any interesting stories about working with some of the other cast members like Corey Feldman or Ted White?

AG: Corey Feldman was very young at the time, I think like ten or in that area. His grandfather was around as his guardian. Corey was a really rambunctious kid, which is another way of saying he was annoying (laughs). But, he was a sweet kid. He was a very nice kid, but very hyper and he was always running around. I felt bad for him. At one point, I turned around and three grips had him by the ankles and were dumping him into a trash can. I thought, "That sucks. You guys are adults!" Then, he popped up out of the trash can just laughing, and that just encouraged them more. I did talk to him a while back at an awards show and he was very nice, a really cool guy. Ted White was one intimidating character. You have to respect that guy. He's been around forever as an actor and a stunt man. His fingers are like the size of two of mine! I remember that Tom Savini was always very anxious to impress him. I remember that Tom was showing him a VHS tape of some of the various stunts that he had done in Romero movies and Ted was just not interested. Tom just kept wanting to talk shop with him about the stunts and all that. At one point, Ted waved his finger in Tom's face and told him, "Let me tell you something Savini, you don't even approach the hair on a stunt man's ass". To his credit, Tom didn't back down. He put his hand on Ted's finger and said, "Now wait a minute Ted, let me explain." (laughs) It was like a baby's hand on an adult's finger. Ted really liked Kevin Yagher, who was doing all the applications of the Jason pieces. Kevin had to leave for some personal family thing he had planned for months, and when he left, Ted was really concerned. He really didn't want to go into the make-up unless Kevin was applying it. I thought it was very cool and a very loyal thing. Ted was pretty awesome. He was like the alpha male around there.

RA: Were you there when the incident happened between Ted and the director over the girl getting hypothermia?

AG: I didn't know that. I knew that she got the hypothermia. Judie (Aronson) was a real sweetheart. We did a body mold of her, but she was out in that stupid lake in Topanga Canyon. I don't remember what month it was, but she was a real trooper. I didn't realize that Ted came to her defense. She was like one hundred pounds and it doesn't take very long for that heat to leave your body. She was on the raft and we were all in wetsuits, so we were fine, but she wasn't.

RA: Yeah, Ted has said that it got pretty ugly and he threatened to walk off the set if she wasn't cared for and had a fight with director Joe Zito.

AG: I could imagine. Ted is a very traditional guy. He goes way back and has worked with all the greats like John Wayne, then here he is in the eighties working on a slasher movie. I'm sure he was thinking "Oh my God, what has my career come to?" (laughs)

ANDREW J. LEDERER
(BODY COUNT)

(Andrew Lederer: back right)

RA: How did you get into the acting business?

AL: I was doing stand-up as a teenager and people just recommended me to things. I had an agent, but I didn't have enough money to get pictures. I would go in and the agent drew pictures of me. It was the typical half-assed way that somebody stumbles into things. Even this movie I got because of this agent, Mike Greenfield, who knew me from another movie that one of his clients, Sherilyn Fenn, had been in. When she was introduced to us in this other movie, she was introduced as Sheri Lynn Quatro, because she was a cousin of Susie Quatro and they were trying to push her just on that basis. You can imagine that, even then, being a cousin to someone like that is not exactly a feather to have in your cap. She fired him when we were doing the other movie and went back to her regular name. But, he remembered me from this thing and I guess that the producers in Italy needed an every-man, kind of a chubby boy character. He said that he knew someone and I went over to a Hollywood studio and dropped off a tape of stuff that I had done. Then, they showed it to Ruggero Deodato and a couple of weeks later, I'm on a plane to Rome.

RA: Cool. So, they filmed it in Italy?

AL: Yeah. It's funny because a typical way of shooting movies in Italy was to shoot it without live sound and dub it later. They had a huge dubbing industry in Italy. The great innovation that they were so enthusiastic about was that they were going to be shooting this one with live sound. If you look at the earlier Italian movies, the voices are always dubbed and layered into them. So, this was going to be some crazy innovation, shooting it with live sound. That meant that they kind of wanted a lot of the people to be American. In the teenagers, it was me, Bruce Penhall and Cindy Thompson, as well as a few others. Then, David Hess and Mimsy Farmer and so forth would be the other faction of that. Mimsy lived over there, so she kind of fulfilled both mandates, being a kind of homegrown talent and that she could act without an accent. Then, they brought in Chuck Napier. He was the ringer. They paid him for a few days and he flew in, in the middle of doing some other movie. We had to get his stuff out of the way fast. Maybe David was a little bit like that too, and fulfilled that genre connection to appeal more to fans. It never came out in the United States though, so I'm not sure who it was supposed to be appealing to.

RA: How did that work then, was everybody speaking English on set?

AL: Everybody spoke English. I'm not sure if they really had to dub anybody. We were actually synchronized with our own voices. I haven't seen it in so long, I don't think it was dubbed at all. Maybe some of the other actors may have been looped, I'm not sure. Italy already had a tremendous movie industry, but at that time, it was kind of withering away and dying. I guess they were trying to make movies that looked more like what they look like in the international market, but in their own idiosyncratic Italian way. I'm sure that we did not help to save the Italian movie industry (laughs).

RA: Were you familiar with Deodato's work already?

AL: No, but people told me all about the cannibal stuff.

RA: Have you seen *Cannibal Holocaust* since?

AL: I have never seen any of Ruggero's other films. Maybe I saw a couple of minutes of *The Barbarians*, just because he was going to make that afterward, with The Barbarian Brothers. I think Cindy may have been in a relationship with one of them and was supposed to be in that. I don't know how any of that worked out for her, but I saw her some years later in a health food store in Los Angeles with a baby and a husband and it wasn't one of the Barbarian Brothers.

RA: How was Ruggero to work with as a director?

AL: Ruggero was a lovely, lovely man ... who did not speak English. (laughs) When I saw the movie for the first time at the market for independent films of the genre in Los Angeles, to me it didn't even look like a film. It looked like pieces of a film. It seemed like a pile of celluloid stapled together with neither rhyme nor reason. (laughs) I'm not sure that I ever read the entire script, but some things just didn't fall into place for me, like the opening parts had other people in it that I never even met. I was wondering if they had just made it up since our filming. Maybe they didn't. Maybe it was in the script. That script was just impossible to read. It was incoherent, because it had been translated back and forth between Italian and English and had passed through different hands along the way. So, it made it almost unreadable to me. One day, there was a scene where I got angry, something with a milk carton. Ruggero was asking why I was and I said, "I'll tell you why". I mean it wasn't so much of a straight forward conversation because Ruggero spoke little English, but I managed to communicate to him that I had to act that way here because this other thing just happened in the previous scene. How could I now be so happy go lucky? He smiled and said (in slow Italian accent), "That's the first time you have shown true concern about the script."

RA: How were David Hess and Charles Napier to work with?

AL: Napier was a fun guy who liked to tell us stories. He told us about how Hitchcock signed him to Universal and then he never saw him again. Apparently, somebody told Hitchcock that there was this guy in the Russ Meyer movies and he was someone that Hitchcock might like. He was called to go to Universal and he went there and into Hitchcock's screening room. They told him to go up to the screen and Hitchcock came in and said (in Hitchcock voice) "Turn left." Then, Hitchcock leaves. The next day, he signs a contract to Universal and never sees Hitchcock again. He would tell stories like that and it was great. (laughs) I remember Mimsy Farmer said that he was a slobbery kisser. I'm not sure why she was saying that, though. I can't remember what the context was of that. I saw her in Rome after we finished the movie, before going back to New York. We went to see *The Blues Brothers* in this English language revival house in Rome, with one of the Italian kids from the movie. She's a lovely person. I really liked her a lot. The fact that she was a name actress was exciting to me and she was just great, probably one of my favorite people there. She was kind of a star over there and very comfortable to be around. David and I also got along very well. David was a nice guy. I remember we went and bought sneakers together. After a party near the end, maybe the wrap party, I remember we came back to the hotel and he jumped up on a glass table and it broke to pieces. Everybody in the hotel was so angry. I did feel that David had a certain bit of explosiveness to him. I don't know if it had anything to do with that situation, though. I mean, he's a big guy, we were a little drunk and the table got broken. Still, there was something about him that felt explosive. I think, as an actor, it's good to have that bubbling undercurrent of explosiveness underneath the surface, though. Maybe that's why it comes across so well on film and it works for him.

RA: Now, I want to ask … (laughs), you did the one scene in the movie …

AL: The naked scene, right?

RA: Right! (laughs) How did you feel about having to do that when they asked you?

AL: Well, I didn't want to do it! (laughs) The cinematographer, Emilio Loffredo, betrayed me. He told me, (in Italian accent) "No, it only in shadow. Nobody see anything." Of course, when I saw the movie, I was like "This is full frontal nudity for God sake!" Thankfully it didn't come out in the theater and my parents didn't see it, so I didn't have to worry about that, but it did bother me. It doesn't bother me so much now, but then it did. I just felt so betrayed. It's funny though, I mean how many chubby boys get to be naked in the movies? I know that some people say they'll do it if it's essential to the story. I'll say that it does make sense and it is essential to the story, so that justifies it on an "artistic" basis. I wasn't happy when it happened. I said I would not do it and they promised me that it would be discreet and that was bullshit. They lied. That is annoying, but it's not the worst thing that ever happened.

RA: I personally thought that scene was hilarious. As a matter of fact, I have you listed under my top ten comic relief characters in this second book.

AL: Because of my cute little penis, right? (laughs) In that case, I'm grateful and retroactively glad that it went down the way that it did. Any time that I make a list that is intended to be complimentary, I'm perfectly happy about it.

RA: Yeah, I really liked the character and got a kick out of your part. It was really kind of sad to see him die.

AL: Yeah, it was. Plus, it hurt too because they didn't strap that thing (the spike trap) on me well enough, so when the thing was activated, the tape vibrated on my chest and it burnt me a little bit. I got hurt twice on that movie. I could have gotten crippled on the scene where I'm naked and slip on the floor. I'm embarrassed and I take the tablecloth to cover myself. We did that scene twice and they didn't clean up properly after the first take. I came running in the second time and I slipped and my feet went straight up into the air and I landed flat on my back. I could have been crippled the rest of my life. We already did the take already, so I said "You know, I thought you guys were looking out for me. Apparently not, so that means I have to look out for myself and I will from now on. But, not today. For now, I'm leaving and going back to the hotel." Then, I regally draped the tablecloth over myself and walked away with my head held high. I was so proud of myself for making that point, which probably mattered to no one, but me. (laughs)

RA: Could you tell me some more about your comedy career and some of the highlights of it?

AL: I'll say that the highlight is that I've done ten Edinburgh Festivals, doing solo shows. The most recent was three years ago. I know that I'm called a pioneer in the whole alternative, storytelling comedy in America, I suppose, that whole '90s alternative comedy that people like Janeane Garofolo were at the forefront of. I think that a lot of people respect me, but I'm a fairly invisible character when you get down to it. I work, I perform, I like it, it's artistically satisfying and it's not likely that anytime soon anyone will be calling to interview me on a book about that. Although maybe that is not entirely true. I've been in proximity to a number of intriguing scenes. I may not have been the focal point, but maybe if you were to just pan the camera slightly to the left, you'd see me.

RA: Are you still doing comedy these days?

AL: Oh yeah. I am the same man that I have always been artistically and personally.

RA: Do you have any current projects that you have coming up?

AL: I've been working on a big show idea that I'm going to be taking back to the United Kingdom. I wanted to have it ready by this August, but it isn't. Unlike America, where you can do short sets and work on material, there's really no institution set up over there where you can showcase these idea snippets of a work in progress one bit at a time. Maybe I can do some kind of podcast where I can throw out little five minute segments at a time. I'm hoping this doesn't sound like pipe dreams and desperation. If it happens, then great. If not, well that's not so great, but life is in living, right?

RA: Right you are. How do you look back on *Body Count* these days and the time you spent on it?

AL: The time I spent on it was great. I was in the mountains outside of Rome and working with great people. I think my best friends on the set were David and Nicola Ferrin. I was a very close friend on the set with Dardano Sacchetti, who wrote the film, even though he didn't speak much English. When I was making that movie, almost everyone on the crew was Italian. Half of them didn't even speak English and if you wanted to make yourself understood, you had to speak English the way that they did, saying it slowly and with an Italian accent. Except for

97

when the cameras were rolling, I had a lot of time off on that movie. When you would speak to them, you would speak in this fashion (slow Italian accent), "Well, I believe that I may going into the dining area for a bit because I won't be having much to do for the foreseeable future and I am looking perhaps to have a bit of a snack." So, I was speaking that way for weeks. I began to wonder whether I would ever speak like an American again! I did when the cameras were rolling, but that was acting. But, all of my normal speaking (Italian accent), even the way that I thought in my mind, was to speak in this fashion. I was given a lift out to Rome one weekend with Dardano and his wife and his kids. He sent his two kids to the American school in Rome because he felt that it would give them an advantage in the world. They spoke English like Americans. I really liked talking to them because they were like American kids. It reminds me of those World War II movies where they train these German spies to speak like Americans and then they give themselves away by smoking a cigarette the wrong way. These kids seemed American, but they weren't, they were Italian! The only way that gave themselves away was when they referred to cookies as biscuits. I was like "Oh my God, Italian spies! You tricked me, you rat bastards!" I was in the car with them when that happened and somewhere along the way, I spoke to them like an American, just to see if I still could. I was like "Hooray! I can still do it!" As a whole, the whole experience was like this glorious vacation from normalcy, from the normalcy of my identity as an American. They invited me to their house and they knew that I loved lasagna, because that's what you say as an American who knows nothing else of Italy, "Oh yeah, I love … lasagna." So, they made me lasagna and what I didn't know is that lasagna is different in Northern Italy than it is in Southern Italy, the type that we know. They put this thing proudly down in front of me and I put it in my mouth and it was repulsive. I was so desperate to get out of having to eat more and somehow, I did. It's funny, because now I like that kind of lasagna. You know that feeling where you're expecting to taste something and you taste something else? I think that has a lot to do with it and that it really wasn't that bad. It's like opening up a can of beer and getting soda instead. That's my thought on it.

I've managed to run into a lot of the people from the movie over the years in Los Angeles and had a chance to catch up with them. One of the girls from the movie became kind of a star over there, Nancy Brilli. I remember Ruggero actually offered to let me stay at his place after we were done, for a month! I didn't realize that it was something that one would do over there. Of course, I had a ridiculous response, when my response should have been "Of course! I would love to stay with you for a month!" I did run into him later on and he hooked me up with his agent. I got to go over to the studio over there and walk around and check out some of the sets and got to meet with him. He asked me to get him some pictures. I guess they like the kind of chubby American comic relief type guys over there. But, none of that ever happened, perhaps mainly because of my own inactivity on my behalf. I feel bad about telling you that I wasn't exactly the best merchant of my own wares. For years now, I have been thinking about doing that and taking him up on the offer. He's probably been in the grave now going on eighteen years (laughs).

I think they still owe me some money from the film, by the way. My agent, Mike Greenfield put me in the movie. I never got a chance to sign the contract, so he signed it for me. (laughs) He signed my name! It wasn't that much money, I mean I got $1500 a week for a per diem. After the movie was over, they put me up at a hotel in Rome for a few days. I ended up staying one extra day. When I came back to the hotel, they wanted me to pay for that one extra day, so I went over to the producer's house, which was just a few blocks away. I asked him to cover the one night and just take it out of the check that they owed me ... and then they just took it all out! (laughs) It was just one night, one fucking night! So, I never got that last check. I asked the guy on the American side about it and he said he would look into it, but I don't think there was really any looking into it. When I ran into the producer years later, it was really not a good time to ask. I still want my money, damn it. Someday, I will rule them all (Andrew wants everyone to know that this rant was in good humor and asked I put a smiley next to it, just to show that, so ... :)

RA: That's one expensive hotel room.

AL: Yeah it was! You know, the movie is always confused with the Dick Sargent movie of the same name that was released around that time. It was even handled by the same video company, so that couldn't have helped. This one also has like a dozen different names, so that adds to the confusion even more.

RA: Yeah, it's a tough one to find, too. It took me quite a while to track down a copy.

AL: I think I'll have to give it a watch again. I mean, it's not exactly what I was hoping to be in. I wanted to be in a real *Friday the 13th* movie. Apparently, years earlier when they were making Part 3, somebody called The Comedy Store to ask if I would like to audition for it, but they never gave me the message.

RA: Oh man! I know what part you would have got!

AL: Yeah, I know! I mean, it was still fun to be in a *Friday the 13th* style of movie. It was like a cheap-ass little excursion. Plus, it was great when we were shooting during Halloween. To be shooting a horror movie in the mountains of Italy on Halloween, with all the trees ablaze with all of the leafy, autumnal goodness, was kind of thrilling and significant.

RA: That is very cool. My final question is, if you could say anything to the fans of *Body Count*, what would you say?

AL: (laughs) I would just say "Hi, how are ya? Tell me what you like about it. Tell me more about my eyes." I'm glad they like "my work". Haha, listen to me, (in deep, diabolical voice) my work.

BERT DRAGIN
(Writer/Director of Twice Dead and Summer Camp Nightmare)

RA: How did you get started in the film business?

BD: I'm from Cleveland, Ohio and I had a furniture business. I sold the business in about 1981. I had always done community theater, both acting and directing, so I had an interest in the movie business. I moved to California with my wife and children and decided to go into the movie business. I met with Penelope Spheeris, who was doing a movie called *Suburbia* and I liked the integrity of it and I told her I would put up the money and produce the movie if she would teach me how to make a movie. Roger Corman at that time was interested, so he and I made a deal where he would distribute and I would produce and that's how I learned how to make a movie. It was after this that I made *The Butterfly Revolution*, which later became *Summer Camp Nightmare*.

Summer Camp Nightmare

RA: Where did the idea for *Summer Camp Nightmare* come from?

BD: After *Suburbia*, I wanted another project and my kids had read a book in school called *The Butterfly Revolution*. I re-read it and thought it would make a good movie. I contacted the author and I made a deal with him for the movie rights. I needed to write a screenplay, so I went back to Penelope and she taught me how to write a screenplay. After writing it, Roger Corman was interested, and with his attorney we went to a company and they said they would put up the money if they could have the distribution rights. So, I made the deal with them and Roger and I went partners on it. A short time later I met them. They agreed to finance the film, so we took an office and started hiring people. We then made *Butterfly Revolution* with Chuck Connors taking the role of the head of the summer camp. We sold the movie rights to a company whose name escapes me at the moment, and they did really well with it. I was trying to find the money to make the movie and there was an attorney who I worked with and played tennis with. I asked him to read the screenplay for *Butterfly Revolution* and later on he said he gave it to some people he knew and that they really liked it and they wanted to make the movie. I said, "That's great, can you tell me about it?" He said, "Well, let's play tennis first and I'll tell you about it later." I lost the game, by the way. (laughs) Then, afterward, he told me all about it. We met with this couple and they were a rather interesting couple. They were not involved in the making of the movie, but were a bit crazy about it. They later wound up in a magazine in an article titled "Hollywood's Dirtiest Divorce", and they fought during the making of the movie, in front of me. I had an office with them and they were quite an interesting couple. I remember I told them when I first met with them that I wanted to direct the movie as part of the deal and they agreed to let me do it. I went to Roger and he gave me some tips on directing. I also had a good camera man and assistant director who helped me make the movie. The first day we drove out to the set, I got two camp sites out in Malibu to film at. On the way out, they said, "Bert, this is your first time directing, so all you have to remember to say ACTION and CUT. We'll do everything else." So, toward the end of the day, we were filming some kids coming out of the water and my mind strayed, I was looking away and after a while the assistant director poked me in the ribs and said "Say cut! Say cut!" and then I finally did. (laughs)

RA: Where did you film it and what are your memories of the on-location filming?

BD: It was over in Malibu at a campsite. There were two campsites that we found and it was off season, so I leased the camps for the couple weeks that we needed to make the movie. One we used only for the rope bridge. I had it written into the movie and when I toured the campsite, lo and behold, there was a rope bridge. I rented that one just so we could film that sequence. We strengthened the rope bridge so that it was secure and used it. It was called Camp JCA.

RA: Where exactly did the idea for that gauntlet sequence come from?

BD: I believe it came from the book. If not, it was something I made up. Some of it was based on the book and other things I made up to make it more exciting. We made it and showed it to Roger Corman and he liked it and showed it to this company, who said that if we would spend so much on advertising that they would reimburse us if they could have the video rights. So, we made a deal with them and we had all the other rights. Roger ended up renaming it *Summer Camp Nightmare*. He thought it would be a better title.

RA: How was your experience working with Tom Fridley?

BD: He was the one who was sort of the evil kid in the movie, not the main one, but the one they claimed raped a girl. I remember he was related to John Travolta, and was his nephew. He was a good kid. I liked working with him. He had a lot of energy and ideas. One night I was dining with my wife in a restaurant and Travolta came in with his entourage. I went over and talked to him. I told him I just wanted to say hello and that I was working with a young man that said he's your nephew. He said (excitedly) "That's right! How's he doing in the movie?". I told him that he's doing great and he was very happy to hear that and told me he was glad to see him acting.

RA: What are your favorite memories of making the film?

BD: I had a lot of fun on all of the movies. I got to learn a lot about punk rock for *Suburbia* and got to work with Chuck Connors on *Butterfly*, who was a really great guy. I remember the first day of shooting that we were driving with the kids on the bus and it was getting towards dusk and we needed the light. The bus broke down and I was getting off the bus to see what the problem was and running all around, getting all excited. I remember I came back on the bus and Chuck said "Bert, sit down here. Look, just relax. You're the director. You're not supposed to be starting the bus when it breaks down. So, sit here and learn to sit and relax every chance you get". So, that was great of him. Then, there was a scene where he gets killed in the movie when the kid accidentally stabs him. He said, "Bert, I have bad hips I really don't want to fall down, can we work something else out?" I said, "Chuck, you've gotta fall. We need this shot. You won't get hurt", so he says "Fine, one time. For you, I'll fall down one time." So, the kid chases him, hits him with the knife and he falls, then I yell cut and take a look at it. The cameraman says, "Bert, it didn't come out good". I had to say, "Chuck, listen ..." and he said, "I know, you want me to do it again. Alright, one more time, but that's it." The next time, the glasses didn't fall off a certain way, so we had to do it again. We ended up doing it six times and he was a good enough sport to do it six times. Of course, he was cussing me, but in a good way. (laughs)

Twice Dead

RA: Where did the idea for *Twice Dead* come from?

BD: I sat down with Bob McDonald who helped me write *Butterfly Revolution*, after it was finished and told them I had a new idea. It was about a gang of thugs, street toughs, and what if they got involved with a ghost in a haunted house and got tricked into getting scared themselves. So, we sat down together and wrote it. He had ideas and I had ideas. The company that bought the rights for *Butterfly* was also interested in this one. I would bring the woman their sections to read and approve and she liked what I was doing, and got Roger involved, with his attorney, who is now head of one of the big studios. He got them to put up the money and came through. Then, we had the money to make the movie and they had the video rights. When we made the movie, it was a lot of work, but a lot of fun. I really had a great time.

RA: It's a beautiful house in the film. How did you find that location?

BD: We got lucky. We found two homes, one across from the other. One was just the front that you see there in the movie. The rest was burnt out. It was a burned down house with the front still standing. We used that for the exterior and then the house across the street had a great interior. There was only one person living there and they were a caretaker, so we used that one for the interior shots. So, it was really easy filming because you could film all of the outside street shots on one side. The kids would go in the house and they would open the door and you'd see them from the back walking in, then we'd go to the other side and film the other one from the inside. It worked really well, much better than a Hollywood set. We kept all of our equipment in the driveway and on the street and filmed there day and night. The cast was really great, very cooperative young people eager to please. I had very little problem with them.

RA: What went into making some of the effects for the film?

BD: We had a great effects guy come in for the movie and I knew what I wanted and he was able to make it all happen. (laughs) This is bringing back some funny memories. I remember I had this idea of having the gang kill the girl's cat by stabbing it to the door. My assistant director said it's a great idea, but was asking me where I was going to find a dead cat. I told him we can do it, because they're gonna make me one. So, they worked and worked on it, but said that they can't do it. Then one of them told me that at UCLA they have these dead specimens that they use for the veterinary program. We called them and sure enough, they had a dead cat. So, we bought one and they sent it over. The special effects guy comes up to me while we're filming and whispers, "Bert, we've got the cat, but it's frozen." (laughs) So they sent us a frozen cat! So I said, "Well, we'll defrost it", so they put it in a microwave oven and tried to defrost the cat and it came out looking like hell (we're both laughing hysterically). After that, I asked them to see what they can do to dress it up. They tried to dress it up, but we just took a very quick shot of it. If you look at it closely, it looks horrible. (laughs) There's another scene where Jill comes home and she's going up the side steps to the house, and the gang is there all in masks. The scene wasn't originally in the movie, but I was walking down Hollywood Boulevard one day and I came across this store that had all of these different masks in it. I thought it was great and that I could put them to good use, so I bought them and made the scene out of it. They put on the masks and we kind of just made up the scene on the spot.

RA: The thing that I really liked in the film was the use of the dumb waiter in various parts and how one gang member gets killed by it. It was very innovative.

BD: Yeah, that was another idea I had. I thought it up and wrote it in, but when it came to it, I thought, "Geez, how are we going to do that?" My special effects guy told me not to worry and that they were going to build one. So, they built this wood tunnel and it was in the middle of the living room. We used that and then faked it in the kitchen. What the main character gets into in the kitchen wasn't really anything. It didn't go anywhere. I can't remember exactly how it worked. Then, we had the part where it drops on the guy's head. That was another fun effect. We killed them off in various ways and did some other funny scenes with them. I like the one where the big guy, Travis (McKenna), winds up in a dump truck, with all of the garbage pouring on him.

RA: (laughs) That was my favorite part.

BD: Yeah, it was a good one. Travis was a good guy to work with. I remember too, that I was taking this course at UCLA on movie art around the time we filmed *Twice Dead*. I remember approaching the guy who taught this course and told him about the movie we were making and asked if he could come down to help with the design of the movie and he agreed and came out to the set. He said that what I want to do is work with the colors. As you get into the fun parts of the movie, or the parts where these people get killed, you want to brighten up the colors and get them really splashy and bright. The scene where Travis drives the motorcycle into the wall, we made it bright yellow. Then, the attic scene had different greens. He sort of went through with me and said which colors should be used to make the scenes more vivid. The scene where they have our hero tied up under the light, I did that with a special blue light I remember. It worked out really well. He really inspired me.

RA: Jonathan Chapin talked about some of the scenes that were not used in the final cut. Could you recall some of the scenes that didn't make it?

BD: No, I'm sorry, but I really can't recall. I know that every movie has scenes cut out. We probably did. Actually, the editor, when we finished the movie, had said to me, "Bert, instead of us doing this together, why don't you just sit back and let me make the first cut? Then, if you don't like it, I can change anything you want." I said okay, and that's what he did. So, he edited it and I came in and looked it over and made a few adjustments and changes. If he left out some stuff, I couldn't recall. But, Jonathan was a good kid, nice to work with. One interesting story is that I had a friend in Cleveland who had directed me in a lot of theater. His name is Dick Meadows. He was an actor too, so I called him up and asked if he wanted to be in a movie and he said it sounds great. I had him come to California and put him in the film and he was thrilled about that. He was one of the gentlemen in the opening of the movie that is called to the house. They come up to the house in an old car and they knock on the door, then they hear the screams and go through the door. Some of the other movies I have put old friends in as well, in non-speaking parts.

RA: What was Todd Bridges like to work with?

BD: (laughs) Well, Todd had gone through a tough time around then. We just needed someone and he was available. He had a great sense of humor. One evening, we were filming the scene where he comes to the house and they warn him about the gang. They were inside the house and he was supposed to go out the door. Somehow, the door jammed and he couldn't open it and they started laughing about it. I yelled cut and we did it again. I said "Okay, the door's fixed now." So, on the second take, he goes to the door and it won't open again and they all start laughing again hysterically. I yelled cut again and told them we were going to get it right this time, and if they can't we would just call it a night and the scene won't be in it. Sure enough, they start to giggle again. I said, "Okay, that's it. Wrap it up, we're through." Todd says, "No, no, no. Please, let's do it again. We'll be serious this time." So we did it again, and he broke up laughing again. That was just Todd. He kept making jokes despite the fact that I wanted to get out of there and finish up. We did like five or six takes before I said, "let's just wrap it up. We'll do it another time." (laughs) That night he caused me some aggravation, but it was all humorous and we were all laughing. Outside of that, he was fine. He kept a good sense of humor throughout the whole thing. The scene where he gets hit by the car, we had a double for him.

RA: Are there any plans for a big re-release with extras in the making for either film?

BD: No. That would be something that I would have to actively do and raise the funds for. I just don't really have the energy anymore, so I'm content to just leave them as they are. I do have good memories and enjoyed doing it, but just want to keep it where it is.

RA: You really made some great movies in your time. I just wish that more people knew about them.

BD: Funny story actually. It was right after doing *Summer Camp Nightmare* that my wife and I were on vacation in Europe. We were in Denmark, I believe, on a tennis tour. My wife and I played a lot of tennis. We were playing tennis at some club there and I walked out and there were a couple young people on bikes. I asked if anyone spoke English and they said yes, they speak English. I asked them if they watch movies and if they had ever seen *The Butterfly Revolution*. The kid asked me what it's about and I told him and he says, "Oh yeah! I saw that. It's a good movie." I asked him how he saw it and he said that he rented it. I asked him if he could show me the video store and he said, "Yeah, get on the bike", so I got on the bike and he took me down there and I saw it in the window. He told me "Over here, we call it The Revolution of the Boys." That was the title on the video. I was very pleased to see that it was being distributed. I was getting the royalties from all of these different countries, but to actually be there and see it and talk to someone who had seen it was very exciting to me. With *Suburbia*, after making that movie, my wife and I were again traveling and we were in a disco In France and the subject came up with some French people there. When they had heard that I produced it, they all gathered around and wanted to hear about it. With that one too, just about a year ago, I had a workman over at my house to do some work. He came into my office and I had a *Suburbia* poster up. He asked me about it and I told him I produced it and he said, "You produced it? Oh wow, that's my favorite movie!" He said he would really like a poster, so I had some around and I gave him one. He was just thrilled. So, people do know about those movies. *Twice Dead*, like you said, is not very well known, but it was successful financially. They all were. I mean it wasn't a lot, but I was able to at least make my money back, so breaking even is pretty good. (laughs)

RA: I see that those are the only two you wrote/directed, which is sad to me because I loved them! Why didn't you make any more films after these two?

BD: Well, after the three movies came out, I tried to do something else, but it's really difficult. It's really difficult to find a good screenplay and I really didn't feel like writing another one. So, I worked on that and I worked on promoting another screenplay idea. After about three more years of that, I just let it fade away and did other things with my life, but I spent a good ten years in the 1980s making the films, and it was probably the best time of my life.

RA: What are you up to now?

BD: Since then, I've been doing volunteer work. That's very satisfying. My wife and I both became para-professional therapists. We work in the area counseling people. (we talk about counseling and helping people). We talk with people of all ages. It's very gratifying and we have helped a lot of people over the years. We don't have degrees, but we did take courses in that, which the majority of the people there did, as well. We've taken a lot of courses and been through a lot of training.

RA: Do you have anything else you would like to say to the fans?

BD: I'm glad that there are fans of the movies out there. I'm glad that they appreciate all of the work and effort that went into it by all of the people involved. I hope that our efforts made the lives of some people a little brighter and gave them something to remember.

BOB DESIMONE
(Friday the 13th: A New Beginning)

BD: Before we get started, there are two things that you should know. I only worked on the movie for two days and I only saw the movie twice, once at the wrap party and once at the premiere.

RA: Okay, no problem! I can work with that. Let's start at the beginning. How did you get into the movie business?

BD: My first love, as you might know, is drumming. I came to California when I was twenty years old. I was working in the studios and the clubs. I played for a lot of people and we opened for a lot of big people like Linda Ronstadt and Fleetwood Mac. The band thing fell apart due to a lot of in- fighting with the management and the record company. So, I went into my second love, which was comedy. I was working at The Comedy Store doing a show called *Make Me Laugh*. I did ten shows for them and it led to a couple of little parts in movies. That's how I got my start. The music business, the comedy and the acting. Comedy and acting are very close, while the music thing is a whole different thing, but it's all show business.

RA: I just wanted to touch on that a little bit. When you said you did comedy, there was a lot going on at that time down in the LA area. Do you have any good stories from that or interesting people the you worked with?

BD: Well, I gotta tell you, I got to work with all of them. I've worked with David Letterman, Jay Leno, Jerry Seinfeld. My biggest problem was that I had the talent, but I was not aware of the business end of show business. I didn't really like hanging with the crowd, either. I didn't go out to Canter's Deli afterward and hang out with the other comedians, telling jokes and such. This is something that I have never told another interviewer. Mitzi Shore was the proprietor of The Comedy Store back in the day. She came up to me one night and said, "You're ready. Give me five minutes of stuff you can use on TV and I'll call the (Johnny) Carson people and have them see you", and I never said to her I could do it. In the club, you can easily do five minutes, but when you're on TV, you've got to be very careful, with the censors, especially back then, not that my work was really dirty. I never did it. She came up to me like she came up to some of the other guys. I don't know whether it was fear of failure or fear of success, I don't know. I had gotten stung in the music business. We were right there, opening for those big names and after that whole thing fell apart, I kind of got stung. I really can't say what it was, but I always kept putting it off, saying I'll get to it later. I kept performing with these guys night after night, but I never went over to her office during the day and said, "I'm ready to go." That was something that I'll never know. Who knows, maybe I would have gotten even more famous and overdosed (laughs).

RA: I have to ask, did you ever run into Sam Kinison when you were doing that?

BD: Oh yeah. In fact, Sam used to sell tickets at the door because Mitzi told him, "You have no act." His act was so out there. I mean, she loved him, she loved all the guys and was very sweet to everyone, but she told Kinison that he had no act and that he should work up a good solid act and put something together and she would put him on. So, I would be going to The Comedy Store two or three nights a week and he would be selling tickets and I would just say hello to him, and go in and hang out until it was my time to go on. He was an intense character. It's too bad though, because he cleaned up and then he got killed in a car wreck. It was like Stevie Ray Vaughn. Stevie cleaned up and then he got killed in a helicopter crash, which is too bad.

RA: Yeah, that is too bad. He was a hell of a talented guy. Can you talk about your brother Tom (director Tom DeSimone) and his involvement in the business? What are your memories of that?

BD: Tom had always wanted to be a director. He went to Emerson College in Boston and he came out here and did post grad work at UCLA. He won a Golden Eagle Award for a student film that he did while he was there. He got involved the hard way, knocking on doors and such. You know, you do these films, these B films, whether you're an actor or director or whatever you do in this business to keep moving your way up the food chain. But, he was so good at bringing movies in either on or under budget that they kept bringing those kinds of movies to him, those B movies.

RA: Yeah, like *Chatterbox*? (laughs)

BD: (laughs) Yeah, he wrote that one. He wrote some of those like *Chatterbox* and *Reform School Girls*, as well. Then he also did *Hell Night* with Linda Blair. I'm not sure if he wrote that one or not. Anyways, he got involved in the B Movies, then he started doing television, doing *Swamp Thing* and such. In this business, you get known for something and then you're typecast. If you're a director, they will ask you to direct the same type of thing in the same genre over and over again. You'll keep getting the horror movies or maybe the sexploitation films. But he's done quite a few films and he did well. He's retired now. We actually just bought a summer place in Cape Cod and every time we go there, he comes and it's just a riot. He's a great cook, so he hangs out and cooks for us (laughs).

RA: How did you come on board for *Friday the 13th Part 5*?

BD: My brother was directing a film called *Savage Streets*. He did not get along with the producer. The producer was just a strange character, so he bowed out of the film and they brought Danny Steinmann in. Danny directed the film, I shot my part and then he came to me and told me that he likes what I do, and that he liked my acting. I played Mr. Meeker, the teacher. I played him full blown, really funny, and as a goofy character. When they brought it to the daily rushes, to them they thought I was hysterical, but it wasn't what they wanted in the film. They wanted just a real, regular teacher. I went back and I shot the scene again, but did it straight. There's one part though, where a fight breaks out among the kids and my character is a lot more animated from where they kept the first character in that I did. So, he saw me play a character two different ways, so he told me, "I would like to keep you in my book, so that whenever I do a film, I would like to call you." I thought it was great, because it's what you're looking for. You're hoping that he could get a better film and call me and that I'll get to work in bigger, better films and so forth.
Well, a year or so went by and I opened my own business and I just quit the acting. I said, "I'm done with show business." My brother had called me and said that he had read in Variety that Danny was scheduled to do *Friday* 5. So, I called him and he said, "Where were you? I called your agent and they said you were no longer working. What's going on?" So, there were no more parts left in the film and he was like tearing his hair out. He said that he has to work with me and wanted to put me in the film. There were only two parts left, the guy who drives up in the beginning in the van and the guy who comes to pick up Lana at the diner. He asked me if I could write something to make those two characters into one person and I said, "Of course I can." So, I read the script and I just made the guy who was riding in the van Billy, simply by saying the line, when Lana asks who wants her and Billy says, "The pride of the Unger Mental Institute, who has just emptied his last bed pan", so that made me the same guy and it didn't look weird at all. So, the script basically just said "Billy does cocaine while

waiting for Lana", and Danny told me I can improvise and that once we start rolling, I can basically do what I want and say what I want. So, the stunt man pulled the car up and did the doughnut, stopped and got out, then they took the right door off and mounted the camera on it. Then, I set it all up with the cocaine in the visor and everything. They yelled "Action!" and I just kind of goofed around while I was there. So, that was the scene and it ended up making all this noise, which was a surprise.

RA: I always thought that Billy was quite the sleazy character. He may in fact be one of the sleaziest in the series.

BD: Thank you

RA: (laughs) You're welcome. What did you think about playing a character like that?

BD: I didn't mind at all. I was fine with it. Also, in the very opening of the film I had no lines and Danny told me I could do whatever I wanted to do. When I opened the van door, my only line was "Tommy". When he just sat there, I threw in, "Okay, sit there. I don't give a shit." It was all okay with Danny. He knew that I did a lot of improv and a lot of comedy, so he said to just do whatever I felt like saying. Then, of course, the tongue thing that I did with the girl (Melanie Kinnaman), I just threw that in. I just did what I wanted because there were really no lines, so I came up with most of it.

RA: I always thought that was funny how you were on the way to Pinehurst, at work, and you're reading porn.

BD: (laughs) Yeah, well, that's what they gave me.

RA: I've heard some funny stories on this. What was your relationship with Melanie Kinnaman like on set?

BD: Oh gee, here I am trying to avoid this (laughs). Well, in acting, if something happens that's out of the ordinary, it's better to go with it. Unless of course something happens like a lighting structure falls on your head, but if something unplanned happens, that's really in the moment. As it was, we pulled up, I got out, and said my lines. So, I'm standing there and while she's talking to him, I wasn't sure if it was a wide shot or not, but I was chewing my gum and I was eyeballing her up and down. I mean, I was a sleaze bag. I was just reading porn for Christ's sake (laughs). So, I stayed in character and while she was delivering her lines to the camera that was in the truck that was supposed to be the kid, she became unnerved by the way I was doing that. She saw me out of the corner of her eye and stopped and said "I can't do this. He's making me crazy!" Danny actually snapped his pencil and said, "Why do you just stop? If he's bothering you, use it!" So, we did the scene again and that's why, because I was miffed that she missed the scene, that's why when she turns I do my line "Anytime doll" and pull my ear and wiggle my tongue at her (laughs). It just made my character sleazier when I did that and when they said cut, Danny was just rolling.

RA: What exactly was the coke that you were using there?

BD: It was baby laxative, Minit. I wouldn't know about this, mind you, but back in the seventies when I was a musician, people used to cut cocaine with that. It's super mild, but it's white and its crystalline. Most of the time when people bought cocaine, they would ask how much of it was in there. So, it was just that and I put it on the thing and I snorted that. I've had a lot of people ask me that.

RA: I noticed you were wearing a wedding ring in the film. What's up with that? Was that part of anything or just an oversight?

BD: Oh my God! You know something, no one has ever brought that up! I wasn't married then. It's on my right hand now and it's a gold ring with a diamond on it. It's an interesting ring. I got married in 1994. Way back, my father was at one time a bookie to make ends meet during tough times. He went to law school, graduated, but the depression came. He went to work to support his parents and the rest of the family. He did a lot of things and later became a lawyer, but during hard times he was a bookie. Some guy owed him money and gave him some jewelry because he couldn't come up with the money he owed him. My father took the jewelry and had a ring made for himself, which is what I was wearing on my left hand then and had a ring made for my mother. He had a jeweler appraise all of the jewelry and he called the guy up and he gave the guy the difference in cash. Bookies don't do that. If you owe a bookie a thousand bucks and you give them five thousand bucks worth of jewelry, you lost the jewelry. That's just the kind of man my father was. He was just doing it to keep the family alive. So, he told me when he died I would get this ring. But, the morning I was leaving on a plane to come out here, he took the ring off and he gave it to me then. I've had it all this time.

RA: That is a great story! I love it. Was there anything else done with your death? I know many were heavily edited down from what I hear.

BD: I think I did two takes. They always do that as a safety. I do remember that I said a couple of other things in there that are not in the final cut. There was some talk about my body with an axe in my head, but they never did it.

111

RA: Do you still keep in touch with anyone?

BD: No. Honest to God, I had no idea that these films would take off like they did. It's constant. I get autograph requests and people mailing me pictures. One just came in today. It just blew my mind. I had no idea that those took off as the cult classics they are. It's pretty amazing.

RA: What are you up to now?

BD: I'm just about retired. I still play in a band here and there. I put a band together recently. I play for fun. I'm getting ready to sell my business to my manager and getting ready to retire. I'm in the office now literally about two or three hours a day, just to make sure things are running smooth. That and golf. I've started golfing again.

RA: Final question. If you could say anything to the fans out there, what would you say to them?

BD: Honestly, the way I've been treated, I love them all. I've got nothing but great letters from everyone. They're just a great bunch. When my birthday rolls around, I just get a ton of birthday wishes from them and cards. I think it's great. It's funny, I've got a lot of parents with kids now who will watch the movies together. I appreciate all of them. I never charge for an autograph. If they're going to be nice enough to ask me for an autograph, that's enough. I love them all.

BOB ELMORE
(TEXAS CHAINSAW MASSACRE PART 2)

Texas Chainsaw Massacre Part 2

RA: I've Heard some horror stories form the set and have heard it was pretty brutal at times. Can you elaborate on that?

BE: Oh yes, get this, it was 110 degrees during the day in Austin, Texas. It was 100 percent humidity. Then, when you got onto the set with all of the lights and everything, it was about 140-150 degrees. It was just miserable. We, as a stunt group would work six days a week, then on Sunday, we would come in and prep for Monday. We really never stopped. It was so bad that we would send people out to buy new underwear, because we didn't have a way to wash our clothes. Toward the end of the movie, I think we did two or three days straight without stopping. They brought in another crew and everything. We moved out of the hotel because we were supposed to go home. Nobody knew where we were at and our luggage was at the set. My poor wife kept calling the hotel trying to find out where I was. When we finally left that, we were all crazy. It was miserable.

RA: I had heard that some of the effects went really bad on the set.

BE: Yeah, they were using meat bones from cattle. They had a scene in there with all of these cow guts that came out of a wall when Dennis Hopper kicks it. It had been in there for days, loaded up and ready to go, but we never got to it. When we finally did, it was just a horrendous smell. The whole thing was like that. The blood mix would start to smell and it was just sticky and nasty. Everything just melted from the heat. Every time we tried to set up and do the dinner scene, the stuff would go bad quickly.

RA: What was your experience working with Dennis Hopper like?

BE: (laughs) He was really kind of stuck in doing this movie. It was like a deal that he had for two or three movies or something like that. He was still partaking of whatever it was that he was taking at the time. I mean, he was such a gentleman and he gave it 110 percent, but it was really something that he didn't want to do. Trying to get him to do that fight scene was really, really hard. He just couldn't comprehend what we were doing for whatever reason. It was just an honor for me, though. I mean, how many people can get to say that they got to work with Dennis Hopper? He went on after that and did *Blue Velvet* and got his career back on track. When he was doing *Colors* down in Venice, I went down there to talk with him and he said that this movie was one of the most miserable experiences of his life (laughs).

RA: What was your experience working with Tom Savini like?

BE: Tom was great, a really nice guy. He was running around like a madman all the time because he had so much stuff to do. One of the stunt guys I talked about, Dan Berenger, doubled Bill Moseley on it. He would come in at 3 in the morning for a six o'clock call to do his make-up, because it took about three or four hours to put all that stuff on. It was quite the ordeal for him and I don't think he went to sleep for like three or four days because of how long it took to do the Chop Top stuff. It was the same thing for Bill Moseley, it took him just as long.

RA: Did you do the cut scene with Joe Bob Briggs?

BE: Yeah, the part where we jumped out of the van. Yes, that was me again. That was one of those things that was part of the last two or three days. They would just load us up and say, "okay, we're gonna go here", and they'd set us up. We were just in a daze, just drinking coffee just to try and stay awake.

RA: I've always wondered this. What all is you and what all is Bill Johnson in the movie?

BE: That's a good question. Like I said, I'm a stunt man and not an actor. I was hired to double Bill Johnson. The first scene we did was the bridge scene with Nubbins and the truck, so that was me and that was when I broke my wrist. The very last scene on the truck of it pulling away, Tom Morga got on there and did that for a second. In a nutshell, I did just about every scene in the movie except for about two or three close-ups that Bill did. He didn't do much in it, but he got the credit, which is fine. I still got my credit. I did the "chainsaw love" scene with Caroline Williams. I did the part at the end at the dinner table where I jumped in and did the fight with Dennis Hopper, also. There was a close-up he did at the dinner table and another at the end of the love scene that he did, which were just seconds long.

RA: Wow, so you were him for the majority of the movie then.

BE: Exactly. That's what I've been trying to get out to everybody. A guy came in and interviewed me for a new Blu-Ray that just came out. I sat down with him and did a timeline of who's on and who's not. I really don't care anymore. I got my money and I know what I did. Bill did not do much in the movie, so if people want to see the real Leatherface, it's me.

RA: It sounds a lot like Steve Dash's situation from *Friday the 13th Part 2*.

BE: Exactly, and it's something we deal with a lot as stunt people. I have doubled for many people over the years, but I don't go around saying, "Yeah, that's me" because you're not on screen much and the actors are acting their parts. But, in this instance, Bill couldn't lift the chainsaw and didn't want to because he was against violence, so it was mainly me doing the work. People go around saying "that's Bill" and I have to tell them, "no, that's not Bill.

RA: I have to say that my favorite scene in the movie is that opening one on the truck.

BE: That was a crazy one. I had a wire and had to lean over the edge of the truck with the chainsaw. We had a couple of stunt guys driving, doubling for the young college kids. The chainsaw was a real one and weighed about 75 pounds. They couldn't make a lighter one because they wanted to see the chain move. That's how I broke my wrist, trying not to kill those two kids in there while I was leaned over the edge.

RA: The other person I wanted to ask you about is Lou Perryman, who is no longer with us. By all accounts, I heard that he was a very nice guy. Tell me what you remember about him?

BE: Yes, he was very nice. He was another actor that did whatever he was asked to do. He always gave a hundred percent in whatever he was doing. Everybody was extremely good in it. Caroline(Williams) is crazy (laughs). I've ran into her so many times over the years and she hasn't changed a bit. She told me later on that she was a bit concerned because when we were doing the chainsaw love scene, I had to put that chainsaw up on her thigh. I had to reassure her that I would be very careful and kept telling her that. But, Lou was just always joking around, just a nice person all around. He was always there on time and always did what he was supposed to do. Jim Siedow was another one who was a gentleman in a half. In fact, we shared a room and a honey wagon right next to each other, so we always got to talk a little bit. Unfortunately, they would change the script on him and he would have to get new sides and go rehearse and rehearse, and then they'd change it. It was much harder on him, being older. We were all in our prime.

RA: What was your most difficult scene to do in the movie?

BE: Well, it was probably one of my worst experiences on a film and also one of my best. I guess it's one of those love-hate relationships. I don't know how we made it through, but we did.

In General

RA: I know that you've been in the movie stunt business for years, with many projects under your belt. How did you break into the stunt business?

BE: Well, I started out at an amusement park, Knott's Berry Farm. They had a show called the Wild West Stunt Show. I never proclaimed to be an actor or anything like that, but I got into that and then years later, I said I want to try this, if it's possible. From there, that's what I did. I put in the work, training all the time to get to that point and got a break, and the rest is history. There were a lot of people that came out of Knott's Berry Farm, actually. Nick Rogers, who is a very famous stunt man came from there. Scott Mann, second unit director; Carl Cefalio, John Casino, Keith Tez, who doubled Dustin Horffman; Mary Yonka, who is still working today; Stan Berenger, who worked on all of the *Pirates of the Caribbean* shows; the whole group.

RA: I have to ask. There's somebody in my mind I want to ask about. He was a very famous stunt man in the 80s and he played a villain in the movie *Stick* with Burt Reynolds. I know he did this stunt in the movie falling from the building that was almost unheard of at the time.

BE: Oh, I know who you're talking about. Dar Robinson. I seem to recall he did something up there in Seattle falling off the Space Needle or something, too. It was a wire fall from the top almost to the bottom, which was a first at that time. That's the kind of thing he did on *Stick* when he played the albino villain. It was a wire descent that he came up with. Nobody had ever done it before.

RA: Yeah, just watching that stunt is crazy, even to this day.

BE: Yeah, he was probably one of the best high wire high men in the business. Unfortunately, he killed himself just doing a little motorcycle ride by a camera. He fell and impaled himself out in the middle of nowhere and bled to death before they could get him to a hospital.

RA: Wow, that's horrible. It's a risky business. What would you say was your most dangerous stunt?

BE: You know, I've been beat up and killed in almost everything I've ever done. I was doing a John Candy movie and I had to do a back fall down a set of stairs. The stairs were one of the old loading ramps that they used to use years ago to get to the planes. So, it was about sixty feet in the air and I had to throw myself backwards down it, which I did. There was going to be two cameras. I did it once the first time. I threw myself back pretty far and ended up right in front of the camera and the assistant camera operator jumped in front of the camera because he thought I was going to hit him. I just beat myself to death on that, so I got really upset with him and said we had to do it again, and if he did it again, me and him were going to have to have a little talk out behind the bushes. So, I did it again and I beat myself up. I had to go with the paramedics to the hospital and get some x-rays. Nothing was broken, but man it sure hurt. I've talked to several people about it, about concussions and things. It's more well known today, but back then, you got a little head ringer and that's it. That was a concussion. Who knows how many stunt men have gotten concussions over the years. It was a very dangerous deal going on. So, that was probably the worst one I ever did. I went through a window and got cut up pretty bad before, but this one just beat me to death.

RA: I can only imagine how many injuries there were back in the day.

BE: Yeah, well it happened and you just would either brush it off and get back to work or you just didn't work. That's how it goes, unless you were seriously injured with broken bones or something like that. When I was doing *Texas Chainsaw,* I broke my wrist and there was nobody there to take up the slack, so I ended up working with a broken wrist for a long time on it. I had to wear a half cast and I would take it off during a shoot, come back and put ice on it and put it back in the cast. It was back and forth like that for months.

RA: Yeah, I don't know if you were aware of this, but I did a similar business for ten years as a pro wrestler and those injuries are very real, as well.

BE: Oh yeah? That brings up a good point. I studied with Gene Lebell, who was a professional wrestler. He's still doing stunts to this day. He's been a stunt man for 30-40 years. He would really get irate about people saying it's fake. I also got to work out with Rowdy Roddy Piper before and that was pretty neat. It's a designed dance, but the dance hurts. I have a lot of respect for wrestlers. I got to talk to Diamond Dallas Page a lot and about what he went through and the regiment he uses to this day, the yoga. It's a stretching of muscles that's so important, and if you don't stretch, they tighten up over time and you can't move after a while.

RA: Oh yeah, I've seen it a lot with a lot of the old timers who can barely walk now.

BE: You would see it a lot in stunt men, too. A lot of the original stunt men were old cowboys who did a lot of the westerns at the time. Over time, you heard of people needing new hips, knees, shoulders and so on. That's the price you pay.

RA: I want to go back to something from earlier. I see that you doubled for John Candy a lot. What are your memories of John?

BE: I think I did about six or seven movies for him. The first one I did, Dick Warlock hired me to double him on *Spaceballs.* He called me up and asked if I can do a forward roll. It was a jump over a door that was coming down. I said, "Yeah, I think so", so we went and rehearsed it and I did it. Once we got all of the stuff on and the make-up and the costumes, nobody could tell the difference. I had people come up and talk to me like I was John. I would have to tell them I wasn't him. It was a very unique experience. I got to work with Mel Brooks. Everybody was really great. From there I went and did *Who's Harry Crumb?* In Vancouver, which was a five-month shoot. That's the one I was talking about earlier where I had to do that fall. Then, I went on to do a bunch of other ones and we went all over the place. John was one of the most gracious people I ever met in all my life. When you got into his inner circle of people, you were in. He eventually put me in his contract, which was unique. When he made a movie, I made a movie. I was supposed to go do *Wagon's East* in Mexico, but it was a lot of horsebacking, and I'm not much of a rider. I can ride, but I wasn't what they needed. I won't do stuff that I'm not comfortable with. In the business, if you say you can do something and you can't, you'll never work again. He went and did that and unfortunately, he had a massive heart attack and died. Like I said, he was so gracious, not just to the people he worked with but to the fans. He would sign anybody's autograph and would take time for everyone. He was so recognizable that people would gather for him and it was always such a unique experience. We were doing *Uncle Buck* in Chicago one year and he said, "What are you doing tomorrow?", and I told him it's the one day off so I had no plans. He said "Well, it's the Super Bowl. We're going to leave early in the morning, you want to go?" So, we did. We took a private jet down to Miami. He would do that kind of stuff. It was unreal. I have a million stories about him. It was a unique experience to be around somebody like that, when you work for them. He was my employer and I worked for John, but he was also a very good friend.

RA: With the rise of CGI, do you think the stuntman will still have a place in Hollywood?

BE: I think that there will always be a place for the stunt man. The audiences today are too sophisticated and they can tell the difference. I know that they weren't happy with a lot of the CGI. When it first came out, it saturated everything and people were not buying it. What you see now is a lot of the thing where the actors are filmed in the green suit with all of the points on them. They would get the facial expressions and then transcribe it into whatever creature or character they have, so then you can see actual face movements and things like that. It was the same thing for stunts. You could take a body and do whatever you want with it and put it on screen, but it would just look like a fake body. Now, they're going back to where they have to take the stunt man and put them in the green suit and then put it on screen as the character. They've been using a lot more stunt people in that capacity. You know, a human moves a certain way and you can't duplicate it for CGI. You just can't.

RA: Are you still actively involved in the movie business, doing stunts?

BE: No, I'm retired. Like I said, I got beat up so much that it's hard to walk around anymore. I'm getting too old for that. I get called every once in a while, but can't do much. I'm still doing a bit here and there, but I've got a few more years before I officially retire. I still do conventions. I've been to Germany three times and been all over the United States, and it's great to meet people and let everyone know what went down on *Texas Chainsaw Massacre Part 2.*

RA: Do you have any final words you would like to say to the fans out there?

BE: I didn't realize with horror fans, how many there were and what a great, great, great group of people that they are. I've never met anybody who wasn't extremely kind and gracious to me. It's been a very unique experience for me, personally. They say nothing but kind words and that's been very nice to me. It's what makes it fun and all worth it for me, personally.

BRIAN MATTHEWS
(THE BURNING)

RA: How did you get into acting?

BM: I was almost always performing when I was younger. I was more of a singer than I was an actor. I was in choirs and musicals and things of that nature. I went to a little college in Minnesota, not for music necessarily, but I ended up switching majors in my Junior Year. Then, I went to a conservatory in Boston after I graduated college. Originally, I had studied biology in college and accumulated enough credits to graduate with that as my major. I went to the music conservatory for a year in Boston, then I went to Juliard in New York for a couple of years. I was a classically trained singer for Opera. While I was in New York, my hope was more along the lines of Broadway, than it was in film acting. I was in a musical called *Sarave*, where I was the understudy of the lead, in New York. It was written by the fellow who wrote *Man of La Mancha*. It wasn't doing all that great. I was about to replace the lead, a fellow who was about to go into the musical of the day called *La Vita*. I was doing chorus and then went on take the lead for him when he moved on. That went on for about six months. After it ended up closing, I was out of work for a while, then I ended up going to an audition for a movie in 1979, which was one of many auditions that I went to. That ended up being *The Burning* and I managed to get the role of Todd, somehow. We filmed that in the summer of 1980 and I was twenty-seven at the time. After that, I got on another musical where I got to be the star, called *Copperfield*. Both of these were amazing achievements that I had when I was twenty-seven. Of course, nobody knew that *The Burning* would go on to become what it has, and be a slasher cult classic. I never thought that it would still be on people's minds in 2016.

RA: Could you take me through your audition and tell me what it was that you had to do for *The Burning*?

BM: I have trouble remembering, but I believe that I had one reading for the casting director, a woman named Joy Todd. I believe that I had the first audition with her and then came back for a second audition with the director, who was Tony Maylam. They must have seen something in me. Back in those days, there was no screen test or anything like that. I do recall them asking about my film history. I told them that I had done some commercials, but that was about it. I think that they really wanted a cast of unknowns and they wanted the story to be more important than who was starring in it.

RA: I've always thought that your character of Todd is the most important and kind of the glue that holds together the other characters, like the leader and the voice of reason basically. Can you give me a bit of your insight into the character and playing him?

BM: (pauses, laughs) Oh man, you're taking me back to a twenty-seven-year-old kid. The guy you're talking to now is a sixty-three-year-old man. I do remember recalling, who is this guy and what is his character like? What kind of fellow is he? Obviously, he is the leader and he does project that leadership beyond his young years. In my mind though, he was sort of playing the part of the leader as he was leading. He really just got done what needed to be done and to get the other kids in line, like with the bully characters and the other characters. He's the boss and he knew how to be romantic. He just kind of fell into these things that were very natural for him. I don't know if I really modeled him after anyone, but I just remember thinking, "If I were looked at to lead this group of young people someplace, how can I do that?" He needed to be very protective of the others in that role.

RA: What do you remember about working with Lou David, as he was playing Cropsy?

BM: That ending scene was about the only interaction that Lou and I got to have. He shot most of his stuff when I was not around. It was really those ending moments when we were together, and all that I really remember is a guy in this crazy looking Tom Savini makeup job. I bet if I were to run into him a week later in New York, I probably wouldn't have recognized him in person. I didn't get to see much of the man or really get to know him at all. It's an unfortunate part of the acting business. You work with people, you say hello, they say action, you do your thing, they say cut and then you leave. It's just the way it is. You know what you're doing and they know what they're doing. In effect, it actually reflected the actual relationship of Cropsy and Todd. They really didn't know each other. Obviously, he had a bit of vengeful thing for Todd, but there was not much interaction.

RA: I always thought that was another interesting thing about Todd, that he does have this deep secret about Cropsy and this regret for what he did to him. I thought it was a very nice addition to the story, where it comes back and says that you were one of the kids that did that to him.

BM: Oh yeah, and we would not have even been able to know that, had it not said so at the end. I do certainly think that it deepens the character of Todd and the movie itself. There was a reason for this. It wasn't just some crazy person doing it to be doing it. He was doing it for a purpose. Todd, unbeknownst to anyone else, knew what that purpose was.

RA: What do you remember about working with Tom Savini and some of the effects that went into the film?

BM: I do remember Tom working on them a lot, but I wasn't really too into the process of it, so I didn't see much at the time. Of course, when I saw the final product, I was simply amazed by what he had done. There were virtually no special effects done with me. No effects, no makeup, nothing too special. I was impressed by the wonderful way that the scenes were cut together, like the scene on the raft, but I was not there that day. I would just hang around my hotel when I wasn't called to the set. With Tom and I, we were working on the same movie, but we really didn't have a lot to do with each other. We really didn't get a chance to see any of the dailies. That was the crew and Tom doing that. We just did what we had to do and what they needed us to do.

RA: What do you remember most about working on the set?

BM: (pauses) I do remember that everyone there, except for me and a couple of others, were very young. The movie *Fame* had just come out and that soundtrack was just being played over and over again by people on their boomboxes. There was a lot of waiting, as there tends to be in acting, while you're waiting for the shots to get set up. I just remember that being a huge part of my time up there. People were just dancing and singing to it. That was fun. I mainly recall just being this young guy that was thrown into his first movie and had the lead role. I had lot of self-doubt and wondered what kind of impression I would make. I worked very hard on the movie. Some of the more difficult parts for me were some of the longer bits of monologue, like with the campfire scene. All eyes were on me. There might have been maybe fifteen kids around the fire and maybe twenty people behind the cameras doing things. You work so hard to remember everything and go over it in your head a thousand times, then all of a sudden, they say "action!" Within a heartbeat, the entire dialogue just goes right out of your head because you can't remember what the first word is. Once you get that first word out, you can just roll from there. I just remember that because it was a monologue and it was all on me, it was the scene I was most anxious about and the most nerve wracking. The other scenes were easier as it was just Todd doing a lot of things and more action, as opposed to just talking.

RA: I was reading your bio and I see that you did a lot of TV shows in the 80s. What were some of the key differences between working on a TV show and working on a movie set?

BM: Probably the most difficult job that there is as an actor in Hollywood, or at least it was back then, was doing soap operas. I did three of them. I did *Young and the Restless* for about a year, *Days of our Lives* for about six months and *Santa Barbara* for another six months. You could work one day in a week, or you could possibly work five days in a week. You would start the day at about seven in the morning and you were expected to come to the studio with your dialogue already memorized, and there was a great deal of dialogue. If you talk to anyone from soaps, they would tell you that it's very hard to start memorizing Wednesday's script while you're working on Tuesday's script. You start to get very good at letting one go and focusing on them one step at a time. It's a more grueling process because they do expect to shoot one whole show in a day. Although you're treated like a king on set, the more difficult part is the memorization of the script in a short time and the expectation of moving through things quickly. They usually only want one or two takes. It's more difficult than working on a film where you have the opportunity to do more takes. You get to tweak your performance a bit and get some input from the director. I did TV more than films when I was there. I was never really able to break through from the B+ actor area. There's the different rankings of the guys in acting. It's not necessarily that they were any better at the higher level or that they would act any different. They just happened to be at the right place at the right time, got the right show and something worked out for them. It just never did for me. I was able to make a really nice living in LA when I was there. I actually made most of my living doing commercials there. I probably did around two hundred plus commercials while I was there. I would walk down to the mailbox and there would be a check there, from the residual payments for these commercials. Back in the day, if you could get on a national commercial that played a lot, you could make a lot of money off of that. That would actually qualify in Hollywood as a pretty successful acting career. There's thousands of actors currently in the screen actor's guild, but I think only a small percent of them are constantly working. Most are barely working or not working at all, so they have to have other forms of income.

RA: Is that what made you leave acting in the early Nineties?

BM: Yes. It was kind of a struggle. I just began maturing and got married. Psychology was just something that held an interest in me, so I just went back to school and got my Master's Degree and I've been doing that ever since. When you're working as an actor, it's wonderful. You're really doing what you want to do, but for the most part, the job of most actors is auditioning. You just audition and audition. It's a process. That's the main job of an actor, in terms of time. It came to the point where I wanted to be doing something that I could call my own, and that was clinical psychology, so I went into that. It's been wonderful. Every once in a while, I kind of regret not being able to go to the mailbox and get those checks, but every once in a while, I will get a little residual check from *The Burning*. It's always fun to see that when it comes. They'll do some form of distribution or showing on some channel and I'll get a check for like thirteen cents. It's just fun for me to see that it's from *The Burning*.

RA: I see that there's a reunion coming up this year in Florida for *The Burning* at the Bay of Blood convention.

BM: Yes, I'm going to be there. Some guy just called me up and got in touch in a similar way that you did. He got in touch and told me what he was putting together and asked if I would like to do it. I thought, "Well, it's been thirty-five years. Why not?" It will be fun to hang out with the fans who want to see us, and catch up with some of the other cast members.

RA: What are your thoughts on the film now and the growing fanbase that it has? Is it surprising to you?

BM: I have to admit that it does surprise me. I'm always surprised when I hear anyone saying that they've even seen it. I'm surprised that you're writing about it and that they're dedicating this thing in Florida to it. From what I hear, it's been getting a great response. I'm totally flabbergasted by the whole thing. To be honest, I have not even seen the movie in about twenty years. My children have never seen it, either. I've just never stressed that their dad was an actor. They just know me as dad, the psychologist. Some of their friends have seen it. They'll say, "Dude, your dad is famous! "We have this local arthouse cinema called The Alamo Drafthouse. When my wife and children went to go see a movie there one day, they saw a poster on the wall of the theater for *The Burning*. She pointed out to my children that their dad starred in this movie. They just couldn't believe that their dad was so famous that his poster was up at The Alamo Drafthouse. (laughs)

RA: That is really cool! I just have one last question to ask you. If you had anything that you could say to the fans out there, what would you say?

BM: I would say that we made it for fun, and apparently, it really was! I'm so happy that it has been so well received by so many people. It's just so unbelievable to me. I loved doing it. I don't have any negative memories of my time on the film or how it was received by anyone who has seen the film. Everyone who has seen it tells me how great it is and that it's one of their favorite slasher movies. You know what? It really is. They did a really great job on the movie. It was just a really fun experience getting to make that movie.

BRIAN PATRICK CLARKE
(SLEEPAWAY CAMP II)

(Brian Patrick Clarke: on right)

SLEEPAWAY CAMP 2: UNHAPPY CAMPERS
A Double Helix Films Production
directed by Michael A. Simpson.

RA: How did you get into the acting business?

BPC: For me, it was a late in life decision. It was all a consequence of lasting all of three weeks in training camp for the World Football League. That was originally what I thought I would be doing for a time when I got out of college. I was lucky enough that I had a good education and had some success as an actor at Yale. I had some expectations that I would have some success in the World Football League, not realizing that a while was going to be three weeks. When I got released from training camp in June of 1974, I went back to Cleveland and a part of me was obviously pretty depressed at the outcome. I figured there wasn't much of a future there in that, but thankfully I did have a few opportunities with Yale alumni for business. I ended up taking a job with a steel company that was based in my hometown of Cleveland, Republic Steel. At the time, we were one of the biggest steel companies in the country. They had these executive management sales positions and a training program and I got hired. So,

I took this job and went through the management training program, and for a time I actually enjoyed it. The more that I look back on it, it was playing a role. I went from being this guy, a college football player, to having this opportunity to be a more stable, contributing member of society. Suddenly, I found myself wearing suits and ties, carrying a briefcase and going to work on the mass transit system. It was kind of fun. I did that for a year and a half and over the passage of time, I just found myself less and less inclined to want to do that for the rest of my life. They then sent me to Oklahoma City in 1976. I was there for three months, then I was supposed to come back to Cleveland. It was while I was there that I realized that I did not want to spend the rest of my life in Cleveland. I like to be outside and did not like the weather at all. I was in Oklahoma and decided I did not want to go back to Cleveland. The gal that I had been dating before in Cleveland was into the plays that they would do at the Great Lakes Shakespeare festival. When we would go watch these things, there was a part of me that said "Well, I can do that. How hard can it be?" There was always a part of me that was a class clown, and I played drums in bands when I was younger. It was an outlet. Even with sports, I always loved the performance aspect of it.

So, I decided then that I did not want to go back to Cleveland and I called and thanked the people I had been working for and I told them I couldn't do it anymore. They said that if I like Oklahoma City so much, they could transfer me there. I told them it's not about Oklahoma City, I just need a fresh start. They asked me what I was going to do and I decided that I would move to the west coast and try becoming an actor. That's how I decided. There was a lot of reflection involved. When I ended up moving out to LA, my brother and I drove like 29 hours straight, save for a little nap break. We packed up everything that I had in my little 1974 Chevy Malibu and moved out to LA, never having been to the west coast or even west of Oklahoma. I knew a couple people there that I made arrangements with to crash with there and arrived on my 24th birthday in August of 1976. We stayed with a friend for a few days, then found a little dump of a place we could afford that was already furnished, in East Hollywood. I didn't really know what the hell to do or how to get started as an actor. I seriously looked up production companies in the Yellow Pages (laughs). I ended up going to a couple of them. I actually went around knocking on doors, not realizing until years later how asinine I must have looked. (laughs) "I'm here to become an actor." "Great, you and everyone else in town." (laughs)

At one of the stops I made, the woman was nice enough to direct me to Universal Studios, where I got a job as a tour guide, which is where a lot of young people start. I wasn't exactly raking it in, but life was an adventure, and it was a good time to be on one. My little brother ended up leaving after a little while, and I was eating very little, like on a dollar a day. I got very lucky because the woman who headed up the tour guide division called me in one day and asked me what I wanted to do with my life. I told her what I wanted to do and she told me that I have a very commercial look and that her daughter is represented by Nina Blanchard, who was primarily a modeling agent at the time, and one of the most notable modeling agents on the west coast. This woman told me to get some pictures of myself and go see Nina. This is how clueless I was, I had my friend take some pictures of me and printed them out at a drugstore to take with me. I had no idea what a headshot or a portfolio was. I didn't realize what a big deal she was. I walked in, in a dress shirt and with these 3x5 pictures in my breast pocket and saw all of these people sitting in the waiting area with portfolios on their laps. I was completely clueless. I went to the receptionist and she asked if I was in the Screen Actors Guild. I said no and she said they weren't interested. As I was leaving, this gruff voiced woman came out of her office and said, "Wait a second!" It was Nina. All of a sudden, I bypass all of these people that were waiting. She brought me and the next thing I know I have all of these agents telling me why I should sign with Nina rather than whoever I was going to see next, not that I had anyone else to see. (laughs) I ended up signing then and there. I was just at the right time to be that "All American, Southern California" looking guy. I just had the right look, and when it came to modeling, I was the right size. They ended up getting me auditions and modeling gigs rather quickly. I continued working at Universal for a while to bring in an income, but I never realized how lucky I was to get signed so quickly. There were others I worked with who had been hoping for a break for years. It had been their lifelong dream. Some eventually got their break, while others didn't and moved on with their lives. One of my first modeling gigs was for Pierre Cardin. I went from making three something an hour to making six hundred dollars a day. It was a very different world! My first commercial was a Dodge commercial, then I got a last-minute call to audition for a TV movie called *Eleanor and Franklin: The White House Years*. It was to play John Roosevelt, the President's youngest son. It wasn't a huge role, but they felt I looked the part. I felt very lucky to get the part, even though I felt pretty clueless when I went in to read for them. Suddenly, I felt like I was in fantasy land. I had print work, commercial work and now an acting gig! This all happened within just a couple months of arriving in LA. One of the things that I'll always be thankful for is when Nina hooked me up with the esteemed acting coach Vincent Chase around that time. I met with him and he agreed to take me on. He was great, truly an actor's acting coach.

I had been in LA just over a year and I went up to do *Blood & Guts* in Canada. We were shooting in a town called Branford outside of Toronto that was Wayne Gretzky's home town. The first time I saw the dailies, I could not believe what a fucking stiff I was. I was just hyper aware of my angles and what I looked like. I just thought wow, I have been doing way too much standing in front of a still camera and I need to get that shit out of my life. So, when I went back to LA, I went to Nina and told her that I'm not modeling anymore. She asked why and I told her it's because I'm a stiff. I came out to LA to be an actor and now I was looking like a mechanical man on screen. It was actually a nice lesson for me and I look back at how nice everyone was to me on that set. They were all very supportive and very helpful. I always try to be that guy once that I had been in the business longer. It's something that I picked up from a lot of the old timers in the business. They were always very nice and supportive.

RA: Wow! Now, that is an amazing story! Very informative. Now, of course the one movie that I really want to ask you about here for the book is *Sleepaway Camp II*.

BPC: Yes! It's funny how this movie that was shot almost thirty years ago still captures an audience. It's pretty amazing. On the Facebook fan page, when I've seen clips that people have posted or sent to me, there's one principal thing that I still tend to kick myself in the ass over. It's a constant recurring thought … why did I ever think that stupid mullet was a good look?

RA: (laughs)

BPC: That has to be one of the ugliest hairdos of all time. I think maybe most of us were either fixated on the look of Billy Ray Cyrus or Barry Melrose, who was coaching the Kings around that time. What an absolutely asinine hairdo.

RA: (laughs) Hey, it was the eighties man. I don't know why, but it was a big thing back then.

BPC: Yeah. There's one scene where I go jogging off to go find out what the hell is going on, and the camera follows me briefly on the jog. I've got that stupid looking thing flopping along on the back of my head. It looks like a dead rat or something. (laughs) I just think, wow, that was a bad choice.

RA: Well, at least you can recognize that now. Some people still don't.

BPC: Oh yeah, I know. We live in the South now and I think that a lot of the people here that still wear that 'do still have the Stars and Bars in their rear windshield. It's like the theme from *Deliverance* is their family theme. There's a real crowd here in some parts that leads one to believe that the clock has not advanced past 1950.

RA: (laughs) Definitely. Were you familiar with the first movie when you went in?

BPC: No, I had no clue. I have heard that the first one was much more serious and ours was more campy. I thought Pamela Springsteen did a great job as Angela. It was still gore driven, but there was more humor to it. I know that with Michael (Simpson) directing it, he gave me a lot of latitude with things. I would just improvise things and he would laugh about it and we would go with it. You know, there's the scene in the dining hall where I'm reading out the list and get to the missing bras and panties, and I look over at one of the actors and say "Oh, we've been a busy boy, haven't we?" Even the one where Angela kind of blows me off and she walks away and then I sniff under my pits and I'm like, is it something I said or the way I smell? That was one of those improvised moments. Even the thing where I'm staring at the photos that the boys took of the girls in their lingerie through the window, and as I'm looking at the picture of Angela in her bra, she's very upset and says her line about it, and I'm just looking at the photos and I go "nice tits." (laughs) She was very good about it. I had a lot of fun on that shoot. I never had great expectations of what it would do commercially. Like I said, what's funny to me is that almost thirty years later, it still has some life.

RA: Yeah, for sure. How did you come on board for the movie anyways?

BPC: Straight audition. I was lucky enough that I had worked a pretty fair amount. After *Delta House*, I had done several years on *Eight Is Enough*. At the point where I had done *Sleepaway Camp*, I had done three years of *General Hospital*. *Sleepaway Camp* was in the fall of 87. I left *General Hospital* of my choosing when my three-year contract was up. It shows how stupid I am when it comes to finances, but I didn't want to be one of those people stuck doing soaps for thirty years. No offense to them, but the reason I became an actor was to not be doing the same thing for thirty years. I had been lucky enough that I got to play two characters on the show and got to work four or five days a week, but it was just time to move on. I did come back a few years later for a three-month storyline as a bad guy. That summer in 87, I had worked on another B-movie called *Private Road: No Trespassing*. I played George Kennedy's hapless son in law, which was a thrill for me because I loved *Cool Hand Luke*. I was working with George Kennedy and that was incredible for me, even if my character was kind of a hapless dick (laughs). I enjoyed working on the thing. Then, that summer, we shot the *Eight Is Enough* reunion movie, that was very successful. They did another one two years later, but I passed on it. We hadn't worked together for years, so it was really cool to reconvene. Then, very shortly after I finished that in September, I flew out to Atlanta to do *Sleepaway Camp*. I knew nothing about it. I had met with the producers and the writer. I don't even think that I auditioned per se, I just met with them. I got the offer and thought, okay, this could be fun. It was a time that I really wasn't doing anything else except for getting ready to run the Marine Corps marathon in November, so I thought I could go to Georgia and get to do my running and have some fun and get paid for it. I knew nothing about the project or the other actors. I think I was so dense initially that I didn't even make the connection who Pamela Springsteen was. As uncommon a name as it is, I didn't even immediately draw the connection. I also didn't make the connection that Renee Estevez was Charlie and Emilio's sister. I really enjoyed working with them and I also really enjoyed working with all of the young people on the film. It was a fun shoot.

RA: Being a summer camp film, were there any pranks or things like that going on during filming?

BPC: There probably were, but I was either too stupid to remember them or I was still in a lot of pain. I was actually in a hellacious car accident as a passenger the morning that I arrived in Atlanta. I got picked up by a PA (production assistant) and I was being driven out to the location. It was about forty-five minutes outside of Atlanta. I had flown on a red eye, so when I got in, I was really tired. When I got up, I was starving because I had slept through the meal on the plane. I asked the assistant if she would mind pulling through a McDonald's. When we pulled in, she noticed I didn't have my seatbelt on, so I put it on. I took my first bite of the Big Mac as we left and were going 45 miles an hour, when a car pulled out and turned right in front of us. It turns out that it was a stolen car with three joyriding teens. They jumped out of the window and fled. My driver's response was to naturally turn the wheel away from her, but in doing so, she turned my side right into it and ended up broadsiding this stolen car. It was unreal, it felt like the hardest I had ever been hit. I just couldn't get a breath. My glasses went flying, my Big Mac went flying, my knee went through the glove compartment. It was insane. I couldn't really see because my vision sucks, but I could only hear the noise around me and the traffic coming to a screeching halt. It was a major scene. I look over at the poor young girl driving and she was just sobbing and apologizing. I was trying to tell her that it was okay and not her fault but it just came out like (barely intelligible, trying to say the words). It was then that I found out that I couldn't even get the air in my lungs to speak. I unbuckled my seatbelt and I looked down and I had a big tear in my shirt. I lifted my shirt and didn't see an immediate wound, but what I saw was a pronounced black and blue stripe on my sternum from the blood collecting and the bruising from where the seatbelt was. It ended up breaking two of my ribs. We thought it may have broken my sternum, but it didn't. It wasn't funny at the time, but looking back it's kind of funny. Here we are, on a major roadway, a horrible accident, the people responsible have jumped out the windows and fled, I have this hysterical driver, I can't speak and they had to use the jaws of life to get me out of the car. The window was down and I could hear people outside say "Whoa! Aren't you Grant Putnam from *General Hospital*?" I was just thinking, fuck man, does this really seem like a good time to ask that question? Then, this big guy reaches his hand through the window and puts his hand on my chest and he starts praying. I was like, "What the fuck, am I dying or something? Do I have injuries that I'm not aware of?" Was he giving me some form of last rights? He wasn't even praying in any kind of recognizable English tongue. It was like he was speaking in tongues as he has his hand on my chest and then I hear somebody else say that I threw up all over the car, but I hadn't thrown up. It was all of that special sauce from my Big Mac that exploded all over the dashboard. I couldn't even get out the words that I wanted to say which was "Fuck you, I did not throw up. That's my god damn Big Mac!" It was one of those moments where you're sitting there thinking, what the hell just happened? Then the firemen and the paramedics arrived and they had to use the jaws of life just to get the damn door open, then they immobilized my neck and put me on a board and put me on a gurney, then they wheeled me down to the ambulance. As they left me in the ambulance to go back and check on the driver, I couldn't speak, I had that collar on and I'm completely immobilized. Then, this fucking bee gets in the back of the ambulance and is buzzing around my face! I just kept thinking how fucked up this is, that I'm going to die and worse yet, I'm going to get stung in the face by this bee that I can't do anything about. It was extreme. So, they took me to the hospital and they x-rayed my neck. Thank God, after all of the years of football and having a fat neck, I was okay. They told me how lucky I was that I had my head rest up. My sternum was okay and all of my vital organs were okay, but when I went to get off the x-ray table, I realized something definitely wasn't right in my ribcage. Sure enough, I had broken three ribs. I was extremely lucky, though. I had gone from doing a sixteen-mile run at the Hollywood reservoir the day before, training for the marathon, to feeling like I could barely walk. After I was released and taken out to the location, they told me to take as much time as I need and they can shoot around me. I was in a small hotel and there wasn't a whole hell of a lot to do and I was on muscle relaxers and some form of painkiller. I just couldn't stand it after a day or two like that. I think I actually asked them the next day to take me out to the set so that I can visit and introduce myself to people. They were very reassuring that it would be fine and that I need to rest. On the third day, I went out to jog and I think I went a total of two miles. I went from being a guy who could run a three-hour marathon on cruise control three days earlier to stumbling, tumbling and thrusting my arms and legs in every direction. It was bad. I do know that when coming back from an injury, it's best to get moving again as soon as you can. I went to work the next day. Thank God I didn't have any stunts to do. I think the greatest stunt for me was trying to act like I wasn't severely debilitated. I had a great time, though. As Pamela and anyone who knows me came to know, almost every line that someone says sparks a song lyric in my head, typically sixties rock and roll. Everybody on set got used to me turning everything into song. It became a joke on set, I had a song for everything. We went out one night in Atlanta to one of those Fifties cafes. Pam and I were out there dancing and as we are, a song by her brother comes on. I knew who he is of course, but I didn't know his lyrics. I was singing along to every other song, but when that came on, I just stopped singing and I was like embarrassingly mute. She just looked at me, realizing that I don't know her brother's music. She looked at me and told me that she wants to hear every word. I was caught. I pretty much had to hold my hands up in surrender and admit I don't know them (laughs). The good news is that his career doesn't seem to be hurting over my lack of buying his CDs. I think he might stick around.

RA: Do you remember some of the effects that went into the movie, like your death scene?

BPC: No, I really don't. I mean, I got hit with battery acid which I've been told wouldn't actually kill you, but it was fun to do. I do know that I got fitted for that prosthetic before I left LA. They were pretty well prepared beforehand. I think the effects people did a really great job. It looked like my face was melting on screen. I first saw the final film at a screening that they had at the Beverly Center, for cast and crew and I thought that they did a hell of a good job with it. I think that Pamela did a great job in it and carried a fine line between being one seriously fucked up bitch and having a great sense of humor. That certainly was the driving force for this and Part III as well, which I've never seen.

RA: You know what's funny? This is a personal story. I first saw this when I was about twelve. My family moved around a lot and we were moving to a new town called Cortez, Colorado. Until then, I had been kind of a straight A student, a teacher's pet, a nerd really and got crap a lot. I had decided that since it would be a new town I was going to change my image and become a bad boy I had always secretly wanted to be. On the first day of class, when they did roll call, they called my name and I just said, "Call me TC", just out of nowhere and I got that from your character in the movie!

BPC: (laughs) That's great, man! Of course, you know where TC comes from right? Every name in the movie was kind of a take-off from all of the young stars in Hollywood and TC was Tom Cruise. TC was a good man, not a bad dude. He certainly had a bad haircut and died an inglorious death. I think he was a pretty good counselor and tried to be responsible. Then, of course there's Walter (Gotell), from the *James Bond* film. I thought it was really cool getting to work with him. That's the cool thing about the business is that sometimes you actually get to work with these people that you admire and you grew up watching. On a film like this, you never know who you're going to see. I know that Pamela has gone on to great success as a photographer. It makes me happy when I see these people go on to productive lives. It made me sad when Walter died. It really saddened me a few years back when I found out that Benji Wilhoite died. I remember him as an older teenager on the movie. I don't even know if he was eighteen yet at the time of filming. Finding out that he left behind a wife and kid was sad. Depression and suicide took his life. It's very sad. He was a talented musician and that was his thing. The world of entertainment isn't always entertaining. I've seen far too many people fall victim to that. I just know that my time on the set was hazy at times after the accident. I'm sure that some of the people may have thought that I was one of those Hollywood drug addicts, but I was one of the older veterans in the cast, alongside Walter, so I really hope that I was able to help out the younger cast as much as I could. I have to say that I had a great time doing it, despite almost dying.

RA: If you had anything you could say to the fans out there, what would you say?

BPC: I would say thank you. Anybody that ever takes an interest in anything that I've ever done is great in my book. I'm incredibly flattered and touched that anybody would take an interest in my work like that.

BROOKE BUNDY
(A NIGHTMARE ON ELM STREET 3/4)

RA: How did you get into the acting business?

BB: Well, I never wanted to be an actress. I started modeling when I was thirteen. From then, I started doing commercials at about fifteen and I was really successful at that. I was going to The Professional Children's School in New York and I was in class with Ronnie Walken. You would know him as Christopher Walken. He and his friend Michael and myself were like the Three Musketeers. He was in this play called *JB* on Broadway and he told me that one of the girls was leaving and asked me if I would like to come and audition. We looked kind of alike, because all of the kids in the show were supposed to be blonde haired and blue eyed. So, I went over and I auditioned, but I didn't know how to audition. Elia Kazan was the director and I think that he was kind of charmed by the fact that I didn't know what I was doing and that I had so much nerve. He asked if I could sing and I said yeah. Then, he asked if I could dance and I said "yeah, I can do the twist." (laughs) So, he said I was hired and I thought, "wow, that was easy." So, I started doing plays. It was a multiple Tony award winning play. It had an incredible cast. I would stand in the wings every night and watch the performers perform and that's how I learned how to act, by watching them. Every night they were different and it was really amazing. So, that was the start. Then, I came out to Hollywood when I was eighteen. I could play like I was fourteen, so for someone who could do that and had a Broadway credit and a SAG card, the doors were just flying open.

RA: What would you say were some of the highlights for you in your early career?

BB: The first thing that I did when I got here, right before I turned eighteen, my soon to be sister in law and myself were hired to model the dresses for the Academy Awards. I won for *West Side Story* and she won for *La Dolce Vita*. That was all cool, coming on stage in those different dresses, standing next to the designers as they were getting their gold statues. That was definitely a highlight.

RA: Looking through your resume, I noticed that you got to work on *The Mod Squad* for a while. Can you tell me more about that?

BB: Yeah, I did the pilot and then one episode a year. Nowadays, if you've worked on one episode of a series, you can't do another episode. In those days, people who watched television knew that you were an actress and that you were playing a role. Now, it's very difficult for guest stars to make a living and I was doing a lot of guest star roles and making a lot of money. Every year I would do *The Mod Squad* and *Kildare* and all the westerns. You would just play a different character every time and it was totally okay back then.

RA: That's funny, you don't see that very often these days

BB: Yeah, you don't see it at all unless somebody is already a major star, like you see on *Law & Order* and those shows where one year, somebody plays an attorney and the next year they play a bad guy and on and on. I was an agent and a manager for so long and I came up against this problem and attempted to talk to casting directors about it and they would tell me sorry, the door is shut. It's not the casting directors, though. It's the producers and also the network.

RA: How did the *Nightmare on Elm Street* films come about?

BB: Well, I didn't do horror movies. I didn't really want any part of a piece that could be interpreted as somebody sitting back in a dark movie house, watching some horrible stuff on the screen. I didn't want them thinking that it looks like fun and it being an influence on their behavior. I just didn't want that karma in my life. But then, *Nightmare* came along and I don't think that I was really working too much then. My agent told me to give it a shot and just go in. I'm not involved in anything awful in it. Of course, they didn't tell me about the head part (laughs), but they just said to go in, so I went in and I got it. The interesting thing was that

I had never seen these movies before. I just didn't like horror. Not because I'm prudish or anything, I just didn't see any value to it, although I do like scary movies, just not horror. So, I was sitting on set, working at a little studio in downtown LA, and we were waiting to go on. Somebody came out and there was a little bit of whispering and I found out that someone had broken into the studio at night and had stolen Freddy's sweater. That made me think, "wait a second, this is important. Somehow, I'm involved in something that is bigger than I could imagine." Who would do that? I mean, it's very risky. There are dogs, security, alarms, all kinds of stuff. Who knows, it could have been an inside job, but the point is, that it made me aware of the fact that I was involved in something that was enormous.

RA: I actually wrote about your character, Elaine Parker in the last book. It was a list of the top ten … let's say, most undesirable characters in these films (laughs).

BB: (laughs) Oh that's great! Yeah, Elaine was someone that was not exactly someone that you liked a lot. Somebody wrote this whole thing for me, about Elaine and it was so funny, and it was about what Elaine does after Kristin dies. She uses her room for a large walk-in closet (we both laugh). It was so funny! So, I guess that Elaine just has a bad rep.

RA: (laughs) Yep! A walk-in closet, that's great. Well, I imagine after she got the smell out of the room anyways.

BB: (laughs) Yep, like it never even happened. It's like that commercial where the guys hose things down if there was a fire. Like it never even happened.

RA: You mentioned earlier about the head scene. I'm always interested in how they do the effects on these. How did they make that happen?

BB: We green-screened it, because CGI was not in existence yet. So, we did it the old-fashioned way. They made a head for me and then we green screened it, and kind of superimposed the head. We couldn't use blue screen, because my eyes are really bright blue. What happens when you use a blue screen with me is that my eyes disappear. When we did the head thing, we had to go through this whole process for the mold. They put straws in your nose and they have to keep talking to you because you can get very claustrophobic, so they just keep chatting away. I was surprised when I saw the head because I didn't think my head was that small (laughs). With the scene itself, we did it all in one take. They had the camera on a trolley and everything and they didn't want to cut. So, Freddy turns to me and he uses the razors to decapitate me and then he reaches to the other side of the hall, I pull back, and then he brings the head out, and then he comes back into her room and rips up the bed. We rehearsed it over and over again. I tend to be kind of clumsy, so I fall sometimes and he was using real razors because he had to go into the room and slice up the pillows. So, it was the real deal. I was scared because I had to pull my head back and leave my body where it was, so he could just swoop down with it. But, he is just so incredible. I cannot say enough good things about Robert Englund. He is just an absolute prince. We choreographed it over and over and he was just so careful. I had to take off my shoes so I wouldn't slip. It was a long take, because they did not want any editing. My favorite thing about Robert is that when I came back to do Part 4 and we were doing a scene together. We were on stage and I said, "Robert, I don't understand something. You killed me, right? How am I back?" He just looked at me and said "Brooke", I said "Yeah?", and he just said, "Shut up", and I said, "Okay, Gotcha" (laughs). Yeah, he's just the coolest guy ever.

RA: (laughs) That's great

BB: Yeah, really the whole cast, both casts, were just incredible. It was just fun to do. Again, I didn't realize the enormity of it, but when we were shooting up by the house and I'm screaming at Kristin to get away from the house, there were just so many people who came and wanted to see the house. A lot of people were just standing around in the front yards, just watching. It was really cool, mostly kids and stuff, but that was another big tip off to me. It was like who are all these people and why are they so excited that we're here? Word got out very fast.

RA: I wanted to say too, that it's kind of ironic that both you and your daughter (Tiffany Helm) have both done horror movies. It's almost like a family business

BB: Oh God, don't say that. No, no, no! (laughs) Tiff has done a lot as well. I think that the genre is just so popular and I think that most actors and actresses have done a horror movie at some point in their career, whether they want to capitalize on it or not. Back then, they were doing a lot of them too, because it was a different time and a different type of audience that wanted to see them. I think that every generation goes through the phases and whatever they go through. I love doing the horror conventions, though. Every single person I have ran into has just been so nice and so respectful. I have wanted to do a soap convention as well and have looked into that because of all the soap opera work I've done. I've also looked into doing one for the westerns that I used to do.

RA: That's something else that I wanted to talk with you about. Could you touch on that a little bit and share your memories of doing the westerns?

BB: I love doing westerns. I don't know, maybe I was in the Old West in another lifetime. I also used to ride. I would ride English, which of course is a whole different thing from riding Western. So, I had to learn how to shoot and ride and duck at the same time. I was really good at it (laughs). It was just so much fun! They were all so much fun to do, like the *Wyatt Earps* and *Gunsmoke*. Again, it was a different time and it was just very embracing. I did a bunch of episodes of *Bonanza*. The big one that I did was when they went to an hour or hour and a half format and it was in color. It was a big breakthrough. I had a really great, big part in it and they were showing it on all the big screens during the dinner for the Emmy Awards. So, they had this humongous dinner in this huge ballroom with these great big screens and everyone was eating dinner and there I was.

The incredible good fortune I've had is just unbelievable. My agent was screaming, he was so happy (laughs). I had no idea what was going on. I was completely clueless, which is usually how I operate anyways (laughs). They called me up and explained the whole thing. Needless to say, after that I worked a lot. Then, working with Jimmy Stewart was just one of those great treasures. We were doing *Fire Creek* and I was supposed to be sitting next to him on a buckwagon. I was having a very awful problem legally and he found out about it. We were sitting on the buckwagon and he looked at me and asked why I'm there. I said because I'm in the scene. He said "Yeah, I know you're in the scene, but when you're having something going on like that, you shouldn't have to be here. We could use a body double. Get your clothes together and get downtown so you can deal with this. We'll get you a car and driver". So, they got me a car and a driver and I was able to get downtown and take care of it. He was an incredible person. You just didn't hear about it a lot and it showed a lot of warmth and compassion for his fellow actors. He was very special.

RA: Do you think the scene in Hollywood has changed a lot since then, like do you think it was closer back then?

BB: Oh yeah, much closer. It was a real community. I think that it's become global now, especially with reality TV. It's certainly changed the nature of the beast. I was teaching in New York and I was playing this game with my students. I asked one of my students who their favorite actor or actress was and they said Kim Kardashian. I looked at him and I said she's not an actress. He looked at me like I had just started speaking in Chinese. I think we kind of hit rock bottom for a while, but now with Amazon Prime and Netflix and whatnot, I think that a lot of the networks have really had to change their views and the way that they approach stories. I think we hit a low, but now we're coming back.

RA: Yeah, the reality shows really got out of hand.

BB: Yeah, it's a shame. Who are these people and why do we care? You know, there is a level of script to them, too. I don't want to name names, but if some of that stuff on these shows had happened back then, it would have been something that is hidden or shameful (laughs). It's weird, it's like this whole flip.

RA: Definitely. There's another movie that I'm a big fan of that I want to ask you about. I've already interviewed three people from it, and that's *Twice Dead*. Can you tell me what your memories are of that?

BB: You're kidding me? Wow! I honestly don't remember much about it. I should watch it again. I wish I had more to say about it. I do remember the house. We shot it in these old great mansions. I just love looking at houses, so I remember that. These houses were so incredible. Kind of dilapidated which is really sad, but you can really see their former glory, what they once were. They're also a bit strange to be in because you don't know how strong the floorboards are, especially when they start bringing in heavy equipment. It was just incredible, these mansions with like three floors, a grand ballroom and a basement. I do remember that and going out and spending lots of time in the garden. I wouldn't want to be there at night, but it was really cool.

RA: Looking back, what would you say have been some of your favorite memories in the business?

BB: Well, in general, there's a feeling that I always used to have when I left the studio at night. It's kind of a quiet time, just walking to your car. There's a certain light and it just kind of fills me with a different feeling. It's just a different, amazing feeling. I remember walking a million times to my car, whether it was after doing *General Hospital* all day or some crazy movie or a TV show. There's just something solitary about it and self-reflective. It's just really nice. It's just a general feeling, but not connected to any one show. There's just something about it and I can still feel it when I drive by a studio on a summer night, when there's still a little bit of light. I just can look at the studio signs and kind of revisit that feeling and it's kind of nice. I loved all of the studios and it's hard to say which was my favorite. When I was at Paramount, I would always get there early so I could do a run through the lot before I had to be on set. Seeing the studios just makes me happy.

RA: What would say that you're most proud of or your favorite project?

BB: It's going to sound strange, but it's a play I did, a one woman play. It was just such a wonderful piece and there was such a connection to the audience. I just loved doing it. It was a play called *Second Lady*. It was about the Vice President's wife and she has to go in place of the Vice President during a national disaster. It was just a wonderful part for an actress and I just loved doing it. It's hard doing a one woman show because there's no one there to save you or that you can blame. You're just out there flying on your own. It was really great.

RA: If you could say anything to the fans out there, what would you say?

BB: I would say never give up. I think victory is in continuing. It's hard and if somebody wants to act, they should be prepared. It is very hard, but also do whatever you have to do. Take classes. You're going to have to give up things, like parties at night, but if this is what you want, go for it and don't give up. The same goes for singing and music or even being an architect. Just don't ever give up.

CHRISTINE ELISE
(CHILD'S PLAY 2)

RA: How did you first get involved in the film business?

CE: I was interested in Film Noir and collecting pulp fiction novels. I saw *Blade Runner* when it first came out and thought it was a nice modernization of the film noir genre. I then thought that I wanted to become a director and carry that torch. So, I went into film school in Boston and it didn't seem to make much sense to me to go to school in a town that didn't have a film industry, so after that I moved to Los Angeles when I was 19. I was intending to finish film school here, but I couldn't afford to. I had to work sixty hours a week just to pay the rent. Two and a half years later, I was working as a cashier on Rodeo Drive and thinking of how I could get involved in the film industry. I thought I could be actor and learn all about the industry and get paid to do it! So, I decided to try out acting at about 21 or 22 and started working pretty quickly. Then, I realized that acting was a lot more fun than I thought it would be and more of a responsibility than I could ever imagine.

RA: Were there any roles that you may have passed up that you wish you didn't?

CE: No, I'm not that kind of an actor. Like most working actors, you audition for things and you take the jobs that they give you. You don't really get things offered to you. You have to go out and do the grunt work and hit the auditions and do that whole process. I've never been in a position to make a big mistake like that. I just say yes to everything.

RA: How did you get involved in *Child's Play 2*?

CE: Like I said, it's all about the auditions. They were looking for a girl to play a seventeen-year-old and I auditioned for it. They actually didn't like what I did the first time and they kept looking and they couldn't find what they wanted they came back and said "Well, who were the people that came closest?", so I went back in the second time and they gave it to me. Most of my jobs came about that way, through auditions. In some cases, I auditioned with people that I worked for before, like when I did *ER*, I did *China Beach* earlier with those same people. I still had to audition though, I never got gifted the part.

RA: I know some people do different things to prepare and immerse themselves in the role. Did you do anything special beforehand?

CE: I've never really had a type of role that was so different from a regular person that it required anything like that. I was really playing just a kid with an attitude, so I didn't need much for that. Plus, there's certainly no way to practice getting chased by a killer doll. You can't really recreate circumstances, so you just try to play the person with as much honesty as possible and make it as convincing as possible.

RA: Did you improvise much or throw in your own things?

CE: It was so early in my career, I really didn't even know you could do that kind of thing. Also, in *Child's Play*, it was not an ad-libbing scenario for a couple of reasons. One, Chucky can't ad-lib because all of his dialogue is written and recorded beforehand, so there's no changing that. And the other person I worked with was seven years old and not a very trained actor himself, and neither was I. The other thing was that Chucky took several puppeteers to work his various components. So, Chucky cost seven times what I cost to hire all of those people to make him work. Also, Alex being seven, he had child labor laws so that he could only work so much in a day. So, they would work Alex and he would go home, then they would shoot Chucky stuff, then they would shoot my stuff and everybody else would be gone, so it was impossible to act when there was nobody to act with (laughs). So, unless you see me in the frame with Chucky or with Alex, and I'm interacting with them off camera, they probably weren't there. They would say "That blue piece of tape on the wall, that's Chucky or that red piece of tape on the floor is Alex" and the script supervisor would be reading their dialogue and I would be just acting like I'm interacting.

RA: So, you said Chucky required all of those puppeteers. I was wondering what exactly Chucky was and what brought him to life.

CE: There was one guy named Ed Gale there. Ed Gale is a little person, and they used him for things like to have Chucky run through the background quickly and that kind of thing. So, when they wanted Chucky to move quickly, which the doll couldn't do, it was him. Then there was the Chucky that was tied to my back that was mechanical and all it would do is kick its legs. So, in the bedroom scene when Chucky attacks me, that's that doll. Then, there's the full doll where everything is, and everything is controlled like his eyes and his mouth and the fingers and that's the one that takes all of the puppeteers to work.

RA: What was Alex (Vincent) like to work with?

CE: Alex was cool. He's just a little boy. He was seven years old and it was his second film. I treated him like a little brother. I really didn't talk to him again until like three years ago when I saw him at a horror convention. His memory of that is that I'm the person that he has the fondest memories of on set and I was the nicest to him. But, I mean, it's a seven-year-old boy. What am I going to do, be a dick to him? (laughs)

RA: That's cool. It sounds like you too had a relationship in real life that was almost like the one on screen.

CE: Yeah, it was really sweet to hear that his memories of me are that fond. He's a good guy now too. I'm really proud of the guy that he's grown up to be.

RA: What was your experience working with Gerrit (Graham) and Jenny (Agutter) (the step parents) like?

CE: Any actor I've worked with really, the experience is about the same. Then, it was really early in my career so I was really blown away to be on the set at all. Being at Universal on one of the stages that had one of the oldest remaining sets in America, which was the theater from the original *Phantom of the Opera*. I can't believe I didn't take any photographs of it. It was so crazy that I had the access to that and could be up in those seats. I think it actually burned down, so it's not there anymore, but to be on that Universal lot where all of the classic monster movies were made, was really exciting. As far as actors go, I've been lucky enough not to have any bad experiences with actors. They have all been very professional and easy to get along with. Jenny and Gerrit both were great.

RA: So, you said it was filmed at the Universal lot? Was all of it filmed there?

CE: Some of it. The house that we lived in was on a stage in the lot. The toy factory was filmed in a warehouse north of Los Angeles.

RA: Were you on hand to see some of the death scenes and they were made?

CE: I didn't get to see much. I mean, I was there for the ones that my character witnesses, but none were very gruesome, just make-up and fake blood. It was almost hard to believe that it would be convincing, because it looks so fake when you're there. I know Chucky was not scary to me and you know the effects are just effects. Jenny would be sitting there with her throat cut open and then stand up and go smoke a cigarette. It's a bit surreal.

RA: That brings something to mind. I talked to someone a while back who said that smoking on camera in one of the most horrible experiences because of all the takes and how much you smoke and having to match it up perfectly for the next shot. What was your experience like for that?

CE: Well, what they gave me was herbal cigarettes and not real cigarettes. I just can't imagine someone not being given fake cigarettes. Matching where the cigarettes burn down to, yeah, but I think a lot of movies don't even bother trying to go that far. Eating is also a very tricky thing to do on camera because trying to get it to match and it can get very distracting. I only had to smoke in two scenes, though. I'm not a good smoker. I don't smoke in real life, so you can tell that every time I smoke, I'm not really a smoker. I hold a cigarette funny and I look awkward.

RA: How do you look back on your experience in *Child's Play* now and the series as a whole and your part in it?

CE: It's nostalgic for me. It was a great job. It was one of my earliest ones and it was really fun. It's got a bit of a cult following which is really fun. I'm really grateful to have been a part of it. It's great to be part of a franchise, instead of just a one-off. It's really kind of an honor.

RA: Have you seen the other ones?

CE: Mine, the first one and the last one, *Curse of Chucky*. I liked that one a lot! The other ones I really didn't want to see by watching the trailers, they seemed campy. I'm not that big of a horror fan in the first place, but I'm especially not a fan of the campy ones. I'm glad that the last one got back to the original tone and was a straight-ahead horror film. It was cool to see Brad Dourif's daughter in it, too. I liked how they put her in a wheelchair, because sometimes it's hard to believe that a full-size adult can't out maneuver a three-foot doll, it takes a lot to believe that a full-size adult can't overpower it. Put that person in a wheelchair and suddenly it's on the level more and you can understand how vulnerable she is.

RA: I agree. I think it's disappointing that it went direct to DVD. I wish it was played in the theater.

CE: I agree. I think it could have done well. I think that the budget to advertise that kind of thing though is enormous and that kind of thing can really make the possibility of making money less possible. Publicity is a very expensive thing.

COREY PARKER
(Friday the 13th Part V)

RA: How did you get involved in *Friday the 13th*. Take us through your audition process and what you feel won them over.

CP: This was a very interesting story, actually. I was In Los Angeles. I think it was the first time I was ever there. I didn't have a car, and as you can imagine, you need a car to get pretty much anywhere there. I got the audition, and I called a friend of mine named Perry Lang, who is an actor and a director. He was living up on Mulholland with Brian Dennehy and a bunch of other guys in this big house. It was a pretty nice house. You could see the valley on one side and Hollywood on the other. He had this old Buick and he came and picked me up and we went over to the audition down in Hollywood. I wasn't thinking much about it. I had the sides, I didn't know about *Friday the 13th*, I just wanted to do a good job. I just wanted to go in there and try to create this character. My connection is always to the acting part of it. The audition was very simple. I think Danny was in there, which isn't always the case, but he was there and I went over the part a few times. He was very nice and gave me a few adjustments, but that was it and I left. I didn't know if I got it or not. I really hoped so, and obviously, I was incredibly thrilled to get the job.

RA: Were you familiar with the other films beforehand or a fan of them?

CP: No, I wasn't familiar. I mean, I knew about them beforehand, but I had never seen them.

RA: The characters of Vinnie and Pete seemed quite randomly picked for victims. Where do you feel the characters fit in, as in why they are there?

CP: I think my feeling about that is that the stakes had to be raised in the story. So somebody had to be killed for suspense. It just so happened to be these two guys. Where they came from, I don't know. These were just two guys that were stuck in the woods and they didn't know what was going to happen. So, it just keeps building and building,

RA: Describe Pete for me and his character. What went into bringing him to life?

CP: Pete for me was a lot of fun. There was this thing about him, being into the fifties. My mother grew up as a teenager in the fifties, so I grew up with a lot of those songs. For me, that love of the fifties was the real root of him. With "Ready, Teddy, Ready" that was the song I did. Danny said he needed me to come up with something that was like "ready, ready, ready to rock and roll" and he said that we don't have the lyrics to make the song and that's when I started making those funny sounds and throwing things in.

RA: What went into making your death scene, effects wise?

CP: That was cool for me. I just had the machete. It had two sides and space in the middle for liquids. It was cut so that it looks like it's going into your neck, but it's not at all. There's a plastic tube that goes into the handle and there's a guy in the seat behind me who's pumping the blood. So, we had one guy who was pulling the knife around and another guy who was pumping the blood so that it slowly comes out. Now for Vinnie, they made a whole cast of his face, that was made of rubber. Then they took the flare and stuck it right in its mouth, and it made it light up.

RA: Were there any other scenes that you were able to stick around for or any interaction with the rest of the cast?

CP: No, that was it. We were there for a while and were up in Coldwater Canyon. We were where they shot the introduction of the *Andy Griffith* show. At night, it's just woods in there, so it's really cool.

RA: What are your memories of working with Danny Steinmann?

CP: I thought Danny was a sweetheart, a real great guy. He had a lot of energy. Later on, I was asked if he had been taking coke or whatnot. I personally didn't see that at all, but it wouldn't have been unusual at the time in LA in the eighties. He may have, I really don't know, but he was very positive, he was respectful and I thought he was great to work with.

RA: What are your favorite memories of working on the film?

CP: There was actually a little bit of spookiness to it at times. Vinnie at one point had tripped over something and hurt his toe, so they had to take him in to the hospital so I had to do some things by myself. There's a real freakiness to it being out there in the woods at night. It was spooky, even when you had the lights and everything because the lights are just surrounded by more darkness. It was actually kind of cool.

RA: What are you up to now?

CP: Now, I still act and I teach. I'm an acting teacher. My website is Coreyparkeractor.com. I've been doing this in New York and I've trained a lot of people in Memphis and for TV in LA. I do a lot of things through Skype and I'll go and teach classes. So, I try to stay real busy with teaching.

RA: Any final words you would like to say to the *Friday the 13th* fans out there?

CP: You guys rock! For me, through my life I have worked on a lot of projects and its just amazing how enthusiastic you guys are. You guys just rock, you're like rock fans and are totally into it. It's cool to have been a part of it and I'm humbled to be a part of it. I really appreciate how much your fans love it and the energy you pour into it. It's certainly let me appreciate it on a whole new level. Thank you.

DAN KAMIN
(OL' CHIEF WOODINHEAD FROM CREEPSHOW 2)

RA: Let's start at the beginning. How did you get started in the business?

DK: It all started when I was twelve, and I got fascinated with magic. I saw a movie about Houdini with Tony Curtis in it. I became a boy magician by the age of twelve and I was doing shows around town. That's when I started performing. It's a special kind of performing because you don't really have a script like an actor does. You kind of have to make up your own character within the scope of what a magician does. I did a lot of children's birthday parties and you very quickly find that you have to think on your feet. You have to learn what really compels people because kids aren't really polite. They'll shoot you down if they're bored and shout it out if they know what you're doing. After graduation, I went to college. Then, about midway through I saw another movie that just stopped me in my tracks, which was a Charlie Chaplin film. Within a few months, I had found someone on the campus who was a teacher in the drama department, who was also a great mime artist and I realized that this is where that silent art of acting has gone. Mime is another odd entry into the world of acting, because it's limited to silent acting. At first you just learn some technique and some tricks of the trade, but there were no books on it. You couldn't just go find a script on it, so you have to make up your own characters and stories. When I started doing that in my head, the only way to find out if it works was to go out there and to try it out, so I started doing it all over town at schools, mental hospitals, things like that. I was attending school at the time in Pittsburgh at Carnegie Mellon. I'm still doing shows out there, but now instead of doing them at birthday parties, I do them with symphonies all over the world.

RA: I wanted to touch on something interesting that you said. What was it about Charlie Chaplin that really piqued your interest and drew you in?

DK: Our culture is obsessed with movies. It's in a sense where you go to the movies to see a model of how to act in the world. It's our imaginary avatars on the screen. You identify with different people. It's like how certain slasher movies appeal to you. I don't know if there's an easy answer to that question, but when I saw that Chaplin movie, something just knocked me out. I thought it was the best movie I had ever seen. It was a funny movie, but it was more than that, because it was about serious stuff. The film I saw was *The Gold Rush*, a film made in 1925. Charlie Chaplin had been looking at these stereo cards, which were like the view masters of the period, and some views of where the Donner Party got stranded in the 1800s. Charlie saw that and he read a book about it and he thought it would be a great idea for a comedy, with cannibalism and desperation. *The Gold Rush* is a comedy about people who are starving and it's almost like a horror movie in a sense. In one scene, he's stuck in a cabin with another guy and the other guy wants to eat him. Chaplin turned it into a comic scene by having the other guy visualize him as a big chicken. It's very funny, but underneath the funny is the fact that there are these two-people starving and they're in a battle for survival, so in a sense, it very much tore apart the genres. Is this a comedy or a tragedy, or is it a horror film? It was all of those things.

RA: Sounds like he was kind of ahead of his time there.

DK: He was. The other thing that is unique is that there's not a word spoken, since it's a silent movie, so the only words are in the silent movie subtitles and there aren't very many of them. So, everything had to be thought in visual terms, it had to be dramatized through action in the way that the actors are acting. There's no words, but we know everything that we need to know. The next thing you know, the guy is seeing him as a big chicken and then he's chasing him around with a big butcher knife. There you go, it's almost like the plot of *Night of the Living Dead*. These zombies have to eat to survive, so it's similar. *Night of the Living Dead* and many other horror movies also have that macabre comedy aspect to them as well. It's funny too how some of these old ones become camp and funny, like *Phantom of the Opera*. Parts of it are still quite good and spooky. I mean, that makeup he has on is as good of horror makeup as anyone has ever had. But, some parts of it are hokey now, partially because we have seen the same thing over and over. It was so good that people imitated it, but things wear out. The funny thing about some of these silent movies with Chaplin is that they don't wear out. Nobody has really been able to imitate him. His mobility and his movement skill was another special feature of these movies. Sometimes, he looks like he's a dancer or like he's a puppet. His physical skill required a high degree of acting ability. You're just in awe at his physical skill. What spoke to me was kind of this combination of this sort of magical quality of doing surprising things with a high degree of physical skill and telling stories with it. Everything kind of came together when I saw that. Afterwards, when I saw my mime mentor perform on the campus, it was a magical form of storytelling and acting that involved a lot of comedy and surprise. That's my particular approach to acting and to the shows that I have done through my career.

RA: How did you make the transition over into film?

DK: When I started doing shows around town, Pittsburgh had become a center for horror films because of the presence of George Romero. When I was an art student, in graphic design, George used to come to my campus, before he even made *Night of the Living Dead,* to show us these industrial films that he had been making. *Creepshow 2* was written by George Romero and based on Stephen King's stories. His director of photography, Mike Gornick was assigned to direct it. Michael had seen some of my performances around town and for the Indian part, they wanted somebody who could move in interesting ways and be convincing as a wooden Indian that had come to life, so they wanted somebody thin, so that they could build the Indian costume around him. It was made of essentially, foam rubber. So, they brought me in and that's how it happened.

RA: Where was it that they filmed your segment at?

DK: It was mostly in Prescott, Arizona. Most of the film was shot there and they also did some of the shooting for the hitchhiker sequence in Maine. A part of my sequence was also done in Maine.

RA: Did you get to see some of the other segments being shot or was it just yours?

DK: They were being shot while I was there. Things were running a bit late because they were having a lot of problems with the lake sequence. One of the actors developed some serious hypothermia. There was a lot of technical problems that they were having. I was actually there for several weeks. I wasn't there at the lake to see it shot, but I was meeting with and having lunch with all of the actors. I don't think I met the people in the hitchhiker sequence, but I have since met them. In fact, one of the conventions I went to was a reunion of myself, Tom Wright who played the hitchhiker, and Daniel Beer from the lake scene. They both have had really nice careers in Hollywood as actors and both have been very successful.

RA: I got to meet the director, Michael Gornick at a convention a few years back and he was

151

very nice. What was your experience working with him on the set?

DK: He was a very nice man. I liked him. It was a little nerve wracking, I must say. I had to have the explosive squibs on my person and a window shattering behind my back, and also the costume was a challenge. It was essentially like being put into a giant rubber condom (laughs). I couldn't breathe and I couldn't see or hear. They had to have an air hose from an aqualung piped in so that I could breathe. I had to have an earpiece in so that I could hear and so that Mike could talk to me because the airstream was loud and made it hard to hear. Plus, the eyes were mechanical and there was no way I could control the movements of the face. There were motors inside the head. So, essentially, I was blind and deaf as I was doing that performance.

RA: Wow, that must have made it pretty difficult.

DK: It was a bit unnerving when I would have to stand on the stump in front of the general store. The stump was a couple feet high and it was on a porch, so I was about four feet off the ground, hoping I could keep my balance, being blind and deaf. The first day I was in the costume I was put in the get ready position where I had the costume on me and I had it on for about fourteen hours and they never ended up using me that day. When they peeled the costume off, the seams of the arms were attached with glue, and whether it was because of the friction or because I had some of the glue on my skin, my whole arm was blistered. I had these one inch high blisters all up and down my arm, which got me a lot of attention and a trip to the emergency room, and some better treatment from then on (laughs). Daniel was the one who really suffered, though. Daniel had a genuine case of hypothermia and still has some effects from it. There can be a real danger when you're making movies. Sometimes people are doing things that can be putting actors in danger, like with him, spending hours in very cold water. The actors all suffered, but Daniel mostly. He was just a teenager at the time, only nineteen I think, and he was just doing what he was told and his body said no. He was very moving at this recent convention that we did in West Virginia. We had a panel discussion and he was really so grateful to Mike because after he had developed hypothermia, Mike was very protective of him. Mike just made sure that he was very well taken care of, in terms of dealing with the after effects of his hypothermia.

RA: Wow, that's crazy. I'm sure with you, it was especially bad in the heat with that costume on.

DK: The heat wasn't so bad. It was more just odd to be in that big rubber costume. Once we were done with that sequence on the porch, it was actually pretty straight forward, where I could actually move. I got off fairly easy compared to Daniel.

RA: One of the things that I always loved about the chief is the way that he moved. It was just very unique. I just wanted to ask you about what went into that, his movement.

DK: That's a good question. When I got fascinated with the Chaplin film, I noticed that the body control was underlying most of the gags, like when he is pretending to be frozen stiff, or the scene where he sticks two forks into these little bread rolls and makes them do a little dance. His head is right over his hands, so it looks almost like a giant puppet image of himself, with the forks like these little spindly legs and the rolls as like his oversized feet. It's so charming and so amazing and just so amazingly skillful. In his case, the acting became almost like a physical sport where he was at the top of his game doing these amazing things. When I was learning mime from my teacher on my campus, I learned how to break down movement almost like music. In that, it's like learning music as you essentially learn to play one note at a time. What I mean by that is instead of just tilting your head to the side, you would learn all of the points at which the movement originates, so you would be able to focus on each area of the body. It's almost like creating the scales of movement. You learn to control each part of your body separately and independently of all the other parts. That's why, out of that kind of training came what the break dancers started to do afterwards, these uncanny sort of robot moves and things like that. That's how I came up with the physical ability to imagine what it would look like, with a wooden figure coming to life. When you start to move with great precision, it looks unhuman. In normal life, we blur our movements together. From years of doing these scales, I have a kind of awareness to how my body moves, which allows me to do what I did in movies like *Creepshow 2* and some of the other movies that I did. In other instances, I was working for other people and teaching them how to do those physical comedy movements, like Johnny Depp and Robert Downey, Jr. With them I had to break down these routines to show it to them and teach them how. It's not something you can just improvise. You have to build up to them.

RA: What were they like to work with?

DK: Well, both of them were very great to work with. They were both consummate professionals who had a great respect for the craft. With Robert Downey, he was so excited about learning some of the techniques that we talked about here. To play Charlie Chaplin, he literally had to change his posture and the way he moved. After seeing and studying the Chaplin films, I realized that nobody had written about those aspects (his performance) before, so I thought the only way to truly have that out there was to write it myself. Eventually I put those thoughts together in a book called Charlie Chaplin's One Man Show. It was a book guaranteed to sell maybe four copies and one of those copies went to Robert Downey, Jr, who called me in Pittsburgh when he read it. He had been hired for the Chaplin film and knew that he was facing the defining challenge of his career. It was the highest budget film he had been in and he was playing a legend, who many people thought was the best actor who ever lived. So, he called me and told me that he thinks I could be the only person who could help him pull it off. In two weeks, he flew to Pittsburgh. The first thing that he said when he met me was "I want you to tell me how to hold my fork", because he realized that to play Chaplin, he had to embody that incredible physical control and gracefulness. He always looked like he was choreographed, even away from the screen and had a certain gracefulness and ease about his movement. It's not natural to most people. So, we began that task of turning him into Chaplin that first day and we worked for several months before the shooting began. The really cool thing was that they wanted him to do new Chaplin routines for the needs of the film, so I ended up having to help him create new routines, which was a daunting task, like rewriting Shakespeare.

RA: That's awesome. Going back to *Creepshow,* you had the experience of working with another Hollywood legend in George Kennedy. What was that experience like?

DK: He was very soft spoken. I didn't really interact with him very much. One of my regrets is actually Dorothy Lamour, who plays his wife in the sequence. She had a trailer and she would be sitting on the steps of the trailer looking rather forlorn. I was younger and I was just too shy, but I really regret that I didn't go over there and just talk to her. I knew her old movies and I have sheet music from some of her old movies. She was in all the Bob Hope and Bing Crosby movies. I know now that she would have been delighted to have a young person that was interested in her to talk to. That was towards the end of her career and the end of her life and I regret not making the effort to befriend her or at least talk with her. The same thing with George Kennedy. In retrospect, I didn't want to bother them. I was too shy.

RA: There was another one in the sequence who really stood out and went on to do a lot, Holt McAllany. What was he like?

DK: He was scary looking. He really did look like he was a thug. He was very good in that part.

RA: Do you remember what went into the parts where you are tracking down the guys and killing them?

DK: Well that was fun, because I could really start to move a lot more than I could on the platform. That part was fun for me and allowed me more of a chance to move around and do more stuff than before. One of the things that really helped me a lot was when I was back at the college doing performances. They told me that I really had to go out there and find a way to draw people into the shows around the campus, so I developed a character that I called Mr. Slo-Mo. I would dress in a business suit and have a briefcase. I would simply walk through crowded public spaces, like school cafeterias, in extreme slow motion. So, I had been doing this for a while before *Creepshow*. I had already been working on walking in these weird, slow ways. In fact, when I met Robert Downey, that first day I had a show at an arts festival, so I just got him in the car and I wanted him to see me do that and the effects of how just walking slowly can get people's attention. I looked like sort of a corporate drone in the outfit. You can see some of those on YouTube or on my website. I actually did that in front of the White House once and that video is online.

RA: Cool, I'll have to check that out. I also read that you worked on *Mars Attacks* helping Lisa Marie in her role.

DK: That's right. All of the Martians in *Mars Attacks* were CGI. They considered doing them in stop motion at first, but Tim (Burton) ultimately elected to have them done in CGI, except for the one played by Lisa Marie. So, the challenge there again, was to give her a very interesting way of moving. It would look reasonably like how those Martians looked. The way that her and I started was we went to the zoo in LA to find an animal that would remind her of the look. She found a certain type of lizard, like an iguana, that she thought was a good model, so we started to work on capturing those kinds of movements. I would teach her certain ways with how to turn with a certain precision and articulation. It took a lot of painstaking work to get that type of movement down.

RA: Looking back, what are your favorite memories of working on *Creepshow* and how do you view it now?

DK: I have an interesting story. When I was on the set, my daughter was about ten years old and she was on the set. It was partially because I was staying weeks longer than I had planned and they said I should just bring out my family. So, they flew my wife and daughter out to spend time with me. When the movie came out, my daughter had never seen any horror movie before because of course, I didn't want her having nightmares like I did when I was a kid and regularly watching horror films when I shouldn't have been. When it came out, she said that she has to see it since I'm in it. I took her to the cinema with me to see it and whispered to her, "Now remember, you saw this in the creature shop. It's not real." After the movie was over, she turned to me and said, "Dad, I don't want to hurt your feelings, but that was the worst movie I've ever seen."

RA: Awwwwww

DK: Yeah, I've told a lot of people that. Anyways, I went to a horror convention last year and they had a *Creepshow* reunion with Daniel Beer, Tom Wright and me. There was a panel discussion and when I walked into the room, the audience response to us walking in was amazing. It was like a love fest. They were crazy about this movie. People were just talking in the most moving way about what this movie had meant to them. People grew up on it and have bonded over it over the years and were attached to it, much in the same way that I was attached to the Chaplin movies. Somebody there was saying how all of the stories in *Creepshow 2* were essentially all moral stories, about crime and punishment. It gave me so much more respect for the film and the fans. It was very refreshing. I came out realizing that this is a movie that has a great meaning and a great value to many people.

RA: If you had anything that you could say to the fans personally, what would you say?

DK: Well, I would just like to urge everybody to find their inner creep. (laughs)

DANIEL BEER
(CREEPSHOW 2~ THE RAFT)

RA: How did you get your start in the acting industry and get into movies?

DB: I moved to New York at age eighteen on my own. I got into an acting class right away. I moved from a very small town called Pontiac Falls, New York. It had a population of 2,000. Then, in New York, I found an agent and went through the whole process.

RA: Was it hard for you making that move on your own?

DB: I was actually excited to go and do that. Was it difficult the first few months in New York? Oh yeah. I was a struggling actor. I lost about fifteen pounds the first month I was there. It was difficult, but I loved the journey I was setting out for. When you're eighteen, the struggle doesn't quite register though, because you're so excited to go out and do what you wanted to do. Nobody from where I grew up ever did anything like that. It was like me saying I was going to go to Mars.

RA: One of the first films that you did was another horror film called *Hell High*. Can you give

me some details of what it was like working on that?

DB: I got that the first month I was in New York. I was a starting quarterback on my high school football team and that's who I played in the movie. We shot it up in upstate New York. It was an accomplishment to get something like that your first month. I remember there was a scene where the car drives across the football field and I'm playing quarterback, and they intercept the pass in their convertible. They used the quarterback of that team and I told them that I can really throw a football. He was struggling to throw it, so I got behind center and the car went across and I threw a perfect thirty-yard strike and I got it to the lead actor in the car. Everybody's jaw just dropped. I don't think that they used that in the final cut though. Maybe it didn't turn out. I just turned to everybody on set after that and said, "I told you I could play football." Some people have actually commented and told me that it doesn't look like me in the part on the movie. I was like, "no kidding." (laughs)

RA: I wanted to save the *Creepshow* questions for a bit later, so I went to jump ahead a bit to some of your other work. You were on *Point Break* as one of the cops, Babbit. Tell me about your experience on that.

DB: Please tell me you watched the original film version and not the edited TV version. (Me: (laughs) "definitely") That TV version is absolutely butchered. I was one of the leads in it. I played opposite Keanu in it and was sort of his nemesis. I'll give you a great bit of trivia. It was the scene where we were switching spots for a stakeout. He and Busey come up and say something and walk away and I kind of roll my middle finger up. Well, I am pretty sure that I invented that on the screen. I had been in bars and places like that afterward and people had done that to me and they said that they got it from me. Somebody said that they did that in *Wayne's World*, but that came out after *Point Break*. I did that in the movie and it wasn't in the script. Katheryn Bigelow asked me why I did it afterward and I explained it to her and she said to keep it in. It was something that we used to do to each other in high school and I incorporated that in there. I don't think anybody had ever done that in a movie before me. I'm not positive. If anybody can find out if someone did it before me, I'm more than willing to step aside and let someone else have the first-time credit for that, but for now it's mine.

RA: Cool! What was Gary Busey like to work with? I've heard a lot of stories about him.

DB: He's exactly what all those stories are. (laughs) He's a beautiful lunatic, just absolutely wonderful. He's truly one of a kind. I mean, he's a professional. He shows up and does his work. He just has a different personality and that's what makes him very talented. I've run into him over the years and he's a very high energy guy.

RA: What about Keanu?

DB: We really hit it off. He's probably one of the sweetest guys I've ever met. I don't think that there's a mean bone in his body. Fun story, I used to have this old Bronco with no top on it and I was running into him a lot. He would be on his motorcycle and I would always hear him call my name, yelling "Danny boy!", like at a stop light. He loves football and I remember he would always go into my trailer and play my guitar. When he was working, he would always come and hang out in my trailer.

RA: How about Patrick? Did you have much interaction with him?

DB: I only met him briefly. I just went up and asked him where lunch was (laughs). We Introduced ourselves and just talked briefly. He was awesome though and I think that was one of his best performances.

RA: I definitely agree with that. It's a great movie all around.

DB: Yes, it's a classic. I've been very fortunate in my career. I've been in a horror classic with *Creepshow,* and an iconic classic in *Point Break*. As a creative person, you hope that your work stands the test of time and that you're a part of film that also stands the test of time.

RA: Another one that you were in was *Dying Young*, where you got to act opposite Julia Roberts.

DB: Yes. I just love Joel Schumacher. He gave me so many compliments. Julia was one of the smartest people I had ever met and one of the most curious people I ever met. We had the same thing, like with Keanu, where I would always run into her. I remember being in a diner and everyone was just surprised and like, "Julia Roberts is yelling your name out and waving to you". She was just totally unaffected by the attention. My role is *Dying Young* was originally much bigger, but they cut some stuff out because they didn't need it to move the film forward. I saw it and think Joel was right to do that, though.

CREEPSHOW 2

RA: How did you get involved in the movie?

DB: My agent, Michael Kingman, walked me into the casting office. They didn't want to see me at first. He passed away in 1999 and I have to say, he was the best agent I ever had, just a good person. He would call me Bubba. He called me up and told me he was going to get me on this project. The first character that they submitted me for was the character of Deke. I was just way too skinny, but they couldn't find anybody to play Randy. Michael just walked me in there and said we weren't going anywhere until they set up an appointment to see me. He was just tremendous. I just went in and auditioned and got the part.

RA: What was it like filming on location down in Arizona for you?

DB: It was absolutely brutal. I've talked about this a lot before. The weather was brutal, the conditions were brutal and the water was brutal. Working with the cast and crew was absolutely fantastic and I just absolutely love Michael Gornick. He was like a father to me. I had hypothermia almost the entire shoot and I had to go to the hospital and have medical assistants. I could have easily gone into shock and died. My core temperature got down so low. That was a freshwater lake and I think it was like fifty degrees. I was skinny, so it affected me the worst. Standing on that raft, with the wind blowing and having to have the water on me to match was just brutal, but I never complained and I fought my way through it. I was an athlete, so I had that athletic mindset, where you're being paid to keep playing through it. I had to have oxygen after doing those swimming scenes. I could only do two or three and then I would pass out. I never took naps and I would just pass out, then they would wake me up and we would go do it again. We got through it though. When everybody was gone was when it got really bad. Michael just totally had my back. I have a permanent cold weather injury from it and I get cold easily. After you've had hypothermia, you get colder much quicker. Anytime you're shooting anything on the water, it's just so difficult. We also had weather conditions like hail and all kinds of stuff. It was just nuts. Michael was incredible. The producers wanted to keep working me and he said he would walk off the set because I wouldn't have made it. I was only eighteen or nineteen and the director was my only support. I almost killed myself to get it completed and so did everyone else who worked on the segment. There's a documentary on the making of it online.

RA: So, were you the only one that suffered that bad?

DB: No, the other ones got it. They shut us down because of it all, but I had it the worst. I think Page (Hannah) was next, but mine was definitely the worst.

RA: What was the rest of the cast like? I imagine there was a certain bond as you were all going through this.

DB: Absolutely, that is right. It was fun. We made a road trip to the Grand Canyon together and that was a ball. We all hit it off.

RA: I've always wondered, what exactly was the monster on it?

DB: Well, they had a different blob before and it didn't work in the water, so they came up with that thing with like two weeks notice. That whole crew on that segment had so many obstacles that they had to overcome. It's really impressive. I think fans actually like that, that it's a little rough around the edges. But, I really don't know what it was. It was some oil slick that ate people, some blob that lived out in the water. Fans could contact me with their theories on what it is. (laughs)

RA: I always thought it was funny at the end how you were stuck on the raft and going to get eaten by this monster, so what do you do? Try to have sex with the girl (laughs).

DB: Well, you know why they do that in horror movies. If I didn't do something shady like that, then there's no justification for me dying at the end.

RA: That makes a lot of sense now. What do you think of the notoriety of it now and the fact that it has such a big fan base?

DB: Stunning. Whenever you're working on a film or a TV show, you really don't have any idea how it's going to connect with the audience. At that time, horror movies weren't given the respect like they are now. I think they have gotten more legitimate and have more respect these days. Wouldn't you agree?

RA: Definitely, and I have a theory on that. Being a kid of the eighties myself, I know that we all grew up in this sort of Halloween culture. I refer to the eighties as The Dark Ages. I mean, our cartoons were dark, Halloween was like the greatest day of the year and horror was at an all-time high. Everything seemed horror influenced, even the cartoons and family films. I think that's why it's more appreciated these days.

DB: Very true. I also think that it's like the older movies like *The Shining* or *The Exorcist,* in that it has a lot of story to it and doesn't rely on gore. I think the most recent movie like that is *The Conjuring*. It got to a point where they were just throwing blood at the walls with the horror porn. I think the fact that people can look back on it and see the story and the scares is a big part of it. Even movies like *Halloween* don't have a lot of gore, but they have a lot of tension built in. To Michael Gornick's credit, *Creepshow 2* opened up at number two at the box office and made double its budget in the first week. If we did something like that now, it would be off the charts. Nobody contacted me at the time for an interview or any of us. If that happened today, we would have been doing interviews left and right, off the bat. I remember going into an audition at the time and they told me that my movie was number two at the box office and the producers were very impressed by that. It just goes to show you how it wasn't considered legitimate in a way. Then, those special effects guys are some of the top guys in Hollywood now.

RA: I also read something online about you boxing. Can you tell me more about that?

DB: Yeah, I used to do that for exercise. Freddy Roach was one of the top trainers around and I would box at every one of his gyms. I remember being at the first one in Los Angeles and Mickey Rourke was working out next to me. I fought an exhibition in front of like a hundred people and would get in there and spar, things like that. One guy actually asked me to turn pro, but I said no way. It's just a great way to work out. You can box at any age too. There was people there in their seventies.

RA: Can you tell me a bit about your writing?

DB: I wrote a novel called *The Silence of Remembering*. I'm doing a crowd funding thing on Ink Shares, which is an innovative platform that combines publishing and crowdfunding. The novel is pulled from the point of view of Tara, whose nickname is Twigs, who is in purgatory and she acts as a guide for her brother Alex. It tells the story of her tragic death and how Alex has a postponed grieving process. He has to return home for the ten-year anniversary. He's an up and coming actor who is having to navigate stardom in Hollywood while carrying around this terrible secret of what happened the night of her tragic death, the night they walked home from school together. He finally gets a sort of peace about what happened that night, but you don't know if Twigs is really in purgatory or not or whether she exists or not. Fundamentally, it's a story about the grieving process and becoming integrated with your dark side. I think all great stories are ghost stories. In all of them, the characters are haunted by something. I think everyone has something in their life that they're haunted by and they have a hard time dealing with it. If he doesn't become healed over the events, she won't go to heaven. It's considered literary fiction, which is considered intelligent and I think the horror community would really identify with it. It has story and I listen to my fans and hear what people love, which is good story. The horror community is very intelligent. It deals with a young man's emotions, which not a lot of stories do these days and I think many could identify with it. I think men are often left out when it comes to these deep feelings, so it touches on that nerve as well. Also, you get an insider's view on Hollywood, because I've been there. You can go to Ink Shares and look it up and pre-order it. I've also been published before in the magazine *34th Parallel*. It was loosely based on my experience working with the late Patty Duke.

RA: I like it. I know I want to read it now. I just have one last question to ask. If you had

anything you could say to the fans out there, what would it be?

DB: Thank you. It's connecting. It's really amazing how books and music and TV shows and the arts mean so much to people and how it makes them feel connected and not alone. When you're working in Hollywood, you can lose sight of that, but it's really all about the audience connecting and feeling like they are a part of something. I thank my fans for educating me.

DANNY HICKS
(INTRUDER, EVIL DEAD 2)

RA: How did you get started in the acting business?

DH: Kind of accidentally. I was a heavy equipment operator, a crane operator. I was 28 years old and hurt myself on the job. While I was recuperating, a friend of mine said they were doing something at a community playhouse and asked if I would be interested in doing something. So, I said sure. I got on stage for about twelve seconds and didn't look back, and did that for about five years. From there, people started asking me to do television commercials, radio commercials and student films, then I got the part of Jake in *Evil Dead 2*. From that point on, I said that was what I wanted to do. I wanted to do feature films.

RA: How did you meet Sam Raimi and become friends with him?

DH: I actually met Sam when I auditioned for the part of Jake. I had never met him before, even though we were all from the same area. Those guys were more in the film industry part of it and I was into theater, so we had never crossed paths before, except for Ted Raimi. I had met Ted before. I just met him and Bruce Campbell when I auditioned for the film. That's also how I met Scott Spiegel. I went in for the audition and there was this guy in my agent's office who I had never seen before. I knew my agent didn't represent him, so I introduced myself and asked what he was doing there. He told me he was auditioning for the part of Jake. I asked him how he got the audition and he told me that he kind of co-wrote it. I ended up getting the part and Scott thought enough of me to cast me in the role of Bill in *Intruder.*

RA: That must have been exciting for you to be able to be a part of something that big out of the gate, because the first one was a cult classic already.

DH: I'm not so sure if it was then. I know *Evil Dead* is certainly a cult classic now and Part Two is definitely a cult classic. In fact, it's considered one of the best horror films ever made. When we made it, I don't think any of us were thinking that. We had no idea. In fact, it really didn't get much attention until maybe fifteen years ago, then it really took off. Some people knew it, but most people didn't. Many hadn't heard of it until recently and then it just went crazy.

RA: What were some of the highlights of working on the film for you?

DH: The whole thing was a highlight for me, honestly. Even though I had been in the business for five years and was already pretty well known in the theater area in the Great Lakes area, I had never done a feature film before. I didn't really know what to expect, but the whole thing was just great, especially working for Sam Raimi. You're like a bunch of kids with a lot of money just having fun and throwing fake blood all over the place. It was just an absolute blast. We all had so much fun, even though some of the working conditions were absolutely horrible. It was so hot, especially for poor Ted in that Henrietta suit. I thought the poor guy was going to stroke out on us. I think a couple of times he came close. It was just great though and a brand new experience for me.

RA: What do you remember about some of the amazing effects in the film and them putting those together?

DH: That was Mark Showstrom, who was the head of the special effects on it. It was great. Some of the effects were so real, it's unbelievable. With Henrietta, just making a whole monster suit like that and getting to play with it was just cool. And then there was the hand. That was the creepiest damn thing in the world, because it actually did move a bit. I mean, it didn't run around like they show in the movie, but if you held it in your hand, it would squeeze yours. It was just creepy and it looked so real. Probably the most incredible thing I have ever been a part of in my thirty plus years in acting was Bruce Campbell beating himself up in the kitchen. That was just amazing. Everybody that was working on the film came to watch him do that. It was just incredible the stuff he put himself through.

RA: Another one I want to talk with you about is a true slasher film through and through and that's *Intruder*. How did that one come about?

DH: That came about because of Scott Spiegel and his co-writing of *Evil Dead 2*. He had actually done a no budget version of that earlier. I believe it was called *Night Crew*. I've never seen it, but I think it's out there some place. So, years later he re-wrote it and got the money to make it and he cast me in the role of Bill. It's kind of funny that even though Scott wrote the script with me in mind, I still had to audition for it about five times. In fact, at the last audition I went to I was straight up with him and said, "You know, I don't know what else I could do for you guys", so I did the whole Parker speech with an English accent. I ended up getting the part, though.

RA: Do you remember where they filmed it and what it was like filming in the store?

DH: We filmed it in Bell, California which is definitely on the wrong side of the tracks. It's one of those places in California where you really don't want to be after dark. It's a pretty dangerous location. We were inside this grocery store that was actually a functioning grocery store. I think that they had just gone out of business, so there wasn't any actual work going on there. A lot of the stuff was left, like the dog food aisle, and I gotta tell you, you would never imagine how bad dog food could smell. You leave it out for three months though and it's pretty damn awful. So, we had to deal with that. There were actually a couple sides of beef still hung in the freezer and they stunk to high heaven too.

RA: One of the things that always stuck out to me is that it's possibly one of, if not the goriest slasher film out there.

DH: It's possible and the special effects were so real. I'll never forget this. The script supervisor was there when they crushed the guy's head in the trash compactor. It popped and the blood squirted out and she actually fainted. She knew that it was a special effect, but it was so real that she still fainted. I think it was KNB's first movie, which is Greg Nicotero's company. I could be wrong. I'll never forget the scene where I have to beat the guy with a severed head. There was really no way to hold on to it, except by the hair and that was just a wig. It was hard to hold because I had to swing that thing pretty hard. So, I went over to Greg and I asked him if we could drill some holes in the head. He was saying it's a work of art and he really didn't want to do it at first, but he ended up drilling three holes in it through the hair, so I could hold the head like a bowling ball. (laughs) The special effects were really amazing in it. Unfortunately, it's one of the things that really hurt the movie, because it was so bloody and so violent. A lot of people wouldn't have it. Paramount bought it and they cut the movie so bad that it didn't even make sense. It was edited so horribly that people didn't like it. It took several years, but finally there's a good version out there on Blu-Ray from Synapse. It's just incredible to see that movie compared to what was originally released. It's like a different movie.

RA: What was your thought of playing the role of the killer in *Intruder* and just getting that opportunity to go bonkers?

DH: I thought it was great. That's one of the great things about being a character actor. I can be anybody that I want to be. It's not really me, just a lunatic named Bill. To me, it was just all in fun.

RA: I think my favorite scene of yours is one where you talk about it earlier in the film, where you tell the story of the man with the head in one hand and the sandwich in the other hand and then later in the film, you get to do just that.

DH: That's a funny story, actually. When we were rehearsing that scene, a few of the actors from *Green Acres* came in because they had some small cameo roles in it. They saw us rehearsing that, and when we shot it, they actually asked if they could get out of wardrobe and come watch us film it. So, they actually came down and watched us film that scene. To me that was just an incredible compliment because I was a big *Green Acres* fan and here's Mr. Kimball and Ed watching me do this scene. That was pretty cool. Actually, that speech about Parker and I was done in another movie that Scott borrowed from, with Nicholas Cage in it (*Raising Arizona*). I've never seen it personally, but I'd like to see it.

RA: I know what you're talking about. I actually had to go back and watch *Raising Arizona* again after hearing that. Cage's co-worker is telling him the story. It's not really the same story, but it's very close.

DH: Cool, I'll have to go watch that.

RA: Yeah, it's a great movie. What was your favorite part of doing *Intruder*?

DH: I think just the fact that I got to play Bill and got to be just as crazy as I wanted to be. My whole role was over the top and it was a lot of fun to be able to do that. It was a lot of fun to do the part and to work with Scott, because he's so creative. He'll let you try anything.

RA: I think it's funny how on my DVD version it says in big letters at the top STARRING BRUCE CAMPBELL. I had a friend pick that up and thought it was cool, but I told them not to get too excited about that role (laughs)

167

DH: Yeah, I've seen that. It says starring Bruce Campbell and Sam Raimi at the top. There's a few versions out there like that. There's one version out there that actually gave away the ending and the fact that I'm the killer right on the cover. Whoever owned it at the time really didn't put much thought into it. Maybe they didn't even watch the movie, I don't know. It was silly to spoil the surprise like that.

RA: And it was a good surprise. You really didn't know who the killer was. I remember it caught me off guard.

DH: Yeah, it was a good one and it was well hidden, unless of course you looked at that cover (laughs)

RA: Now, I was reading that you also had a small part in *Maniac Cop*. Could you tell me more about that?

DH: I did. That was the second time I got to beat the hell out of Bruce Campbell (laughs). I made a mini career out of beating him up. I kicked the hell out of him in *Evil Dead 2* and then in *Maniac Cop,* I arrest him. I got to put him in the Paddy Wagon. I can't remember what the dialogue was, but he was cuffed behind his back and I slammed him up against the side. I slammed him into it so hard, the whole truck shook! We finished the scene and asked the director Bill Lustig how it looked. He said it was pretty good, but asked if I could do it harder! (laughs) I said, "I don't know. I need to talk to Bruce about this", and Bruce said sure we could do it harder. We did another take and I slammed him into it even harder. We ended up doing four or five takes of that. I thought I was going to kill poor Bruce.

RA: Wow. *Maniac Cop* is still another favorite of mine. Robert Z'Dar did a great job in it as Cordell.

DH: Yeah, he was great in it and a great person. May he rest in peace.

RA: Another one that you did that was very significant is *Darkman*. Can you tell me about that?

DH: Speaking of Rest in Peace, we recently lost Larry Drake as well. He was probably one of the finest actors I ever had the pleasure of working with. He was also one of the smartest human beings I have ever known, which is ironic because his main claim to fame was playing a character with special needs in *LA Law*. In fact, it's funny how I met him. I got out of wardrobe and I had this tie on. It was pink and purple and black and it was just outrageous. I walked in the make-up room and Larry is sitting there getting his make-up done. I asked the make-up lady what she thought of the tie and Larry said, "It's kind of just like you. Fucking boring, drab, dull". I looked at him and I said, "Geez, you really are retarded, aren't you?" (laughs) So, we really hit it off. Larry had an amazing sense of humor and was just a great guy. It was great working with him and I'm honored that I had that chance.

RA: (laughs) That's a great story! What was Liam Neeson like to work with?

DH: Liam was fine. I don't know if you realize it, but my character doesn't die in the movie. That's because they had some technical difficulties and they had to cut a bunch of my work out. I spent like a whole week working on that with just Liam and I. It was fun working with him. He's incredibly talented, even if he does have a horrible accent (laughs). As soon as they say cut you can barely understand him. In fact, he always called me Donny all the time. He spent a whole week killing me. We actually found a real one-legged stuntman to do a stunt for me, which didn't even make it in the movie!

RA: Yeah, that was something I had always wondered that I wanted to ask about, is what happened to him?

DH: Well, originally what happened is that Darkman grabbed me by the throat and he threw me the entire length of my apartment and I slammed against the wall. When they did that, they built the apartment so that the floor was the wall. Then, they found a one-legged stuntman who resembled me and then they dropped my false leg past three high speed cameras and then they dropped the stuntman. He fell eighteen feet onto this wall. He hit so hard on his stump that everybody thought that it killed him, but he was fine. He got up, brushed himself off and went back to his trailer. The problem was that then Darkman grabs me and he starts punching holes through the concrete wall around my head while asking me questions. While doing that, you could unfortunately see the mechanical apparatus, so it never got done and they didn't use it. I don't know if the footage exists anymore, but I've never seen it. It was a shame.

RA: What went into playing that role anyways? It was a very interesting part to play.

DH: It really was. It was before CGI, so I actually had to wear a harness to tie my leg up like that. It was very painful. I could do it for like an hour, but then I would need to take my leg out of the harness and have it massaged and everything because the cramps were just horrible. When I first knew that I was going to do the part and knew I would only have one leg, I started stretching my ligaments and getting limber enough to where I could do that. It really looked very good, like I only had one leg.

RA: It was very cleverly done too. It was like, oh we don't have any guns with us and then, surprise!

DH: Oh yeah, when we shot that scene, it was supposed to be one afternoon of work. They looked at the dailies and they kept saying that they wanted to do some more. We ended up spending a whole week in that warehouse, doing explosions and gunshots. It just kept getting bigger and bigger. It was pretty cool.

RA: What would you say is your favorite project that you've worked on?

DH: It's hard to say what my favorite one is. I did a student film here in LA, a short film called *The Lutheran*. It's about a Lutheran priest who leaves the flock because he doesn't think that they do or act the way that they're supposed to. It's a very interesting film. It won several awards and there was some talk about making it into a television series, but it never happened. I think that was probably one of my favorite roles. It was a fun little movie. I remember my agent calling me and asking me to read the script and was a bit hesitant, wondering if I could make it work and make it funny. I gave it a shot and I think it worked well. It's an interesting little film. That was one of the favorites. Jake of course in *Evil Dead 2* was another favorite for a number of reasons. For one, it introduced me to the filmgoing public. Strangely enough, to this day people still think I have a Southern accent. Then, there's a film that I just finished last summer that's set to be released soon called *Elder Island*. I got to play a character that has absolutely no redeeming qualities, which I just loved doing. The director and producer originally wanted me to play a different role, but I was like, "I've done that role before. Let me do this guy." They asked me why I wanted to play that one and I said it's because he has no redeeming qualities. I thought it would be fun to play him. I haven't seen it yet, but I think it went well.

RA: What else are you working on lately?

DH: That's about it. I've kind of semi-retired lately. I'm doing a lot of horror conventions all over the country and that's a lot of fun. One of the reasons it's so much fun is that I get to meet so many fans. That's been cool. So, I've been doing that and working on some music, collaborating with Tim-O, a very talented musician who I met at one of the conventions a while back. I've been writing and recording for a little project called The Tim-O and Danny Hicks Brain Invasion. We're currently working on our fourth album and it should be finished this summer. I'm having a lot of fun doing that. You can find some of our videos on YouTube.

RA: If you had anything to say to the fans out there, what would you say?

SLASHED DREAMS PART 2

DH: Thank you. Without them, I would still be a crane operator. It was a good job, but it wasn't nearly as much fun as making feature films. I have to say that you guys are the real stars, not me.

DAVID Z. STAMP
(Easter Bunny, Kill Kill!)

I start out by reading him the following excerpt from the book regarding his performance in the movie, *Easter Bunny, Kill Kill!*

RA: "He is so genuinely creepy, that I felt uncomfortable watching his parts. That's the mark of a great actor though, the ability to evoke a feeling like that. I really hope that he gets more work. God damn, he made me shudder!"

DS: Wow, that's a really wonderful review. Thank you.

RA: No problem. Like I said, you were really good in that movie and genuinely creepy in the part! My first question is a general one. How did you get into the acting industry?

DS: Well, when I was 39 I decided I wanted to try to do something with my life other than just being a regular guy going to work every day to pay the bills. So, I was thinking of a few different things that I thought I would try. I ended up just deciding on acting as a thing I would try. Now I'm 53, so it's been like fourteen years since I started. I haven't become successful, but I can say I've made a good living off of it. I'm glad though, because I at least wanted to try to do something different with my life, so at least I can say that I've tried something instead of being insecure to step out and try something different. Growing up, I had the kind of dad that would

172

say I'm nothing and it didn't leave me with a lot of self-confidence. But then when I was 39, I don't know if you'd call it a mid-life crisis, but I said I at least want to make an attempt to make something more with my life.

RA: What were you doing before acting?

DS: Just before it I was working at a call center for AT&T in Sacramento. It was probably the best job I had to that point. I also had your usual delivery jobs, working at 7-11, those types of things, the working poor.

RA: What were some of the steps you took to make the acting dream a reality?

DS: First, I lived in Sacramento and would just look on the internet, just word search for auditions. I would just go to auditions. I didn't even have a head-shot or know what I was doing yet. It was just to try it. Then I got into a program and took an acting class at a local college to learn more about it. Then, I moved to LA. First, I was in Reno for about a year, then I came to Southern California and was stuck in Orange County for about three years before I got to Los Angeles.

RA: How did you get involved with *Easter Bunny, Kill Kill*?

DS: I looked at some of the websites like LA Casting. I think they were the ones that had a casting notice for it. So, I went to the audition and I had to scream. They liked the screaming and just thought I would be right for that part.

RA: About how long did it take to film your parts?

DS: I think we did it all in one day. It was just a one day thing. I didn't really have a big part, so we were just at somebody's house. Somebody was letting us use their house and they put paper on the walls, trying to get the right look for the lighting. My part included the scene on the phone and pulling up in the car. Most of it we would do in the house during the day, then we would have lunch and in the evening, we would do the car pulling up scene.

RA: Like I said, it's a very creepy, disturbing role as the pedophile. What were your thoughts on playing a character like that? Did you have any reservations?

DS: Well, it's not really a real person like say, a Catholic priest or Michael Jackson. It's just a cartoony type of character. It didn't seem to me like a real person, like they're trying to do a serious dramatic piece or anything. So, to me it just seemed like a cartoony character to the extreme. Of course, some people's perceptions might be that the character is real.

173

RA: What did you bring to the role as far as improvising or your own little quirks to add to the character?

DS: Well, Chad (the director) had said that he wanted me to have kind of a high-pitched voice. When I showed up, he kind of sprung it on me, that he wants that voice. To me, it was kind of like Michael Jackson, how he talked. When I think of that voice, that's what I think of. When you're ready to do it one way and they kind of throw it on you like that last second, it was kind of hard, but it went good. He was happy with it. As far as the walking goes, it was just those crutches that I was using, so obviously, you're going to walk funny on those. And when he directed me, he said that when I walk, I need to drag my feet deep down into the floor, like I'm really struggling to get down the hallway.

RA: What went into doing your death scene?

DS: Like I said, that's how I got the role, because they liked the screaming so much. When they did the knife in the eye, they have a long knife and then another knife that's cut off and you keep your hand on it and hold it so it appears that the knife is stuck in your eye. Then they come up with the drill behind me. I had an idea, and I play to extremes in movies. I wanted a board on the back of my neck and have them drill into the board but they thought it might be too dangerous. So, they just did the thing where it looked like I was getting drilled in the back of the head. The person who stabbed me in the eye wasn't even there that day that we did that part. I wasn't even in the room when you see the blade come through the fire, when they were filming that. I just did the part later where now I have a knife in the eye. It was pretty interesting. It took a while to do the blood. I had to sit down and the makeup person put blood on the face and then on the shirt One interesting thing I want to bring up is the shirt. Did you see what it says on the shirt?

RA: I can't recall what it was. What is it?

DS: It's a shirt for The Golden Cup. Years ago, when I was in High School, I remember reading an article about a place in Hollywood called The Golden Cup, where things like pedophilia was going on, where like teenage men were getting picked up by older men. That name always stayed with me. The police eventually shut it down years ago. I thought it was cool to have that shirt. Probably only a very old Hollywood vice cop would know what that means. It was just a coffee shop where a lot of male prostitution was going on. I asked Chad what year this would be taking place and he said no specific year, so I went and got the shirt made with that on it.

RA: Wow, that is very interesting. I did not know about any of that. Did you have any interaction with the rest of the cast?

DS: Most of my scenes I'm not really interacting with anybody. Even the actor that was playing the kid wasn't there that day. The funny thing with him is that I think he felt uncomfortable playing that mentally challenged character. At one time, they had a showing at a film festival in LA and as soon as it was over, people were looking around for him and he was just gone! When I talked to him later, it seemed like he felt uncomfortable playing that role.

RA: What are you up to now?

DS: Still acting. I mostly do background work, driving jobs, focus groups. Whatever you can do to make money to pay the rent. Just going to auditions and hoping that I'll get something that will be a break.

DEAN CAMERON
(BAD DREAMS, SUMMER SCHOOL, ROCKULA)

RA: How did you get your start in acting and catch that big break?

DC: I spent my summers in Santa Barbara, California as a kid. My parents are divorced, so I grew up in Norman, Oklahoma, but would come over in the summer and Christmas and visit my dad. Santa Barbara had this great summer theater program called Youth Theater, so when I was about ten years old, I started doing musicals and plays. Some of the other guys that I did shows with were Anthony Edwards and Eric Stoltz. By about the time we got into high school, they started going down to LA and doing commercials and things like that. I was in Oklahoma finishing the school year and I thought if they could do that, I could do that. I wanted to be an actor and I knew it was possible. So, when I got out of High School, I moved to LA. Eric, Tony and I were roommates for a couple of years with this other guy named Scott. I basically starved. I managed to get an agent. I had really no experience other than doing theater in high school. I was signed by this commercial agency and for the next four years, I was doing these odd jobs on the side. I worked at Shakey's Pizza, I worked at the Chinese Theatre (Mann's) for two years as the head usher there, I parked cars, I bartended. I was in this great acting class run by Peggy Furey, and I was in with these great actors like Sean

Penn and Michelle Pfeiffer and Crispin Glover. Just great, great people and being around that environment meant it was actually possible to do that work and get movies and things like that. I did a couple of small parts on TV shows like *The Facts of Life* and some commercials, and I ended up getting a part on a show called *Spencer* with Chad Lowe. That was sort of the beginning of the career. From that show, I got interest from the William Morris Agency and they courted me for a while and I ended up signing with them. Then, the following year, I did the *Fast Times* TV show and I played Spicolli on that and that really put me on the map in Hollywood. Everyone wanted to know who would be the poor fucker to play Spicolli on TV, and I was that poor fucker. (laughs) I sort of pulled it off. I didn't suck too badly and that was really the launching pad for me. That led directly to *Summer School* and everything after that and the rest is history. Also in that time, I had booked a pilot and had gotten fired from it, and I landed a movie that got shut down because the producer had been wanted by the FBI. There were some heartbreaks in there too, but I persevered. When I first started, my manager told me that one of the most important things is tenacity and sticking with it, so I stuck with it through all of the adversity and managed to get lucky.

RA: That was the first movie that I wanted to talk with you about was *Summer School*. You're almost like a young Tom Savini in that movie. Were you a horror fan before doing that?

DC: Not really. I appreciated that it was a definite genre, but what was nice is that we had about a month before we started shooting. So, during that time I got to immerse myself in horror films and became a connoisseur. In fact, right before that, there was some sort of anniversary of *Texas Chainsaw Massacre* and *Fangoria* had done a special issue on it, so I learned everything I could. I also bought a subscription to *Fangoria* as Frances Gremp. It confused my postman. Rick Baker did the make-up on our movie and the funny thing was, the guys who did all the grunt work looked just like Chainsaw and Dave. Apparently, they're still in the business. They were very excited because they had not been represented in the movies and it was nice to get to represent that. The writing of it was so good.

RA: Did you get a lot of leeway with the script?

DC: Yeah. Carl Reiner really liked me and I got lucky with that. It was my big break. I was working hard and he recognized that and let me improvise a lot.

RA: Can you tell me a bit about another one you did, *Rockula?*

DC: Yeah, *Rockula* was movie number three for me. *Rockula* was pretty amazing. Every actor, when they move to Hollywood, dreams of being number one on the call sheet; the star of the movie and *Rockula* was the first time that I was number one on the call sheet. I was in the title role and that was a big deal to me. It was heartbreaking because Cannon went under right before the movie was supposed to be released, which is also why there's no soundtrack. There was just no money. It ended up on video, but there was supposed to be a big push for the movie and a big push for me, but it just never happened. Still, I had such a blast doing it. It was so much fun. I'm a musician and I got to write a couple songs for the movie and play guitar and sing. Every actor wants to be a rockstar and I was no different, so that was really fun.

RA: There's another one I wanted to ask you about and it's kind of funny because it's one of my dad's favorite movies, *Men at Work*.

DC: Oh cool. Funny about *Men at Work*, I was such a snob then. Back at the time, there was this group in Hollywood referred to as The Brat Pack. And Emilio was one of them. He had directed this other movie, Wisdom, that I thought was just horrible. Dismissing, of course, that he had written and directed a movie... Anyway, I got the script for *Men at Work* and I thought it was pretty good, but I was being snobby. So, they made the offer and I kept turning it down. I was being such a dick about the whole thing. Finally, I had lunch with Andy Fleming, the writer/director of *Bad Dreams*, and I told him all about it.... (At this point they were offering me a lot of money for a pretty small part.) I told Andy I didn't want to do it and he said "Dude, you're an actor. You're being an idiot. Just do the movie." (laughs).

So, I went home and told my agent that I'll do it. I ended up just having a great time and Emilio was just the nicest guy in the world and Charlie was very sweet. It was just a very fun time. The one thing that was crazy about it was that most of the work I did on it was at night. I was on the movie for like eight weeks and I was just there a lot. They would schedule me and I'd just be there. Some nights, they wouldn't get to my scenes and I would just hang out, so I ended up not seeing any of my friends. Everyone got kind of crazy because we were shooting at night all the time and sleeping during the day. It's basically the graveyard shift. But, doing the movie was a great time. Audiences had pre-conceived notions about what the movie was going to be, so it didn't do that well when it was released. Which was unfortunate, but I had a great time making it and I think it's a funny movie. Also, NWA had released *Straight Outta Compton*. Emilio and I loved that record and we would bust out NWA. Keith David, who is the greatest guy, had no idea what the fuck we were doing. So, I played it for him and he was, well, suitably entertained and horrified at the same time. (laughs).

RA: What was it like doing the part where you get beat up by him in the apartment?

DC: (laughs) It was fun ... simple. The "extra cheese?" line was Emilio's suggestion. I'm very lucky, most of the stuff I've done I've had a great time on.

BAD DREAMS

RA: Right on. Now, of course, this being a slasher movie book, the main one I wanted to talk with you about is *Bad Dreams*. How did you get involved in that one?

DC: I was talking with Grant Heslov on the phone and he told me that he'd read for it. I called my agent and asked about it. They were a little reluctant… "Well, it's a slasher film. I don't know if you want to do that." After Summer School, I'd gotten a development deal with Paramount for a feature film and a TV series. A writer's strike came along and shut down Hollywood long enough to kill any momentum that I had built up. *Bad Dreams* had been greenlit right before the strike happened.

Anyway… I read for it and later that afternoon they offered me the part and worked everything out with Paramount.

RA: How was working with the rest of the cast on the film?

DC: Wonderful. It was Andy Fleming's first film and he was young and idealistic. What was great about is him is that he had taken an intense acting class, so he could become a better director, which I really admired. So, he really listened to his actors and let them help make his movie better. It's one of those things where you have so many talented people on the set with great ideas and you as the director are going to get credit for it, so why not take those ideas and use them? To his credit, he did. He listened to people and was really open. I really admired that. It was a fun time. There are these dressing rooms that they call two bangers, where they have these trailers with two rooms in them, and Richard Lynch and I shared one. We had a common wall and he was learning to play the saxophone, so he had that there and I would tease him about his horrible sax playing. (laughs)

RA: What was he like to be around and to work with?

DC: He was really sweet. He was really hoping that it would become a franchise like *Nightmare on Elm Street* and hoping it would go on. He was a sweet, gentle guy. He was a little freaked out by the burn make-up when they first put it on him, and all of the fire, because he was a burn victim. That first day that they put the make-up on, it took him back a little bit. A few months before he died, I did one of those autograph conventions and he was there. He was a good guy and a great actor. Should have done better and more people should have known about him. Then, there was Harris Yulin. Apparently, he had ad-libbed over a very important plot point. It was so late in the shooting and they were trying to make the day and they didn't realize until they got the dailies back that they had missed a very important plot point, so they had to do some re-shoots. Sometimes, there can be a disadvantage to listening to actors

179

too much. Everyone was great. Jennifer Rubin was very sweet, beautiful and awesome. I had been in class with Elizabeth Daily, or EG as many know her. Coincidentally, she had done songs for *Summer School*. Hollywood is really one big, weird, connected mass of people.

RA: I was wondering about the direction in the movie, for example, there's a scene where you pretty much just flip the fuck out. You're running around like crazy and ranting and basically tearing down the walls. I just wonder, because it was so involved, what was the direction there? Did the director just tell you to go nuts?

DC: Good question. We shot that for two days. He had pretty much mapped out where stuff was going to happen and we walked through it. He knew that I would do stuff that would just come off spontaneously, so he had like two or three cameras set up, which doesn't happen much these days. So, he was telling me I could be here, and over here, and here, then run over there. The dialogue was pretty much set. The name of the movie at the time was actually *Unity*. There was the whole thing with the cult and unity and that's what I carve on my arm. Obviously, that's a horrible title for a horror film. So, we mapped it out and he was very protective of me and Jennifer during that scene. He would tell me when to really go for it and he knew when I could really mark through it and save my voice and my energy, until I really had to go for it. He was very respectful of me being able to find the places where I could go crazy. It was great.

RA: I always thought you were very good in that part, throwing things left and right and knocking things over. That was very good acting there.

DC: Thank you. You know, scenes like that I almost think are easier than like playing a lawyer in a courtroom scene or things like that. All I really had to do was just go nuts. If that's available to you, it's simple and just a matter of pacing yourself for something like that. There was another one I did, a cop show where I committed suicide and had a similar freakout. It wasn't quite as involved, but I went nuts on that.

RA: Another one that I wanted to ask about is a scene that is so realistic that it's uncomfortable and that's the knife through the hand scene that you do to yourself.

DC: Right! My mom freaked the fuck out when she saw that. It's a good effect, isn't it? It's just a little fake arm and a knife, but man, it's really effective. I liked that scene. That's one of those scenes that I'm really proud of in that movie. There's that and then the scene where I'm talking to her during the rehab and I show her the scars on my stomach. Those are two scenes that I'm really happy with. They're short and I don't do a lot, but I just remember being really connected to the role at that point. I hadn't watched it in a long time, but when

I did watch it, I just remember thinking it was pretty damn good.

GENERAL QUESTIONS

RA: I have a few other questions that I wanted to ask you about other things you've been involved with away from film. First off, what exactly is Coreyoke?

DC: (laughs) Well, it's a karaoke band and originally, we just played eighties covers. The idea was that we were the Coreys from the eighties and that Michael Jackson had molested all of us and so, to pay us back, he said that he would get us to be his backing band on his comeback tour. We got a call from an attorney saying that they wanted to make sure that people knew that we weren't the actual Coreys. Corey Haim and Corey Feldman were great young actors, but they sort of went to hell. I always enjoyed making fun of them (laughs).

RA: Did you run across them much in Hollywood back in the eighties?

DC: A little bit. I'm sorry I did, but I actually turned down a part in *Rock N' Roll High School Forever*. Feldman was in it and that was the one where he was driving home from the wrap party and he got busted for drugs for the first time. That was pretty much the beginning of the end for him. I know someone who was in the movie and the Corey stories are legion. That's kind of why I wish I had done the movie is so that I could have experienced some of those stories for myself. But, I just didn't want to do another movie with school in the title at that point.

RA: Another interesting fact I found out is that you were born on Christmas. So, did you have to experience that whole "This is both a Christmas and a birthday gift" thing?

DC: Absolutely. I think that may have contributed to my bitter outlook on life (laughs). It's funny, the woman who is now my wife, when we were first dating, on the first Christmas that we had together with her family, they made a point to have a birthday tree and not a Christmas tree and everyone got me two presents. I think it had to do with me whining to her about much I hated Christmas because of that. So, it was really nice and one of the things that just made me love her to death. I do think that the Birthday-Christmas is a drag. However, I think it's better to have a birthday on Christmas than around Christmas. I think maybe January 4th would be the worst birthday to have, because everyone is just so done with the holidays and it's so close to New Year's. Everyone's tired and getting back to work and it's like, "Another fucking party? No." So, at least I can say that I was born on Christmas and that's kind of cool.

RA: (laughs) Very true. I saw too that you got to work with Steel Panther on a couple videos?

DC: Yes, I played in a band with one of their guitar players and the drummer called The Thornbirds. We actually have a record out that you can probably find for a penny on Amazon, if you're interested. Actually, the drummer was the one who came up with the name Coreyoke. So, while we were doing The Thornbirds, they were in this group that was doing a lot of cover bands. They had a disco one and this one called Metal Shop. They mainly played these eighties covers and I started doing the artwork for their covers when they started doing originals. Russ, the guy who is Satchel, is a musical genius. When they wanted to do a video for their first song, they really didn't know anybody who knew how to direct except for me, so I directed their first video and it went really well. Then, as time went along they got a record deal and budgets for other videos and I directed an idea for a reality show for them. It's another iron in my show business fire. I co-wrote a couple of their songs with them.

RA: Can you tell me about your comedy show?

DC: Yeah, The Nigerian Spam Scam. For about a year, I fucked with a Nigerian scammer online and would send the correspondence to friends of mine. After about three months of this, they said I should make it into a show. A few months later, I did. I got together with a friend of mine from a theater I was working at called Sacred Fools Theater, and they had this late-night program where you could put up whatever you wanted for ten or twenty minutes and try it out. So, over a few weeks, I tried this out and would put up this correspondence with this guy and show pictures. It went really well and we got Paul Provenza, who directed this movie called *The Aristocrats*. He had been to the fringe festival in Edinborough and hooked me up with a producer there, who brought the show over, even before we really had a show put together. On the plane over and the week before the show, we really honed it and got it tight. So, I've been performing that since 2005. We did the *Just for Laughs* festival in Montreal and played a bunch of theaters around the country. It's a hilarious show. The ending was never really satisfying to me. I tried to get the scammer to send me a dollar through all of this roundabout reasoning and he had agreed to, but he never did. It always sort of nagged at me and there's a moment in the show where he says he's going to send me a dollar and people really responded to that, so I thought that I'm really going to try to get that money from him. After about four or five years, I contacted him again. I had sent him a couple packages and called him over the phone a few times over the years. I play the calls and show the contents of the packages on the show, so I knew where he lived and I contacted him again. One of the characters I was writing as was Perry Mason, the lawyer. He had found the website for the show and that was initially the end of the show is where he found the website. So, I wrote him back as this lawyer and told him that the show is now a hit, and that he's technically a co-writer of the show and entitled to some of the money. I told him that I, Perry Mason, am horrified by Dean Cameron's behavior and that I would like to represent him in the claim against Dean. So, this went on for a while and I got his trust and I eventually got him back, and got him to send me a retainer for my services of three dollars and fifty cents. So, that's now the new ending of the show. It's a really funny show and really fun to do and easy to set up. Every now and then I'll put it on when I get antsy.

RA: What else are you currently working on?

DC: Working on getting other jobs. There's a movie coming out called *The Waiting*. I think I'm still in it. It's an independent film and James Caan is in it. I just was on *It's Always Sunny in Philadelphia*. I stopped working for about ten years. I got sick of the business and wasn't getting the jobs that I wanted to get, so I left and started working as a front-end web developer. I worked at Legal Zoom and Ticketmaster and places like that. A few years ago, I realized that I hated doing that and that also the people who grew up watching me are now running showbiz. So, some very smart young managers reached out to me and got me working again. I've been doing that and rebuilding my career. It's almost like starting from scratch, which is frustrating and weird, but necessary. I am Mr. Mom to my son and my wife works as an editor on the show *Major Crimes*. I have a nice little existence. I play music every Wednesday night and am enjoying myself.

RA: How do you look back on your place in pop culture? Chainsaw, for example has been a big part of it and is even mentioned on *Robot Chicken*. How do you feel about that, looking back at your career?

DC: It's nice. I always knew that I was very lucky to be working actor and I was always very appreciative of the work I had, but as an ambitious young person, you're always looking to the next thing and always comparing yourself to those around you. I do wish that I had appreciated it a little more than I did, but I'm proud of all the work I did and happy that I did it. I'll be happy when my son is old enough to see the stuff I did. I think it's a fine legacy. If I never work again, I'm fine with that, but I think I have a lot more to offer and I hope that other people feel the same way.

RA: If you had anything you could say to the fans, what would you say?

DC: Thank you. I just recently went to San Francisco because the Alamo Drafthouse was doing this thing called Midnight for Maniacs. They showed *Summer School, Ski School* and *Rockula* over a night. They had me come up and talk in between the movies and there were so many people there. I had no idea. It was overwhelming and I was really touched. I know

183

almost every day, somebody recognizes me. There were like 300 people there who spent money to go see these twenty-five-year-old movies and loved them. I was just very touched and overwhelmed to know that people feel that way about the work I did. It was a lot of fun making them and I'm glad it meant something to so many people. Thank you.

DEBORAH VOORHEES
(FRIDAY THE 13th PART V)

RA: How did you get involved in the acting business?

DV: Well, it was one of those things. I had been working at the Playboy Club in Dallas. I had heard that the show *Dallas* was in town and my agent sent me out for an audition and I was hired for a speaking part. The first time I was hired was as an extra role and then they put me in as a regular stand in for all the brunettes like Linda Gray and Victoria Principal. From there, I ended up doing several speaking roles on the show. I really enjoyed it. It was a lot of fun. Larry Hagman was a blast. When I would walk on set, he would sing Debbie Sue, I love you. It was a really great experience. I feel pretty lucky as I look back because I have been a part of several iconic American institutions like being a Playboy bunny, being in *Friday the 13th* and being on *Dallas*. I probably actually enjoyed working as a stand-in more than anything because you're a part of the crew and you get to be involved in everything. I'm into filmmaking now, so it was a great opportunity for me. I didn't just hang on the set and chat with people. I was always busy paying attention, looking, listening, seeing what people are doing and how they're doing it. I was just that quiet little fly on the wall. It was just a wonderful experience. After working on *Dallas*, I just put everything into my Pontiac, which was belching black smoke and took off to Los Angeles, having to run the heater full blast through the desert so I didn't overheat. It wasn't fun. I was sweating like crazy (laughs). Plus, it was summer, so it was brutal. Getting to Los Angeles was the first time in my life that I felt like I was on foreign soil. Now, I have to say that Los Angeles feels very much so like home, even though it's been years since I've been there. One of my screenplays was an official selection at The Beverly Hills Film Festival and I went back for that. There's something about it that just feels like home to me, which is a stark contrast from when I first got there. Everything is so different there, like you look around and the billboards are movies. There's nothing about it that feels like another city anywhere else.

RA: What was it that won you the part on *Friday the 13th*?

DV: I think there were a few things. When I first went in to audition, of course they recognized my name immediately. They were like, "Well, we knew that we definitely had to see you" (laughs). At the time that I went in for my first audition, the producer had already picked someone else. The director still wasn't happy because this individual, as well as most of the actresses that came in for it, didn't understand that Tina was flirting when she told her boyfriend to fuck off. The other ones would be angry and mad and I was like, well this is your boyfriend, you like him. He's asking you to go fool around. You're not going to be mad.

RA: What was your experience working with Danny Steinmann? What kind of a director was he?

DV: I found him to be really nice. I had a tough role to play because the very first day ended up being the nude scene. So, obviously the first day on the set, that's a little stressful. He was super easy going and kind of walked me through it, making me feel secure and comfortable.

RA: I wanted to ask about that, doing such a nude scene. Was that tough to do, with the crew there and everything? I imagine it could be awkward.

DV: They do a closed set, so it's only the people that absolutely have to be there. However, that number is still pretty high! (laughs) So yeah, it's a little bit nerve-wracking, but once you get into the scene, things relax pretty quickly. It wasn't like I was shaking nervous or anything like that. I was just kind of, la la la. (laughs) Also, with Robert and I, they gave us each other's numbers, so we met up close to the beach in the Santa Monica area for a little while and visited, so it would be a little bit less awkward when the actual day came.

RA: What are your memories of the late Mark Venturini?

DV: I don't remember much specifically about him, but I didn't have a problem with anybody on the set. I can tell you that he was very nice guy for the time I knew him, though. We didn't really hang out on an intimate basis, but he was nice.

RA: I know the movie was heavily edited. What all went into your death scene and what was cut out?

DV: I honestly couldn't tell you what was cut or anything. I've heard different people say different things. Some you just hear about years later and its news to me. I really didn't notice much, but it was a challenging scene to shoot for many reasons. Just the make-up alone took several hours. I look at the shots in the film and that's pretty much what we got. I'm sure that there's some angles and things that they didn't use, but for the most part it's there.

RA: Was that a tough make-up job to sit through? I imagine that especially with it over the eyes, it could have been uncomfortable.

DV: Right, yeah it was. Before we even got to the film set, I went to the guys that were creating the mask and doing the props. The first thing they had me do was to put on this very cold consistency that was basically making the cast. I just remember that it was thick and extremely cold. It was like one of those brain freezes that you get when you drink an Icee, only you couldn't stop it. So, that was kind of freaky and of course they didn't warn me first. Then, they take that and they make what is like a rubber mask. I can't remember the exact time, but I think it was in the neighborhood of about three to four hours in the make-up. Once all of that was done, it would be time. Thankfully, they waited until the last minute to put the blood in, but I still had the blood in my eyes for several hours. That burned. It really hurt. That's one of the things that really took some time too and needed to be re-shot, because once the shot was done, they would have to touch up the make-up again.

RA: What are your favorite memories of making the film?

DV: There were a couple of things. One was going to lunch and seeing people holding their head or their arm from their death scenes. That was kind of funny (laughs). We had a producer on the show who was really nice. Overall, it was fun. Most everyone was really nice. I honestly didn't know that anybody was fighting behind the scenes. It wasn't until a couple of decades later that I knew about that. It was very funny in the scene where the guy was about to put the garden shears through my eyes. Of course, it wasn't really the guy playing the killer there, it was just a stand-in. I just remember waking up and looking up seeing this sweet smile on his face (laughs). He was kind of humored by the whole situation. There was another show I did where I was supposed to be being killed and I opened the door and there's just a grip smiling and sitting on the counter eating a burger. It was too funny. I had them re-take that shot (laughs).

RA: Do you still keep in touch with any of the cast?

DV: I've said hello here and there. I've spoken to Shavar Ross a few times and chatted with him on Facebook. He's just a very nice, kind man. I got to see and talk with John Shephard at a convention and I've just always liked him. I really respected him on set. He really put time and effort into making his character real. He was a real method actor and I respected that. He put a lot of time and effort into something that, honestly, is a bit campy. He made it real and you actually feel for him as a character. I did get to see Danny Steinmann before he passed away, at the same convention. It's the only one I've ever been to. I didn't mind it once I got there. I think I'm pretty well known for being afraid of scary movies. I just don't like them, they're just … they're just scary (laughs). I'm actually starting to make myself watch some more scary movies. I'm planning to watch *The Sixth Sense* and my husband has pledged to sit next to me and hold my hand. I've heard it's good and I've wanted to see it, but I'm a massive chicken when it comes to that sort of thing. But, I am so lucky to have such nice fans. Somebody contacts me almost every day of my life at this point, which is very surprising. They're just very nice, lovely people.

I've been making films lately and I thought to myself, what would be a film I could do to make them smile? So, I'm working on one now which is a *Faust* story. It's something I would actually like to make into a series. I'm finishing up the final touches on the first episode now. Obviously, it's about the devil, being a *Faust* story and it has some scary parts in it. It also has some comedy and it will have a cliffhanger at the end of episode. I've been playing with that and having a lot of fun with it. I'm good at twists, but I feel I really need to sit down and watch more horror and see the story structure and different things like that. So, we'll see how I do.

RA: Why did you leave the acting industry?

DV: A couple things. I had been taking classes at the junior college in Los Angeles. Initially, I started doing it because I just didn't want to work in bars anymore. I thought I'd go get a real estate license or something where I could do the work and still go to my auditions. I just absolutely hated working in nightclubs. What I've learned since I've gotten older is that most men are really lovely creatures that are a delight to be around, but when you look a certain way, they can make life very uncomfortable. I would actually like to go back and do a study on that. I wonder if it would have been different with a smaller breast size or a different look, or if they treated all girls that age that way. It would be interesting to see. Being in a nightclub where people were drinking, and they were just being rude and inappropriate, I just said I don't want to do this anymore. I wanted to be treated with respect. So, that was one of the things. Another thing that I noticed was that Hollywood was really tough on women. I was in my early twenties and I would see women in their forties trying to compete for the same roles. They would have all of their plastic surgery and everything worked on, and staying in the tanning booth and putting oil and glitter on. I felt bad for them. It really hurt me to see because they couldn't compete with us. I didn't want to be that person to be so desperate to cling to my looks because I needed it for my job. It was particularly bad in the eighties. That was a big thing. I also got a tiny taste of what it was like to be known. I wasn't very comfortable with it, but I'm still very glad I did it. Being in Hollywood prepared me for what I do now.

When I started taking classes, I really was loving it. I took pretty much everything and I ended up with two years of nothing. I think they should have given me something for that (laughs). I do have my degree now, but at the time, I just took what I found interesting or something that I thought could be beneficial. I took all kinds of classes. I started to notice that I would start to get annoyed when I had an audition and had a class. At first, the acting came first. I always thought that college was just for kids that were really smart. I didn't know how smart I was then until I had my IQ tested and found out it was at 145. That's no slacker. When I realized that, I had this deep desire to go to college, so one day I was walking by this place that had a college entrance exam and I thought, "Hmm, I wonder what would happen if I really studied ... ". I mean, I had good grades, but could have applied myself better. I walked in and signed up for the test and told myself that if I fail, it's my secret and no one has to ever know. After I turned it in, I waited for the results and not only did I pass, I did very well. I was thrilled. It was one of those moments when I passed where I said "Wow, I actually am intelligent", and it was a wonderful feeling. Within two weeks, I was packed up and went back to Texas and went to school. I was working full time and going to school full time and it was brutal, but I graduated at the top of my class in the top five percent. I was very proud of myself. I went on and worked at some newspapers as a journalist for many years.

RA: I also read that you did some teaching. Can you tell me about that?

DV: I did. I taught for four years at a high school in Texas. I did advanced placement and specialized in British Literature for seniors. I did the advanced placement, which is college preparation, in both Texas and New Mexico. I also taught journalism. In New Mexico, I also taught at Eastern New Mexico University for acting for film.

RA: I was reading somewhere that unfortunately you lost a teaching job due to your role in the film and the nudity involved. Could you talk about that?

DV: Two actually. I was thrown out of two high schools. (laughs) When I first left journalism, I had it in the back of mind that I was very grateful for the people who had taught me. Getting my degree was huge in helping me feel good about myself and like I could do anything. I just thought that at some point I wanted to teach because I wanted to give back where other people gave to me. After leaving journalism, I went back to school again to get my teaching certification. It took about nine months to take all the classes and exams. I was probably about two weeks from starting my first job, when someone who knew my past asked if I was worried about *Friday the 13th*. It was the first time I ever thought of that and I said "No. Why?", and they said, "Well, you know the whole morality thing of school boards". Well, I thought I doubt anyone would even recognize me, but then I wondered if they did and if I may have picked the wrong profession. I knew not to go into politics (laughs), but it never crossed my mind. Well, I was at Decatur High School for quite a while, when apparently, some of the boys had a *Friday the 13th* watching party and they recognized me from it. I was in my forties and thought nobody would, but I was wrong. It got around school very fast and it was a really brutal situation. Most of my kids were good about it, but there were some of the other faculty. My first principal was great. She really tried to protect me, but then I had another one who came in and he was brutal. You know when you're under attack and I was under attack. Unfortunately, the principal before was also released. I don't know if it was solely because of me, which I really hope wasn't the case. She was a wonderful principal. For the most part, the teachers were complete jerks. They let me finish up my year, but very few of them would talk to me and they were very rude. It was like something out of a movie! You would think that nobody could be that ugly. So, I decided to move to New Mexico, which I had wanted to do anyway, because the area is lovely. I thought it would be okay because nobody knew me there. I kind of had it in my head that maybe a rumor had started, and the same thing ended up happening there, but this time it was in the first year. In some ways, the principal was fine there. It was more the vice principal that was more problematic and once again I came under attack, going from being highly thought of to being attacked at every angle. I had problems with teachers, administration, faculty, parents. You could write a movie script on it, because my kids really came to my aid. They went to the principal and the school board, and they tried to fight to get me back. I mean not a few, but a lot. I had so many letters and phone calls and kids that would run into me and just start crying. The mere fact that I had so many kids fighting for me says a lot. There were a lot of illegal things that were happening too, like the vice principal broke into my computer and got into my grade books and changed every student's grades. They even tried to forbid me from going to graduation. I told them that these are my kids and I'm going, no matter what. When I got there, it was like I wasn't respectable enough to sit with the teachers. I just said fine, I'll sit with the parents. It was like that old Harper Valley PTA song. (laughs)People were giving me ugly looks. It was nice though, a couple came over and said that they wanted to sit with me. They were trying to show their support. At the end of it, I went down on the football field because I was going to congratulate my kids. To hell with anyone else and what they thought or what they felt. These were still my kids. I went down there and hugged them and congratulated them. One of the boys had caused me grief before because of the situation. I wasn't mad at him, he was being a boy. How can you not be excited to find out that your teacher was topless in a major motion picture? (Note: I mention how it's like the Van Halen song Hot for Teacher and we have a laugh) I remember he was text messaging my boobs around the classroom and I'd tell him to put the phone away and get back to work. That was one of the things that helped spread the whole rumor and led to my release. Anyways, I heard his voice calling out from across the football field to me and I turned and he was running for me with tears just streaming down his face, saying "I am so sorry I hurt you". He said that he really didn't mean to hurt me and I just hugged him and told him that it's okay. It was just a wonderful moment between me and him. Of course, I balled my eyes out too. I had a couple of kids run into me at the grocery store and they told me they thought I would leave town. I said, "What, do you think I'd hang my head in shame and leave? Hell no!" No, not gonna do that.

RA: Wow, from listening to that, it sounds like that needs to be made into a movie, for real!

DV: It really is, especially since it went from the principal at first telling me "You're the kind of teacher they make movies about" to being damned the way I was and them coming after me the way they did. You know, I had kids in my classroom who were painting murals on the wall and making songs. You could always do a book report and some did, but I also gave them an opportunity to be creative and write a song or paint or write a fictional story. They did all kinds of things. It's really quite the detailed story and has a lot of twists and turns, so yeah, it could make a great movie. (laughs)

RA: Maybe that should be your next project.

DV: One of these days, maybe (laughs) It's one of those things I can look back as a good thing, though. Anything that really gives us life experience and gives us a different way of looking at life is very valuable. All of these things bring new and interesting ways of seeing the world. Plus, it brought me back to film making. I decided I was not going to try teaching again because it was a painful situation to go through. I don't want to work and be with people who are that judgmental. I hear people like that rail against Hollywood and the products they put out, but you know what? The demon is in your own house. It's not Hollywood. Hollywood is very open minded. If you have something they want, they don't care what your background is. In a Hollywood business office, the only thing they would say about my past is "Okay, cool." (laughs) Granted, getting to that office and in with the right people can be difficult, but if you really have a drive and something to offer, you can do it. I mean, what can be better than entertaining people? Something where you can make someone smile and just put away all of their problems for a while. Isn't that a wonderful thing? It's amazing how something that you can create like that can have such an impact on the world.

RA: If you had anything you could say to the fans out there, what would you say?

DV: Thank you for being so lovely.

DEBRA LAMB
(EVIL SPIRITS)

RA: How did you get into acting and get your start?

DL: When I was a kid, I was extremely creative. I would write poetry, draw, write songs, write children's plays and this was all when I was just a little kid. I would draw out these long elaborate scenarios on those long rolls of paper. I would make puppets and put on these little plays. When I was seven, I had this favorite children's record called Tina the Ballerina and I would just play it over and over. I had always wanted to be a ballet dancer since I was little and would beg my mom to let me do it. So, finally she said okay and I started taking ballet. I was able to dance in a lot of different productions during that time in ballet. I did that from the time I was seven until I was fourteen and had to quit when we moved from Portland down to LA. We were so poor. We finally found a little place behind a bigger house in Beverly Hills and I went to Beverly Hills High School. It was such a culture shock! It was so big, I thought it was the college when I first saw it! Once there, I took dance and drama, but then we moved to Santa Monica and I went to High School there for two years. I took dance classes there and did musical theater, so by the time I was a senior, I had been doing dance almost my whole life, but I really wanted to be an actor. So, I graduated, but I wasn't able to go to acting school right away because I was dirt poor. I had to work my ass off. Eventually after a couple of years I got myself into an acting school. It was a very reputable school in Hollywood and I went there for a few years. Actually, I had been going there a while and Traci Lords ended up joining my class and we actually became friends. Another guy that was in was my class went on to do a lot, his name is Tommy Lister and he goes by the name Tiny. Everybody knew that he would make it and of course, he did. I stayed there for three years, but then I moved on. Meanwhile, while I was busy doing that and being poor, I got into dancing and was working at bikini bars and waitressing and doing improv, just doing whatever I could to make money to survive. I also did a little modeling. Somewhere along the line, someone recommended me to Fred Olen Ray, the director. The first movie I did with him was called *Warlords* and it starred David Carradine and Sid Haig. I just had a small part, but it

SLASHED DREAMS PART 2

was a great experience. The next movie I did with him was *Beverly Hills Vamp*. Then, he had me come back to do a small part in *Mob Boss*. I got to work with a lot of different directors on a lot of different things. I even got to work with Paul Verhoven on *Robocop … but* I got cut out. (sad voice)

RA: Really?

DL: Yeah, you know those funny commercials where the guy says, "I'd buy that for a dollar!"?

RA: Of course!

DL: Well, they did a few of those and I did one of the commercials. But then, when they did the final release of the film, they only used one of the commercials and they used the same one over and over. I was a pizza dough juggling girl, or a juggling pizza dough girl, however you would say that (laughs). I also worked with David Lynch before.

RA: Yeah, I wanted to ask you about that. How was that experience?

DL: Well, I did that film *Wild at Heart*. I was so thrilled to work on that film and I didn't get cut out either! (laughs)

RA: I was also reading that you were able to work with John Hughes before as well. What was that like?

DL: Oh yeah! That was awesome. Unfortunately, I got cut out of *Planes, Trains and Automobiles*. I went in one day and was working as a dancer in this scene at a strip club. At one point, they wanted to add a scene and do an improv scene, so they asked which one of the girls would like to do it. I said that I'll do it and they said great, so I got to do it! (laughs) I already had experience with improv at this point, so I just did improv on a scene with John Candy and then Steve Martin comes up and I'm insulting his character. It was really silly. When we were done, everybody just howled. They were just laughing their asses off and they were clapping. It was so much fun. I was actually able to get my SAG card from doing that job. John Candy was the nicest person on the planet. He was just so sweet.

RA: That's what I've heard

DL: Yeah, he was so nice to every single person. It didn't matter who you were, he was just a sweetheart. Steve Martin was a bit more reserved. Anyways, then I was invited to go to the screening of it at Paramount. When we got to the door, they were handing out these sheets

193

with all of the cast and crew listed on them and my name was on it, so I figured that I'm still in the movie. I sat right in front of one of the editors who recognized me from that scene and he told me I was so funny and it was such a great scene, so I'm thinking "Yay! That's good. It means I'm still in it". So, we watch the film and my scene is right after the one where their car catches on fire. But, the scene wasn't there. After it ended, the guy behind me said how sorry he was. When he was working on it, the scene was still in it, but he didn't know that they had cut it out. He was just consoling me and we were both devastated.

RA: Aw, that's too bad they cut that out. Do you know why or what happened to it?

DL: I don't know what happened to it, but I figure that it's because it's a family movie, a holiday movie where the whole thing is him trying to get home to his family for Thanksgiving and I think they didn't want that topless scene in there. That's probably why. I just wish somebody would contact me and say "Hey, the lost footage is out there. We found it!" (laughs)

RA: I really hope they find that, too. Another one I want to ask you about is another horror film and I read the credits and I know exactly who you are in that one, *American Scream*.

DL: (shocked) You saw that? Wow! Where did you see that?

RA: I actually have a copy of that.

DL: Wow, you have a copy of that? What made you get a copy of that? That's one of the ones that hardly anybody knows about.

RA: Oh yeah. It's one I always remember seeing on the video store shelf as a little kid, but as I got older, it just became impossible to find, so I kind of searched around until I finally found a copy and I jumped on it.

DL: Wow, that's so cool! Yeah, that was right toward the beginning of my film career. That was a good one and a lot of fun. It's so funny too, because when I got on the set, one of the guys on the cast turned out to be somebody that I knew from High School. I don't think he's done anything since (laughs). We filmed that way up in the mountains. I think it possibly could have been Big Bear or one of the other mountains in that general area. It was winter and there was a lot of snow. You know the scene where the girl is running through the forest and then falls down and gets captured by the bad guy? Okay, so there's snow everywhere and I'm wearing nothing but this little negligee and these little shoes. So, I remember falling in the snow and then the killer gets me and later on has me in the shower. They wrapped me in cellophane or saran wrap and I get gutted by the killer. It was a fun film. The director was really happy with me.

RA: Nice. Now, the one I really want to talk with you about the most here is *Evil Spirits,* a personal favorite of mine. How did you get involved in that one?

DL: Oh yes! I know exactly how I got involved in that one. So, Gary Graver is the director. He was the cinematographer for some of Fred's films and I knew him from that. So, he knew me and every once in a blue moon I would pop into his office. One of these times, I came over to drop off these newer pictures and a resume. He was looking at them and really liked one of the pictures because I look really young. He told me I would be really good for this movie that he was doing. Apparently, he had an actress to play Tina. When she was hired, she understood that there was some topless scenes and seemed fine with it, but all of a sudden after they hired her, she didn't want to do a topless scene. Luckily, I came down to his office at the right time and I said I would do it and I got the part. He asked if I had any problem coloring my hair and I said no problem, so I colored my hair to an auburn color.

RA: I always thought that your character was very interesting in the movie. I love how she would just pretty much glide into the scene from out of nowhere and kind of dance around for no reason.

DL: (laughs) Yeah, I was always popping up in the background just dancing around. There's this opening scene where Karen Black had just killed someone and is washing up in the kitchen and it's the first time you see me. I just kind of glide into the kitchen and twirl around. When I first did it, I just danced into the kitchen and she says I should be in my room, I just sulked and walked out, but then Gary said "No, I want her to be dancing all the time. Never stop dancing.", so I'm like "Okay, whatever you want" (laughs). So, every time you see me, that's what I'm doing. It's pretty funny.

RA: Yeah, for sure. One of the things that I have always loved about the movie is Michael Berryman's performance in it. I mean, my God, he should have won an award for that. It was one of the best performances I've seen and just so weird!

DL: Oh yeah! That was good. I remember doing a Monsterpalooza convention back in 2012 and I ran into him there and it was the first time I had seen him since we had done *Evil Spirits*. He totally recognized and remembered me. He was really shy on the set and didn't really say a lot. He kind of kept to himself. He was very nice, just kind of quiet.

RA: Were you able to see the whole finished version of the film after it was done?

DL: Yes, I actually did. It's so funny, with a lot of the other films that I did like *Beverly Hills Vamp* and *Mob Boss*, I would get a video tape with maybe a clip or two of my scenes, but I wouldn't get the whole movie, so a lot of these movies I never saw until decades later. With *Evil Spirits* though, I was given my own copy on videotape, so I did get to see the whole thing.

RA: Cool. I always have thought it was a very interesting movie and it did some very clever things like having the drunk character in it who always escapes getting killed by Karen Black just because he's drunk.

DL: (laughs) I know, it's pretty funny. You know, he's the writer, Mikel Angel.

RA: Wow, I did not know that. He was just one of many interesting characters in the movie.

DL: Oh yeah, another one was Virginia Mayo. She was quite the famous movie star at one time. She was in *White Heat* with James Cagney. She was huge. When she came to work on *Evil Spirits*, I didn't know who she was, but somebody told me. She kept to herself and was a bit standoffish. I can understand why, I mean, she had such an illustrious career and here she is doing a low budget horror film (laughs). But, that film had some really great people in it, like Arte Johnson and Karen Black.

RA: For sure! Karen is a legend herself. What was it like getting to work with her and playing her daughter in that?

DL: She was really nice and so great to work with. She really knew what she was doing. She was so professional. There's that end scene where I'm crying and she picks me up. We did that in one take and she just whisked me right up (laughs). Before we did the scene, I asked if she was sure she could pick me up and she said it wouldn't be a problem. (laughs) Oh yeah, she was strong! She had a very young child at the time, maybe a couple years old. I remember thinking that she must have been lifting that kid all over the place. I loved working with her. I would have really loved working with her again. I just can't say enough good things about her.

RA: What would you say was your favorite memory of working on the movie?

DL: I would say getting to slash Arte Johnson's throat (laughs). I really got into that. I loved all of my scenes with Michael Berryman. It was so funny because he was so quiet, but for some reason I just wanted to be around him all the time. We had scenes like where we're at the breakfast table or where I blow out his candle on the stairs. We had a lot of scenes together and it was just so much fun to work with him. He and Karen Black were my favorites to work with. I also really liked Martine Beswick, as well.

RA: Another one that you did is *Point Break* where you have a scene at the party doing

firebreathing. Could you tell me more about doing that?

DL: Oh yeah. Around that time, I was doing a lot of performance art. There was a restaurant where I was doing the fire eating and I had done it in a couple music videos. Some casting people had seen me doing that. I was going through my Madonna phase, so I had this platinum blonde, curly hair. It was so cool. They're having the party and I spit fire right as Keanu Reeves and Lori Petty walk into the party. In between takes, I was chatting with them. Keanu was asking me about the fire eating and how I do it. They were really nice. We did a bunch of different takes for that scene and then after I was just hanging around. It was getting into the wee hours of the night and I walked up to Katheryn Bigelow, the director, and I asked if she wanted me to stick around and she said yes, so I just kind of hung out in the room that's supposed to be Bodie's room. Patrick Swayze was there, but I didn't really get to talk to him, but it was really great, a lot of fun. I really loved working on that.
(Note: at this point I'm sharing stories of myself in wrestling and my mentor doing fire breathing. She starts to interview me and ask me questions about my career and where the Ronnie Angel name comes from, then we talk a bit about our personal lives :)

RA: I am looking at your IMDB and I see that you played Elizabeth Bathory a few years back on *A Blood Story*. What can you tell me about that?

DL: It was great working with Camden Toy again. I had previously worked with him on *Disciples*. I had a chance to get to know him better on this one, since I didn't really get a chance to on *Disciples*. It was a great film to work on. I was an executive producer, producer, plus I had quite a few other behind the camera roles on this one. I really enjoyed playing Elizabeth Bathory. My character is not the focus of the film, however, she is the pinnacle character. I'm in there throughout the film in little bits here and there, and then more towards the end. The movie is about these deviant characters that are after the fountain of youth, but what they find is evil. It's pure evil! (laughs)

RA: Looking back over your career, what would you say has been your favorite project?

DL: Let's see. I have a couple favorites. One of my favorites is on my YouTube channel. It's a short film called *Kissing Time*, in black and white. It was a student film from 1993 or something like that. That has got to be my favorite. It's so beautiful. It won the award that year for best film and director at UCLA and won the Jack Nicholson award and was featured on the show Fine Cut. I also really liked working with Katt Shea on *Stripped to Kill II*. She was just an amazing director to work for. Another one was *Planes, Trains and Automobiles*. I mean, how can you beat that? How can you beat working with John Candy and Steve Martin and getting to improv a scene with them? I would say it doesn't get better than that, but it would be better if I was still in the film, so I guess it could get better than that (laughs). Another one that I really enjoyed was *The Invisible Maniac*. It is so funny and it was so much fun to work on. The whole movie is really funny and still makes me laugh. That may be my favorite, in fact.

RA: If you had anything you could say to the fans out there, what would you say?

DL: When people say that they owe it all to the fans, I say, well of course they do. It's true. I do owe it all to my fans. I got out of acting for a while and was just working a 9-5 job and was getting kind of depressed. I had done quite a few psychic readings early in the nineties and decided to do that again and my friend suggested getting on Facebook to promote myself. Well, once I got on there, I started getting all of these fans who recognized me and remembered me for my movies and they started sending me all of these messages telling me how much they loved my work and asking if I would be doing more work. When I say, I owe it all to my fans, I literally mean that I owe it all to the fans. If I hadn't have gotten on Facebook and received that kind of a welcoming and response from all of these people, who had grown up watching these movies, I wouldn't be where I am now. Many of these people that grew up as fans are filmmakers now and have sent me scripts and wanted me to be in their movies, so I finally started to do films again, so I do literally owe it all to my fans. I have the best fans, they are all such great people, and many of them have become good friends. It's amazing. I'm really excited for what the future holds.

(Author's note: You can find out more about Debra and her current projects by visiting her on the net on these websites: The official Debra Lamb/Lamblight website: **thedebralamb.com** or at Debra's Psychic page: **debralambpsychic.com)**

ELAINE WILKES
(KILLER PARTY)

RA: How did you get into the acting industry? Can you tell me some of the steps that you took?

EW: I always tell people that want to get into the acting business, that it's all in how you think. People think that it's so hard to get started in LA, but it's really a state of mind. I would just visualize getting work and believe in myself, so I would get work. I started in commercials and then I got into acting after that. Everything just all kind of fell into place for me.

RA: One of your first acting roles was in *Sixteen Candles*. It's a big way to start off a career! Tell me about your time making that film.

EW: Oh yes. It was a little film. Who would have known that it went on to become so well known? John Hughes was the most awesome director ever. I just had one line where I was supposed to say, "what is it?", and cut her hair. He came up with the idea to do more and have the fur coats on. We improvised the whole thing, and John had me pretend to be drunk and crawl into the scene. We just improvised it. There was something that was so magical about John Hughes and what he did. He would make you feel so comfortable and he was so creative. You would forget that you were working. He would yell "Cut!" and you would forget it was a movie. People will still come up to me and ask me about that scene. It was really fun and just an amazing experience. I loved John Hughes.

RA: You played a role in a movie that dealt with real life horror, about serial killer Ted Bundy (who Mark Harmon played to perfection), *The Deliberate Stranger*. Can you share your thoughts on working on that subject? Were you uneasy about it?

EW: It's interesting because each set is always a different experience. That set was really serious. Mark Harmon was a very nice person, very sweet and very professional. It was one of those things that was just done very fast. My part was done in just a few days. It was very straight forward. It's interesting, sometimes you go to an audition and you think you nailed it, while other times you think you did terrible. I thought I blew it and I was so bummed out that I wouldn't get the job, but then they called me and told me I got the job. You never know! Sometimes you think you did a great job and they never call you back, but other times you think you did a horrible job and you get it. Go figure. (laughs)

KILLER PARTY

RA: This is one of my favorite guilty pleasures of the slasher world. It's a fun movie all around and very underrated, in my opinion. How did you get involved on this film, and what was your audition like?

EW: You know, it's funny. I don't really remember auditioning for that one much. I really think that what won me the part is that I visualized myself getting the part and working on it. I think that if you can really believe in yourself and visualize yourself doing it, it gives you an advantage over the others auditioning for it. I think that wins you the part more than anything, because there's something about having that confidence. I mentally prepared for getting the job. I think that's what helped me land the jobs over the years. Another thing is that I really liked auditioning. I think that if you really enjoy it and people see you having genuine fun, I think you've got a chance to get booked. I think that I just really enjoyed the process and wasn't like, "Oh my God, I have to get this part!" I would just go have fun. If I get the job, great. I think that's why I got the part.

RA: What are some of your favorite memories of filming *Killer Party*?

EW: I really liked it. I have such good memories of filming there. We all got along great and it was fun being in Canada. We were all put up and transported in to one spot, therefore, we were all kind of in the same boat. When you film in LA, you all go home afterward and don't get as close. We were all in the hotel together and we all got along really well. It was such a lovely time.

RA: I love that the movie has such a funny vibe running through it and that a lot of the jokes still work to this day. Was there a lot of fun and shenanigans to be had on the set?

EW: Oh yes, totally. Although sometimes I think that the director would take it out. I would be like, "No, it's great! Why not leave it in?" I remember there was one time that I tripped and fell. He said we have to go back and do it again, and I thought it was funny. Everyone started laughing, but he said they should take it out. But, it was just fun like that. It was a very easy time. There was really no pressure. What was really funny is that they kept changing the script all the time. For example, one time they said that all my friends have died in a scene and I'm supposed to be looking at them. When you shoot, they'll tell you what you're looking at, but you're really just looking at a blank wall. They would tell you what you're supposed to be looking at, but really, you're looking at nothing. Sometimes you wouldn't know what you were looking at until you watch it later. It's like when we would walk into the bathroom and we're supposed to see a dead body and react, but really, we were just looking at a bathroom. They did that scene and I was crying, then they cut that part out, so when you watch the movie now, you're like "what is she crying about?" I was crying about a part that was totally cut out (laughs). They totally removed that part. While we were on the set, they changed parts and changed the scenes all the time. Then, after the movie was finished, more things changed. That part where I'm crying looks so ridiculous. Now, it just looks like I'm overacting for nothing (laughs).

RA: Speaking of which, I remember reading an article in *Fangoria* about *Killer Party*, years ago, and it actually showed pictures from scenes that were never even used in the final film. I know that it was heavily edited and many of the death scenes were cut out. Do you have any insight into that, or what happened?

EW: Things just kept changing. It was originally supposed to be called *April Fool's Day*, which makes no sense because it was at the beginning of school in the fall. There was already a movie coming out with that title, so they just changed it to *Killer Party* and kept changing things. I would love to see the edits that they took out. That would be really fun. That's what happens in movies, they just keep changing things and think that maybe one thing will work better than another. They also test it with people. Here in LA, you can sign up to watch movies and test them. You watch the movie for free and then you give them your feedback and they take all of that feedback to the director or producer, and they re-cut the movie, depending on what the audiences say. That could have happened. I know that it was released much later than it should have been, too.

RA: Speaking of which, I've read that there were many production problems that led to the delay of the film being released and it led to many problems down the road, which sadly caused it to be overlooked by many. Can you recall some of these problems? Did you kind of wonder what was happening with it?

EW: Oh yeah, you're correct. The thing is, as an actor, once you do something you kind of have to move on and forget about it. Sometimes things happen, like they decide not to air something. I just remember that all of a sudden, it finally came out. I don't know all of the things that happened with it or why, but they changed a lot of things. I think they changed companies and there were a lot of things going on afterwards. That's really the business of the movies though. It happens a lot. It doesn't always go so smoothly. I really don't know what happened, but it's interesting to see how it turned out.

RA: What do you remember about working with Paul Bartel?

EW: Just a lovely person. He was so nice and such a wonderful actor.

RA: SPOILER ALERT! You got to be one of the lucky ones to play the killer in the movie, and it led to some very interesting moments in the last half. The movie really did a complete 360. Tell me what it was like playing that part, when you're possessed?

EW: Yeah, I remember that night very clearly. They had to put these contacts in my eyes and the person that would do it would push their finger toward my eyes and every time that they would do it, I would flinch and blink my eyes. They would tell me not to blink, but it was hard when you see this big finger coming at your eye. It was so hard to get those contacts in. Back then, they were hard and they hurt to put in. I remember we would shoot at nights for that and we would go until like five in the morning. I remember crying and shaking from being up so long and eating all of this candy to try and stay up for those scenes. It was one of those things we did towards the end, and we kind of just decided to have her look all disheveled and just stare like that. It was really fun to do.

RA: Looking back, what are your favorite memories of working on *Killer Party*?

EW: I think just being with everyone. It felt like a family and I felt very comfortable with everyone. Everyone just seemed to be helping each other on the set. There was no awkwardness or ego there. I remember laughing a lot, and all of going back to the hotel after shooting and hanging out. It was nice weather and we just explored Toronto. It was a nice time all around. We all liked each other and it came through on the screen. We all really looked like friends.

RA: If you could say anything special to the fans out there, what would you say?

EW: I think it's so lovely that they enjoy the movie. I'm happy that they enjoy it and it makes me very happy. I've had people tell me how many times they've seen it or that they do certain lines or characteristics that some of the characters do in the movie because they like it so much. I think that's awesome. I realize more and more how important it is to entertain people. I will be working at the hospital and see the patients and family members watching their TVs. I'll be walking through the hospital and think, "right now, those TVs are helping people." I think it gets them out of their world for a little while. I think it's great to have that opportunity to entertain people.

HELENE UDY
(My Bloody Valentine)

My Bloody Valentine

RA: How did you get involved on the film?

HU: I had done a film called *Pick-Up Summer* with the director. So, for *My Bloody Valentine*, I just had to go in and scream as loud as I could. He just wanted to make sure that I was a good screamer because I had a lot of screaming to do. So, I passed the screaming test and the rest is history.

RA: One of the things that always stood out to me about the movie is that the location is so unique. What do you remember about the location, like the town and the mine itself?

HU: It was really a beautiful little town. It was just a really quaint little Victorian town. It was very old fashioned. We all stayed in this great old fashioned hotel that was just absolutely beautiful. We had a wonderful time. It was a real band of brothers. The whole cast was just great. It was early on in Canadian film making and we were all very new to acting and new to films. It was a very exciting time and we all took it very seriously. We were all determined to make it a great project and were very dedicated.

RA: You were involved in, what is in my mind, one of the scariest scenes in the room with all of the miner suits. What did you go through filming that scene?

HU: That was very exciting. I was a young actor and I was a real method actor, so I was doing my best to scare myself and it was a very emotional day for me because I spent the whole day trying to scare myself. It was really fun and very realistic. The coats came down and I just … well, screamed as loud as I could.

RA: You talk about making yourself scared for that. What was it you used in particular to do that?

HU: It wasn't really anything in general. It was just putting yourself in the situation and getting emotional. There was really no trick to it, just trying to be in the moment and conjure up that emotion. It really was kind of spooky, Honestly, I love to be in horror movies, I just don't like to see them.

RA: Not a big fan of horror movies?

HU: No, I don't like to be scared watching them. It's better to be scared in the movies than watching them for me.

RA: Your death scene on *My Bloody Valentine* was one of the more intense, honestly. What went into making it happen and the affects you had to go through with it?

HU: I took a plane out to Los Angeles and went to a very, very big special effects company. They had just been doing special effects for David Bowie in *The Man Who Fell to Earth* and then they were doing me next. They had just spent the day with Bowie previous to me. It was a really exciting time for me, getting to take a plane to Los Angeles and they put me up in a hotel and brought me to a studio and then they wrapped me up in a kind of cloth and created a mold, then the rest they built. It was really great.

RA: What was Peter Cowper, The Miner, like when he was in full costume?

HU: Peter was really great to work with. He had to lift me up so many times. Even though I was not that heavy, still, lifting me so many times repeatedly by the elbows like he did, couldn't have been easy. He was just a great guy. He's a massage therapist now. He was the furthest thing from a killer, just a very kind, thoughtful, tenderhearted and careful person. He was very, very careful with me. He was very good at it.

RA: Did the shooting of the movie take a long time?

HU: Relative to nowadays, no. We didn't have a long time to shoot it. I think we had about fourteen days to shoot the movie, I can't remember. In terms of that kind of movie now, we had no time at all. We still did manage to do multiple takes. It was a thing of precision and everything had to work properly in order for it to look good.

RA: The other person I wanted to ask about, who is unfortunately no longer with us is Keith Knight. What was he like?

HU: Such a lovely guy. Just a nice guy, really. He was very embracing of people and soft spoken. He had a great sense of humor and a bit of quietness to him. He was just a really stable person and a very nice guy. It's very sad that he died so young. He was a very good actor and very well trained and very dedicated.

RA: Did you get to any of the other death scenes take place?

HU: No, I didn't really. We weren't really invited on set when it wasn't our turn. I never even really got down in the mine. My death scene was actually shot in some kind of a warehouse. I think they really tried to limit the amount of people going down there into the mine, trying to limit the people put in danger.

RA: Do you still keep in contacting with any of your co-stars from the movie?

HU: I do. Lori Hallier and I are good friends and I'm going to be staying with her soon when I travel back home. I have a love for everybody from it. I have a love for Alf and Rob and Carl and Neil and Tom. Cynthia Dale I haven't seen much of. She's kind of extricated herself from the group. I've never seen her at a convention, but I do have fond memories of her. She's a lovely person. Paul is lovely too and I do keep in touch with him.

RA: How do you view these movies you were in now?

HU: I view them with much fondness because they're part of my personal history.

PIN

RA: What are your memories of working on *PIN*?

HU: It was wonderful as well, Sandor Stern was a wonderful director. That movie was more character driven. It was a small cast. I remember the lead actor David Hewlett was very special, a wonderful actor. Canadians take the work very seriously because we don't get as much of it as Americans do and don't get chances at leads very often, so we handle it with care. It was a really enjoyable experience all around and everybody was great.

RA: It's a very unique film too and very psychological.

HU: Yeah, it's very creepy. It's such a good movie.

RA: The Doll in it in itself was very creepy. What do you remember of working with that?

HU: I don't recall doing much with it. It was David that killed me, not the doll. I remember seeing it. It was like a man-sized mannequin. I didn't really have to deal much with it, though.

The Dead Zone

RA: How did you get involved on the movie?

HU: I was doing a Soap Opera in New York and I sent them a videotape audition. The casting directors already knew me pretty well. They were Canadian casting directors.

RA: What was it like working on *The Dead Zone*?

HU: Oh, it was lots and lots of fun. I was really honored. The closest I got to Christopher Walken was when he was getting his makeup done while I was getting mine done in the trailer. That was very exciting. It was a great experience. It was a beautiful set and it felt very real.

RA: What projects are you currently working on?

HU: I'm actually doing a lot of comedy right now. I have a comedy show called Vas Is Das? that we do in Los Angeles once a month at a place called The Three Of Clubs, which is a wonderful venue. It's very odd comedy. There's clowns and cabaret, and there's storytelling and puppets. It's my biggest focus right now. I've also done two movies recently with David Decoteau, who is a wonderful horror director in his own right. He is very prolific and it's amazing what he can do with the money. I'm just very grateful to work with him.

RA: Do you have a final message to the fans out there of these films?

HU: Thanks for keeping them alive all these years. It's great to hear from people.

HOWARD BUSGANG
(KILLER PARTY, TERROR TRAIN)

RA: How did you get involved on *Terror Train*?

HB: It's funny. It was a very big deal for me and I was very excited to do it. I was a comic for many years. I got it from being a comic. The makers came to see me perform at a comedy club in Montreal. They saw my stand-up routine. I don't remember my audition, but I remember that's how I got the job. What was ironic about the whole thing was the part that I was in, which was at the beginning of the movie, they shot last. So, when I finally showed up to film, everybody was kind of at the end of their rope. They're already thinking about wrapping up and here I am going like "All right! Let's do this!" So, here was this young kid, so excited to be making a movie, and by then they were all tired and exhausted from too much partying and shooting. Also, the scene at the beginning of the film was all shot outdoors, so we shot outdoors in Montreal just before Christmas. So, it was freezing! But, for me it was so exciting, but for everyone else, they pretty much just wanted it to be over (laughs).

RA: So, from the sounds of it, it seems like your character of Ed was pretty close to home then.

HB: Yeah, they just wanted me to put some stupid jokes in. The jokes are kind of lame, but I just did some of my own shtick. It's nothing from my act, but just things that I put in that I figured the class clown would be doing. So, I wrote those lines and used them. Trust me, it's not *Gone with The Wind*, but that's what they were looking for. I was just this class clown who dies first. I think that's my claim to fame in that movie is that I'm the first one to go (laughs).

RA: Yeah (laughs). You know what's funny? I was working on lists for this book and I have you listed as one my top comic relief characters. I thought Ed was very funny.

HB: Oh wow, thank you. Yeah, Ed Rubinske was my character. I had a lot of fun. When I came in, I was really impressed by the quality of the cast. To film in Montreal, there had been a lot of things filmed of a really dubious quality, but this one had a really great cast and a great director and crew. Jamie Lee Curtis was in it, Ben Johnson was in it. I got to know Hart Bochner a bit. When I got to LA, I hung out with him a little bit. He was a great guy. I'm really not in touch with any of them now. It's funny, a buddy of mine was working sound engineering and not too long ago, he recorded the director Roger Spottiswoode recording commentary for a Blu-Ray release recently.

RA: Cool! What was it like working with David Copperfield? It's interesting that he's in it and I think may be the only movie that he did.

HB: I really didn't have much of a chance to interact with him. I had the one scene with him where I joked about him making my girlfriend disappear and he kind of shrugged me off (laughs). But it was a big deal to me. He was a star, even in those days.
(Howard is looking up all of his co-stars on the film and seeing what they're up to now. He mentions that Sandee Currie has since passed away and asks about Hart's recent work)

RA: I actually mentioned Hart in my last book and said that he was so good at being an asshole in this and that he played another great asshole in *Die Hard*.

HB: Oh yeah, and he definitely was an asshole in this. He had that vibe, but in hanging out, he was actually a really nice guy. He was a good guy to hang out with and he was very welcoming to me. I have some very fond memories of Hart. But, again like I said before, I was in there late in the filming. I went in and did my part and then I remember that they called me back about three months later. They needed a pick-up shot of somebody taking the mask from me. They had to go find some train tracks that we could shoot on, so we went to Vermont. It was just me and a small crew. We were there for a couple of days at some train museum. There we shot the insert where I've been harpooned and I'm lying on the track and the killer takes my mask. They were just missing that moment that connected the killer from taking my mask.

RA: What do you remember about working with Jamie Lee Curtis?

HB: I don't know if we had a scene together. I do remember that because I came in so late, they didn't have a dressing room for me, so I remember using her dressing room. I said to myself, "Oh my God, I'm undressing in front of Jamie Lee Curtis". (laughs) I just remember thinking, oh well, she can see my underwear, no big deal I guess. I didn't get to know her that well. I just know that everyone else had so much fun on it and there was so much partying going on, but I missed all of it! I feel like that's the story of my life (laughs).

RA: You were in the opening bonfire scene if I can remember correctly, right?

HB: Yes, I was there too. Again, we were shooting outside and my biggest memory of that is just how cold it was and trying not to die. I think was the coldest winter we had on record. It was all right before Christmas, so the rush was on to get it all done by Christmas.

RA: Another slasher movie that you were in, that I would like to talk about is _Killer Party_

HB: (laughs) Oh my God yes, _Killer Party_. Yet another movie that I get killed in. It seems that they killed me in every movie. I think if they weren't going to kill me before, once they saw me acting, they would decide to kill me later (laughs). _Killer Party_ was fun too. I think that with these things for every actor, the idea that you get to die is fantastic. Having a harpoon shoved up your ass through your head is also quite the thing to have on your resume. I'm sure my wife would like to recreate that moment.

RA: (laughs) Oh my God, that's great. Yeah, with that death, it was kind of hard to tell what had happened with how badly the movie was edited and the deaths were cut.

HB: Yeah, that was a movie that frankly had a great director on it, in a sense that he was a well-respected guy at the time and had done quite a bit of television. But, you can tell with the cast that it didn't quite have the lineage of _Terror Train_ obviously. It was fun though. We shot that in Toronto. I think that yes, they did a lot of editing to it. I don't think that it had the budget behind it to go back and re-shoot things. As for the kill, I don't know exactly it worked. I know that we just had these harpoons shoved up our butts, me and Jason Warren. We were just known as The Bee Boys.

RA: Yeah! That was odd to me too, that you're just credited as that. I mean, that was just one part of the movie and you had other scenes. Did you guys even get character names in the script or were you just called that?

HB: You know, that's kind of funny. I can't really recall, but that's a good question. I will have to ask someone. I'm still friends with Jeff Pustil. I know that he married Terri Hawkes, who in the movie, too. Honestly, it was not the most memorable film, but we all know that. I think that it was fun and that it was an interesting way to die. I mean, we were sitting on a grate and we get these harpoons shoved up our asses and through our heads. I think that would be the best thing that could be said about that movie for me (laughs).

RA: You know, I also like the part where you guys do the prank on the girls by releasing the bees and your frat brothers lifted you up and carried you.

HB: I do remember that. I don't remember them lifting me up, but I do remember the prank. I remember reading that part and it just said, "a bunch of horny frat guys dump bees in the back yard while the sorority girls are in the hot tub". (laughs) I think that's all that needs to be said.

(Howard is looking up co-stars from *Killer Party* now)

HB: Oh, that's right! Paul Bartel was in that!

RA: Yeah, he was! He was another great actor. How was he to work with?

HB: He was great. He was obviously already pretty well known for a lot of the quirky stuff that he did. You don't ever forget a guy like that. He was a real character and it was a real honor to work with him. I just liked the fact that he was in that movie.

RA: Me too. I'll admit, it's not the best movie in the world, but it is an interesting movie. I remember reading that they had a lot of production issues with it. Were you aware of any of that?

HB: I wasn't aware of any of that. You know, Jeff may be the man to talk to about it. Honestly, nobody has ever asked me about this movie before (laughs).

RA: Cool, I'm the first! Was that actually filmed at a college campus?

HB: Yeah, that was filmed at the University of Toronto, which is very cool. I don't think that the house itself was on the campus, but I think it was very close. It was in an area called The Annex, sort of the student housing area.

RA: Cool, I wanted to move on to a couple of other things that you did apart from the slasher thing. I wanted to ask about your work as a television writer.

HB: Yeah. When I did all of these films and acted, I was a stand-up comic. I came right out of the university and became a stand-up comic. I worked right up until about 2000 as a stand-up comic, but in the early nineties, I transitioned from acting to writing. I became a writer and the longest one that I did was *Boy Meets World.* I did that for four years and rose up the ranks and eventually became Executive Producer for that show. Then, when I left that I did a series of less memorable shows, but have made a decent living and that's how I'm making my living now. I've worked in Canada a lot and created a bunch of shows up there. The show that I'm best known for there is a show called *The Tournament,* which was a mockumentary about a kid's hockey team, but it was really more about the parents. In the world of hockey, it's one of those things that has become a cult classic and something I'm very proud of. Parents who are into hockey all know about this show. Not long ago, I had a friend invite me to a hockey arena in Burbank and he introduced me to a lot of the people there. You should have seen the smiles on their faces. It was crazy, that this was in Burbank, far away from Montreal, where we shot it. Just seeing those smiles is one of those things where you know that you worked to make a difference and that people do see it and it affects them. One guy even showed me his jacket that had Barry embroidered on it after the lead character in the show Barry. That was very cool to see. It's what I'm most well-known for and one that's been a great part of my life. I'm very proud of it.

RA: What was your experience working on *Boy Meets World* like?

HB: Well, that was a great experience. I learned how to make TV from that show and from working with the creative team and Michael Jacobs. It was a good team of people and again, we created a show that really resonated deeply with kids of that generation.

RA: Are you involved in the follow-up to the show that's on now?

HB: No, I didn't take part in that. I've been working on some of my own projects lately.

RA: What are you currently working on?

HB: Well, I'm doing a few things. I'm writing a pilot for Disney right now, and two for networks in Canada. Most of my work has been in Canada.

RA: (reading) *Single White Spenny* ... Is that the guy from *Kenny vs. Spenny*? (Canadian cult classic comedy show) Oh, it is! I remember watching that show a lot when I was wrestling up in Canada years ago.

HB: Oh yeah? Yeah, they were crazy. When that show went off the air, the network in Canada gave each of them their own show. I got Spenny (laughs). Neither of them lasted. I think that the real magic with these guys was them working together. We did six episodes of it, but I think that nobody really wanted to see Spenny act. They just wanted to see Spenny humiliated.

RA: Looking back on some of these early slasher films, how do you view them now?

HB: I find it incredibly fascinating that anybody would care, honestly, but on the other hand, it's a life moment for me. It's realizing that whatever you do, these things get out there and the people do care. It matters to people and it has an effect on them. If it inspires somebody or somebody got some kind of enjoyment out of the films, the fact that there is a feedback is amazing. I'm glad to have been a part of it. I wish I could have done more, but there's still more to come.

RA: Along those lines, if you had anything you could say to the fans, what would you say?

HB: I wouldn't have had the opportunity for these great experiences if it wasn't for the fans, so I appreciate everybody's appreciation so much and with all my heart. It's fantastic to know that there are people out there who really treasure these films. When we made it, we treasured all of those moments too. As long as they're watching, people will still be making these films. I want to give a great big hug to every single person that has ever watched *Terror Train*.

JACK SHOLDER
(Director of Alone in The Dark, A Nightmare on Elm Street 2)

RA: How did you come to be involved in the film business?

JS: When I was in High School, I wanted to be a musician. I was a very serious trumpet player. At a certain point, I realized that wasn't going to be the right thing for me to do. I was very good, but somewhere out there, there was someone who was better. It's like being the best golfer in town, then you run into Tiger Woods. So, I decided that I had some other options and that I would become a writer, but then I decided that I really didn't like writing, although ironically, I've written several screenplays. Then, I was studying at The University of Edinburgh, where I had a girlfriend who really loved film. I started watching these films and thought I could do that, be a film director. It was kind of a crazy idea. That's basically what I did. I went back to school at Antioch College, a liberal arts college in Ohio. At that point, nobody had film programs unless you went someplace like NYU or USC. So, I just started making films on my own without any knowledge of what I was doing. Then, I moved to New York where I started working as a film editor. Soon after, I got introduced to the head of a small film distribution company that just started called New Line Cinema. I met the owner and he asked if he knew anybody that could edit trailers and I said, "Me." He said okay and hired me to edit a trailer for him. We soon became best friends. I tried counting once, I think I edited about eighty movie trailers during that time. I cut trailers for the *Street Fighter* films, for *The Evil Dead*, and a lot of other ones. It was a really good way to learn how to do different films like horror and action, so I learned a lot by doing that. Anytime that they needed anything done with a film, they would always call me. Bob Shaye always liked to get other people's opinions about stuff. Whenever they would have a film, they would screen it and usually invite me and ask me what I thought. Then, eventually New Line grew and they decided to start producing their own films, rather than just distributing them. They said that they would specialize in the college age market and said that they knew the youth market. We were sitting around one night and they said that if they could make a low budget horror film, they could make a ton of money. This was right around the time of the slasher craze. So, I thought about it and I came up with an idea. They said okay and that they'll pay me to write it, and if they liked it, they would hire me to direct it. So, I came up with the idea and wrote the screenplay for *Alone in The Dark*. Nothing happened, then I got hired by the Weinstein brothers to edit their first film, *The Burning*. I learned a lot about how horror films work from that and I went back and re-wrote a lot of *Alone in The Dark*. New Line would raise the money and that was my first feature.

RA: What was the inspiration for the story that became *Alone in The Dark*?

JS: In retrospect, it was M, the Fritz Lang movie. I had been talking with a friend and we came up with this idea. There had been a blackout in New York a few years prior to that, and parts of Manhattan, including the part that I lived in, had no power for about three days. There had also been other places where blackouts would happen and there would be riots and looting. It was this whole breakdown of society. Everyone was doing these antisocial acts when as soon as something that we took for granted like electricity went out, it seemed like everyone kind of gave up on their idea of social contract. So, I thought that was kind of an interesting idea. I didn't think much about it at the time, but this and many of my other films all seemed to have a social commentary. So, the idea was that a bunch of homicidal maniacs escape from a mental institution during a blackout and they would terrorize Little Italy before they're rounded up by the mafia, which was sort of along the lines of *M*. That was the original idea, but then New Line said that it's too expensive to shoot it in New York, so they told me to come up with something else aside from the mafia and New York. So, I took the idea of the blackout and the guys escaping during it and kept that. There was a famous psychiatrist at the time, by the name of RD Lang, who had a mental institution in Scotland. His idea was that there are no crazy people, but that they have simply adapted to a crazy world, and that you should not treat them like they're crazy and if you treat them like they're normal, they would get better. So, I worked that in, where the guy that runs the mental institution has that philosophy, that eventually gets him killed, so there was a certain amount of irony there. That was all the stuff that kind of fed into the story. I loved the irony that they would lay siege to their psychiatrist's house, because they mistakenly believe that he killed their previous doctor. When they find out that's not the case of course, they say, oh well, never mind. (laughs) So, there was a lot of irony and a lot of social commentary about what's normal and what's not. So, wrapped up in this film, there's a lot of ideas that I was trying to deal with, within that format.

RA: Did you already have certain people in mind to play the roles when it came about? How did the casting come about?

JS: Well, Palance and Landau I guess were at a point in their careers where they would do anything to make a buck. (laughs) So, we were able to get them for not that much money. The producer asked me at one point, "How would you like to have Jack Palance in the movie?", and I said, "Wow! That would be fantastic." Then, apparently, Landau's agent called us and solicited the role for him. Then, someone said that we could get Donald Pleasence to play the psychiatrist. For me, Donald Pleasence was one of the greatest actors in the world, so I was the most excited about working with him. I had been a huge fan of his for years. I was just thrilled to get him.

RA: Yeah, he truly is one of the greatest, and I must say, even though he is more well known for playing Dr. Loomis on *Halloween*, I still think that his role in *Alone in The Dark* was his best. He was just phenomenal in it.

JS: Oh yes, he was fantastic. I was a little nervous about working with him. I think that the first day, we shot some stuff out on a road. It was just some driving things and we didn't really have any of the main actors there. In fact, it was a low budget, non-union production. We had a union cameraman who was shooting outside of the union, which you're not supposed to do, and we were shooting somewhere out in the wilds of New Jersey. We showed up and there was a bunch of union guys standing there, so that made a lot of the crew nervous. (laughs) On day two, we started at the mental institution with Pleasence. I was pretty nervous, this being my first feature and here I was working with this actor who I have always had this enormous admiration for. We did the first scene and ran it through, and my mind was completely blank. I had no idea what had just happened. So, I called for us to run it through again afterward and that time I was actually able to focus on what was happening. I gave him a note on something to change and he said okay, so I thought, "Wow, this is going pretty good. I'm directing Donald Pleasence. I ask him to do something and he does it." So, it wasn't bad, and that's how we got started.

Then, there's that scene where he first meets Dr. Potter and he's smoking a hookah. I had planned everything out, every bit of staging, every shot that I was going to do. I planned it all out meticulously. Partly that was out of fear. If I were to walk out there and not know what to do, I could just look at this piece of paper and go okay. I had this whole elaborate thing: on this line, he walks over to the window, on this line he sits down, on this line he does this. I had this whole complicated scene completely worked out and we rehearsed the scene. Then he said, "You know, I've always thought of this scene as being like the caterpillar in Alice In Wonderland, and that I should just sit on a cushion in the middle of the room smoking a hookah." So, I panicked, because it was a totally different idea that what I was setting up, but it was actually better and made it easier. So, we changed it around and basically did it the way he wanted to do it, and it worked out.

Then, the next day, Palance showed up. He was scary, you know his persona. Apparently, he had shown up the day before and met with Bob Shaye. Bob said he was very angry and told him that he didn't want to be in the movie. In between the time that we cast him and the time that he showed up, he had done a pilot for Ripley's Believe it or Not TV series and he was supposed to go to Florence. Instead, we insisted that he come to New Jersey or we would sue him (laughs). So, he wasn't happy to be there. It was a low budget horror film for a company that nobody had ever heard of, with a director that nobody had ever heard of. He wasn't a happy camper, so that was pretty scary. Also, we were walking down the street and somebody said, "Hey, aren't you Jack Palance?" and he almost punched the guy. I almost had an anxiety attack.

Then, I had to meet Martin Landau that evening for dinner. I'm normally a very good eater, but I ended up ordering consommé. I was so nervous, that was the only thing I could keep down. Landau told me that he had worked with Palance before, and they did a stunt where he was supposed to hit a guy with a lead pipe. They gave him a fake one and Jack said, "I don't want to use this, I want to use a real one!" He convinced them that it would be better and that he would come close, but miss. They asked the other guy and he said he was okay with it, so they did the scene and Palance ended up cracking the guy's head open! So, I thought long and hard about it that night and I woke up the next day and said, "I'm the fucking director. It's my film and nobody's gonna push me around." So, I came in with that attitude. We shot in the morning and Palance was scheduled to do the walk and talk scene when he first meets Dr. Potter and they're walking through the grounds of the mental hospital. He told us that he couldn't possibly do that scene. He said that nobody had told him about it, and he had a hard time memorizing it and so forth. In the evening, we were supposed to shoot the scene where they escape from the hospital and steal a car. He was supposed to kill the guy and said that he didn't want to, because he doesn't believe in violence. So, that was the day's work there and we had to shoot the dialogue scene because it was our only chance to shoot it. I told him that we could do it later in the afternoon so that he had time to work on his lines, and if we had to break it up into smaller pieces, we could do that, too. I told him we'll just focus on that scene and talk about the escape scene after that. So, we set up for the dialogue scene after lunch and he did it. If you see the film, he's fantastic (I agree). I was blown away, and I told him that it was really good. He just looked at me and said, "Ah, you're full of shit." That was his way of saying thank you. (laughs) We met again later on after the afternoon filming had wrapped, before the night scenes, and by that point, he was a lot more cordial. He was a big opera fan and I knew a bit about opera, so we were able to talk about that a little bit and he was more relaxed.

I told him, "You've been in the business a long time. Why can't you do the part where you kill the guy and take the car?", and he said, "Why, what's the point?" I told him that we need to know that his character is capable of murder. He just looked at me with that intense face of his and said, "They'll know." (Laughs) So, I thought about it and came to the conclusion that he's right. You just have to look at him and you know he's capable of murder. He suggested having the fat guy kill him, so that's what we did.

RA: Yep! It's funny that you mention that, because from watching the movie, you can tell that he's capable, but he plays more of a ringleader and seems to have Martin Landau and Erland Van Lith do the dirty work for him.

JS: Right! That was also a great lesson in filmmaking for me. Like we had a line in the script where someone says that Erland, or Fatty, is very powerful. You didn't need to say that, you just look at the guy and know. You don't need to say that he's capable of murder, you just look at him. That's the beauty of film, you don't have to explain those things. I actually learned a lot working with him. It was a great privilege, particularly on my first film, to work with people who had that experience and knowledge and who were also such great actors.

RA: One of the most interesting characters to me is The Bleeder. It's a very interesting coincidence that this was the same year that Jason got his hockey mask in *Friday the 13th* and he wears the mask as well. Can you tell me a little bit about that character and where that idea came from?

JS: Bob Shaye had this idea that we should have a character who we wouldn't know who he was, and then later we would find out. That's where the idea for The Bleeder came in. If you notice, we never really see his face, and then at one point he seems to be a normal guy who gets inside the house and gets close to the family, then at one point, he goes crazy. The hockey mask was another way to hide his face during the shopping center looting scene. The whole shopping center scene one of those great moments. The lights and the power go out and now, you have all of these normally law abiding citizens taking to crime and the world goes crazy, and of course the crazy people fit right in. Nobody even notices.

RA: How did the band The Sic Fucks come into the picture?

JS: Well, I had written in a band. One day, the producer came in and said he found this band called The Sic Fucks and that they should be in the movie. He had a tape from them, and they had a song on it called *Chop Up Your Mother* (laughs), which seemed to be a good fit for the film. They were pretty ironic themselves and it all appealed to me. They showed up and I met them. The girls were dressed like trashy nuns, and it just seemed like a perfect fit, so I said yeah, by all means.

RA: (I relay the legendary story of the singer of The Sick Fucks running into Jack Palance years later, where he tells Jack that he was in the film with him, as one of the Sic Fucks, to which Palance replied, "We were all sick fucks in that movie.")

JS: (laughs)That's funny, I never heard that. I actually have a picture of Jack from the set that he signed for me, that had a funny inscription on it. (he starts looking through some things, trying to find the picture) Here it is. "Jack, it wasn't funny, but it was fun."

RA: (laughs) That's awesome

JS: Yeah. It was a real thrill for me to work with him. I actually ended up doing two more films with Landau, he became sort of a mentor to me. He was a really nice guy. It was a very difficult shoot. It was mostly nights and, in fact, somebody had told Palance that there would be no night shooting. I think it was the producer. Yeah, on a film called *Alone in the Dark*, there would be no night shooting. (laughs) I think on his second day, we shot the scene in the club. We started at like 4 in the afternoon and ended at about 7 the next morning, so again, he was not a happy camper.

RA: I can imagine! Now, after *Alone in the Dark*, you went on to direct *Nightmare on Elm Street Part 2*. I know many fans go back and forth on this one, they like it or they don't. I had to go back and do a second take on it. I came to realize that it's unique take on the series and not the norm of what we are used to from Freddy, and I have come to respect the fact that it is so different from the rest of the franchise.

JS: Thank you. Well, at that point, we have to remember that there was no franchise yet. They were just trying to squeeze a little bit more money out of the film. Back then, we had a whole different view on sequels that what we have now. Now, you have a hit film and you rush out to make a sequel and expect it to make more than the original film. At that point, the idea was to make a sequel just to suck a little more money out of the first film. Normally, the sequel was not as good and was not expected to be as good, and that was the expectation. The head of distribution at New Line had said that if the sequel could do eighty percent of what the original did, they would be thrilled. In the end, it actually made more money than the original. New Line really didn't know what they had. They didn't really know why it had done so well. In fact, if you look at the original poster, Freddy's not on it. You better believe

Freddy was on all of the other posters. So, why wasn't Freddy on the first poster? They didn't have much faith in it. In fact, for the second one, they didn't even want to bring Robert Englund back. It wasn't that they didn't like him, his agent just wanted more money. They felt that the agent was trying to screw them and take advantage of them. They felt they could get any old person to play the part.

Back then, they usually had anyone to play the monster, usually a stuntman, or an extra. You just needed somebody to come in and slash somebody. There wasn't much thought to that person as a character. One of the great things that Wes did was to cast a real character actor. Normally, if they were to go the way they usually went with these things, they would go for some 250-pound scary looking stuntman, as opposed to somebody like Robert Englund, who was more of a character guy. If you see him in real life, he doesn't look particularly scary, but he's a fantastic actor who brought a lot of dimension to the role. They eventually hired him and brought him back. I was telling them that he's really good at it. Eventually, they managed to work a deal out with him, but he wasn't available the first week that we shot, so the scene that we shot in the shower didn't have Robert in it. We had this extra for some of the scenes and not a very good one. I had to keep telling him to stop walking like a monster. When we finally got Robert there, it was like night and day. He just had this tremendous power about him, just the way that he moved.

I had very little input on the script. It was already there when I got there. Wes had worked on it a bit, but he didn't like it. It violated one of his key things, that Freddy only appears in your dreams. In this movie, Freddy shows up at the pool party when everyone is wide awake, so it violated his concept, but nobody gave a shit about his concept. All that they cared about was making more money off of this thing. There really was no franchise by that point, so there was no need to adhere to the mythology of the original. I was just trying to make something that I thought would work and could be reasonably scary.

RA: Of course, I have to ask about this, and I asked Mark (Patton) the same thing, about some of the hidden subtext of the film. Where did that come from exactly?

JS: (laughs) Well…basically, it never really occurred to me. I never thought about it and didn't think about it…supposedly, the writer thought about it…and he has said that, that was part of what was going through his mind at the time, but we didn't talk about it. Honestly, we didn't talk about very much. I got hired six weeks before shooting was supposed to start, and there was a huge amount of stuff to do to make this film. I got handed like seven pages of effects, none of which I had any idea how to do, so I was basically just bobbing in the water trying not to drown.

Normally I have a fair amount of input on a script, but in this case, I did not. When it came out, there was a review in the Village Voice, and they called it "The gayest horror film of all time." I actually got a call from Sarah Richard, who was in charge of production at New Line, and we both laughed at that because we both thought that it was kind of ridiculous that anyone would see it that way. None of us had ever thought about that. There was a screening last year in Denver that I went over for. I hadn't seen the film since around the time that it was made. There's been a lot of discussion about the "gay subtext". Upon viewing it again, I have to say that it's clearly there and I picked up on it. Again, there's a social commentary to that, as well, which I picked up on. I had lived in the East Village during a period where all of a sudden gay life was out in the street and in the open everywhere. That was just my life. I would walk out my door and that's what I would see. A lot of it to me was kind of funny and ironic. You would some guy dressed like Marlon Brando in *The Wild One* walking down the street with another guy who was on a leash. A lot of it kind of struck me as absurd and funny. So, it was an aspect of it and that life from living in that area that I saw in the subtext.

When they screened the film, I think that the thing that really struck me, I mean you can pick up on some of the other things, but I think the thing that really drove the point home was the casting of Mark. It's funny, it never occurred to me that he's gay and I never even thought about it. I guess you could either look at that and say I was naive, or that I was just never interested in having that discussion and I didn't care. A lot of people came in and read for that part. Someone even told me, and I want to back and see if I can find it, that Brad Pitt read for the role. It's entirely possible that he did. I saw over a hundred people, who came in and read for that role, but what I liked about Mark is that he was very vulnerable. In this film, it kind of turned the table, because the role of the victim is usually played by the girl. In this one, it's reversed and he has to be saved by the girl. It's a role reversal. Mark was playing the part that normally a female would. I never really thought that I needed someone with a feminine quality, but instinctively that's where I went. New Line went along with the casting choice and they liked him as well.

For instance, he wasn't right for the role, but if Robert Rusler had been cast in that role, I don't think that people would be so quick to call it a gay movie. But, because Mark has this feminine aspect about him, I think that that's what's part of what moves it into that sphere. You can make the argument that the same subtext is brought out in other films, but it's not brought out as much, but with Mark in that role, I think it highlights it. I think I heard the writer claim that that was part of the intent. It's funny how I never thought about it. Some are so obvious, like the S&M bar, but that was like the neighborhood bar where I was from, so it wasn't weird and I thought it was kind of funny. Bob Shaye actually plays the bartender in that scene. He wanted to be in the movie and wanted to be one of the people that got killed and he was pissed off that I wouldn't let him do it. I think he was offended that I wanted a real actor and thought he wasn't a real actor, which he's not. So, I put him in during the bar scene and I had him kiss another guy in it, some friend of his. It's amazing what people will do to be in a movie. I just did it to fuck with the guy and was just having a little bit of fun with that. (laughs)

RA: Beyond these two movies, I know that you have had quite the history in horror, with movies like *The Hidden, Wishmaster*, etc. I consider you one of the unsung heroes of the genre. In summary, I wanted to ask what are your thoughts on the horror genre as a whole, and your place in horror history?

JS: There are people who really express themselves through horror movies, and there are people who express themselves in spite of horror films. I think I fall into the latter. I was never really a big horror film fan. I used to watch the creature features when I was younger, but I was always more drawn to the artier films. Horror was never really my genre, but it was a way for me to get in and in a way, it's kind of suited me because I have a sort of anarchical view of things. I have kind of a skewed view of life and that fits very well into the genre. Plus, it is kind of fun. The gore aspect doesn't interest me at all and I'm not into that.

RA: Neither am I

JS: Yeah, I'm not into the whole coming up with creative ways to kill somebody thing. That holds very little interest for me, but it lends itself to certain kinds of stories. Like I said before, the social commentary that I'm interested in, I've been able to do within the confines of the horror genre. In films like *Alone in the Dark* and *Wishmaster*, which I wrote, I can really express a lot of the ideas that I have and there's ideas I can play around with. It's given me a way to express certain things that I might not have been able to otherwise. I think the real heart of my films, is that there's so much more going on than just the horror. That's how I like to think of it. I'm always interested in the characters. A lot of other films have characters that are very shallow and don't have much to say. For me, that was never very interesting and I like the characters to have more depth.

RA: For the last question, is there anything you would like to say to the fans out there?

JS: I think one of the things that I enjoy about the genre is that the fans are very, very loyal. I don't know what directors of other genres go through, but as a director of horror films, there is always a huge amount of enthusiasm about the genre. I certainly appreciate that. I also appreciate when people get what I'm trying to do, when it's more than just a scare and it really connects.

JACK VERBOIS
(Legendary Hollywood Stuntman, "Ben Tramer" on Halloween II)

(excerpt from a letter that I received from the veteran Hollywood stunt man Jack Verbois, where he specifically discussed his short, but significant role in *Halloween II*. This is his story of how they made the iconic scene in the film with the fake Michael Myers death.)

JV: That stunt was pretty easy on me because they let me set it up. I had done a car hit in 1976 on a TV show called *The Feather and Father Gang*. It hurt a little. The car hit me at twenty miles per hour and even though I slapped the hood to take the weight off my feet, it caught my thighs pretty good. When they showed it on TV, they left the actual hit out because they said it looked too violent. I wasn't going to waste my body again, so when Dick Warlock (Michael Myers/ Stunt Coordinator) called me for this one, I told him that I wanted a platform on front of the car, four inches off the ground. They had a camera inside the car for the hit. Dick took off from a dead stop six feet away, and I turned and I took the hit. It worked like a charm.

Later on, in the picture, I set Dick on fire in a hospital hallway. They had to bring in the fire department to put the fire out on set before the whole place went up in flames. In thirty-two years, I had many days like that. After retiring in 1997, I'm still getting around pretty well.

JAMES SHYMAN
(Writer/Director of Hollywood's New Blood/ Slashdance)

RA: How did you get involved in the film business?

JS: My background was as a television announcer for ABC in Hollywood. That was ending due to technology changes and I also had a pretty good run as a commercial actor, but I was getting older, so I started thinking of stuff to do. I looked into low budget movies. In the 80s, they were looking for new videos for the stores, to fill the shelves. I thought I'd try that and it turned out to be a rather unsuccessful venture for me.

RA: You mentioned something about working in wrestling before?

JS: Yes, my brother has been in the wrestling business for several years. I tried to entrepreneur with several things and the one thing that did work was doing a 900 number called Pro Wrestling's Hottest Hotline and that thing ran for over 20 years. 900 numbers are pretty much obsolete now, but it turned out to be a really good run. I tried the low budget movies and that didn't work too well, but the hotline was very successful. It was especially good during the pre-internet days. In the Hulk Hogan era, the wrestling was a hot commodity. It (the hotline) started in LA and ended up nationwide. Once the internet came around, it kind of did a slow nosedive into oblivion.
(we talked wrestling for quite a bit)

Hollywood's New Blood

RA: Where did the idea come from for the story?

JS: I wrote it. Blood is a lot cheaper than gun powder and explosions and everybody seemed to like to make the horror movies. I knew my way around Hollywood pretty good because I had been there a long time, so I was familiar with casting situations and pretty knowledgeable of the business.

RA: What was the process from paper to the screen on making the movie for you? Any challenges or roadblocks?
JS: This one was actually pretty easy because we just cast it, put it together, got a crew and

224

went up to Lake Arrowhead and shot it up there. It was pretty easy to cast. We put an ad in the Hollywood Reporter, so that wasn't a problem. Getting the money from the syndicators and all that, there lies the problem, getting it distributed and everything else.

RA: What inspired the look of the killers?

JS: Well, actually the concept was not that bad. The movie was, but everything else wasn't that bad. We actually had several decent actors, so some of the actors were good, but the overall product was far from great.

RA: What was your favorite scene to film?

JS: It's hard to say. When you shoot with a budget so low, you shoot ultra-fast. Who knows how many set ups you're doing in a day, just as many as you can squeeze in. We did get rained out one day and that was the non-fun part of it. You work with a lot of young people on stuff like that and they're very enthusiastic and hard working. You have so many assets in the LA area, be it on-camera or off-camera talent. Most of the people we had were pretty good.

RA: What kind of distribution went into it? It's a bit hard to come by these days, unfortunately.

JS: I was with some company, but I believe that they folded years ago. I'm surprised there's even any copies of it around anymore. I think it (the company) was called Radon, I'm not sure. It's funny, Radon is a type of poisoning, so that should have been a hint right there. I'm probably glad they're not around more, honestly (laughs).

Slashdance

RA: Where did the idea for *Slashdance* come from?

JS: It was just looking for another idea for a product. It was a *Flashdance* take off that was catered to the slasher market. We shot it on location in Hollywood. We found a place to shoot that was pretty good. Again, it didn't really make any money, either, so I don't have fond recollections of it. The distribution was the main challenge on this one, too.

RA: The flasher scene is one that always cracks me up.

JS: Yeah, that guy that did that weird part was a really good actor. I wonder what ever happened to him. He was very strange, but I hope he did well somewhere. He had an interesting, strange appeal to him.

RA: Now, I noticed on the movie that you used a lot of the women wrestlers of the time.

JS: Yes, we did. We used some of the GLOW girls. I knew them through various things and they were in the area. We had a few like Beastie and Queen Kong, and our lead was America. They were very nice.

RA: Talk about the choreography for the dance scenes

JS: One of the girls helped us out with that. She was a dancer in the area.

RA: How do you view the films these days?

JS: I haven't seen them probably since back when they were made. By the time they finished, it was when the 900 number came along, fortunately, because I never made much money off of these.

RA: What are you up to these days?

JS: I'm pretty much retired these days. That's fine though. I certainly had a great run and I'm very pleased. Right now, I'm just enjoying life in Northern California.

JENNIFER RUNYON-CORMAN
(TO ALL A GOODNIGHT, GHOSTBUSTERS)

RA: How did you get into acting?

JRC: I first started because my mother and her friend were so concerned at how shy I was. They put me in an acting class, just thinking that it would get me to open up. They thought that maybe it could at least get me to talk to people (laughs). I was very painfully shy. So, I was scared to death to go, but I went to the class and I thought that it was so much fun getting to watch all the people up there having fun and being someone else. It was just so interesting to me. I kept going back and I ended up being in that class four years. I really wasn't sure what I was going to do and a casting director came to our class one day to tell us about the business. He brought me in for a soap opera and I got it. (laughs) Then, I went to New York and I was on a soap opera for about three years. That's how I got started. It was kind of a fluke. I did one thing before that and that was the movie *To All a Good Night*.

RA: Cool. How did that one come about?

JRC: A friend of mine had already been cast in it. She was like another mother to me and she told the casting director that they have to see me. So, it was really my first thing. It was really low budget and non-union. I did that and I honestly never even thought it would come out.

RA: One of the interesting things about the movie is that it was directed by another horror icon, David Hess (*Last House on the Left*). What was he like to work with?

JRC: Yes, it was. I loved David. He was just great. He gave me my first opportunity and he was

227

so kind to me. He was so encouraging. I was really lost and really just a baby. He was very good to me and helped me a lot. I think he was a very talented guy.

RA: Something funny about *To All a Good Night* is that when *Silent Night, Deadly Night* came out in 1984, everyone went crazy about it, but they seem to forget that your movie and *Christmas Evil* were the first to do that.

JRC: Exactly, we had the very first Santa slasher movie. It seems like now everyone knows that. It's funny how I thought that this movie would never see the light of day and now it has such a following! It's so funny how people still message me about it all the time. I just find it funny how, as time goes by, some of these things can take on a life of their own. It's pretty cool.

RA: Do you get a lot of people that come up to you at conventions about the movie?

JRC: I've only done a few, like three in six years. It always surprises me when somebody brings up *To All a Good Night.* I keep getting asked if I have any photos from that and I'm starting to think of how I can do that.

RA: One thing I have always noticed when I watch the movie is that it's so dark, it's hard to see much of what's going on.

JRC: Have you seen the new one?

RA: No I haven't. Is there a new transfer?

JRC: Yeah, there's a new transfer. It's brand new and I did commentary for it. That was my thing when I first saw it. When I first got a VHS of it, I was like "You can't even see this thing." But, they've completely color corrected it and you actually see the movie. It's kind of amazing. It's funny, I just got invited a few months back to a comedy club that does a horrible movie night. It has a big following here in LA. They watch the movie and a lot of comics go and they shout out funny things at the screen. They invited me to come and do a Q and A after and it was the first time I had seen it on DVD and I couldn't believe how much better it looks. It's still a bad movie (laughs). I think it's one of those "so bad they're good movies" though. You've got to have a sense of humor about these things.

RA: Definitely. Another one I want to ask you about is of course the classic, *Ghostbusters.* How did you get involved on that one?

JRC: It was the typical get a call and go on an audition thing. They said that it wasn't a very big part, but I said I don't care. I mean, it's Bill Murray, come on! (laughs) So, I went and they put me on tape. Then, they had me come back and Ivan Reitman was there, as well as some of the other producers. I didn't hear anything for a really long time, so I just figured I didn't get it, but I did. I really didn't know the extent of the movie because I didn't have the script or anything. I just had the part that I read for, so I was pretty surprised when I finally saw the end result at the premiere.

RA: What was it like working with Bill Murray?

JRC: Oh, he was wonderful. It was probably the best day I ever had on a set. He just keeps it going and he makes you feel so comfortable. He's a joy to work with.

RA: Did he do a lot of improvising?

JRC: A little bit, here and there. It all worked out really well, the way that the final scene ended up.

RA: One thing I have to ask is, do you ever think that Venkman followed up with your character?

JRC: (laughs) I get asked that question a lot. I would like to say that they did, but I think he got busy with the library thing. I think she was probably waiting, but he was busy hunting ghosts (laughs).

RA: (laughs) That's great! Another one you did is *Charles In Charge,* a show you had a long run on. What was your experience like working on that show?

JRC: I had so much fun on *Charles In Charge.* Scott Baio was great and Willie Aames is one of my best friends to this day. I learned a lot from both of them and they had so much experience. They really taught me a lot about the sitcom field. I had never done a sitcom before and I think that it's my favorite genre to work. I love working in front of a live audience. I just adored everybody on that show and we just had the greatest time. It was sad when it ended. I was very surprised and I think we all thought that it would get at least one more year, but they did end up coming back with a new cast and I did a couple of episodes. I loved the new cast too.

RA: Another early movie that you did is one that I just recently saw, *Up the Creek.* Can you tell me about working on that?

JRC: It was great. I got to learn how to whitewater raft and we got to film that up in Bend, Oregon. I actually ended up living in Idaho and Oregon later in life, raising our kids, which is funny. I got to go back to Bend a lot. The cast was great, just a lot of funny guys in that movie. It was fun rafting but also a little frightening because even though we had stunt people, we did do a lot of things ourselves.

RA: Can you tell me about working on *Carnosaur?*

JRC: I was honored to be asked to work on a Roger Corman film. The pace was fast, but I was used to that from working on a soap opera. I was also five months pregnant. I kept that a secret, but it was figured out pretty quick. I really enjoyed working with Raphael Sparge. The budget was low and there were no fancy trailers. It was bare bones and I loved the experience.

RA: What was it that made you want to step away from Hollywood?

JRC: I retired from the business to raise my children. I really didn't want a nanny telling me that my child took their first steps or said their first words. Family to me is everything.

RA: How do you view your experiences now and the notoriety from *Ghostbusters?*

JRC: Being a small part of film history is amazing. I'm still amazed that people recognize me all these years later. It's pretty awesome.

RA: If you could say anything to the fans out there, what would you say?

JRC: If I could say anything to my fans, it would be Thank You. They have always treated me with such kindness. I'm humbled and honored that you all have enjoyed my work. You have no idea how much you touch my heart.

JOHN GRISMER
(Director of Blood Rage)

RA: How did you get started in the film business?

JG: A friend of mine from Graduate School, Larry Strasser, was doing a movie for Otto Preminger called *Such Good Friends.* There was a gentleman on that picture named Jean Marie Pellissie, who was from France and he wanted to make a film, so he, Larry and I teamed up to make a company called Golden Gate Films. Jean Marie had a novel that he liked that he thought would make a good movie. It was called The Golden Gate and was a murder mystery set in San Francisco. It wound up that we were never able to get the rights to it. So, Jean and I were driving around the countryside and we found this house, this big, weird looking house and we thought we should make a movie about this house and it turned into *The House That Cried Murder.* We used our Golden Gate Films company and whipped up a story and it starred Larry's wife Robin Strasser. At the time, she was a star on a soap opera. The original title was called *The Bride.* That was the first feature I made.

Blood Rage

RA: *Blood Rage* is by far one of my all-time favorite slasher films. It really sets itself apart from the rest.

JG: Yes, in a way it does. You know, my favorite quote from a review about it describes the movie as "a steaming pile of crap." (both laugh)

RA: Really?

JG: Yes! (laughing) So, everybody has their own different point of view. To me though, I thought that particular review was very funny. I still quote it to people all the time.

RA: Well, I always thought that the movie set itself apart from the rest because there's a lot of heart to it.

JG: That's a very interesting thing that you should say. I think, in a way, I understand what you're saying. There really was a lot of heart in it.

RA: Yeah, like there's the scene with the "good brother" taking care of the mother and some of those scenes

JG: Yeah, well that's actually my favorite scene, when he puts her to bed, and she says, "Maybe Todd has gone far, far away". Of course, she's totally mistaken of which brother is which all the way through. It's really a tender scene and the music works well into that. I think it's a heartfelt scene. That's my favorite scene in the whole film.

RA: Mine too

JG: It's very emotional. It's him dealing with his mother and his mother is totally screwed up in her perception of him and it's sad. It's really sad.

RA: It is. What was it that made you get involved on *Blood Rage*?

JG: I was hired by Marianne Kanter, the producer of it. She saw *Scalpel* and she saw in *Scalpel* that I dealt with two characters that looked alike and that's what was going on with her film. She met with Joe Weintraub and through him, she called me up and asked me to come in for a meeting. We had a lot of meetings talking about it before she decided she wanted to have me direct it. She was very intellectually astute about her planning of that script. The script was her doing. She hired Bruce Rubin to write it, but everything in that script is from her. She wanted it the way she wanted it. She was the boss of it and she got what she wanted. She knew exactly what she wanted. She wanted nudity, she wanted a lot of blood, she wanted to make a horror film and make money on it. We spent a lot of time looking at other slasher films. We looked and we noted things. We looked at *Halloween* and *Friday the 13th*, and everything else like that over and over again.

RA: How did you feel about making a slasher film?

JG: I felt it was a job and I was lucky to get hired to do it. Now, I wasn't emotionally wrapped up in it. There's a quote from famous director John Ford where he said, "It's a job of work" and that's what it was. I tried to do the best I could. I knew exactly what she wanted and I was given an assignment, and I tried to carry it out the best I could.

RA: The ending to *Blood Rage* is by far one of the more harrowing and clever endings in slasher history. Talk about your thoughts on that, looking back.

JG: There's a quote from a critic in Chicago where he called it the "Who's on first? Of Slasher Films". I quoted that on my Facebook page. I thought it was very amusing. It was because Annie, the mother continually mistakes which twin is which throughout the film, even to the point of shooting the right one which she thinks is the wrong one. That's why I agree with you and think the ending is just cool. It was devised that way.

RG: I thought the ending was also very sad.

JG: Oh, of course it is. I call it "The Greek Ending". It's a Greek tragedy. The mother's face, if you notice, becomes a mask of tragedy when she realizes that she was wrong.

RA: Some of the deaths in the film are some of the other things that really stand out and I liked the effects that went into them.

JG: Mary Anne hired Ed French to do the effects. She was very careful about hiring him. We interviewed him and he showed us samples of his work. From the get go, she wanted some of those more photogenic horror deaths and they were all carefully plotted out by her.

RA: *Blood Rage* was recently released on Blu-Ray with tons of extras. Did you oversee it or get any special input?

JG: It's through Arrow Films, and run by a British gentleman who is a fan. I sat down with

Mary Anne's lawyer and him and made some comments for the disc that was released. Then I was interviewed for it, as well. It was interesting.

Scalpel

RA: Going back, the other one that I wanted to chat with you about is *Scalpel*. How did you get involved with that one?

JG: After my first film, I really liked the experience, so I next teamed up with Joe Weintraub, who was an editor and he had this story that developed into *Scalpel*. It took a lot of time and a lot of detail to develop the story and we finally had some access to some money from family and people we knew, so we went down to Georgia and made the picture.

RA: Was it an expensive movie to put together?

JG: It was about $400,000. It was done in an economical way. We paid the actors some deferments, and eventually got paid off. We did make some foreign money on the movie and were able to pay off the deferments. It went very well, but as usual when you make an independent film and you don't have a distributor, you've kind of painted yourself into a corner. It's not a good position to be in. Then you have to go out and find your own distribution and that's a whole other story. But, eventually we got it done and got it to the company known as Avco Embassy. It was a lot of work to get that done. The hardest thing about it is not in making the film, but once you've made the film, what do you do with it? How do you get it distributed? The making of it is not that hard, it's what you do with it after. We're still doing it now with Arrow films, who is working at putting it out on Blu-Ray. We're hoping to get it on Television and sold in the stores.

RA: Although it's not a horror or slasher film, but a very good film in general, I was impressed by *Scalpel*. Where did the idea behind this come from?

JG: Yes, it is. I'm very proud of it. Yes, it's more of a psychological thriller. The idea for it came from my producing partner Joe Weintraub. He knew of some kind of story that covered this situation and so we used that story premise and wrote up the script. It turns out that there is another film out there along those lines, a French film. I think the translation is something along the lines of *Mask of Blood*. It's a funny thing too, last night on CBS on a crime show, there was a story about a guy who was kidnapping people and changing their faces. A friend of mine said "Maybe you should watch this. You may have a case". So, I looked at it to see and no, there's no problem with it. It was similar in parts, but in no way a problem of copyright. It was interesting, though.

RA: It was quite funny, when my fiancé and I were watching *Scalpel*, we noticed something odd in the story. Now, the main character makes the girl look like his daughter for the inheritance, but then he starts a relationship with her. So, we looked at that and said "Okay, that's a bit messed up", I mean sleeping with a girl you made to look like your daughter. There's some deep psychological issues there

JG: Yeah, that's right! That's what he did, he was crossing a line. That really contributes to the creepiness of the movie. He had his problems. That was intentional.

RA: What are your favorite memories of making *Scalpel*?

JG: Just in general. We had a wonderful line producer and he had that thing organized beautifully. We just had a wonderful crew and it was all very organized, perfectly. It just went very smoothly. The director of photography was Ed Lachman. He was making his first feature film in that capacity and has gone on to a great career. He was up for an Oscar this year and was at The Academy Awards. I guess the Oscar went to the guy who did *The Revenant*, I believe. Ed did an excellent job on the film Carol, which he was up for. I saw it and the images were wonderful.

RA: One of the other things that I loved about *Scalpel* was the twist at the end and the main character's comeuppance.

JG: Yes, it was kind of an idea like *The Sting*.

RA: Let's talk about some of your other projects. I read that you are an author now. Tell me more about that

JG: I have one book that's out. It's called *The Ghosts of Antietam*. I think it could make a great TV series. It's a story about the Civil War general George McLellan. He was the political enemy of Abraham Lincoln. He ran against Lincoln in 1864 and lost. It's a bit of speculative history or "what if" history. The premise of it is Lincoln dies two weeks into office and the Vice President Hannibal Hamlin becomes the president. Hamlin then goes down to Charleston and negotiates a deal with Jefferson Davis to avoid the Civil War. It's a bit of "what if this happened instead of what really happened?" I think that story of how they avoided the Civil War could make a stand-alone movie. It was hard enough to write, but I was very fortunate I had a very good editor working on it.

RA: Sounds great! Looking back, how you view your time in the director's chair and the projects you worked on?

JG: I'm happy and I'm proud of the films that I made. I probably should have made more, but that's just the way it worked out. There's a quote out there that says "John Grismer is a good writer and a good director. It's a shame he didn't make more". Of course, there were other stories we were trying to get made, like a Science Fiction Western that we pitched around a lot that never got made. The recent movie *Cowboys and Aliens* kind of reminded me of that. It was along the same lines. Some things get made and some things don't. There's a famous filmmaker out there quoted as saying that "Every time I make a movie, I'm scared" and I can relate to that. It is a scary process. You wonder if you're going to screw up. You just don't know.

JORDAN LADD
(CLUB DREAD, DEATH PROOF, CABIN FEVER)

Jordan was kind enough to sit down with me at Days of The Dead in Los Angeles to discuss *Club Dread* and her as Penelope in the film in depth.

RA: I realize that you have a massive filmography, and I'm a fan of many of the films. However, the one film that I really want to ask you about your involvement in is the Broken Lizard cult classic *Club Dread*. Tell me about your involvement in this underrated film.

JL: It really is underrated. What I like about it is that it's a slasher and a comedy at the same time.

RA: That's what I love about it too! It can be funny and scary at the same time.

JL: I will say that it's the most fun that I've ever had on a set. We were in a remote resort in Mexico, kind of sequestered in the country. We had a good time. There was a lot of tequila and a lot of hanging out, and after work we would strip down to our bathing suits and jump in the ocean and wade around in the ocean and goof off for a few hours, then take a little power nap, shower and head down for dinner and margaritas. It was truly the best time I've ever had on a set.

RA: How were the Broken Lizard guys to work with? I'm a big fan of theirs.

JL: Hilarious! They're a riot. It's like joining a fraternity with them, especially in that kind of location. I kind of started out being a bit of a goody two shoes, and they eventually broke me down.

RA: Did you ever watch any of their other movies?

JL: Yeah, *Super Troopers* I was a big fan of. My friend Joey Kern of *Cabin Fever* was in *Super Troopers* with them. It was a really good, fun opportunity working with them.

RA: How did you come about working on the film?

JL: I auditioned for it. They had some awareness meeting that I had been in, and knew I had been in the genre and worked on *Cabin Fever*. Actually, you know what, I'm not entirely sure they knew that at that point, because the movie hadn't been released yet. So, I just went in and auditioned for it and the good news was that the role was for a gymnast, and as we know, gymnasts are quite small. So, I auditioned two or three times and I got the job. I thought "what a far out, crazy, weird character it is." I just fully wanted to embrace it. So, I was pretty excited when I got the job.

RA: Did you already have an experience in gymnastics going into it?

JL: No, I had a double that actually knew how to do all of that stuff. But, it's the one and only time that I ever appear topless in a movie. I kind of had a rule about it and thought "Do I really want to disrobe for anyone but Martin Scorsese?" (laughs), but in this situation, I thought that this is a go for it character and a go for it moment and I thought that it's funny, you know, topless gymnastics. So, I just embraced it.

RA: Plus, there was the thing where they thought that you might have the killer too for a while.

JL: Yeah, there was that too, kind of a red herring moment, which was great. So, that was fun too. She's someone that is weird enough and enough of a mystery that it's possible she could be the killer. She's stalking Juan enough and is just a little off.

RA: Of course, there was the possibility it could be your trainer too.

JL: You thought it could have been my coach? I forgot about that. I guess maybe it was a red herring within a red herring. That's interesting. I didn't think about that.

RA: I thought that the most amazing thing in the movie is the transformation of Bill Paxton into the character of Coconut Pete.

JL: Oh my God, yes! It's one of my favorite things that he's done. I think that he's such a fine actor and he was fantastic in it.

RA: Did he actually do the songs himself?

JL: He did! Yeah, he sang the songs. He went into a studio and sang. He didn't write the songs, the guys wrote them, but I think that it's a very under appreciated performance.

RA: It totally is! Did you get to see any of the kill scenes of the effects that went into the movie?

JL: A little bit. Because we were all in such close quarters, we would get to see the torsos and bodies. There's a scene where myself and Brittany Daniel run into the dance floor area and we look around and other character's bodies are strewn about, so I remember them setting all of that out. I thought that was pretty cool.

RA: Awesome. Do you have anything else you want to add?

JL: I just think that's its really under appreciated and I hope more people check it out.

KANE HODDER~ SLASHER LEGEND
(From Crypticon 2016)

RA: (to Kane) Welcome Kane. Thank you for joining us. (to the audience) Now, we all know Kane for playing one of the most iconic masked characters in horror history. Am I right? (crowd nods and agrees) ... Of course, I'm talking about the gorilla from *House Part 2* (the whole room, including Kane, burst out laughing).

KH: Hey, who saw that scene? (hands up) Okay, what happened to me as the gorilla and what did I do? (a person in the crowd says he fell over the banister). Yes, I got bumped into by the big guy, pulled my gorilla mask off and said "Hey!", and then he punched me and I flew over the balcony. That's not an easy fall to do either because I had to rotate over the banister. It's a two-part thing. I went over the banister. It was big and wide, so I had to kind of flip over and then went down into my boxes which is what I prefer to land in when doing a fall. Then they had to put in a platform where I fell and landed on my back on the couch.

RA: Cool. What was it that got you into stunts in the first and got you interested in that line of work?

KH: Well, I was going to college and majoring in geography. In between semesters, I went to visit a buddy of mine from high school who was down in LA. I wanted to do some tourist stuff, so we went to Universal Studios. I saw the Wild West Stunt Show and I just became enthralled by it because I thought they're doing these things and getting paid for it and it looks like they're just having fun. When I was a kid and growing up, I used to love to pretend like I got hurt. I would ride my bike and I would go toward a sign and hit the sign with my hand and then fall off my bike, like I hit my head. They would see that and run over and say "Oh my God! Are you okay?", then I'd just get up and laugh at them (laughs). I just always loved doing stuff like that. Then, when I saw people making a living doing that, I thought I should look into it. I waited until the show was over and I asked one of the guys how he got started and he told me about a stunt school in Santa Monica that helped you learn the basics that you need to know to do stunt work. So, I decided to take a semester off and went there. I figured I would take a few months off to try it out and see if I liked it, but if not, I could always go back to college. I never went back. I wouldn't recommend it to anyone. I never got my degree and if it hadn't of worked out in stunts, I would have been screwed. You gotta have something to fall back on. Even when I started in stunts and for the first eight years, I didn't make a living. I loved every minute of it that I got, but I just didn't work enough to make a living at it. It takes so long to build a career in the stunt business, much harder than acting. In acting, you do your auditions, but in stunts, there is no audition. You get hired by a stunt coordinator based on your work. They're not going to hire you to do something dangerous if you're unknown and they don't know if you're any good. It takes forever to get any kind of credibility and I didn't know anybody in the business. But, I loved doing it. I got into the Screen Actors Guild, the union for acting and stunts, in January of 1977 and in July I got burned. So, six months after starting in my professional career, I almost died in a fire stunt that didn't go right.

RA: What was the stunt for?

KH: For many years, I used to say it was for a TV pilot that never aired because I didn't want to admit how it really happened. If I had admitted it then, how ridiculously stupid I was, I probably wouldn't have been hired again. I was doing it for publicity. There was a newspaper reporter who wanted to do a story about me for the newspaper, so I said I would do a fire stunt for them, just to get some photos. I had done it this way several times before and just thought, no big deal, I'll just do it the same. Fire is so unpredictable. It went out of control and burned 45 percent of my body. I was in the hospital for five and a half months and then outpatient for six months after that. There is so much that happens to your body when you get burned that even when you are out of the hospital is where the real work begins. You can still see the scars to this day.

RA: What would you say is the sketchiest stunt you have ever been asked to do on set?

KH: There's been a few. Fortunately, a competent, confident director will let you as a stunt performer design the stunt so that it's as safe as possible and still looks as good as what they want to see. I can think of one in particular that was a movie I did called *Fair Game* with Cindy Crawford that we shot in Miami. Before I got down there, the stunt coordinator told me that it would be him and his brother, myself and a stunt woman doing the stunt. I was playing a character, a hit man, and the other three were doubling the actors. The stunt was, we were flying in a helicopter at night and we would be flying over a moving train and we were supposed to jump from the helicopter to the top of the train, one by one. The first two guys jumped from the skid on the helicopter and when you do that, the pilot has to balance out to compensate for that weight loss which makes it veer off. The woman then jumped from the deck, which was about three and a half feet higher. I saw that and knew that now I had to jump from there. I couldn't let her be the only one. Three and a half feet doesn't seem like much of a difference, but when you're eighteen feet above a train, it's a huge difference. I really couldn't come to a conclusion of how I would land, it being a moving train, until I did it. I didn't know if I would kick back because of the speed of the train, or what. It worked out fine, though. That's what I love about stunts, is that you have to know the physics of it and anticipate what can happen and what could go wrong. That's what I love about doing stunts. You have to really think about these things. It's not just a mindless idiot doing stuff like they do on *Jackass*. I always found it funny when a stunt person would brag about how many bones they've broken doing stunts. I never got that, because it's like you're bragging about fucking up. You're supposed to do it safely and successfully, not go out and not care about what happens. Anybody can do that. It's about doing something that's scary as hell and walking away from it. I have never broken a bone in my life. Forty years of stunts and I never broke a bone. Maybe it was genetics. My mom fell down a flight of stairs when she was eighty and didn't break anything. I think maybe I got it from her.

RA: Now, that brings up something I want to touch on. There was one famous stunt man named Dar Robinson, who was famous for doing the really high falls. He was unfortunately killed in a motorcycle stunt.

KH: Yes, Dar Robinson. He was what they would call a descender. He pioneered it. He once jumped off of the CN tower even with a cable attached, no air bag or anything. Obviously, at 1,100 feet, an air bag is not going to matter. What a descender does, is it lets you free fall for a while and then it slows your rate before you hit the ground. He perfected that in the stunt business. Then, ironically, he died in a motorcycle accident and even worse, it was going back to one. Going back one means that you do a take and then they cut and tell you to do it again, and you go back to where you started. So, he was going back to one and somehow went off the bike and got gored by a sagebrush. It's so ridiculous with all of the things that he did, that he would get killed doing something so minor.

RA: Wow, it almost is like what happened to Steve Irwin in that sense.

KH: Yeah, exactly.

RA: One of the earliest films that you worked on was *The Hills Have Eyes Part Two*.

KH: Yes, the original one, not the remake. I was stunt doubling a character called The Reaper. That was John Bloom, who was way taller than me. He was like 6'11. He is not with us anymore. I was riding a motorcycle, falling through a skylight and stuff like that.

RA: Another early one that's a favorite of mine is *Prison*. That had some really great effects on it.

KH: That was Renny Harlin's first American film. We shot it in Wyoming. I was the stunt coordinator and had to do most of the stunts myself on it. There were some really cool things that I got to do because they didn't have the budget to bring a lot of people, so I got to double when I could and did a high fall out of the tier of the cell block. The director of photography worked on a lot of Sean Cunningham's films and I also did a lot of stunts in those. On *Prison*, he had enough confidence in me to tell me what he wanted. He said that there's this big sally port, this big giant wooden gate, in front of the prison that he wants me to drive a car through. They packed the gate with primer cord and just as it explodes, they want me to drive through and slide the car right in front of a camera that he would be operating. I thought it was nuts that he wanted to be there operating it because I would be hitting the gate completely blind and couldn't see anything until the gate explodes. It worked out perfectly, though. The car slid very close to the camera. Viggo Mortensen was in the movie. He wasn't very well known. Lane Smith was also in it. They had a very good cast. Toward the end of shooting, John Buechler, who was doing make-up told me about a character in full body make-up that looks like a rotted corpse. He's been strapped to an electric chair and would come out of the ground, open his eyes and scream. Buechler told me that the guy who was going to do it, can't do it and asked if I wouldn't mind doing it. I had never done make-up like that, so I said sure, I'll do it. The guy that the suit was built for was like 5'8, 165 pounds, and I'm ... not that size (laughs), so that had to do all kinds of modifications to get me in the suit. Then, it was prosthetics laid on. It took three and a half hours to get into it. I actually liked being in it. I thought that it was a lot of fun and it's a challenge to act when you're completely covered in latex. You have to exaggerate what you're doing. Before we shot it, Renny said that he wanted to put these big nightcrawlers all over me, for effect. He said that when I look up, he just wants me to scream and I suggested having the worms coming out of my mouth. He liked the idea, so I did that. I don't think you can really tell on the movie. I think my enthusiasm for playing a character like that is what Buechler really liked, so the following year, he was hired to do *Friday the 13th Part 7* and he told them that he wanted me as Jason because he has to do a lot of stunts in the movie. So, he said from the beginning that he wanted me to play Jason. They didn't know who I was, so I had to do a screen test, but eventually it happened. It's all because of Buechler and my work in *Prison.*

RA: So, how was the process of getting suited up as Jason? I know that he looked a lot different in this movie.

KH: Right. He kind of took the same feel from *Prison* and built it into Jason with the rotted look and I thought it looked amazing. Even though I had the hockey mask on for seven of the eight weeks on the movie, I still had to put the prosthetics on every day underneath, because part of the mask was missing. You had to be able to see what my face was, so that was a pain. In all of the other Jason movies I did, I didn't have to have the full prosthetic face. I loved the look of it and still think it was the best look of Jason. I had to do a fire stunt, which was challenging. It's still my favorite fire stunt that I've done. You would think I would never do a fire stunt again after I got out of the hospital, but I always liked doing it, other than that one time (laughs).

RA: Was that your favorite scene to shoot on the movie?

KH: I loved it just because of how it turned out, and how long it went. The sleeping bag kill was amazing, but every single kill was completely cut by the MPAA.

RA: I know, they butchered it.

KH: It was the worst that had ever happened to a horror film that I had done, the most censored. It's still a decent movie, but it would have been so much better with the effects in it. Buechler spent so much time creating these amazing things and then it was all cut out.

RA: Then you went on to do *Jason Takes Manhattan* from there. I know that they used Vancouver as New York. I was curious as to the difference of filming in BC, as opposed to here in the states.

KH: The make-up was much easier for me without all the prosthetics, although I had to be wet every single shot. I loved the city of Vancouver and it was a lot of fun to shoot there, but the exteriors were so cold. We were shooting in February and March, and let's just say, the exteriors there were much colder than in Alabama, where we shot the previous movie. The part that I didn't like was that, because it was Canada, I wasn't the only stunt coordinator.

RA: The one scene that always stuck out to me is the scene where you pop out of the water and grab onto the rope. What did you have to go through for that?

KH: Trying not to shiver. I couldn't do it for long. I got in the water and it was barely above freezing. It was in Britannia Bay, outside of Vancouver in early March. Rob Hedden, the director, wanted me to get in the water, go under, come up and grab on and look around. I said, "You better make this fast. I don't mind getting cold, but the longer I'm in there, if I see myself shivering on camera, it's gonna piss me off." (laughs) Jason wouldn't shiver. I said to roll the cameras and I went in and went under and did my thing, came up like a bad ass, they yelled cut, and I got the hell out of there.

RA: What was your favorite kill in that movie?

KH: Punching the guy's head off probably. Very hard to do in real life.

RA: Have you tried?

KH: Yes. The human neck is very resilient. (laughs) Yeah, but that's a pretty good kill. There were a couple other good ones too. Of course, that's when I started continuing with my practical jokes on set. I used to do things that wouldn't compromise the movie, but things just to entertain myself. Like on part seven. So many times, I was just exhausted and wanted to do something to lighten the mood for myself. I was always known for things, like I would get up really close to someone right before a kill and then say something under the mask like "I just farted" (the whole room cracks up). Then they would laugh and the director would cut and ask why they're laughing. They'd say "Well, he said this!", and I'd say, "No, I didn't". (laughs) I would only say it loud enough for them to hear it. On Part 8, at the beginning, there's a guy and girl on this small boat. I come in, get the mask, grab a speargun, kill him, and then she runs and hides in this hatch in the bow of the boat. So, I take the spear and open the hatch and I slowly stab her. Well, of course there's a point of view shot where the camera is down in the hatch. The camera is looking up and you see the hatch open and see me standing up there. So, I talked to the effects guys beforehand, and when they rolled the camera, and as I opened the hatch, I had a really big prosthetic penis hanging out of my pants (everyone cracks up again). I could see the camera guy laughing. I never did see the footage and I don't think they kept it or anything, but somebody brought a photo of that to a convention recently. I was like, "Where in the world did you get this?" I signed it, of course.

You've gotta do something to keep it light on the set and to entertain yourself when you're so uncomfortable all the time.

RA: That's great (laughing). Now, I wanted to talk about the boxing scene. I heard VC Dupree say that when you did the scene, you really wanted him to lay it in, correct?

KH: Right. I thought it would look better if he made a lot of contact with the punches, so he did. By the time I was ready to punch him, boy was I ready (laughs). I made a movie a couple years ago in Australia called *Charlie's Farm*. Nathan Jones plays Charlie and he is another massive guy like Bloom. We did a fight scene to my death. He's 6'10 and like 360, and used to be a pro wrestler. We both agreed that we should make contact during the fight. I was giving him forearms and stuff and at one point he gets enraged and kicks me in the chest. So, when he did, his wrestler personality came out and he just nailed me. They anticipated that and reinforced the wall of the barn that Nathan was going to kick me into, because they knew he would kick me hard. He just laid it into me and I almost went through the barn wall. The fight looks good, but that was the biggest guy I ever had a fight with, for sure.

RA: I know that when you did publicity for *Jason Takes Manhattan,* you actually did an appearance in full costume on TV for Arsenio Hall. We didn't see the guy for years, so I actually wondered if you really killed him in real life (laughs).

KH: (laughs) Yeah, he had a popular late night talk show and they asked me to be on as a guest in full costume. I was like, "You mean, like to go sit on the couch?", and they said yeah. I was like, "How? I don't fucking talk" (laughs). They told me that's the whole point, he'll make it funny. Before I put the costume on, he came over to introduce himself and said, "I know it sounds stupid, but I'm gonna be scared to death of you when you're in that costume, so please don't fuck with me". Well, that's the wrong thing to say to me. That's why at the end he goes to shake my hand and I held it and pulled him in. He was scared shitless. It was quite funny. I wanted to do more, but they told me to please be careful because they didn't want him to look stupid. I had to restrain myself somewhat.

RA: Here's an interesting one. You did some of the stunt work for *Leatherface,* right?

KH: That's right. I was the stunt coordinator for that movie. RA was perfectly capable of doing everything on his own, but sometimes you have to use a stunt person for legal reasons and for liability reasons. If a person gets hurt by an actor as opposed to a stunt person, it's a much bigger deal, as we try to make it as safe as possible. I did quite a few scenes, like the whole fight scene in the water with Ken Foree. It was me and a stunt double for him.

SLASHED DREAMS PART 2

RA: On *Jason Goes to Hell*, there's a very interesting scene where you actually get to be a victim of whoever Jason possessed at the time.

KH: When I read the script, I saw that Jason's evil spends a good deal of the movie going through other people and told the director that I wanted to be a victim, now. I could never do it before. I would never let somebody else put the Jason costume on to kill me. So, they went for it and I came up with some dialogue that would make fun of him and then I end up dead. Then, of course there's that scene at the end where Freddy's hand comes out of the ground, grabs the hockey mask and pulls it into the ground. That was my hand wearing the Freddy glove, so I did one shot as Freddy too.

RA: Now, that's saying a lot right there, getting to play Jason, Leatherface and Freddy.

KH: Yeah, and I always wanted to play Michael. It's funny because I was being considered to play Michael in *Halloween 5* in 1989. They were considering me, but I was in Vancouver playing Jason for the second time. I never had that chance again. That would be fun, if I could play all four of the main guys.

RA: You know, they are doing a new *Halloween* movie. Maybe you should look into that. John Carpenter is returning to it.

KH: Oh wow, that would be amazing. I always thought that would be a cool character to play. I would have my sleight, different take on it but not much because I know that people want to see what they're used to, with maybe a little added touch. But, I did play Michael in a short with Adam Green. It was a little short called *Driving Lessons*. Joel David Moore is the instructor and I'm the student. I get in with the Michael mask on. It's a real one from part four, I think. It was funny. I don't count that as playing Michael though because it wasn't in a film. Maybe we should get on Twitter and talk John Carpenter into bringing me on board (huge applause).

RA: You mentioned Adam Green. I really appreciate what he does and he seems to have a genuine love for horror and the icons of the past.

KH: Everybody in horror has been in the *Hatchet* movie and I've killed all of them (laughs). (everyone starts listing off the names. Derek Mears is mentioned)

RA: That was my favorite one, was when you fought Derek. It was like the new meeting the old, and kicking his ass.

247

KH: Yeah, and I'm glad that he went along with it. At first, Adam was talking about doing a big fight scene between the two of us. I said that if we do it, it should be quick and totally one sided. Derek was even up for it. It went good. Adam Green always talks about the first time that we met. There was a place I used to go to every October called Spooky World at a farm in Mass. They asked me to come there and sign autographs at this haunted attraction. It was a very cool place. Adam was very young and had his dad bring him there to meet me. He says that they waited like two hours to meet me and right as they were getting up to the table to meet me, they took me away for some reason. I think there has to be some mitigating factor somewhere because I would never leave my table if there was people still waiting. He was so bummed out for years, but it was so cool for him that he came up with a character that I eventually ended up playing in the *Hatchet* movies. It really put me back on the map. I really loved playing that character too, as well as Victor Crowley's father in the flashbacks. There's a flashback scene where I drive young Victor up to a store and go inside and leave him in the truck. These three little kids jump up on the running board to get a look at Victor. Two of those kids are my sons. They were eight and five at the time. Now they're all grown up. It was so cool to see them as little guys harassing my character.

RA: There's another movie I have to mention, and it's another one where you have a death scene, and a very cool one at that, in *Wishmaster*.

KH: That was one of the first times that somebody had asked me to be in a horror film in a completely different character. I still sign that picture all the time from that, with myself, Tony Todd and Robert Englund in it. It was fun just to be a victim, just to see how that side of things worked. I become a glass door as a security guard. That glass door was hand painted by Screaming Mad George. Robert Kurtzman still has it in his house.

RA: Another one that I pulled up while doing research is one that's not horror, but just an amazing action film and a favorite of mine, *Demolition Man*.

KH: Because of the stunts, I was able to work on some really cool, big action movies like *Demolition Man, Enemy of the State, Lethal Weapon 3, Under Seige, Batman Forever. Demolition Man* was fun because it was Stallone and we did a lot of car chases in these really bizarre looking cars. It's nice when you get to work with somebody who's on the level of Stallone and he ends up being a cool guy. Some actors can be assholes, but some of the biggest stars, especially the guys, identify with the stunt people. So, they can kind of be themselves around us and they really like to hang out with the stunt people on the set. It's just fun to see somebody of that stature be themselves. One of the biggest surprises to me was doing the movie *Seven,* with Brad Pitt. There's a scene where Spacey is being chased by Brad Pitt out into the street. We were all out there in cars doing things and they try to avoid them. Brad jumped off of my car and to the stunt car next to me, and he wanted to do a cool slide off the back of the car and continue running. He ended up putting his hand through the back window of the car and cut his hand really bad. He actually ended up having to have surgery. If you see the movie, you'll see that his character suddenly has a big cast on his arm. That was why he had it. What I liked so much is that, even though it was cut bad, even the stunts guys were going wow, he wrapped it up and asked to finish the scene before going to the hospital. That to me is a stunt person's mentality, which I liked. He's a big star and he could have freaked out, but he wanted to get the scene finished and then go. He realized that probably another fifteen minutes really wouldn't matter. I became a big fan of his after that and have a lot of respect for him.

RA: What can you tell us about _Death House_?

KH: Well, it's a lighthearted comedy (laughs). No. It's an interesting story about a prison that appears to be a gateway to hell. I am the leader of the inmates. I've seen some of the footage of it and it looks unbelievable, the way it was shot. The Director of Photography is incredible with lighting and it looks really good. So many friends are in the movie. Unfortunately, they're calling it _The Expendables_ of horror, and I really don't like that term. That would mean that it's these horror stars throughout the movie, but what it is, is that my character is throughout the movie, while most of the other horror people are cameos. As a fan, that would piss me off. But still, I think it will be a really cool movie. A lot of great people are in it, practically everyone you can think of from the horror world. We shot at a prison outside of Philly, in a really amazing looking location.

RA: Who wins in a fight, Jason or Victor Crowley?

KH: Well, I would have to play both characters and that's going to be hard to do. I have been asked that question a lot and I would have to say, character wise, that there would be a very slight edge to Victor. That's only because he's less predictable. They're both the same stature and creative and adept at killing and unstoppable.

RA: Was it different playing Jason for the video game?

KH: Whenever I'm playing Jason, I always feel the same, except this is in a motion capture studio. So, I'm doing horribly violent things to people, but I'm wearing spandex. (laughs) It's not the look you would typically think of, but sometimes I would wear the mask just for fun. Even though I look different, the feel and movement are the same, so location doesn't really matter. It was like how I looked at playing him in _Jason X_. So, I still approach it the same way and don't act any differently. I didn't realize though, that I would be able to stand on the stage in spandex and see my live character animated on a monitor. So, I could look over at the monitor and I'm Jason. There's gonna be different versions of Jason that you can play as. I get to play all of the different versions of Jason. It's interesting.

RA: Did you even get to play Roy from Part 5?

KH: (laughs) No. Thankfully they're not using Roy in the game. You can play as the other ones though, including sackhead from Part 2. I thought that was cool. I've always liked that look.

RA: Can you tell us about the ghost hunting?

KH: Well, there's no more episodes of *Ghost Adventures* that I'm doing, but I've had meetings with producers who want to do something with my group, Hollywood Ghost Hunters. Everyone in the group has something to do with horror and we're all interested in the paranormal, so we investigate places. My approach is to let me have who I pick to be in the group and people will laugh whether or not there's ghosts and it will be a fun show. They like the idea. In between investigating, you can make it more compelling than it ever is.

RA: What scares you?

KH: I used to say that nothing does. I was doing the show *Adam Green's Scary Sleepover*, and he asked me that. I told him that I had an answer, but it's not going to be a fun one. The thing that really scares me the most is dementia. It's scary when someone can't even recognize their own family and a terrifying thing. If you've ever had a family member go through that, you know exactly how sad it can be.

KELLI MARONEY
(CHOPPING MALL)

RA: How did you get your start in acting?

KM: I used to watch old movies with my Mom. I was just in love with it and I always thought it would be great to do that. I just thought it was the absolute pinnacle of life, to be in the movies. I started out watching old horror movies. They would run them on local TV and that was, needless to say, awesome. I did a play in the second grade and I got my first big laugh, and after that I was hooked. We didn't have a drama department in my school or anything like that, so when I was in 8th or 9th grade, I became an apprentice at the Guthrie Theater. Then I went to New York and did conservatory school when I graduated early. I was going to their Manhattan program. I had 500 dollars to my name and I was too young to get a job and too young to rent an apartment. Honestly, it was a disaster. I think maybe God intervened or something because I got on a Soap Opera (laughs). I was really starting to realize that I was in trouble by then. I didn't know anybody really. I was just in this conservatory school and had like two friends there. Finally, I took the subway down to this apartment and the woman there looked at me and said she may be able to find me a roommate situation. Then she said she has a friend who is an agent and she was telling me that they were having a very hard time finding this "Mid-Western nymphet" for a Soap Opera. So, she said I should go over there and asked if I had any pictures of myself. I had one picture of myself. I met the agent and she told me to go in and I auditioned and I got the job. Once I was out there, I was not about to go back home in defeat, so whatever it took, that's what I did. Then, because I had my job, I had more opportunity. When you're on TV every single day, there's nothing like practice, and talk about pressure when you're on national television. It goes so fast and you learn on your feet. Then, the industry took me seriously because I already had a job. I didn't have to go through all of the casting couch crap and all of that, and the abuse that some young actresses take, because I was already there and for real. They treated me like I was for real and I blew past a lot of the stuff, luckily. I hear some stories now and just think, "Oh my God, why did you let them do that?"

RA: That's good. I'm glad to hear that.

KM: Yeah, sometimes these girls just need to hear from somebody who's been there that you don't have to do that, you don't have to degrade yourselves for a role. Some people just need to hear that to snap back to reality and just need that support system. I wish I had that support when I first started. I mean, I didn't know anybody when I started. I came out to New York by myself and then later I came out to California by myself. I didn't really have a network in place and I didn't really know how to create one. In my mind, I was the kid and everyone else was the adult, and I carried that for a long time. I wasn't just the kid, I could have spoken up more. I just think that the soap opera was a great stroke of luck because it placed me in a more professional position. I think the universe did that for me, because I wouldn't have had the self-confidence to make it the hard way. "Give her some encouragement there and see if she can last on her feet after that."

RA: Very cool. I know that you have an impressive resume and have done a lot over the years, but the one that I mainly want to talk with you about for the book is _Chopping Mall_.

KM: Oh yes, speaking of that, some very exciting news, we just found out that Lion's Gate is finally going to do the Blu-Ray. We just found out a couple of days ago. Wynorski called me up and said, "you'll never guess". (laughs) People have been asking for it for a long time, all over social media, and I had no answer for them. Roger Corman has the rights to it. There's some movies people don't really care about and the rights go away, but not so with Roger. This is a guy that made these incredible remote control robots and you want one when you see it. They're awesome. I said, "You've gotta market these!" Anyways, I thought that Roger owned it, but he just wasn't doing anything with it. That was not the case. The rights to a lot of these 80s horror movies were so splintered, like on _Night of the Comet_, the issue was that nobody knew who owned the rights to the music. So, it kind of got splintered. It was kind of similar with *Chopping Mall*, in that Roger owns the rights to distributing for theaters, but Lion's Gate somehow got a hold of the rights to distribute it on DVD. When they were going to do the DVD a long time ago, Barbara (Crampton) and I, Jim and Steve Mitchell did a commentary and they were never able to use it. I didn't know what had happened to it. It was like the lost commentary. Who knows what happened to it? Anyways, long story long, we're gonna do this and it's going to have tons of extras and we'll all have commentaries. It's a really fun cast too, so I'm sure that the commentary is going to be epic. It's great that the fans are finally going to get something that we have been asking for. The fan power is a powerful thing and we pretty much exist just to please the people. People in this industry are people pleasers and that's all we really want to do in life.

RA: I like it! How was working with Wynorski on the movie? I interviewed him in the last book and I've heard different stories of working for him.

KM: I always got along with Jim personally. I mean, he is a screamer and he can yell because he is very passionate about what he does. He knows exactly what he wants. It freaks a lot of people out. I have to tell you, I'm not a huge fan of the screaming, but you've got to go really fast. If he knows that you're doing everything that you're supposed to be doing from an acting standpoint, you're not going to have a problem with him. (laughs) It's funny, when you do a scene, he likes you to talk really fast because he is very easily bored. From an acting standpoint, you just kind of feel like you're yelling your lines as fast as you can. You don't know what it's going to look like later. Sometimes you're doing your thing and he could yell, "Cut! Cut! I'm bored I hate it!" (laughs). If you aren't used to that, I know that you're going to be super taken aback. I think he's gotten worse with age. He wasn't that bad on *Chopping Mall*. I just did *Gila Monster* with him and let me tell you, he has not mellowed with age. But, let's face it, it's his movie and he wants it made his way and he's really been doing this all his life. He knows how to get what he wants as fast as he can.

RA: What was your experience with the rest of the cast like? Who did you really enjoy working with and do you still keep in contact with any of them?

KM: I feel the best part of doing *Chopping Mall*, in retrospect, is that Barbara Crampton and I became really good friends. That's a lifelong friendship, but I liked everybody. I'm still friends with Tony O'Dell. There were no bad people there, there wasn't anybody that we didn't like, no egos. It was really a good cast and a good experience.

RA: What was it like getting to shoot the movie in that mall?

KM: We were going into that mall after they closed at night and basically destroying it. Then, the crew had to put everything back together again before they opened in the morning. Looking back at that, I really had no idea how they did that. There were some issues, like we chipped some marble and things like that, but I didn't have to be privy to it, because I got to go home. I had no idea of the mess that we left. You really didn't think about that stuff after you made a mess like that. Even if you did, they're not going to let you help them. They'd say "Get outta here, we have work to do!" (laughs)

RA: What was your impression of the Killbots?

KM: The robots in the movie are very effective. We only had one that was really fully functional. There was only one that would completely work. I found out that the effects guy for the robots was going to be Robert Short, a great effects guy who did things like Daryl Hannah's tail in *Splash.* I thought that it was going to be awesome since that was one of the greatest effects I had ever seen. That was of course back when the movie had the different title. I don't think any of us would have signed on to do a movie named *Chopping Mall*!

RA: I actually liked the original title, *Killbots.*

KM: Yeah, that was the original title, but it's a weird thing because they would test the movies out, to see if they were going to be popular or not and it was just not generating any interest. Roger was always very smart about this. You can sell a movie on a poster and a title, and then if somebody buys it, they go write it. So, they thought that nobody would want to go see robots, or *Killbots.* Jim tells the story that they were all sitting around and a maintenance guy came in and said, "Why don't you just call it *Chopping Mall*?" Of course, nobody gets chopped up in the movie, but that title sold for whatever reason. I know that we were all mortified.

RA: (laughs) I bet! There's one particular scene that I want to ask about from the movie. I have to ask, are you okay with spiders and snakes?

KM: I actually was fine with that. There was a really cool old Hollywood guy who is a bug wrangler. He brought that tarantula over to me and said "This is Dolores. She's been in the business for years and has worked with all the greats" (laughs). So, that was Dolores and I let her climb in my hair. Wynorski would always say "I'm never going to ask actors to do something that I wouldn't do myself". So, here comes this scorpion and we were like, let's see if Jim will have that on himself. So, they held it over his crotch I guess, and he went "No, no scorpions." (laughs). So, there's no scorpion in the movie. I actually was fine with the snakes.

I really would prefer not to have a tarantula crawling on me, but it was okay for that. I wasn't scared or anything, but I know a lot of people that would freak out over something like that. I personally got lucky and it doesn't bother me all that much. The funny thing is, people always say that it's creepy having them on me, but I was more concerned about hurting the spiders. I was more concerned that I would hurt them. I wasn't concerned that they were going to hurt me. I did not want to be responsible for standing up and hurting them. Then, afterwards they did the sound and added a "squish, squish" sound when I stood up, but no spiders were harmed during the making of this movie. The guy was awesome. It's interesting that you meet these people in show business and they do their thing and that's what they do. Then, they had a guy who did the guns and everything. I just find everything fascinating about it.

RA: It's funny you mention that. You used guns in both movies, *Chopping Mall* and *Night of the Comet*.

KM: Yeah, for a while there it was like that, guns and shopping malls. (laughs)

RA: Did they have you do any special training?

KM: Well, I started shooting on the soap opera. I killed a boy on the soap opera that I did. But, for *Night of the Comet*, they took us out to a real shooting range and they taught us because it's different shooting an Uzi or Mach-10. It's a whole different thing. We worked with the real guns too. You know, everybody laughs at Samantha in *Night of the Comet* because she squats when she shoots. I got that because those guns are so freaking heavy that it's what I had to do. You don't just go knock off an Uzi. It's a heavy, heavy weapon, and the kickback is extreme. So, we had that training and once you learn on Uzi's, you can figure anything else out fast. I actually became a really good shot. But, I'm a pacifist, so I would never. I'm not a fan of guns honestly, with all that's happened in the world like school shootings, though.

RA: Since we're on the subject, I'd like to touch on it briefly. Could you talk about your experience on *Night of the Comet* and your memories of it?

KM: We had a great time on it, Catherine (Mary Stewart) and I. The day we met, we shot the scene where she comes home and finds me getting ready for pep squad practice. It was the first time we ever met each other and we just lucked out. We had great chemistry together. Half a movie is great casting. If you get the right people, the movie shoots itself. We both had been on daytime television, so we both knew about moving fast. I was from Minnesota and she was from Canada and there's a similar sensibility and philosophy of life there. It was really wonderful. Sadly, Wayne Crawford just died, who was the producer. He also did *Valley Girl*.

RA: How do you view the role these days, as one of the scream queen icons of the 80s?

KM: I'm really more of a 'final girl' than Scream Queen. I actually think that I'm more scream queen adjacent (laughs). I'm very pleased to be one of the "scream queens". I would really love to do more horror than I actually do. I like to do comedy too. I am actually doing a play right now. It's all for laughs, but that's not to say that I can't run screaming, too. I'm really pleased that I came up in a time with really strong women characters like the scream queen characters were. We were survivors. I have to say that I'm extremely honored to be a part of that.

RA: Looking back on these projects, how do you view them now and your experience on them?

KM: What a great time. We get older, but our personalities don't change. It's more weird to see how similar it is. I do think that I'm a lot less timid than I used to be. When you're older, you don't let things intimidate you as much as they did when you were a kid. I don't watch a lot of my stuff. I kind of have a hard time watching myself. A lot of actors do, actually. But then, I can look at some and think, "You know, that scene actually works pretty well". What's fun for me is if I have to do a Q and A after a movie is screened. I love watching the audience and seeing their reactions. That's the whole point, we do it for them. The fact that they're enjoying it really inspires me, so by the time we do the questions, my heart is really full.

RA: What are you working on right now?

KM: I'm finishing up a play that I'm doing, which is a comedy. Then, I have a couple other things lined up. I'm really excited about them.

RA: If you could say anything to the fans out there, what would you say?

KM: Thank you. Thank you from the bottom of my heart. I mean, that's who we do it for. It's something you can look at as you go through life, whenever you get discouraged, you can look back at something that you did thirty years ago and know that it made somebody happy and makes them happy to this day. Then, you feel like your life means something. I'm so grateful every time people reach out and tell me that. If it wasn't for the internet, I would never know. At one point, I thought, "You know, you've got to do something else with your life other than sitting around waiting to be cast in a movie". Then, people started asking me if I knew how many fans I had on the internet. I went, "You've got to be kidding me. People still watch that stuff?", and I just found this huge fan base. I'm just in love with my fans. I think they're awesome and I just want to say thank you. It means a lot to me as a performer to hear that they affected people so much. I have had people share so many experiences with me. One person told me, "My mom used to leave that movie (*Night of the Comet*) on when she went out because she couldn't afford a babysitter and you were my babysitter, and I felt safe because you guys had guns". I just feel like I'm luckier than most people. If people can share that with me, I know that I did the right thing with my life.

KEN KIRZINGER
(FREDDY VS. JASON)

RA: How did you get into the film business?

KK: I started by reading an article about stuntmen when I was about eleven or twelve years old. Keeping that in the back of my mind as I got older, I was in University and I wanted to play pro football, but I blew my knee out. I was about 21 years old and I thought it was a good time to look into being a stuntman. So, I went to LA and I met some stunt people there. About a month after I got back to Vancouver, I started working on my first movie, which was *Superman III.*

RA: I have to say that there is a certain irony in the fact that you were able to play both a victim and the killer in the *Friday the 13th* series. How do you look back on that?

KK: It's certainly one of the notable things. Kane Hodder and I are the only two guys who have played both Jason and a victim of Jason. I've been killed so many times being a stunt man in the movies, so that was nothing new to me. Just another day at the office.

RA: How did you get on board for *Jason Takes Manhattan*?

KK: I actually got a phone call from Randy Cheveldave, the production manager on it. I had worked with him before. The first phone call I got was asking if I wanted to be the stunt coordinator and play Jason. I said sure, but the next phone call I got was telling me that Kane would be playing Jason again, so they just needed me as a stunt coordinator. That's when I first met Kane. I worked as the stunt coordinator and as Kane's stunt double and as the fry cook who gets killed in the diner.

RA: You got to play Jason later on in *Freddy vs. Jason*. What was it like working with Robert Englund as Freddy?

KK: I call him the Vincent Price of our time. He's such a sweetheart. I remember when I first met in the make-up trailer, he was getting his three-four hours of make-up put on. Right off the bat he was very warm and genuine and told me that we would be seeing each other for the rest of our lives now. I asked him why and he said because of conventions. I knew nothing about conventions at the time. Now, we see each other three or four times a year. He and his wife have become very good friends. I just can't say enough nice about them.

RA: How were you chosen to take on the role of Jason in that one?

KK: I was interviewing for the stunt coordinator job. The producer was looking at me and said that they have been looking for someone my size and my build and asked if I would be interested in auditioning for the part of Jason. I said sure, so they sent me in and they did a close-up of my eyes and read the opening scene where the girl is swimming naked in the lake. They had me walk around the room and they showed the tape to Ronny Yu, the director. I went in and met with him later and from that, they gave me the job. I was very lucky.

RA: What was your favorite kill scene in the movie?

KK: It was the kill in the bed. It wasn't enough just to stab him over and over again. Folding up the bed on him was just a great afterthought.

RA: Oh yeah, that was brutal. I also really liked the one with Freeburg, the stoner kid. I interviewed Kane a bit ago and I remember hearing years ago that he was kind of upset because he wanted to play Jason in this. What is your relationship with Kane now?

KK: Well, he's let me know that he doesn't bear any animosity towards me anymore.

RA: Well, it wasn't your fault

KK: Yeah, I know. Everybody knew that, but Kane. (laughs) But, I think he's over that. He's moved on to *Hatchet* and still does very well for himself since then and I'm happy for him.

RA: That's good. I ask a lot of the other stunt people this question. What do you think was the hardest or the sketchiest stunt you ever did?

KK: I've been asked that many times before and I always think about the stunts that could go wrong. You count on the equipment and your ability and if one or the other goes wrong, it could be disastrous. I fractured three vertebrae in my back landing on concrete, I flipped a jeep off the side of a mountain and I managed to survive that. Things can go wrong very quickly. For a stuntman, it's the stunt that goes wrong because you never plan to get hurt, but it can happen. Hopefully, you just don't get killed and broken bones is the worst that happens.

RA: I wanted to ask about a couple of the other films you worked on. On *Bad Moon*, one of my favorite werewolf movies, did you get to play the werewolf?

KK: On *Bad Moon,* I was the stunt coordinator and I got to play the werewolf. Michael Pare plays the uncle that turns into the werewolf and I play the werewolf after the transformation. That was a really tough job. The werewolf suit had to be built very tough and strong because I was fighting real attack dogs. I was looking through a hole that was about the size of a fifty-cent piece that was covered in black mesh that was in the mouth of the werewolf. There were the fangs and all the slobber and the animatronics that they built into the back. It was very heavy and I had to be in it for long hours. I forget how many days I wore that, but I started to get a little claustrophobic after a while. It was probably the worst job I ever had as a stuntman.

RA: Wow. What did you do on *Thirteen Ghosts*?

KK: Again, I was the stunt coordinator on it. Also, in the opening sequence, when Breaker attacks all the guys in the wrecking yard, I was one of the guys. I got hit into the side of a car and got sucked up into a car, then the door slams and you see blood splatter everywhere.

RA: Cool, I remember that scene. I just have one last question. If you could say anything to the fans out there, what would you say?

KK: I would like to thank them for all their patronage and love of *Freddy vs. Jason* and I look forward to meeting them all in the future. I'm very thankful to them for loving the movie.

LARRY JOSHUA
(THE BURNING)

RA: How did you get your start in the acting business?

LJ: There were a few women involved. One was a woman named Sally Brophy Goodman down in Princeton, who has passed now. She was an inspiration. Another girl named Rosie O'Neil, who was a playwright and pretty famous now, in New York. They really encouraged me. Another one is a girl named Barbara Colachello. She also encouraged me. So, I took some acting classes in Manhattan and started going to auditions. Later on, I studied at HB Studios and Circle in the Square, and studied with a guy named Win Hanman and another named Warren Robinson. They all contributed. Another wonderful teacher I had was Kim Vaughn. Nikos Sauporapolis was another teacher of mine and so was Michael Kahn. They all contributed to my understanding of acting and theater. It's something that started to work and I started to get jobs. I've had a good run.

RA: How did you get involved on *The Burning*?

LJ: Joy Todd, who is a casting director in New York, brought me and my agent Gene Carsey got me up for the part. I went in and auditioned for Joy, and the director. We got it. I don't remember if Harvey Weinstein was in the audition or not, but we all met with Harvey up in North Tonowanda, where we shot the film. Harvey was a lot of fun to be around, too. I think it was one of the first movies that he produced. He was just a regular guy back then. Now of course, he's a huge star in his own right. Back then, he was just some guy named Harvey who was trying to make a movie. He wrote it and produced it, and shot it in his neck of the woods where he grew up. We had a really great time.

RA: What are your favorite memories that stand out of being up there and working on the film?

LJ: Some of my favorite memories are of hanging out with some of the guys up there, like Fisher Stevens, Jason Alexander and Ned Eisenberg. It was great fun hanging out with them. We had a lot of good times up there. It was like doing a movie and going to summer camp. For a lot of people, it was their first film, like Holly Hunter. It was just a great bunch of people. We hung around and played music and entertained each other.

RA: What do you remember of working with Tom Savini?

LJ: I didn't realize that he was going to become one of the greats. He was one of the highlights, working with him and putting together my death scene. He's just phenomenal, a true artist. He's a positive person and very fun to be around. He deals with blood and gore all the time, but in no way is he like that. He's just a fabulously wonderful guy. I enjoyed working with him a lot, as well as with Tony Maylam, the director. They were all positive to be around. Tom was very important for this particular film. His make-up and effects were amazing and we couldn't have done it without him.

RA: What was it that went into making your death scene happen, with Tom?

LJ: I had never had that fake blood in my mouth before and it was that syrupy, sweet blood mixture. It almost made me want to gag. They put those shears into my throat and putting on that make-up and cutting away was interesting. I was sitting on a dolly on some tracks and the camera was down. If you remember the scene, I'm forced back into a tree by the strength of Cropsy, putting those shears in my throat. That scene took a good part of the evening to do and Tom was very instrumental in getting that to look as good as it did. Tom helped rig up that entire scene.

RA: Glazer was always one of my favorite characters. What was your take on the character and your thoughts on what made him tick?

LJ: I don't know if there's much to him or much thinking involved. It's just one of those teenage boys who sees a pretty girl and wants to be the one to be with her. I just followed the script pretty much, and did what they asked me to do. Boys will be boys. It's one of those guys out there trying to fluff up those feathers, like birds do in nature. I guess you could say that Glazer wanted to be the cock of the walk, and I think he was just a kid who was trying to impress a girl.

RA: When I saw it, my take on him was at first you think that he's kind of an asshole, but once he gets with the girl, you see that facade break down and then you realize that maybe he's not that bad of a guy, or what he puts out to be.

LJ: I'm happy that you picked up on that. I think that's a case of always trying to find that moment of humanity in every character, like The Birdman of Alcatraz. You really want to try to round a character out. It's like seeing someone who's a bad cat, but nice to his elderly mother, you know? There are some villains, and I don't think Glazer is a villain by any means, that are not meant to be redeemed, but it's nice to see that spark of humanity. It's like you or me in real life. There's a public side to your persona and then there's a private side to your persona. If you're able to, when the script allows you, to see the private side of a character, that's gold. It's a special moment and a real gift from the writing. You don't always get that. I think it was fortunate that he was written that way.

RA: I wanted to talk about a few of the other films you did that really stood out to me. You got to do *Sea of Love* with Pacino. What was that experience like?

LJ: Well, there was two other big actors on that stage that I got along with well, being John Goodman, who had just been cast in *Roseanne* and Samuel L Jackson. We got a chance to hang out together. Sam and I had just become fathers for the first time around then. We had been out hanging out in Toronto where it was filmed and we both went out to buy presents for our new babies. I have good memories of that. Al was good to work with, too. He was very inclusive as an actor and he was great to be on the set with, as was Richard Jenkins. We were up in Toronto and just had a huge company of actors and the crew. You really become a family. Of course, like a family, you're closer to some than you are with others, but still a family. Al was not reclusive and we got to hang out and he showed me a few things on the set that helped me because I was still young then.

RA: After that, you did another one that I really enjoyed, *Quick Change* with Bill Murray and Randy Quaid.

LJ: Yeah, that was a fun one (laughs). I auditioned for Bill and the director. Bill just brings a smile to your just being around that guy and thinking about him. He's just so full of life and wit. It's just a pleasure. Randy Quaid was also wonderful and a great actor. He was also very inclusive and fun to work with. He was great in *The Last Detail.*

RA: You also had the honor of being in two Academy Award winners, *Dances with Wolves* and *Unforgiven.*

LJ: I know. It's pretty amazing. In both cases, I had a great time. In one, I was able to work with an iconic actor in Clint Eastwood, and another icon, Richard Harris. I didn't really get to hang around Gene Hackman or Morgan Freeman, but I did get to hang around the other two. That was a real treat. It's great to be around that kind of talent. Then, Kevin Costner was great to be with on *Dances with Wolves* and that was one of the best experiences I ever had on a film set. The whole cast and crew were the best and I really enjoyed working with Kevin. It was great to see both of them win best picture and I don't think that anyone thought that would happen.

RA: Another one you did is *The Shadow*, which I think is a very underrated movie.

LJ: Yeah, I had fun with that one. I think that was the same producer as *Sea of Love*. Alec Baldwin was another one that was fun to be around and one of those great personalities. He's also a Long Island boy and I appreciated his humor. I think I only had a couple of scenes, so it wasn't a big role, but I had a lot of fun. It was a period piece, so being around the old cars and set pieces was amazing. You really get transported in time, which is what I loved about doing the westerns. Once you're there and everything is all set up, you really suspend belief and you're in that time period. We shot *Dances* up in South Dakota near the Black Hills and not much has changed up there. We shot *Unforgiven* up in Northern California. Once they do the set direction and you're standing there and you look out, you feel like you are transported. It's the magic of film, and it's the same when doing a play. It's a real bit of magic going on.

RA: What was your experience playing the wrestling promoter on *Spider Man* like?

LJ: Sam Raimi is an actor's dream, just such a good director. It was great being on set with him. I had two scenes with Toby and he was great to work with, too. I also did *For the Love of the Game* with Sam Raimi and Kevin Costner, as well. He's one of those directors that enables actors to do great work. That's my best memory of *Spider Man*.

RA: You've done a lot over the years. Looking back on that, how do you view your experiences on these projects and as an actor, in general?

LJ: I was lucky and luck definitely had something to do with it. It's been a great ride and I've had fun. I have absolutely no regrets. I don't know what the future holds, but if it's over and this is the end, it's been fun. I met a lot of great people and got to do a lot of great things that

I never imagined doing. I'm glad I took the risk. When you become an actor or a musician or a writer, you kind of take a vow of poverty. Back then, there was no guarantee of making a living when you first start. To learn the craft of acting, that is something everyone should know. If you're lucky, you do make the money and you do make those relationships. You're able to get that next job and sustain yourself. But, you've got to able to live that lifestyle and be a bit of a gypsy. The thing that every actor has to live with, or every craftsman in a trade of the arts, is not knowing. It's hard for some people to do that. I know. Some people want to think that this is the plan and this is what they're going to do, and I can appreciate that linear logical thinking. You can do that, but there's also that big part of when you throw yourself out there, you're in the hands of the angels. You are living in a place where you have to be comfortable with the I don't know factor. Even when you're working, you have to live with that uncertainty. You can have the talent. You can be a really good actor or a really good singer, but if you can't live the life that those pursuits want from you, in not knowing or not getting a paycheck every two weeks, that can make a lot of people decide it's not for them. I know people who were great guitar players, but just couldn't live the life. I knew actors that I went to acting school with in the early seventies, that I thought were just phenomenal, but after a couple of years of trudging around looking for work, they took rejection very personally and left. That's another thing, you're not going to get every gig and you have to think if it's something that will keep you up at night because you didn't get it. When you're up for a big gig or a big part, I'm not saying that it doesn't mean nothing. It does. You can get bummed out, but the day to day money making, what I call hamburger money, is what you need to get by, to pay the rent. When you can't get those smaller gigs just to get by and to live is what makes most people walk away. They go do something else. I've seen so many walk away. When I say I had luck, I think maybe it's lucky that I had this disposition to look at things that way and to live that way. I was able to be frugal when I had to be because I didn't have money coming in, but I was always able to have joy and that's a gift. I went for what I wanted and took classes and took it serious, but it really comes down to that. It's really in the hands of the angels. You go to the auditions and you do your best, but it's really not in your hands anymore. It's hard for a lot of people, but it can be an exciting journey to jump into that world. It becomes a University of itself, not to mention the psychological aspects of the characters you're playing. It's an adventure and it's not about money. Money will come if it does. I'm just lucky that once I started, I didn't have to look for other work on the side. It doesn't work that way for everybody. I was very fortunate and worked as hard as I could, but I got a little help from above.

RA: If you have anything you could say to the fans, what would you say?

LJ: I would say thank you and keep going to the movies. I want to thank everybody who has ever participated in making movies or going to the movies, as well as those who make the plays and enjoy them.

LINNEA QUIGLEY
(LEGENDARY SCREAM QUEEN)

RA: How did you first get involved in the movie business?

LQ: By total accident. Moving to LA with my parents and I worked at Jack LaLane's fitness spa, which doesn't exist anymore. These two girls that were working there were models and said I should try it. They said, "You'd be good at doing it too". I was like, "Oh my God, me doing that? That can't happen" and they talked me into it. They were going to the set of some movie with John Saxon and Jack Palance. I was just on the set. I think they just used the other two girls as doubles. It was funny because Jack Palance was talking to me and I thought he was trying to pick me up. He asked if he could give me a lift and I told him no, my car's in Hollywood, and he told me he could have his helicopter take me there later (laughing). You know, I was like 19 years old and terrified. Then, I went with this agency and started doing extra work, modeling work, got a line here and there and here I am.

RA: Did you actually get to work with Jack LaLane himself at the club?

LQ: I met him, which was really cool. What's really weird is that I've looked at some of his stuff from years ago that he said on TV and some of it's so true. It was like he could see the future.

RA: I'm still amazed by how fit the guy was, right up until the end.

LQ: That's right, his wife too. I remember watching him with my mom and I think my Mom did some exercises to it, and as a little kid I really loved it when they would bring Happy and Lucky, his German Shepherds on. That was a big thing for me.

RA: You worked on *Don't Go Near the Park*, one of the infamous video nasties (though honestly, I don't know why it is lol) and if I may say so, a very weird movie. What are your memories of doing that one?

LQ: I haven't seen it in a long time, but it's more like don't go near the movie! It's terrible (laughs)! The director was at that time one of the youngest directors. He was like a little kid, and was just saying that all the time, "I'm the youngest director!" It was just weird to work for someone who was my age. It was just strange.

RA: Another early slasher film you did was *Graduation Day*. Pretty under rated too in my opinion. What are your memories of that one?

LQ: I remember that I was really excited because I'd gone in to read for it and didn't hear anything, then about a week later I got a call and they said they're replacing this one actress and asked if I would like to be in the movie. I was like "Hmm, let me check my schedule. No, of course I'll do it!", so it almost didn't happen. You never know, you may be the next in line. So, that was fun. It was a lot of fun. I got to meet Vanna White before she did *Wheel of Fortune* and I remember her showing us this newspaper, like a free magazine, and it had her posed in it for mud wrestling. I remember that very vividly.

RA: I see that you were in one of my personal favorites I wasn't aware of, *Fatal Games*! What did you do on that one? Any fun memories of it?

LQ: Oh my God, yes! I remember that, with Sally Kirkland. I think that maybe she's ashamed of it because I did a talk show with her and Lanie Kazan and they were looking at me like "Who are you?", and I mentioned on the interview to Sally that "You and I were on a movie together" and she seemed a little bit like "Oh God, can we just forget about that?" I don't know why. Maybe it's just that at that time, they didn't appreciate horror all that much. It wasn't as big as it is now.

RA: I don't understand that. I would embrace it.

LQ: I know. It used to be horrible. People would ask what I do and sometimes I would say I'm an actress and sometimes I'd say I'm self-employed, because there would be that other question "oh, what movies have you been in?" and I'd say "Well, mainly I do horror films" and they'd say, "Oh, THOSE kinds of movies". They would always say that. It was like they weren't appreciated.

RA: With you though, you've managed to make a great niche out of it and do just one after another and become this icon that everybody recognizes and that in itself is something very cool.

LQ: I think so too, because I loved horror as a kid. I think it's great! Too bad about the other people, but I think that now with horror being so big with *The Walking Dead* and stuff, you have the wannabe horror people that for the most part really don't truly know horror that well.

RA: You did a few movies with Cheech and Chong (*Nice Dreams/ Still Smoking*) back in the early 80s. What was it like working with them?

LQ: It was fun. Cheech is a really nice guy. Tommy I didn't talk to a lot, but Cheech was very nice and funny. They were just a pleasure to work with. That just happened by an interview too. They had a guitar in there and they knew I was in a band and I played the intro to *Charlie's Angels* for them.

RA: So, was there like a big cloud of smoke around them on set?

LQ: (laughs) Not really. Maybe from Tommy. I'm not sure if Cheech so much was really into that. I think Cheech took it as a job, which it was. It's not easy to be funny, that's for sure, and he really was.

RA: You did an absolute slasher classic in the early 80s, *Silent Night, Deadly Night*. Tell us how you got involved in that one and memories of working on it.

LQ: I remember thinking that it was really weird to be working with a director that also directed kid's things like *Grizzly Adams*, and then he was doing this slasher film. There were some problems I had with it, like a woman would not do that. You would always put a top on to answer the door, so it was off to me that I wouldn't and just put my shorts on to go run upstairs and get my cat in (laughs). There was another girl on set that was complaining and going "I don't want to do nudity" and so they bought her this little diamond necklace and I did this really great job there with the antlers and had to be cold and uncomfortable and I didn't get anything. Maybe I should have been difficult! (laughs)

RA: Wasn't it filmed up in Utah?

LQ: Yes, in Utah. There was the wonderful guy who got thrown out the window and had to go lay in the snow when they placed the glass in him and everything. He had it a lot worse than me.

RA: Your death on that one is still one of my all-time favorites. What went into making it, effects and stunt wise?

LQ: All they did was really simple. They took and just put on my stomach these two antler looking things. Then they put me up on this thing that I straddled up there. I couldn't breathe though, or the antlers would move. They decided to stage the fight scene under me, so I really had to hold my breath a long time. It was like, "geez, can't they just fight somewhere else?"

RA: What was your reaction to how *Silent Night* was viewed on release and its boycott?

LQ: I was surprised. I was in Mexico filming *Treasure of the Moon Goddess* with Don Calfa and my manager called me and told me it has all of these people in an uproar and I couldn't figure out why. It was just a scary movie. I didn't really grasp it until I got back. People were upset because it showed on TV and their kids got afraid of Santa and they just wanted to complain. I mean, it helped the movie, so it's kind of good that it happened.

RA: Here's the one we've all been waiting for ... *Return of the Living Dead*! Such a great, classic movie and your role as Thrash is definitely one of the ones that stood out most. What did you have to do to prepare for such a badass role?

LQ: I didn't really do anything for it. I don't really prepare for a part. I just kind of go off what I'm feeling. The way Dan wrote it was just so great and the cast, oh my God, was amazing!

RA: One of the guys that I'm always fascinated to hear about, who is sadly no longer with us, is Mark Venturini. What do you remember about him?

LQ: He was just a really, really nice person. It was just really sad. I didn't find out for a while that he died and there were different stories about what happened. I was really upset because he was so good in it. I think he would have done a lot of good work. And so young. It was surprising.

RA: Of course, one of the scenes everyone will remember most from the film is your grave dance. Tell us how that came about and your memories of it.

LQ: That was probably the scariest part of doing the movie for me. I didn't choreograph it or anything. I just winged it. After all of the rain and everything, it was hard, especially with those short shorts to get off. Plus, it had to be fluid. Then, they had the road flares and that sulphur was coming in my face and I was like "Oh God". I almost passed out from the sulphur. That's nasty stuff.

RA: How did they do the zombie Thrash look? What went into that one?

LQ: Well, there were two different people that did it. The one guy pretty much was fired or walked off, I'm not sure. He was giving me gasoline to take that white make-up off which should never happen. He just had no personality and was very slow, so when they changed over to the other people, they did it a lot faster and I had to get tons of molds done and everything. It took a long time to do. I think that was my first prosthetic piece. I didn't know what to expect. I was okay with the life cast, but I hate prosthetics on my face. It screws up your face and is just horrible.

RA: One of the more offbeat and interesting horror films of the 80s was *Hollywood Chainsaw Hookers*. What are your memories of working on that one and working with another horror legend Gunnar Hansen?

LQ: That was so cool to work with him! I was very afraid because I loved *the Texas Chainsaw Massacre*. I think I was like everyone else, kind of scared to meet him, because I thought he was going to be this mean, scary guy. We all convinced ourselves that, but he was a total sweetheart. I told him "You know, you've been a name since the movie. I bet if you came out here and did a convention, people would go nuts for you.", and he kept saying "I don't know, you really think so?", and I said "Yes! Give it a try". Of course, he did and it turned out great for him and he did that for years. I should get the credit for that (laughs).

RA: *Night of the Demons* is another of my all-time favorites and just an all-around cool movie. From all I've heard from the others, the house itself on *Night of the Demons* was actually a pretty creepy place. What do you remember about it?

LQ: I liked the house. I like that kind of look, though. It was the kind of place where there's dust everywhere. And it feels like nobody has lived there for a long, long time. Of course, it was in the worst area in LA, so we had to have security from gangs and things like that. I just remember that we had to work from like four o'clock in the afternoon until around six in the morning, then hitting rush hour going home. Not fun.

RA: I talked to some of the other cast members and they said the make-up was an absolute

nightmare on the movie and took hours and was very uncomfortable. Is that true?

LQ: Oh yeah. I think that mine took about twelve hours at least. I was just like, "Please let me out of this chair. I don't want to be here anymore". It was really hard. We came in at like three o'clock in the afternoon and they were doing us all up for a dawn shot the next day, so that's how long it took. It's hard to eat with that stuff on. Just having it on your face, I can't stand it, so when they were done I was just kind of ripping at it. I didn't want to wait for the stuff to take it off. I got out of it though for one day, which was really nice. It was the scene where I'm with Jay and I say, "Do you want to have an orgy?" and they run out of the room. I talked to the director and suggested that when I come to the door for Judy, that it would be scarier if I looked just totally fine in my regular makeup. Kevin said, "Wow, that's a great idea. They can change back and forth" and I was like, "YES! "It worked in the movie. I think the main thing behind it was to get out of the misery of another makeup job.

RA: There was another cool iconic moment that you were a part of on this one, the lipstick trick. Tell us about that one and memories of doing that scene.

LQ: They had me come in and they took a mold of me, like a life cast mold. Then, they took it and put like a gelatin in it. They binded me down and then they put on the fake ones. They cut a hole where I'm supposed to put the lipstick in. It looks like I'm topless, but I'm really not. Movie magic. I liked that one. That one didn't bother me, it's just over my face that does. Ugh.

RA: How did the part as a soul come about for *Nightmare on Elm Street* 4? I always wondered why you weren't one of the regular victims on that one. What do you remember about it?

LQ: That it was fun. Again, a lot of hours and a lot of blood.

RA: One that I just watched recently that I really enjoyed, and I met the director recently too, was Sorority Babes in The Slimeball Bowl A' Rama. What was your experience on it?

LQ: That one I really liked a lot. It was so much fun because I got to be the tough girl. It was like, "finally, I'm not the same girl that gets killed!". David showed me the characters and asked me to pick one and I was like, (excitedly) "I want that one!" There was no question about it.

RA: Did you know that they actually used your voice and one of the quotes from that movie in a Static-X song back in the late 90s?

LQ: Yeah? I didn't know that. My God, that is cool! That's kind of neat that anybody caught that. Wow, that is neat. I'm immortalized now! (laughs)

RA: I remember you telling me at Crypticon a very cool thing about trying out for LAPD in the early 90s. Could you elaborate for the fans out there?

LQ: Oh yeah, I wanted to do that so bad. I just got it in my mind that I wanted to do that. I've always been interested in that kind of thing. So, the first step is you have to take a written test. I took it and then after that, they say who can stay and who can go. I was so shocked that I passed it. Then, the other parts are just time consuming, like the physical. The worst one is the background one. For me, I had to bring up all of the movies I had done and some Playboys I was in. They just wanted to know everything. The guy who was interviewing me, they had to ask these questions like "do you ever want to take over the government" and other weird things and they tried to trick me, and were saying oh, I'm sure you went to these Hollywood parties and partied down with them, with coke and stuff like that. I said, "No, I really don't go to many parties or see things like that", and he said, "Oh, it's okay. You can tell me". I just kept saying I didn't know. When we came out, an older officer was there. The guy went up to the older officer and said, "Well, she's in these movies that people masturbate to" and the older guy was laughing and said, "No, that's not right!" I was just laughing. But, I did pass everything, but then I kind of chickened out, which I wish I wouldn't have.

RA: You did an often-forgotten slasher in the mid-90s, *Jack-O,* and did a great job as the babysitter heroine in it. What are your memories of that one?

LQ: Well, it was fun to do it. I played a babysitter and I got to do a lot of behind the scenes stuff. That was the first one I did behind the scenes stuff on and I had fun doing it. It was my first time working with Steve Latshaw and he was a great director. *Jack-O* was actually the second movie I did with him.

RA: This is one I've always wondered. You happen to do a lot of nude scenes in the movies, so I have to ask if it was something that some film makers almost expect it because of previous ones you did?

LQ: Kind of, yeah. That was the formula back then. They had a certain formula that they could pre-sell stuff by and then they would shoot it. Of course, that would include a girl being topless, a lot of blood and having some sort of moral thing, like that the people who did drugs and had sex were usually not going to live. Lately, they've really veered off of that formula and they're making more women being strong in them.

RA: That's what I loved about your character in *Sorority Babes*. She was a total ass kicker.

LQ: Yes, and I really loved that.

RA: What would you say has been your favorite project to work on so far, the most fun?

LQ: That's really hard to say. I know I had a lot of fun working on *Treasure of the Moon Goddess* for some reason and it was really fun doing *Sorority Babes*. A lot of them with David Decoteau were a lot of fun, almost every one of those. I can't really say which one was the most fun. I can probably say which was the worst. I think I had a lot of fun on *Return of the Living Dead* for sure, except for that make-up stuff on my face. All of them have been an adventure.

RA: You still keep VERY busy these days and have lots going on it seems. What's next on your agenda?

LQ: I have a movie that I'm doing now called *Gnats,* and then I'm doing several conventions back to back coming up. I keep it up to date on my website so people will know where I'm at, which is linnea-quigley.com.

RA: Is there anything you would like to say to all of your fans out there?

LQ: Oh my God, yes. I would say that I'm a huge animal activist and I wish that people would maybe get out there and help out more and sign some petitions about it. There's too much animal abuse going on in the world and it's a very frightening thing. I would like to see tougher jail times, fines, firings, and more of that to make it more of a serious crime and not just a slap on the hand.

RA: I agree, I would have to say that I'm an animal lover too. I may even like them more than people.

LQ: I do too. They're definitely more honest and they are more loving. They're always there and they don't care what you look like, or how old you are. They're just the best. I think they're more intelligent than us. They haven't wrecked the planet, they don't have politics and all that.

273

LYNNE GRIFFIN
(BLACK CHRISTMAS, CURTAINS)

RA: How did you get into the acting business?

LG: It started because my dad was a professional photographer, a high fashion photographer. He got me into some modeling when I was a little one, which then became television commercials. Then, my mother became a talent agent and she represented me. I got some acting jobs and I did a couple of series, then I started to grow up and I got some film offers. One of the first films that I did was *Black Christmas*. Then, later on, I did *Curtains*, so I did two horror films during that time.

RA: Very cool. Sounds like it was a natural progression there.

LG: Yeah, I guess I was never meant to do anything else. It's funny because my mother really wasn't a stage mother. She really didn't push me into it, but she certainly encouraged me and took me everywhere. Because she was an agent as well, she could put in a word for me to get jobs and to get seen and have some doors open for me. I just decided that I wanted to start doing it my whole life and I was hooked.

BLACK CHRISTMAS

RA: I just have to start by saying that I actually rank this as my all-time favorite slasher film.

LG: (genuinely surprised) No way! Wow, number one?

RA: Yep, number one! People ask me that all the time and I always tell people that it's my all-time favorite because it's one of those movies that still manages to be scary and effective, even forty years after the fact! It's held up very well over the years.

LG: Yes, it's very true. It really has. I'm witness to the fact that now there have been so many re-releases, so I know that it's been rediscovered. We did a re-release for the twenty-fifth anniversary and then we did another one, and another one. We did special features each time and I've been on the convention circuit promoting it and I'm just so delighted to see that so many people have discovered it and that it has been so enduring. There are people that literally watch it every Christmas! (laughs) I even know that apparently, Quentin Tarantino watches it every Christmas, from what I've been told.

RA: That is so cool! One of the most interesting aspects about your part in the film is that Claire is killed in the opening minutes, yet still is seen throughout the entire film, and you're even on the poster! That's very unique.

LG: It is very unique and not only that, but that image of Claire with the plastic bag over her face has become such an iconic image for the film, and it was always on all of the covers. Little did I know that of all things, that would be the enduring image from *Black Christmas* (laughs). I'm very flattered, even if it isn't the most flattering photograph of myself.

RA: Was that surprising for you, when they chose that image for the poster?

LG: Yeah! I mean, they told me early on as they were putting together the poster, and they showed me the picture that they were going to use and I was very flattered, but I didn't think that it would continue over the many, many years and now, decades. Every time the film is re-released, I'm still gracing the cover in some form.

RA: Your kill scene in the movie is still one of the scariest parts for me. Can you tell me what went into making that scene? Was it a natural surprise for you or something that was scary to film?

LG: Well, it was. I mean, obviously one is directed and told what's going to happen. Bob Clark, the director was always very sweet and kept the set very jolly, and not terrifying and not demanding in ways that you thought were going to frighten you. Obviously, I knew how I was going to meet my demise, but it was quite gently presented to me and then it was kind of hilarious when we did it, because the cameraman Bert Dunk was in the closet. Bob had created this steadicam situation where the POV of the killer is really the camera. It was quite new and revolutionary at that time because steadicams really didn't exist then. Bert kind of fashioned this whole rig and had it belted on himself. So, he was in the closet behind the clothing, so it was actually the cameraman who strangled me. He was filming it the whole time. It's his hands and it was his hands when the killer is crawling up the outside of the house. That's all the cameraman. Just the fact that we didn't just have some actor in there, there was something funny about it being the very man who was shooting the film, and sort of keeping it all in the family. (laughs)

RA: That is definitely unique

LG: Oh yeah, but they were very kind to me. I got the job because I told them that I was a fairly good swimmer, so I could hold my breath for a long time. They said that it would be important when the plastic bag is over my head, sometimes for very long periods of time, like when they would be doing some of the stuff after my death, up in the attic when I would just be sitting there and having to have the cat jump on my lap and not breathe. I'm actually quite impressed when I see the film now, I am impressed that I managed to stay so dead looking under that plastic bag, knowing that I didn't breathe. That's a pretty impressive credit to have on the resume. (laughs) "Can hold her breath for a long time. Plays dead bodies very well." I actually played some other dead bodies as well later on. I did it a couple times, where I had to lie on a slab in the morgue. It's tough when all of the actors and crew are around and giggling, and you're not only trying to keep a straight face, but a dead face. (laughs) In my time, I played quite a few victims.

RA: (laughs) Now, you mentioned the part with the cat. I know that cats are notoriously hard to work with. How exactly did they get Claude to play along with you in the chair?

LG: Oh yes, and Claude was a total diva. Claude was very beautiful and not particularly a trained cat. I don't know exactly where Claude came from. He may have been someone's beloved cat that they wanted to have in the film. He wasn't one that was specially trained to do stunt work. In fact, for that scene when he is supposed to jump on my lap and lick my face, Bob was the one who was sitting opposite of me and he was the one who had his foot on the rocker of the chair, so he could rock it. He was actually the one who would hurl Claude at me, hoping that Claude would land on my lap happily and come lick my face, which of course, Claude didn't want any part of. The first few times, Claude just landed on me with claws extended and kind of screeched down my leg and ran off! Then, Bob decided that it was a good idea, because I had a plastic bag on my face, to spray my face with catnip. That way, Claude would behave and be a little bit more interested. We were really flying by the seat of our pants, hoping that this cat would actually do what we were hoping. In the end, we actually got the take, but yes, I remember being smothered with a plastic bag on my face, sprayed with catnip and having a cat that is not declawed thrown at me (laughs).

RA: (laughs) Wow. That is too funny! Margot Kidder played her part in *Black Christmas* to absolute perfection as the drunken train wreck. What was it like working with her in that role? Was she going "method" on that? Any funny stories of working with her?

LG: (laughs) Now, when you mean method, do you mean something else? (laughs) Well, the answer is yes. She's a riot! There is a certain amount of a wonderfully disciplined actress there, but she is definitely method in a sense, like during the story that she tells about the turtles. There had been … let's just say, maybe some added help. Maybe a bottle of Jack, if you know what I mean (laughs). She was always really … kind of loose, and I don't mean that as in a loose woman, but more like being easily able to access that certain part of her personality. Yeah, this is all put very delicately (laughs), but she was a riot, as was Andrea Martin. Olivia, on the other hand, was a fairly serious and straight forward actress, and she obviously had the burden of carrying the whole film. But, she was great too, because at that time, I was quite a serious Shakespearian actress and had worked at Stratford, so I was very interested in pinning Olivia down to talk about her working on Romeo and Juliet. She was very keen to talk about that and it was fascinating to hear her stories about playing Juliet on film. Come to think of it, I'm not even entirely sure if a lot of the stuff that Margot did was actually scripted. It was just brilliant. I know that the part with the phone number in the police department was scripted. Also, she had such a wonderful cheeky glint to her whenever she was working on it. She enjoyed playing that role. It's funny, one of my dearest and oldest friends from when I had moved and lived in California for twelve years, was Nancy Loomis, who was in the very first Halloween. She was actually the one that said to me, "You've done horror films, you should go out on the convention circuit." I have lots of great horror film friends, the women particularly. Leslie Donaldson and I still remain friends, from *Curtains.*

RA: The other one that is equally as funny in a similar role was Marian Waldman as the drunken, foul mouthed house mother. What are your memories of working with her?

LG: She was wonderful too. I must say that the whole atmosphere on the set was very jovial. That obviously always comes from the top down. That's what's so funny about watching it, to me, because I remember it as being a very joyous time, because everyone was having so much fun. We were all pretending it was Christmas in the fall, and there was no real snow on the ground. Marian Waldman came up with such a wonderful performance in that film, like with all of the hidden bottles in the house. She was a wonderfully comedic talent. Funny story, when they were talking about doing the remake of Black Christmas, which I still haven't seen, I kind of thought that I would be old enough to play the house mother part now and that I would have loved to have had a crack at that. Everyone had a really good time working on the film. It was never spooky, or scary, or seriously horrific. We all laughed a lot, and Marian made us laugh a lot. (pauses for a moment, then laughs) Ha! I just remembered when we put that flannel nightgown on her.

RA: (laughs) That's great to hear. It sounds like it was a really fun environment. Another thing that I really love is that Billy's identity is always kept a secret. You never find out who he is. (Lynne agrees) I remember hearing a rumor that there was an idea of having Art as the killer. Is that right?

LG: (laughs) Really? I think that maybe somebody was trying to solve an unsolvable mystery. At the end of the film, the phone is ringing again. I'm still in the attic, I haven't even been found and obviously, we know that it's not Keir Dullea, because he's lying dead in Olivia's arms, so I think that it was meant to be left ambiguous and never solved. I don't know. Have you seen the remake? Did they give any kind of indication as to who it might be in that film?

RA: Oh yeah. They completely left that one in the open. They said who it is, and why they did it. They pretty much took all of the mystique out of it.

LG: Oh my God, who did they say it was?

RA: (I explain the whole reveal to her. I'm leaving the spoilers out for the readers)

LG: Oh … I don't mean to sound so disappointed, but I kind of like the fact that the original left it so up in the air. (I agree) So often, when we talk about this film, like when Art and I do the Q and As, we like to ask, what is it that frightens people the most? For me, it really is that home invasion, that sort of never knowing aspect. It's much more psychological than just seeing people slashed up, and blood and gore. You know, Black Christmas, the original film, doesn't have a lot of blood in it and it doesn't really have the type of gore in it that most of the films that followed in that genre have. To me, that psychological fear is much scarier, fear in what you don't know or what you can't see or figure out. That to me is much scarier and its what Black Christmas succeeds at so brilliantly. You don't know who it is and you see this weird eyeball and you hear that crazy voice. My favorite moment is when the hand grabs Olivia's hair and pulls her back and you don't know who it is. I think that the things that scare and haunt us the most are the things that we don't know. In the end, we don't know. He's still in the house, whoever it is.

RA: Exactly! Honestly too, those cops were horrible at their jobs for leaving Olivia in the house alone.

LG: (laughs) Weren't they? Yeah, wouldn't you think that there would be a complete search of the house?

RA: (laughs) You would think so!

LG: Well, there's also that the cops are pretty much portrayed as buffoons throughout the film. They're not the brightest pennies in the pot. I think that's another thing that I loved about Bob Clark, is that he worked an awful lot of humor into the film. As well as being a horror film, there's a lot of really funny stuff in it, and there's a lot of incredible things there, as well. One of the most incredible things is that they actually had the thing with a young woman speaking about an abortion.

RA: Oh yeah, I've always thought that that had to be pretty cutting edge stuff at the time.

LG: Oh yeah. But then again, there's still so much fun in it as well, and so much humor. I'm good friends with Doug McGrath, the cop who receives the phony phone number. John Saxon has come out to a few of the conventions over the years, as well. I think that he was sort of a last-minute casting because the original actor wasn't able to be there, so John was flown in. They filmed that scene, where they're searching for the young girl, and it was in the freezing cold outside and that was the first scene they had him shoot. (laughs) Welcome to Canada! Welcome to the Canadian film industry, you're gonna freeze. (laughs)

RA: Can you share your thoughts on the enduring legacy of Black Christmas, and of being a part of that?

LG: You know, it is amazing to me that however many years it was, that it still has that reaction. I remember the initial release and it was fairly successful, but for me, the advent of Facebook and for me when I joined Facebook, there was this outpouring of people who made this connection between me and Claire. All of a sudden, there were so many people who had approached me to come and talk about it and come out to the convention circuit. I made lots and lots of friends through Black Christmas, and most of the time at the conventions, the people who come by to chat with me are younger people so it's just had this outpouring of support, especially since its come out on DVD and so many have rediscovered it. There's a whole new generation of viewers, which I find just extraordinary. They're always very complimentary, which I find amazing because it's one of the first films that I did. I always say, that when it's slow at the conventions and maybe there's not enough people paying attention to me, I just take out a plastic bag and put it over my head. (laughs) We do a lot of selfies then.

RA: (laughs) That's awesome!

LG: Yeah, I actually have a picture of myself that someone took at a convention where I have the plastic bag over my head and I'm actually holding up the DVD with a picture of me with a plastic bag over my head on the cover. It's very funny. Then, I always get people lining up and asking to take my picture. I say, "Okay, but I have to take the bag off at some point, to breathe."

CURTAINS

RA: (laughs) That's always helpful! Now when you do the conventions, do you also get people that come up, who are fans of *Curtains*?

LG: Oh yeah, and with *Curtains*, because it was only brought out on Blu-Ray and DVD a couple years ago. Before that, there was only that awful VHS bootleg on DVD, that had three other films on it as part of some collection, so that was the only way you could see it. When they contacted me to tell me that it was finally getting an official release on DVD and Blu-Ray, I was very excited to see that have a new life. Initially, I was watching it and it had huge sales on Amazon, but I don't know if it caught on the same way and if it's as enduring as *Black Christmas*. I'm not sure if it has the same kind of following, but there's definitely a following. When I do conventions, I have memorabilia from *Curtains* as well and I like to promote both of the films. The remastered version of *Curtains* is so beautiful. They did such a fabulous job on it. Leslie Donaldson and I went to New York and met with Edwin Samuelson and he filmed us just sitting and watching the film together in his studio, for the first time in so many years. It was so much fun. We did the commentary together and it was hilarious to be watching it together and to find moments that we hadn't remembered, and sharing memories of certain scenes and how they were shot. You know, that film had a rougher start, what with the director eventually taking his name off of it. We went back to do re-shoots a couple of years later and it got re-edited. It had a rougher and rockier journey, but I'm so glad that they eventually took it and made a beautiful remastered print of it, and that's what people are seeing now.

RA: I'm glad about that too. *Curtains* is another film that is one of my all-time favorites. Like *Black Christmas*, it's still scary and effective, and a very good movie.

LG: That's good to hear, because when I first saw it, it wasn't at the screening. I was actually in New York and I bought a ticket. It was playing at some … kind of … not very reputable theater (laughs). I went in to see it with maybe about twenty other people. Then, after that, it disappeared for so long. Nobody really knew about that film, so it's really wonderful when films are rediscovered like that, that you did so long ago and that people want to talk about it. People do want to know about the behind the scenes gossip, if there was any. There certainly was more of that on *Curtains* than there was on *Black Christmas* (laughs). Well, that's the nature of the film, really, being about six actresses up for a part and one of them will kill to get it.

RA: It's funny too, for you, going from being the first killed in *Black Christmas* to having such a huge part in *Curtains*, and you had a very interesting, quirky character, as well.

LG: Right! Plus, no spoilers intended, but it was very fun for me to get to live till the end of a project, because, as I said before, I was too often the first to go in many of the projects that I did (laughs). I did another film called The Amateur, which was a wonderful thriller with John Savage and Chris Plummer. In the very beginning of it, I have a horrific early demise as well. So, to get a film where not only do you get to live until the very end, but also, being a serious stage actress, to learn how to do stand-up comedy and to play a comedic role, was very different for me.

RA: Did you actually do your own stand-up bits for *Curtains?*

LG: I did. We filmed it at a very famous comedy bar in Toronto called Yuk-Yuks, which is actually where Jim Carrey started his career. I helped write the stand-up routine and I did it in front of a live audience and we filmed it and it was terrifying (laughs). I had never done anything like that. I've always been a fairly serious actress, working at Stratford and doing Shakespeare, so it very much was a departure for me, but I really enjoyed it. I really just enjoyed Patti's sass and that cheeky reverence that she had about everything.

RA: That brings up another question. When you did the stand-up, how did you come up with some of the bits and how was it received live?

LG: (laughs) Well, like with the joke about the guy from Photo-Mat, I don't remember. It was a long time ago. I'm pretty sure that was mine. They just told me to write something and get up there and do it, and they'll just film it. It just took a courageous plunge to do it. It was interesting because we did do it like a live show. I don't know if the people were extras or if they paid to see it, but they came in and sat and they didn't know what they were going to see. In those days too, they kind of shot things in a guerilla type way. You didn't really know how things were going to be done until you were kind of thrust into it. Obviously, we know that I never pursued a career in stand-up comedy, because it was this terrifying thing (laughs). I'm very in awe of people that can just get up there and riff. I've had friends that do it, and it's so awful when you see them bombing and nobody is laughing and they're getting heckled. (RA: I relate a story of doing security for a stand-up comedian who bombed so badly that everyone walked out on him, leading him to get drunk and angry on stage, challenging people to fight)

That to me is just soul destroying. I don't know how people keep doing it when that happens. It's one thing if you're doing a play and people walk out. You can say, "Hey, I didn't write it". So much of stand-up is about revealing your own personality and what you find funny or odd, so if they're walking out, you would feel like they'd be walking out on you and your personality. They just don't like you (laughs). That hurts! (RA: I relay a wrestling story of the difference between "good heat" and "bad heat", the crowd reacting to what you do vs. Something they find about you specifically to boo you for) When the crowd is against you, I can imagine that you'd just want the Earth to open up and swallow you up.

RA: Definitely! (I relate to her information about the *Troll 2* documentary *Best Worst Movie* and how the director could not understand why people thought his "serious" work was funny)

LG: That makes me think back to the movies of Ed Wood, where people now kind of enjoy them because it's so bad it's good. It's like there's a curiosity factor because of cheap or sleazy they are and the production values are terrible, but it's actually fun to watch because it's so bad. (laughs) Some people have made careers out of it.

RA: (laughs) That is very true! Getting back to *Curtains,* I've always been in love with the location and the snowy landscape of the film. Can you remember the location and your memories of working there?

LG: You know, I don't really remember, because I wasn't at the snowy house. The only place that I really remember where I shot outdoors was the drive up, at the gas station. Everything else was shot in the studio, except for when you see the characters outside in the snow. I don't know where that house is, because I never went to the house. Everything was just built on set in a studio. I do remember that the area where they shot me driving up was very beautiful. Maybe the house was up there too, but I was never there. Of course, the house from *Black Christmas* is still there in Rosedale. I think they might have put a big fence up a while ago. Maybe they're tired of having people come visit (laughs). I remember, Art and I went back there for the special features of one of the releases, which was very cool for us to kind of wander around and talk about filming in there. Although, they did clean up the attic quite a bit. It was much gloomier during *Black Christmas* than it is now.

RA: Did she actually get to play the killer in the kill scenes, with the mask?

LG: (laughs) I think I'm going to leave that to people's curiosity. I don't really want to spoil whether it was me or not. I can say though, that during the scene in the skating rink, they wanted somebody who could skate. I think a lot of people got to wear the mask for various scenes, but I like to think it was me.

RA: What do you remember about working with John Vernon?

LG: Oh, what a wonderful actor. I knew him mainly because I worked on stage and knew him as a stage actor from some of the things that he did. He was really nice, but he was intimidating in exactly the right way. When I got to see the scene between he and I, he was truly an intimidating presence. He was totally great for that part, but very nice in general. I knew him very well because I worked with him in other things, as well. He was a very sweet man and great at what he did. I will say though, on the other hand, that Samantha Eggar was very remote.

RA: I would have to say that the scene between you and John is one of my favorites.

LG: Well, thank you. That was one of my favorites as well, because it was my dramatic scene. I wasn't as comfortable trying to be funny as I was trying to be dramatic. Now, I'm just funny all the time (laughs). I like playing funny parts now.

RA: Without giving too much away, can you tell me a bit about the significance of that final scene, that final shot of you and give me your insight into that?

LG: It's funny because we shot two different endings. Unfortunately, when they went to do the remaster of *Curtains,* I guess they found out that wherever the extra footage had been stored, literally only two or three years prior, someone had thrown it all out.

RA: No!

LG: Oh yeah. The actual ending that I remember shooting is gone forever, although I do have a photograph from that scene, how the original ending was shot. We shot it in a little theatre space and I had gotten all of the women propped up on chairs around me, as I do my stand-up routine for an empty theatre. The evidence that I have is that photograph from when we shot it that day. We shot the new ending about two years later, when we came back and shot me doing the stand-up act at the asylum. I think that the first ending was definitely more chilling, but because it changed direction and it changed directors. The director, Richard Ciupka, had a different idea in mind for the movie, but I think that the producers wanted a true slasher film, which is really not what he had set out to do. I would say that pretty much the last third of the film is not what the original director had intended. All of that stuff with Sandee Currie running around in the costume area was not originally in the movie. The scene at the end with Samantha Eggar and I was not in the original film. It changed a lot, but I don't think that it really hurt the film. Obviously, Richard had a different idea for it and took his name off of it. They put the name Jonathan Stryker on, which is obviously the name of the character of the director in the movie (laughs). I wasn't really aware that there was trouble in the background of that film. I had a very enjoyable shoot both times that I worked on it. When I first saw the completed film, I could tell what was the original director's work and what was not. That's why it seemed a little uneven to me when I first saw it.

RA: That is truly fascinating! I have one last question. If you could say anything to the fans out there, what would you say?

LG: I would say, keep discovering them. Keep discovering some of the films that were made back then. There's a big library of horror films that I think people, or younger generations, aren't aware of. There are lots of them out there that are really quite wonderful. You can go back even further to older films like *Dracula* and *Frankenstein.* These are much older films that are still hugely enduring tales of horror that I think many people aren't aware of because there's such a glut of the modern extreme films now. I say, just keep going back and watching them because you could unearth some fascinating little gems, some that you had no idea existed. Go and watch Boris Karloff and films like that. One of the most terrifying films that I remember seeing as a kid was *The Wolfman.* There's also many great things coming out now, like the horror series they have on Netflix. I loved *Penny Dreadful* and I watched it religiously. There are some very good modern ones that are more psychological, which I find much scarier than any slasher movie. I would also say, definitely go back and watch more Hitchcock films. Don't neglect those films. They'll be around as long as people are still wanting to watch those films. I'm amazed by how many of the younger generation don't know Hitchcock. If you like horror, you should watch them. I say keep watching and maybe we'll have this horror renaissance, where more people will start making even more films that are more terrifying.

MARK HOLTON
(LEPRECHAUN, PEE WEE'S BIG ADVENTURE)

RA: First off, I would like to ask, how did you first get involved in the film business?

MH: I realized that if I was going to make a living beyond regional dinner theater, I would have to try my luck in New York or L.A. I chose Southern California because I would rather rub bumpers than elbows. It was an easier adjustment for someone coming from a small town in Oklahoma. I joined an improv group and did waiver theater to stay sharp. A casting agent asked me to read with the actors auditioning for a pilot called *Webster*. They wrote me a role for an episode in the first season and that's how I got my SAG card.

Pee Wee's Big Adventure

RA: Although it's not horror (okay, Large Marge was quite horrific) this is my personal favorite work of yours, as Francis. How did you get in this film? What did you do to win over your part, and was there anything you personally improvised in it?

MH: I was seen as an alternate, after they had offered the role to another actor. The actor's agent made a counter offer and casting declined, making an offer to me instead. I didn't know this happened until I ran into that actor at an audition months later.

RA: Any funny stories from the set?

MH: There were so many talented and funny people on the set every day, but the set was the most fun when Phil Hartman was there.

Leprechaun

RA: Your character in Leprechaun was very interesting, kind of a man child. Could you describe your thoughts on him and what went into playing the part?

MH: Well, Ozzie needed a new brain. (laughs) Ozzie was partly a caricature of Lenny from *Of Mice and Men*. The director never reigned me in and he probably should have.

RA: What was the atmosphere on the set like and your personal experience in the movie?

MH: It was a very fun and comfortable atmosphere. Jennifer was a hoot. She was very bright and genuinely funny.

RA: What was your experience working with Warwick Davis as the leprechaun like?

MH: Warwick Davis was a trooper. The man was in makeup hell every day. Even when he was sick, he always had a smile and never complained. He was there before the rest of the cast and stayed long after. When he wasn't in front of the camera he was stuck in a chair while makeup got him ready for the next take. Warwick earned everyone's admiration and respect.

Gacy

RA: I have to say that playing John Wayne Gacy, a real life serial killer (who is personally the scariest person in existence to me), is some challenging and controversial territory. I talked with William Forsythe about playing the role and he said it was disturbing at times. What was your experience like playing Gacy and more importantly preparing for the role? Any interesting stories from your preparations?

MH: At the first meeting before starting the film, a production assistant stopped at a branch of the L.A. Library in Hollywood looking for the latest book on Gacy. The book had been checked out three times. On the back of the cover page was a hand drawing in black ink of Gacy on his knees behind a small boyish figure. In blue ink, another "reader" had drawn a rope around the boy's neck leading back to Gacy's hand. Added by the third "reader" in pencil above this scene was the word DREAMS. The word was sketched in wavy lettering. I dropped the book on the table and walked away. I wanted to wash my hands. When asked during filming how it was going, I would answer, "I wash my mind out with a toilet brush at the end of the day and go home to my wife and children." Some disturbing fan mail that I received after the film was released, went unanswered. The fact that there are people like Gacy out there, and those that have *dreams* of following in their footsteps is one of the reasons I sleep with a gun. I wish I had never done the film.

MARK PATTON
(A NIGHTMARE ON ELM STREET 2)

RA: How did you land the role of Jesse on *Nightmare?*

MP: I had previously screen tested for the role of Glen on the first movie. I then came back for this one and auditioned and was chosen through the natural process of auditioning in Los Angeles.

RA: What was your experience working with Robert Englund like?

MP: It was great. I had already known Robert a long time before *Nightmare on Elm Street*, so I knew his work and knew him as a person before I started. I continue to still see him and have had a great lifelong relationship with him. He's just a good friend and I think that he is a wonderful actor.

RA: The one scene in the film that always amazed me, effects wise, is the transformation scene where Freddy rips out of Jesse's body. How was this pulled off?

MP: It's a puppet. It was pre-CGI, so it's all hand built puppets and effects. I was buried in plaster of Paris and they built seven replicas of my body. Then it was a lot of the hand pulled puppets and me acting. Most of it is the eyes of the actors. It really helps to sell the illusion. That was the good old days and how it was done then. There were no computers, so it came down to that and a lot of models. For example, when the bus is falling down at the beginning of the movie, that was a model that was the size of this room (the vendor space in the convention center, which is massive-Ronnie), and tiny, tiny pieces. There were thousands and thousands of pieces to it, and tiny cameras and little buses. They just had to build everything by hand.

RA: I see that you have a book that you wrote called *Jesse's Lost Journals*. Can you tell me more about that?

MP: It's a sub-textural story of Jesse inside of the movie. It's like Nancy's diary in the first. Of course, there was no actual diary in the movies. Nancy didn't have a diary on the first film. That was just an invention for the second part. So, I just invented one for Jesse. I started it as Facebook posts and it was picked up by Static Mass in London and won the best companion piece of fiction for a movie about four years ago. I direct sell it. I think I've sold about five thousand copies of it and it all belongs to me.

RA: One thing I really wanted to touch on and talk about is something interesting I heard you say. You were saying that it was hard at the time to be open about your sexuality in Hollywood. I find this odd because I know that so many people in Hollywood at the time, and now, were gay themselves.

MP: Well, it wasn't hard to be open … it was impossible. There was no out of the closet in the pre-late eighties. The only reason that it became possible to be open ultimately was because of the AIDS epidemic. There was no openness back then, everybody lived in the closet. If you didn't, you didn't work, you were fired. You know, it's funny, there's an old saying in Hollywood that there would be no theater or film industry without Jews or gays. Strangely, they were both two self-hating groups of people. It was odd that there were so many people and the business that were, but they didn't want anybody else to be (gay). It was a very strange dynamic.

RA: It seems very hypocritical to me, as well.

MP: Yeah, it was horrible. Just a terrible time. A lot of people's lives were destroyed over gossip and gay innuendo over the years. So many suicides. Some of the actors that we admire the most, mostly the male stars, were gay, and many of the women were, too. It was a very hypocritical time, from the early days through the seventies in Hollywood. It was a very repressive time and very conservative in the United States in general. It was hard. It was a case of whenever money gets involved and there's a lot of money, people begin to convince you that they have your best interests at heart, and they put you in a cage and they control you. It's really all about the money and there was a lot of it.

RA: Is that what made you step away from Hollywood?

MP: Yeah, it did actually. I was getting ready to play a gay character on television and I was at CBS doing my final contract. I was sitting at a table with fourteen men who were asking me how my girlfriend was going to feel about me playing a gay person and how I would deal with it in public, with people asking me if I was gay and I was supposed to be straight. I looked around the table and I realized that all the people I was talking to were gay. It was fourteen gay men sitting around this table asking me these questions. At the time, there was the AIDS epidemic going on and there was people dying in the street. I just thought that this is bullshit, so I just got up, walked away from the table and I walked away from the whole thing. That was it for me. But, it's almost over now, so that's very cool to see.

RA: On that note, do you Hollywood is now more accepting? It sure seems that way.

MP: Oh God yes. Half of the television stars right now are openly gay in some of the most popular shows in the world. Jim Parsons is out and married to a man. Many talk show hosts are out, like Anderson Cooper and of course, Ellen. You don't even think of people being gay and it mattering anymore. The show *Scandal,* the guy who is the serial killer on there, who is the biggest, brutish, meanest guy on television, is gay and a total sweetheart and married. People just live very openly. The next step will be the first male superstar, like a Tom Cruise, who will come out, but of course, in that case we will never see that happen. It's a completely different world now, but it still has its perils, too.

RA: The one that I like to see is Neil Patrick Harris now and the success that he is having. It's so well-known and he's so open about it, yet nobody cares. It really is the essence of how acceptable it is now.

MP: Oh yeah, of course. Neil Patrick Harris grew up on television. He's a very talented young man. Then, there's other types of gay people too like Kevin Spacey, who doesn't really want to talk about being gay. The reason why he never wants to talk about it has nothing to do with being ashamed about being gay, it's just that he doesn't want to reveal anything about his personal life. He's just that kind of actor and he doesn't want anything to interfere with his art. The level that he works on deserves that type of respect. His personal life shouldn't be discussed because he wants to be an illusion and he's good enough to pull that off. He just stays very private and people should respect his privacy in that return. People have the right to a private life if they want it. All of us do.

RA: How do you view your notoriety these days from *Nightmare on Elm Street* and the massive fanbase that you have, with all of these people following you and coming to meet you?

MP: It's interesting. I'm really good friends with Allison Arngrim, who played Nellie Oleson on *Little House on the Prairie*. She wrote a book called *Confessions of a Prairie Bitch.* After *Little House on the Prairie*, she just couldn't get hired for anything because people thought that she was a bitch, but she turned that into a goldmine. Then, she turned that goldmine into a platform to begin to change laws. She changed the rape laws in California by her fame. She has changed the laws in many of the states by going and talking about her own experiences. I have done the same thing with this movie and my notoriety. I can talk openly about homophobia and HIV to people that don't know anything about it. That's what I use my fame for is to talk about things that are more interesting to me and things that are helpful. So, I'm having fun, but I'm also doing a lot of good.

MICHAEL SWAN
(FRIDAY THE 13th PART VI)

RA: How did you get involved in the acting business?

MS: When I was nine years old, my mother dropped me off at the Palo Alto Children's Theater. That was my start. I did plays at the children's theater, then I moved to the regular community theater as I got older. Then, I got an agent in San Francisco and started to do a lot of extra work in shows like *Streets of San Francisco* and in some movies. Then, I moved down here to LA after I got out of the Army in 1973. I was under contract to MGM Television. I did shows like *Medical Center* and *Bronx* with Jack Palance, a show called *Executive Suite* and then my first guest star role was on *CHIPS*.

RA: Did you find it tough getting work when you first got to LA?

MS: Yeah, relatively. I was very lucky, though. I got started and never stopped. With how the climate is now and how much the business has changed though, I would never attempt it. I'd rather be a delivery driver or sell shoes. (laughs)

RA: How has it changed over the years?

MS: In so many ways. I'll tell you my favorite story about how much the business has changed. Here's an example of how it was. When I was under contract, I would get a call from my agent and they would say they want me to read for such and such show. I would go in at ten o'clock in the morning and everyone that needed to see the actor would be there like the writer, the producer, the director. Everyone was there. You went and read and then by four o'clock in the afternoon, you would know if you had the gig. I went and did a soap opera in New York right after *Friday the 13th*. I did *As the World Turns* and I was on there for ten years. Then I came back here and I started going out on auditions. I had an audition for the show *JAG*. My friend was the executive producer who I worked with before on *The Rockford Files*, so I thought I had a good chance there. I didn't hear anything for a few days and then my agent called and said "Mike, *JAG* called and you've got a callback. They want to see you this afternoon" and my question to her was, "What's a callback?" (laughs) So that's my "how the business has changed" story, but there are so many other things. It's a lot colder now. It's not really about the craft anymore. It's more about how many Twitter followers you have or how many Instagram followers you have. Like I said, if I was starting out now, I wouldn't want to be a traditional actor, except possibly on stage.

FRIDAY THE 13th PART VI: JASON LIVES:
RA: How did you get involved with *Friday the 13th*?

MS: I went on the audition and booked the gig. I then went out to Atlanta and we shot the show in Covington, just south of Atlanta. I had some good times with Tony Goldwyn. Tony and I became friends. We went and had a couple of wild nights in Atlanta together. He went on to his great career and I went on to my soap career. I'll tell you a funny story about me and Tony. One day we were talking about what we wanted to do after the movie. He looked at me and said, "You'd be great for Soap Opera" and I said I would never do a fucking soap opera. I said they just suck, the acting sucks, it's horrible to watch, it's boring and everything. The funny part is, about a week after I said that, I was starting my ten-year role on *As the World Turns!* (laughs)

RA: What was your filming schedule like when you were filming the movie?

MS: We shot at night, so we would go to work when the sun went down and we would come back to the hotel when the sun came up. The guy who owned the hotel also owned the bar next door, so he would open the bar at seven o'clock in the morning. Everybody would go in there and get hammered and then go to sleep, get up about six thirty at night and go back to shooting.

RA: How was your experience working with director Tom McLoughlin? I interviewed him for the first book and he was at my debut book signing. A very nice guy!

MS: I ran into Tommy a couple of years ago when he had a screening of *Friday the 13th Part Six* in the area. I hadn't seen him in like 25 years. I haven't seen him since, but we email back and forth every now and then. He's a cool guy. He really trusted his actors. He would say action and just go. He was just very cool, like a non-director. He was cool to the crew, cool to the actors. Everything was mellow with him.

RA: That's great. I like hearing that. Could you talk about your death scene in it and what went into making that happen?

MS: Well, to be honest with you, it did not come off. It was not as well-lit as we hoped and the effects really didn't do what they were supposed to do. So, I had to go in and they made a cast of my head, and they created this skull that would squeeze and the brain would pop out the top. The way it was conceived, it really didn't come off that way, but it was okay. Obviously, Jason crushes my skull. You can kind of see my brain come out of the top of the skull. It was good effects and the make-up guy was good, so when you see me lying on the ground there with my head all crushed and everything, that took him about two hours to do that make-up. I sat there and drank Brandy the whole time because I didn't have to do much else than lie there, so I thought what difference does it make if I'm hammered? (laughs) That was a real fun evening. I think that was the last night of my part of the shoot. Then after that, I flew to New York and started *As the World Turns*. I started about ten days after *Part Six*.

RA: What was your experience like working with CJ Graham as Jason?

MS: We only had that one scene where he crushes my head. That's the only thing we ever really did together. It was just kind of matter of fact. We did what we had to do and that was that. I don't think I ever had a conversation with CJ besides that. Of course, there were those times at the bar at seven o'clock in the morning where by about eight, I didn't even know who I was having a conversation with anyways! (laughs)

RA: What was your favorite memory of making the movie?

MS: Well, the Tony Goldwyn story and hanging out with him. He and I also rented a car one night and went up to Atlanta to see what kind of trouble we could get into. We went to the Hyatt just for fun and we stumbled into a Dental Assistant's convention. So, there were about four hundred women there and we got there at a time that everyone was pretty well lit. We picked out a couple of girls and started talking and they invited us up to their hotel room. Next thing you know, I'm on the bed with my girl and Tony's there with his. It was then that my girlfriend said to me "Just so you know, my husband is a linebacker for the Miami Dolphins". Well, you never saw a guy get out of a hotel room so fast! (laughs)

RA: (laughs) I bet! I also read that you've done a lot of work with Roger Corman?

MS: I've done four of Roger's pictures- *Dinocroc vs. Supergator, Camel Spiders, Piranhaconda* and another one. They all show up on the SyFi Channel. Roger, for a long time at the end of his career used director Jim Wynorski, who is a … crazy man. (laughs) So, you never knew what was going to come next. He would yell at everybody and scream at them, then he would speak softly, then he would be obsequious the next moment. You never knew what was going to happen, so you were always on your toes with Jim. A lot of times I didn't agree with him and thought he was making bad decisions, like he made a bad decision with my character of *Piranhaconda*. I did some other things with him, but he doesn't work much anymore, so he doesn't call me anymore, so that's okay.

RA: Looking back on it, how do you view your time on *Friday the 13th*, and how do you view the movie now?

MS: I've seen them all and I still think that ours is the best. I liked the remake and thought that it was good, but of the originals, I think that Part Six was the best. My time on it was great and we just had a ball. We worked and did our silly stuff and had fun. We got hammered at seven o'clock in the morning, Tony and I became good friends and it was a fun gig.

RA: If you had anything to say to the fans of the series, what would you say?

MS: God bless you for your dedication to this seminal series. It's the most successful slasher franchise and I think it's great that the fans are so dedicated and still want to see guys like me.

MILES CHAPIN
(THE FUNHOUSE)

RA: Thanks for joining me here. I'm a big fan of *The Funhouse* and that's what I wanted to talk about with you today. I rank it as one of my top favorite slasher films.

MC: Really? That's cool. To me, it's probably the most unscary scary movie. Of course, that may be because I read the script. I think that the terror that was in it was more in the suspense and the buildup than the payoff.

RA: I agree. It is definitely one the more suspenseful, slow burn slasher films. Well, first off I want to start at the beginning and ask you, how did you get into the acting business?

MC: I grew up in New York City. My father worked in the arts, he was in the music business. A family friend of ours, a guy named Stitch Henderson, used to conduct the band on the tonight show with Johnny Carson, and was doing an Opera production at City Center in New York. He asked my parents if it was okay if they could put me in the chorus. This opera had a chorus of little ragamuffin street kids. They said to ask me and I said "sure, I would love to do it." So, I did that, then one thing leads to another. There was a talent scout that came to the rehearsals one day and they were casting a movie called *Ladybug, Ladybug* and I ended up doing that. Then, later I did another movie. Showbiz worked at a different pace back then and there weren't a lot of child actors, so I didn't really concentrate on a career the way other child actors do. I never had an agent, but I fit a specific type. I was sort of fat and funny. By the time I had gotten out of High School, I had done a bunch of movies, TV shows and it was I wanted to do. I had sort of backed into a career and I was very fortunate

RA: How did you get involved with *The Funhouse*?

MC: *The Funhouse* came at a period in my life when I was very busy as a performer. I had just finished a movie and I was in New York doing a play. My agents inquired about my availability for something. They told them I was in New York doing a play and they said "That's great, Tobe Hooper is in New York too. Why don't we get them together?", so they called me and told me that he is interested in having me in this movie and sent the script over. Tobe came to see the show one night and we went out for beers afterwards. I mean, who doesn't want to work with Tobe Hooper, right? I was like, "I'm in, what do I do? Where do I show up?" He was pretty easy.

RA: I've always liked the set on the movie and it's one of my favorites. It's just very cool. What are your memories of working on that carnival set?

MC: Well, that was the thing that was amazing. It was quite remarkable. We were down in Miami, Florida and there was this old movie studio that belonged to Ivan Torres, who was an old-line producer who did the show *Flipper*. They had this small studio and out behind the studio was a vacant lot. Next door to it was a Howard Johnson motel with a Denny's in it. They set up the carnival in that vacant lot behind the studio and we lived in the hotel next door, so we could walk there. We didn't have to get driven to the set, and they hired a carnival! How cool is that? They had an actual carnival back there! It was amazing. We had the run of the joint, so we could go burst balloons or throw darts or shoot the guns if we wanted to. It was full of extras and full of real carnival people. Of course, they had all the tents with all of the grotesque animals and things. The art department had done all of those banners, so that it was so much more than just a traveling carnival. It was like a traveling carnival on steroids. It was perfect. Then, when we filmed the interiors, we moved it into the studio and shot that there. It was very simple.

RA: I want to draw a comparison here: your own personal memories of carnivals growing up as opposed to the one in the movie. Did it enhance the experience for you?

MC: I grew up in New York City, so it's a little different here. I mean, we had Coney Island here and I used to go there a lot. I still do, I take my kids and they go there too on their own. But, that type of traveling carnival I was only able to experience once or twice in New England, where my family used to go in the summertime. So, that kind of a show was very exotic to me. To see a set like that which was an authentic traveling carnival that was directed by a Hollywood art director was where my steroids comment came from. I didn't have many preconceived notions. I really only had the idea of it from what I had seen on TV. A lot of those types of images are what give us that image in our minds eye of what carnivals and those types of experiences are like, even though we haven't really experienced them ourselves, but we've seen them in the movies. My frame of reference was Coney Island and the New

England carnivals, but that kind of Southern circuit carnie thing was new to me and that added to the exotic nature of it and I think that it enhanced the film.

RA: Definitely. What was To be like to work with? Were you already familiar with _Texas Chainsaw_ and some of those movies?

MC: I hadn't seen them, but he screened _Texas Chainsaw Massacre_ for us when we were in pre-production, in that week or two before we started shooting. I loved it. I thought it was one of the funniest films I had ever seen. When I gave him my reaction, that I thought it was hilarious, he thought that was hilarious! He just kind of slapped his knee and said, "God damn it, more people don't understand that about that movie!" I said, "Well, it's scary as hell, of course, but it's funny and it's a riot!" I think we got off on the right foot with that interaction. He's really a remarkable guy. He's really talented and I loved working with him. I think he liked me too, because it seemed he trusted me. There were times where he would say something to all four of us and maybe someone didn't get it, and he'd turn to me and go "You know what I'm talking about" and I'd say, "Sure thing, Tobe. I know exactly what you're talking about, but I'll let you tell them because I have to go do this". I'd say we had a good process and then the four of us got along really well. It was an enjoyable experience.

RA: You got to work with a couple of the legitimate legends of the film business in _The Funhouse_, Kevin Conway (The Barker) and Sylvia Miles (Fortune Teller). What was that like working with them?

MC: I'll start with Kevin. To me, Kevin Conway is one of the great American actors. I had known his work for years and it was a huge honor to work with him. I have to say, when I first met him I was a little intimidated. When I got to know him, I really grew fond of him and I think it's mutual. His work, going back to _The Elephant Man_ where he originated the role of Frederick Treeves, which was a very significant thing, just embodies the essence of American acting. There's a strong, sound, emotional core to his work and believable truthfulness and yet, he's a character actor too. You can give him anything and he can do it. When he came on _The Funhouse,_ to watch him build all of those characters that he had and watch him put them together, with all of the makeup and costume and everything, was just a real lesson in acting. Sylvia, of course, is a legend. I mean, she's Sylvia Miles. What can you say? I had run into her a couple of times in New York and since I have the same first name as her last name, we always remembered each other. I think the first time I knew her work was in _Midnight Cowboy._ She's just a solid professional and it was great to work with a living legend. Then, there was Bill Foley too. _Phantom of The Paradise_ was one of my favorite movies and it was remarkable to watch him come down and put together his character of Dracula. They were all good people and very talented.

RA: I especially liked Kevin Conway in *The Quick and the Dead*. He was amazing in that, as well.

MC: He is an amazingly versatile actor. That's what I was talking about when I said he is one of the great American actors. If you know about acting traditions, you've got like the British tradition and the American kind of rivaling each other in a way. The American way is the method, the deep emotional resonance and the resonant truth, while the British is more refined and kind of outward technical stuff, and more character driven. To me, I've always thought that what needed to be done was to merge the two. To be able to merge the emotional truth at the same time as you have that outward symbolism and the outward things of character acting. That's exactly what I was talking about with Kevin Conway. He does them both. He can play a gnarly sheriff from the south or he can play a carnival barker from God knows where, and at the same time he can play a doctor and be completely believable. He can do anything. Kevin Conway fan society here, sign me up. (laughs)

RA: Definitely! (laughs) Another one that was great in the movie as the monster is Wayne Doba. What was he like playing that role?

MC: Wayne is great. Wayne's physicality is what really sets him apart. He's a brilliant physical comedian, mime, acrobat. I mean, those kinds of skills take talent. I remember when they told us about Wayne when he was coming in and that he was going to be the monster, they looked at us and said, "Well, if you've seen a lot of guys who play clowns in the circus or mimes on the street, wait till you see this guy. He's one of the best of all of that put together." It's true.

RA: I always thought it was interesting about him as the monster that they made him seem like this huge monster, but when you saw certain long shots, you can tell that he actually wasn't that big, in reality.

MC: No, he's really not. He's like my height, which is like 5'7-5'8. He's sleight and skinny and limber, but that's what he does. He was also wearing a mask that didn't have a lot of articulation to it. These days they would do it differently. A couple of years after I did *Funhouse*, I did *Howard The Duck*. We had the same kind of limitations with physical, practical effects. They were very limited, so the way that you got the expressiveness was with full body performance. You couldn't just do it with a computer. So, you really needed someone who was as physically expressive as possible and that's why Wayne was so good.

RA: What was your take on your character, Richie?

MC: Well, he's kind of a doofus. (laughs) He's a nice guy, but he makes several big mistakes through the course of that movie.

RA: I thought he was kind of an idiot at times (Laughs)

MC: Yeah, he was an idiot! (laughs) I mean, he just wanted to get laid. It was his brilliant idea to spend the night in the funhouse, then it was his brilliant idea to smoke weed and then his lighter falls out and betrays their presence. Then, he's the first one to get it, so sayonara Richie!

RA: Plus, he takes the money too, which was a very bad move

MC: There you go! That was the third thing. I mean, what an idiot. And I love playing idiots. He's really the story driver. Richie's character is the one that propels the story forward, because without Richie's brilliant ideas, they would have just gone home. End of movie. (laughs)

RA: Right! (laughs) So, was the funhouse itself, the set, fully functional?

MC: No, the interior of the funhouse was done in bits and pieces. It was very tricky doing that stuff. I also have to give Tobe props. He didn't have a chance because of budgetary restrictions, to fill out those sequences as much as he had envisioned it. He was under a lot of pressure just to get the shoot over with. Movie making can be expensive. There never was a ride like that, it was just in pieces. They had constructed parts of it and then you could do quick adaptations here and there. That's how you make movies. You write it and then you want to go and shoot the script, but there are a lot of constraints along the way. Sometimes you have to improvise and think on your feet. You gotta give props to Tobe for making lemonade out of the lemons he was given for that.

RA: It's funny, I saw the movie at a young age and it sort of built up my idea of what a funhouse would be like. Sadly, the reality is a bit of a letdown with those tiny ones.

MC: True, and you would never get something like this that's that big and complex at a traveling show. I hear you big time. The equivalent for us was the spookhouse out at Coney Island, with the one track and you turn and there's a skeleton. You turn again and, ooh, there's a paper mache Dracula. It is what it is, but that's what growing up is all about. It's kind of like when you find out about the Easter Bunny or Santa Claus. It becomes something bigger the simplicity of what the word gives you. It's like good magic, it's what you bring to it. The magic happens inside your head. That's why we go to the movies.

RA: Now, you got to work with another prominent director of horror in Alfred Sole, who made *Alice Sweet Alice,* on the movie *Pandemoneum.* What was the experience like?

MC: You know *Pandemoneum*? Wow. You know, it's really funny. Movies kind of go in cycles. Sometimes there are genres that never really take off and you wonder why. It's like, how come every studio did a sword and sorcery picture? Or, like how the gang movies were such a big thing in the late seventies. The answer is that Studio A hears that Studio B is doing this kind of a movie and they think they had better do one too. So, in terms of *The Funhouse,* the complimentary movie is *Carnie* with Robbie Robertson. It's not a horror picture, but it has that sort of grit we were talking about. It's actually a better representation of that carnie life. My point is that the comedy horror film was kind of inevitable. Actors of my generation seemed to follow suit and have their ticket punched. You had to do a horror film or a slasher film, like in *Friday the 13th.* My old friend Kevin Bacon did that one. Then, there was this comedy horror genre, and there were several that came out of the gate at the same time. With ours, the script was called Thursday the 12th. Then, Roger Corman announced a movie called *Saturday the 14th* and so they changed ours to Pandemoneum. Well, I got the script and I read it and I thought it could be fun. I didn't know the director and had never heard of him, so I went to see *Alice Sweet Alice* and it scared the shit out of me! It happened to be playing when they were putting together *Pandemoneum*, so I went and saw it in the theater and it scared me so bad.

To work with Alfred Sole was interesting. I think we had some very strong comic performers in that film. I think, maybe we blew his mind a little bit with the things that we brought to it. He was always telling us to go ahead and improvise. I mean, we had Paul Reubens, Tom Smothers, Carol Kane, Donald O'Connor, Kaye Ballard, Judge Reinhold. My God, it was like every day on the set you were thinking "Who's going to be here today?" These are amazing comic performers.

RA: I remember when I did the review for it in the last book, I mentioned a lot of the funny scenes in it, like the whole "Candy, Randy, Andy, Mandy … " scene.

MC: (laughs) Yeah, and then Judge came in with Glen. We made that up on the spot. That's what I was talking about. We were going to do this strip poker scene and were talking about what we could do and we started just riffing on that. Then Alfred suggested doing it in one take and he built a little thing and put the camera in the middle and swiveled it around. When actors know technique, you obviously want to say the line when the camera is on you and you have to be in the light. But, when all of you are firing on all those cylinders and you're all taking advantage of each other's talents, one thing leads to another. That's the essence of collaboration. It's like we're sitting there and riffing on this with the names and we need a button. Obviously, Glen is the button here, so we decide to put it out even more with "Glen

... Dandy" and it's perfect. Then the end too, where we start singing "heaven, I'm in heaven... it's the same thing. It's like, how are we going to end this movie? Well, here's an idea. The thing that was great about Alfred was that he was open to all of these ideas, so we could have fun and be creative. Those experiences happen to be the most fun that I had in the movies. You want to be creative and have your contribution acknowledged.

RA: What was it like getting to work with some of those notable comics like Reubens?

MC: Paul Reubens was amazing because he had been doing Pee Wee Herman at The Groundlings in LA. I had heard a lot about it. It was pretty well known. It was like the coolest thing in town, but I'd never seen it. When I met him, I was a bit underwhelmed, because he is so different from the character. Paul Reubens is completely different from his character. I compare him to Jack Benny. I mean, we know the characters, but who knows what the man is really like? It's like Donald Trump. Is he the same guy when you're talking to him alone as when he's on the podium talking to thousands of people? I don't know. Also, with Tom Smothers, I mean, my brothers and I lived for their records when we were growing up. To meet them out of character is a really different thing. Then, you want to observe them and you want to learn from them. That's one of the pleasures of acting in general, is that you get to work with people whose work you love. With Paul, I didn't know him before, but I later went and saw the show and I thought he was brilliant, just really good. In a way, he was so good that it almost backfired on him, because people just expected him to do that and nothing else. As a performer, that can be frustrating.

RA: What would you say was your favorite project to work on?

MC: I would have to say that my favorite project I worked on has to be *French Postcards*. To me, that was just the dream job. I loved the character and the people I was working with. We shot it in Paris for five or six months, and it's just a gem of a movie.

RA: What are you up to these days?

MC: I'm more doing life than performing right now. I'm working as a residential real estate broker, mostly on the high end, but I work with clients from all walks of life. I have also published two books, one on tropical forests and one on the making of the Steinway piano. I write when I can. I haven't done a movie in years. I mean, I would love to. Acting is great, but I just don't have time to do small parts or go out of town that much, at least until my kids graduate and I'm an empty nester. I know too, that the whole film business has changed so much over the years. Even TV has changed with these long form TV series and it's some really good storytelling. It's exciting to see. I'd love to do something like that in the future. Right now, though, it's mainly taking care of my kids and getting them educated.

RA: Looking back on *The Funhouse*, how do you view it today? Do you still keep in touch with anyone from it?

MC: We keep in touch a little bit. Interestingly enough, you do these movies and kind of move on, but then you find they have a life of their own and I was not aware of it. I got contacted about four or five years ago by a convention organizer and I went to meet the guy and I was asked to come to a convention. I was like, "You mean, people would really want to meet me?" He told me that I have no idea. So, I did it and I've done a few since then. I just love them. To go to those things and to meet people is amazing. To find out that my work has affected people and really touched their lives, it just doesn't get any better than that. That's what it's all about. It's really cool. It's fun too, meeting these other actors your age and finding out that you had this mutual admiration thing going on. It's really great. It's a lot of fun. You know, the fans are who it's all for. Without them, we don't have anything.

RA: If you had anything to say to those fans out there, what would you say?

MC: Bless your hearts. Keep watching. Keep going to the movies. I have a huge and deep gratitude for fans of *The Funhouse*.

NATHAN BAESEL
(BEHIND THE MASK)

RA: First off, how did you get started in the acting business?

NB: I was going to school for acting for a number of years. I actually did ten years of college. The last eight I was focusing more and more on acting as what I wanted to do. After my third year of community college, I felt like it was the track I wanted to go down. I did what a lot of folks around me were doing, which was to go off to UCLA. At the end of my time there, I felt like I had learned a lot, in terms of book smarts, but felt like I lacked practical skills and I felt like I needed some intensive training, so I went to Juliard for four years. When I was done there, I came back to Southern California and just started hustling.

RA: I've heard a few horror stories. Did you find it difficult trying to get work down there at first?

NB: Yeah, it really was, particularly having come from a place where the school's pedigree kind of lends credibility automatically to a lot of people. It felt like despite the cred that I had going in the door, nailing a job down was a completely different problem altogether. It took a long time for me to wrap my head around the fact that it doesn't really matter what you've got on paper. What matters more is what you've got coming through the door. Whether it's an audition or a meeting, that's what is going to be what really matters to folks.

RA: How did *Behind the Mask* come about? What was it about that audition that you think won them over?

NB: I think that what I was doing and the choices that I was making was different than what the other people were doing. Sometimes, that's my default is just to assess what everyone else is doing and just go the opposite direction. Sometimes, it really stands you against the competition. In this case, a lot of the competition was bringing in a lot of menace and a lot of anger and a lot of pent up rage. Every now and then, you could hear that rage being released on the other side of the wall. You could hear the other people auditioning and just hear shouting and all kinds of things. I just kind of felt like it was too (pauses) boring, and I felt like there was something that was a lot more compelling about somebody that you could identify with, who isn't just your typical villain. It's someone that you can almost see yourself kind of liking, or somebody you could pass by on the street without noticing, or if you did notice them, strike up a conversation with them and you might even enjoy their company. That to me was a lot more interesting than the two-dimensional type of approach.

RA: Oh yeah. That was one of the things that I noticed, was that Leslie was just such a friendly guy and completely disarming, like the guy next door, like your neighbor. I just love how you conveyed that.

NB: Well, I think that really the only thing that is menacing or scary when it comes to slasher movies is the relentless pursuit of the villain. That's kind of the thing, is the knowledge that there's this big hulking death machine that is unstoppable. That's kind of where the slasher particularly lives, but I felt like this movie had the potential to live in a way that was more dynamic than just your typical slasher movie. I mean, it had that cinematic 35mm 80s slasher effect to it, that was already taken care of in the script, but for all of the documentary stuff where we're getting to know somebody, it felt like it was a really unique opportunity to endear yourself to an audience and get them to jump on board with you, so when you got to those cinematic slasher elements, it wasn't just watching the film play out. You were forced to confront the fact that this guy had an appeal for you. You may have even developed an affectionate relationship for him, so now you're confronted by his actions because you're seeing how it plays out and this human, real world impact that those actions are having. If felt like that kind of an approach doesn't let the audience off the hook in the way that just playing the guy as evil does.

RA: Speaking of which, that's one of my favorite scenes in the movie and in my mind, the scariest, when you chase the cameraman down and he's trying to reason with you, like he's known you for so long. Just the look on your face and the dead look in your eyes was a turning point for me.

NB: Yeah, it was the only time that you see Leslie in mask mode without the mask on. I felt that it was a very important bridge for what we had been doing between the faux documentary level and what we were doing on the cinematic level. It was where both of them really come together and meet, really the only time that it happens.

RA: Were you a fan of slasher films before doing this and familiar with all of the clichés and rules of the genre?

NB: The extent of my slasher knowledge beforehand would be *Nightmare on Elm Street*. I had seen the first through the third and for me, even though you had the villain as a personable figure and not just a silent vehicle of death behind the mask, there was something really frightening and entertaining at the same time. When I booked this job, I felt like I really had to figure out what it was all about and be as knowledgable about the genre as my character. I tried to get some studying in, but I only got as far as the first *Friday the 13th*. (laughs) I still haven't even seen Halloween.

RA: Really?

NB: (laughs) I know, I should be ashamed. Frankly, horror movies scare me. (laughs) So, usually the ones that I do see are kind of the popcorn flicks, or some of the older classics, The Exorcist being my favorite, in terms of movies that really elicit terror from me. I'm still very illiterate when it comes to the genre. Fortunately, though, everything that Leslie says and that is in the script had been studied thoroughly by Scott Glosserman and David Stevie (sp?), who both wrote the screenplay. They were both well versed in the genre and I felt like, it was already on paper so the work is done. If I memorize the words and deliver them correctly, I will have done everything that I needed to do in terms of presenting this guy in a credible light. I just needed to focus on being alive and responsive to the people around me, and being really excited about my occupation and really happy about sharing the gospel of what it is that I do. That's what I focused my energy on.

RA: Do you remember much about the location? I've heard it was outside of Portland, correct?

NB: Yeah, that's true. We just did one scene, the library scene in Portland itself, downtown. There was a courthouse scene that we did in Portland that never made the final cut. The rest of it was just outside of Portland, to the North (Troutdale, Oregon).

RA: Was there much of a notable difference in the two filming styles used in the movie, the documentary style and the regular style of filming?

NB: Yeah, it was totally different. I had never done a film before Behind the Mask, so it was a real quick orientation into the techniques of both formats. The documentary style was very run and done, trying to move quickly and efficiently. The film, or cinematic shooting was much more production oriented. Everything had to be composed and executed flawlessly. The documentary style allowed us to move quick to get a lot of content done in a relatively short amount of time. The cinematic aspects were a lot more plodding and predetermined. There really wasn't a whole lot of room for improvisation or making things up on the fly.

RA: What would you say were your favorite scenes to film?

NB: (pauses) One of the scenes that I reflect on most often, when I think about how I prefer to work as an actor, is the scene in front of the schoolhouse where Leslie is pointing out the different people and social groups, where he is going on and explaining that he is looking for the group that ties all of those different social groups together, with the one unifying figure being the virgin that could be his survivor girl. We got to the location pretty late in the day. I think that we had gotten there from another shoot that we had wrapped up. We didn't have a whole lot of time and had to get it done, so we only had a certain amount of daylight left. Daylight changes pretty quickly and you can have in a very short amount of time, completely different looks based on light and shadow. If you're not getting the whole thing shot and wrapped in a short amount of time, you're exposing yourself to the possibility that it could look off. Some shots can look lighter or darker.

RA: (laughs) Yeah, I've seen that problem with a few of the older films.

NB: That's the funny thing, too. Because we were working on such a micro budget and had such limited time, we didn't really have the luxury of messing around. We had to get it done. That schoolhouse scene was an example of showing up to a location and executing something that was relatively complex, because you had a lot of choreographed stuff going on in the background and things like the girl exiting the school and walking past the little Nightmare on Elm Street girls with the jump rope. All of that stuff was getting jampacked into one continuous take. Within three takes, we were able to knock out a pretty heavily choreographed sequence involving a number of people outside of the van, while knocking out a scene within the van that had tons of dialogue and information to deliver. Getting all of that content nailed and in the can in about two hours at the most was pretty remarkable and it was a huge sense of accomplishment at the end of the day from a team that had to really hustle and work together in a coordinated group effort. We found ourselves in a number of ways up against time and up against budget restraints. There were times when we felt like, especially during the final cinematic aspects, that we didn't have the luxury of holding and waiting until all of the elements were in place to proceed.

RA: Like what?

NB: For example, a great one is the posthole digger gag. That was supposed to be a close-up shot of a chest cavity, that was in the process of being constructed by our effects designer. He was building this chest cavity that would be puncturable and then we would be actually physically removing a heart that would have been mechanically constructed to still be pumping. Well, the gag wasn't ready and we didn't have the luxury of waiting. We had to lock this scene down and move on. We couldn't come back to it and there was no time to delay. So, the solution ended up being this really wide shot where it looks like the digger is going through him, but really, it's just on the side of him, the side opposite of the camera. Then, they did a close-up shot of a pig's heart with a lot of fake blood on it. For some people, they see a gag like that and it looks cheesy, but for some people, they see a gag like that and they are transported back to the early 80s slashers, where they didn't have the luxury of time or budget, either. The kind of constraints that we were dealing with were exactly the same kind of constraints that they were dealing with. I think that it shows up in our movie in an even more accurate depiction that what we initially set out to do, in referencing those movies.

RA: What were some of the more difficult scenes for you to do?

NB: All of the stuff with the mask was really uncomfortable because it was really cold. It was deep fall in the Pacific Northwest. There was a lot of rain and the area of the location had lots of rocks and puddles. The genius that I am decided that he doesn't have shoes. He's recalling his character, his monster and harkening back to an event that happened when he was a child. The mask has a bit of an embryonic quality to it and in my opinion, he wouldn't wear shoes. That's what we ended up going with, so with a little bit of flannel with some holes in it and some overalls as the exception, I was walking around doing my scenes completely exposed to the elements. That was rough, but it also forced me to develop a kind of Zen approach, of getting into his headspace and to focus on the task at hand. I think that it really helped me psychologically to get into the character's head in a much more profound way than what I had been dealing with before in the documentary style. When we are working with that and the mask was on, that was a whole different type of psychology to explore and that was very fascinating to me as somebody who is interested in the psychology of how and why people do the things that they do.

RA: I know that this was sadly the last film that she did. What was it like working with Zelda Rubinstein?

NB: It was cool. That was the final day of shooting. She was there and Robert Englund was there, too. It was my first time meeting her and working with her. It was just like with Robert, a total class act. They're not about just collecting a paycheck. They're about turning in work that's going to turn people on. That was just fascinating watching a pro like her, and like Robert and Scott Wilson. Their body of work is tremendous. They probably have learned how you can just show up and get the job done with the least amount of energy expended possible, but that's just not what they were about. They were about playing and working. People like that who have a great amount of experience, have learned technique and they have a fallback that is executing work cleanly and efficiently with the least amount of taxing on the body and mind as possible, but there is the ability to work employing that technique that doesn't let the individual off the hook. It doesn't let them rely on the technique as much as employ it as one of the means to accomplish their task at hand. When you see people that have learned over the course of decades about technique and developing their own personal technique and you see them using it not as crutch, but as an instrument to do great work, that's a huge turn on. This movie was great and I couldn't have had a better opportunity to see people executing what was, in my opinion, perfect professionalism, as well as show me what I wanted to be as an actor forty years from now. When I have earned the right to coast, learning from their examples, that you can still bring your A game and see how amazing the results are.

RA: That is great to hear. Another thing that I have always thought was very clever about *Behind the Mask* was the reveal of the final girl, how it was hidden right in front of you the entire time.

NB: Yeah, it's funny, some people will see that moment come and the revelation and say, "Oh God, I saw that coming a mile away", then there's some people that will go, "What? No way!" Mind explosion! (laughs) That kind of covered the whole spectrum of reactions. I think that for the most part, we were able to create a character dynamic, where the focus was on Taylor to the extent where she was intrigued, attracted and drawn into Leslie's way of thinking. Because that was so naturally occurring during the process of the shoot, because I was so intrigued and infatuated with Angela (Goethals) and she was enjoying my goofiness, the chemistry that we were allowed to develop together was a really good distraction for the audience, so that when it came to that moment for most people, it was a surprise. As far as their appreciation was for Taylor and what she was about, it was really easy to forget about anything, including the possibility that she might have been brought in for a specific purpose and not just to document his rise to legendary status.

RA: Another thing that I really appreciated about the film, and it's another slasher staple, is the open ending. I know that there was some talk about it and I've read articles about a sequel to it. Can you tell me what is happening with those plans?

NB: Yeah, we had a script that David Stieve (writer of *Behind the Mask*) wrote and it was really good. This was probably four or five years after *Behind the Mask*. He and I and Scott got together for lunch and chatted about what we imagined a sequel would include. It felt like the compulsion to raise Leslie up as this vaunted figure was too easy and kind of not what made the movie so relevant to us in the first place. What made it so relevant in the first place is that all of us felt like it was going to be a launching pad for all of our careers, just like Leslie felt like he was about to unleash his legend upon the world. I think that we all felt like the movie was going to be doing that for us. Well, that didn't happen unfortunately. Yeah, the movie had a national release, but in most theaters, I would be surprised if it lasted more than a week.

RA: That's sad to me because it was very clever and very different from the other ones that were coming out then.

NB: Yeah, but there was a problem there. Just try describing it to somebody. You really can't. I mean, you can't do it in a sentence. It's not a straight up slasher and it's not a straight up comedy. It doesn't really live fully in either of those worlds, so it's a hard thing to pitch and it's a hard thing for a promotional department to get behind and try to figure out how to leverage the film for the best effect. If you market it as this straight up slasher, slasher fans might get pissed off and if you market it as a straight up comedy, fans of comedy are going to be revolted. It's a tough nut to crack and it was the first theatrical release for Anchor Bay. I don't think that they knew how to handle it. We had done a lot of great leg work on our own on the festival circuit, building a name for ourselves and drawing excited crowds. I think that they were really counting on the web presence that we had been enjoying up until that point to carry it for us, and that didn't happen. We have seen a continued thriving of it on DVD and saw that the film was continuing to turn people on. It hadn't done it quite on the scale that we had hoped, but there were many reasons for that, as well. I think for the sequel's sake, we could use that. How about this? What if Leslie is devastated that his plan didn't come through and that he didn't become this massive deal? Does he retreat, or does he crawl into a hole and disappear, or does he rally and come back bigger, better and stronger? In a way, it's kind of like what a lot of people deal with in losing their job or when they're trying to figure out who they are and what they're doing with their life. It's one of those epic life decisions. If we could try to tap into that and look at how you can rebound when everything seemed perfect and yet it just didn't take off for whatever reason, that's sort of where the sequel script went. Stieve finished it off and polished it and it's a really solid script. I think in a lot of ways, it's actually cleaner than the original, and I felt like the original was one of the cleanest scripts that I had ever read. It was really streamlined. Everything was purpose built, where everything has a purpose and nothing is thrown away. Everything is introduced for a purpose and plays off later on in the movie. I felt like the first script was so much like that and I was so delighted to read the second script and see that it had those same qualities to it, as well, but was also opening up a bit to explore the conventions of sequels and prequels, where budgetary constraints are fewer and you can really blow things up in a way that you couldn't do the first time around. Now, where the film is in production, I'm not really sure. A few weeks ago, it felt like things were looking very promising, but we met a roadblock. So, if things come through, we could start to shoot maybe next year, but it looks like if it happens, it may have to be another independent film fund financing campaign, and that's just a huge amount of work that I wouldn't wish on anybody, but it seems like one that Scott Glosserman is willing to take on. He's really the heart and soul of the machine and provides all the momentum and kinetic energy. It all depends on Scott and it seems like he is really wanting to make it happen. As long as he is committed to that, I think that it could happen. But, as I have told people before who have expressed sadness that it's taken so long for the sequel, I assure them that simply from the things that are being explored convention-wise, it could actually be more effective, the longer that it is between the original and the sequel. The more time that elapses between the two, the more it really helps to emphasize the points that we want to. So, in that sense, it won't break my heart if we don't get it off the ground this year, although it would be very cool just for shits and giggles to get the band back together. It's still coming. It's rolling slow, but it's still rolling.

RA: That's great to hear. I'm very excited to see the sequel. I have one last question here. If you had anything that you could say to the fans out there, what would you say?

NB: Thank you. I really had very little exposure to the genre before I did *Behind the Mask*. Shortly after, I started attending conventions and I still get contacted constantly by people that have seen the movie and been turned on by the work that we were doing. That turn on, in effect has fueled some of their creativity. I have seen so much creative talent pouring out of fans of the genre, in terms of fan art and letters of support. The people that stop me on the street or come up to me at a convention have just shown so much love, and it blows me away. It's something that, if not for this film, I never would have known of. With a horror convention, I probably never would have attended one or even known how special the genre is or how special the people that love the genre are. I have a huge appreciation now and I am grateful for every single person that has made a point of telling me how meaningful the work that we were doing has been for them.

NED EISENBERG
(THE BURNING, LAW AND ORDER: SVU)

RA: How did you get into the acting business?

NE: I got interested in it as a young kid in Junior High and then I auditioned for the High School of the Performing Arts in New York. I got accepted in and from then on, I just kept on that trajectory, getting involved and auditioning. From there, I went to college and then I put myself out there in the world of acting.

RA: I was reading your bio and see that one of your earliest roles is another film I'm very familiar with, *The Exterminator*. Can you tell me about working on that?

NE: That was the first film that I actually got a principal part in. We shot that all-around New York City. That was a big hit when it came out, kind of an international sensation and it was in that *Death Wish* genre. It was a lot of fun at the time. Then, I was in a scene in another movie I did with that director (James Glickenhaus) years later called *Soldier*. Ken Wahl was the lead in it and Klaus Kinski is in it. It was the second film that the director made. I only had one scene in it.

RA: How did you get on board with *The Burning*?

NE: Interestingly enough, it was the same casting director as *The Exterminator*. It was woman named Joy Todd, who was very helpful to me in my early years. She is just a lovely person. I didn't have an agent or manager or anything and she would bring me in for these films. She brought me in for the audition and they ended up casting me. Then, we went up to Upstate New York to film it. That was in August or September of 1980.

RA: Being from that area, were you already familiar with the whole Cropsy legend beforehand?

NE: Well, it was one of those things. When you would go away to sleepaway camp, they would always tell you that story about the Cropsy maniac. So yeah, I had heard it as a kid. Whether it's just something to scare kids around the campfire or an actual criminal case, I don't know. I guess that all of these films take off from some kernel of truth somewhere.

RA: Yeah, there's actually a documentary out there about it called Cropsy. I saw it on Netflix once.

NE: I think I may have scrolled past that before. I didn't realize it was a documentary. I just thought it was some remake of our story. I'll have to check it out.

RA: What did you get to do during your downtime when you weren't filming the movie?

NE: We just had a ball. It was a lovely bunch of young actors. All of us were young, maybe in our early twenties. We just had a lot of laughs up there. We were right by Niagara Falls, I remember. We filmed in a town called North Tonawanda. We visited Niagara Falls one day and then the other town that we filmed in was Buffalo, so we did some sightseeing there. Mostly, we were just on the set, though. I think that it was something where we were pretty much around all the time. I think we were only there a couple weeks to film it.

RA: What was your experience working with Tom Savini like on it for the effects?

NE: Oh, that was wild. I'm even featured on a documentary about the experience somewhere. I mostly worked with him just in the preparation. He had to make the casts for the bodies. You would put your head through something and then below you is what your body is supposed to be. It was the first time I had ever had any sort of body cast made for me. It was a strange experience because he actually used some kind of plaster that created its own heat. Suddenly, they had this thing on me and it kept getting hotter and hotter, and I was thinking, why is this thing getting hot? It was a strange sensation having this thing heat up as well as contract.

RA: What do you remember about doing that late-night swim scene in the movie?

NE: Oh God, I remember that it was very cold. We were in and out of that lake a hundred times. They would have those little portable heaters on the shore and towels, but we just went in and out so much. It was in Upstate New York and it was deep into September and it was not the most comfortable. When she said that it's cold and wanted me to hold her, there wasn't much acting there because it really was cold! (laughs) I think we did that on my last day that I was working on it.

RA: What was your take on your character of Eddy?

NE: Well, he was just a hot headed, angry young man. They have them in all movies. He was just your average city kid out in the country. He was hot to trot, but the girl he was enamored with was not, so he was frustrated.

RA: The scene that is always notorious on *The Burning* is one that you're part of, the raft scene. What went into making that happen?

NE: That's become the money shot for the movie. The big thing that people remember is that scene. We were out on the lake on that raft all day. The camera guys and their equipment was on another boat or raft. They just had us out there rowing and rowing, for hours. Then, they put the scene together. They never had the guy actually leap out of the canoe. They must have shot that at some other time. There wasn't any real interaction between us and the maniac, but the way it was cut together looks like it. I think that some of it was done on the dock. When I get killed, I was in some other area. I had that body cast and a big piece of wood and I would stick my head through a hole in the thing. It's a trick. It's tricking the eye. I think they show that in the Tom Savini documentary.

RA: One thing that always makes me laugh about that raft scene is the physics behind it. You would think that if Cropsy stood straight up in that canoe and lunged forward, it would have a much different outcome in reality.

NE: Oh yeah, you have to suspend your disbelief in that scene, for sure. If somebody were to stand upright in a canoe and then lunge at someone else, that would not happen. (laughs) It really doesn't make much sense. You'd have to be some kind of supernatural being.

RA: (laughs) True that. How do you think *The Burning* holds up these days?

NE: I had no idea. I hadn't seen the movie in decades. Now, there's a Blu-Ray edition with all the extras and everything. Clearly, it has a following. I don't know how to compare it to the other films of the genre, but obviously, it has legs, as they say in the business.

RA: Yeah, it's really nice to see the attention that the movie is getting these days. Shelley Bruce was even telling me about the reunion coming up in Florida for a convention.

NE: I know! I've been talking to a very nice guy who is putting on that event lately. I'm going to try to put it together and get down there, if I can. I have never been to one of these things, but a lot of my friends have and they always say it's a lot of fun and pretty astounding to see all these people that are fans and love the movie.

RA: Are you still in touch with anyone from the film?

NE: Yeah, I am. It was a really great group of people working on that film. It was a lot of fun and friendships were made. I still know people from the crew and the other actors. Some I haven't seen in decades, but others I have kept in touch with. Facebook has really opened up several channels of communication that otherwise wouldn't be there.

RA: I see that you also opened up a theater company with your co-star Fisher Stevens in New York a while back, right?

NE: Yes, that's true. We created this company called Naked Angels in New York City. It was very much on the scene in the late eighties and nineties and it's still going strong to this day.

RA: Another favorite of mine I want to ask about is *Moving Violations*.

NE: (laughs) I knew you'd bring that up! That was a blast, plus I got to play a fan of these kinds of movies. That was a big budget film. We were on that for months in California. It was crazy, working all night. Getting to pay homage to a horror film aficionado with the character I played was a lot of fun, too.

RA: The other one I want to ask about is one that I remember reading about in the local paper when I was a kid living in New Mexico and hearing you were filming there. It's another very cool movie that I still enjoy, *Last Man Standing*.

NE: Really? That's cool it was in the paper there! Yeah, I do remember filming that down there. We shot some of it outside of Los Angeles and then we shot a lot of that outside of El Paso, Texas. We spent like a month and a half out there in the desert. We were all over the Southwest working on that. It was really quite a gig. It was quite something. That was also one hell of a group of remarkable people, getting to work with Walter Hill and so many others. It was an army of men, really. These movies are like armies with the crews and the actors and the equipment and all the extras. It was a really wonderful experience. It could also be some cold terrain out there at 4 or 5 in the morning in the desert. We were deep into the borderland area there. It was fun that it was a period piece, getting to wear those hats and costumes and they made these suits for us. It was a lot of fun. I really liked the Mexican stand-off scene that we had in the middle of the street. That was a good scene. I think it's another one of those movies that went on to a bigger life than when it was released.

RA: What was Christopher Walken like to work with?

NE: At the time, he pretty much kept to himself. He read his books and worked on his character. We had a few laughs. He was the guy that got to shoot me. I got taken down by his machine gun. Other than that, we didn't really do many scenes together. I did a lot of scenes with Bruce Willis and Michael Imperioli. Then there was Alexandra Powers who was the gal that was supposed to be my girlfriend.

RA: One that I know that many people that I know are absolutely obsessed with is *Law & Order: SVU*. Can you talk about that?

NE: Oh yeah, that is quite something. You talk about a following. Good God man, that's on, what, thirty hours a week? (laughs) You can find that on anytime and anywhere. That show has been very good to me. I think I've done about 28 episodes of that show since its inception. I was there the very first day of filming, in the very first pilot episode. Since then, it's always been fun. They'll call me out of the blue and ask if I'm available next week and I'll say, "Yeah okay. I can come on down and put that suit on again." So, that's been a lot of fun. Interestingly enough, in that *Law & Order* empire, the first time I ever got cast in that was in 1997. You'll appreciate this. I was cast in that by the director who had started his way up through the ranks as a camera operator. The real punchline here is that he worked on *The Burning* as either the Gaffer or the Best Boy or something like that. He has gone on to become a producer and done spectacularly well in the film industry. His name is Christopher Misiano. I am not sure if I would have gotten the part if it weren't for knowing him from that and I'm very glad to be part of that family. I've been with them for around twenty years now. So, you could say that this directly came from *The Burning*. Isn't that a trip?

RA: Wow, that is amazing. It really is a small world. If you had anything you could say to the fans out there, what would you say?

NE: Thank you very much for your support and appreciation.

PAGE MOSELEY
(Edge of the Axe, Girl's Nite Out, Open House)
4/13/2016

RA: How did you get into the acting business?

PM: It's so funny. My mom tells this story about me in my underwear and cowboy boots at the age of three trying to wash dishes and sing songs. I think that was probably the beginning of it. As far back as I can remember, that's all that I really wanted to do. I did my first commercial when I was twelve. I rode on my bike and had to hit a mark and go up in the air and they would try to take a picture of the shoot. It was funny. It was at a really early age that I started cutting up and I was always a class clown, getting into trouble for doing that kind of thing. Whenever the teacher would leave the room, I would do the *Gilligan's Island* show from the day before. It was like first or second grade, giving everybody a rundown on what happened on the show the day before.

RA: Did you grow up around the industry, in the LA area?

PM: No, I grew up in North Carolina. I grew up in Raleigh and Charlotte.

RA: Did you suffer any kind of culture shock or difficulties during the first while in acting? I know many people do (I call it Hollyshock. It always makes for interesting stories)

PM: Well, I had been living in New York for a few years after I graduated from school, so I had already done some films, small spots on television shows, some off-Broadway work, and things like that while I was in New York. That was the real culture shock for me. I went to North Carolina School of the Arts and it kind of compares a little bit because my senior year, we had a touring company, so we went around to all of these fancy-pants private schools and were on the road for almost two months our senior year. We had three shows and we rotated the shows, depending on where we were. So, by the time I got to New York, I had a little bit of that under my belt. New York was the culture shock, though. It was loud, busy and you could just feel the energy there. I didn't care for it too much, so when I found the opportunity to move out to LA, I took it. I had been here maybe a year or so when I landed the role on *Santa Barbara*.

Girl's Nite Out

RA: This was your first horror movie in which you played a smaller role as an extra pledge. What all did you get to do on the film and what are your memories of working on it?

PM: That was actually done in my time in New York. It was filmed in and around New York. One of the guys who was a pledge with me in the film owned a really big restaurant and upstairs was a supper club. For a couple of years in a row, there used to be a show called *Night of a Hundred Stars* and after the show, they would all come up to the supper club and perform. Me, doing the film with him, he gave me a job as a Maître D' upstairs. I still have all of these autographs from that from people like Robert De Niro, Christopher Reeve, Liz Taylor, and so many more from when they were up there and I would be opening up their bottle of wine and would ask if they would mind if I got their autograph (laughs). I know that on the movie, only a hundredth of what we did really made it into the film. We were supposed to be the comic relief of the film. We would do panty raids and all of these things like that. Of course, we would always be drunk and trying to get everyone else drunk. They kind of let us run wild and let us improvise a lot. Really, a lot of it didn't end up making it into the film. I don't know why. Either it was bad or they just didn't need it. But, it was fun. I also remember it was so cold! It was really cold when we shot it and probably about ninety percent of the stuff that did was at night. I just remember always being cold.

RA: This one has one of the better killer costumes of all time. Did you get to see it? Thoughts on it?

PM: Yeah, I saw it a couple of times, the bear with the claws coming out. It was kind of spooky and they would always put somebody kind of big in it to make it look bigger. To see those knives sticking out, it was like, you didn't really want to get too close to whoever is wearing it.

RA: I can see that! Where was it filmed at?

PM: I can't really remember, it was so long ago. It was a little school right outside of New York and they would bus us out there in these big vans that held like eighteen people.

Edge of the Axe

RA: This is the one I really wanted to talk about and one I'm a big fan of personally. How did you get involved in it?

PM: Well, it was shot in Spain and the producer was kind of like the Dino De Laurentis of

Spain. He wanted to shoot a horror film that he originally hoped he could release here in the United States and make some money on it. So, he came over here and there was a casting director named Melissa Scoff, who had cast me in a bunch of things, and they had me in to read. So, the main cast was American and they supplemented expatriates over in Spain in Madrid and Barcelona to play some of the other parts. It was kind of grueling because being an actor over here you have certain rights and certain comforts, but shooting over there was different. They would put out a huge spread for breakfast because that's how they did it there, but throughout the day, if you wanted anything else like a bottle of water, it just wasn't around. There were no craft services. Hotel wise, once we got outside of the cities, they would put us in these little hotels that had no air, where it gets to be like a hundred degrees at night. At one point, I kind of led a little revolt. It was around 115 degrees and we were trying to shoot in this. I said, "If there's not water on the set tomorrow, we're not working". So, I was twenty-six years old, leading a revolt (laughs). But, even with that, it was a lot of fun. Anytime you see somebody driving a car, I was either in it or I was driving it. I actually lied and said I did some stunt driving, so they were impressed and told me I could do all of the driving then. I got to drive these old model cars out there in the woods on these dirt roads and I would really push it to make it look good, going faster than I would ever usually go. That part was a lot of fun.

RA: It's odd that they made it in Spain with an American cast. It almost sounds like they were just trying to make it as American as possible to cash in on the slasher craze.

PM: Exactly, that's exactly what they were doing. If you look at the cast list, and you see the man that played the sheriff, he actually became the president of SAG for a while. He and I wrote a script while we were there and we were trying to get this guy to produce it. It was going to be called Bogey Men. It was about a guy who was a pro golfer. His brother shows up and his brother is a criminal. These guys were after him and he involves his golfer brother and there was all this action and these high jinks like golf cart chases, guys getting hit with golf balls and silly things like that. We pitched it to him and he said he would think about it, but we never heard anything. It was funny, we actually took our golf clubs over there and played a lot. Every day that we weren't shooting, we would catch a train to this golf course that was in the middle of absolute nowhere and get hooked up with guys who couldn't speak our language. But hey, golf is the universal language.

RA: What was it like working for director Jose Ramon Larraz? What kind of director was he?

PM: Well, he was cool and very lenient when it came to many things. There was a lot of ad-libbing. Staying within the words on the script, anybody that let you be creative within that, is really great. Anybody can say words, but when you can ad-lib and play off of what's going on, that's really good. In that case, it was a lot of fun. I think that he knew though that I couldn't really stunt drive (laughs). There's a scene where I'm throwing a hatchet at a tree and that was all ad-libbed. It was all spur of the moment. He was just a really nice guy. The whole crew was. I remember being invited over to people's houses that didn't even really speak English, but I was invited over to meet their families and have dinner. All in all, except for the conditions sometimes, it was a great experience.

RA: It's funny that you mentioned that back there. It was almost like they set up your character a couple of times to look like he could be the killer.

PM: Well, it's interesting because I don't think that they had really decided who it was going to be. That was fun too, because sometimes they would have us do a scene one way and then turn it around and have us do it a completely different way, just in case they went that route, so at times it was even kind of confusing to us. We didn't even know who the killer would be.

RA: Yeah, I thought for sure it would be you, but then they threw that curve ball in there with the girl.

PM: Oh yeah, with that creepy smile! Oh, that girl was like a deer in the headlights. I think that was her first … anything, really. She turned eighteen right before we were taking off to go over there. I think that was the only way her parents would let her come over and do it. We kind of tortured her. She was really straight laced and we were just a wild bunch over there going crazy. We did everything we could to try to get her in a little trouble with us, but we rarely succeeded (laughs). She was nice though, a really nice girl.

RA: It's one of those movies that actually still manages to be scary to this day. The killer is just, simply put, amazing and one of the best killer disguises I've ever seen.

PM: Yeah it is. It's creepy. It's funny, I was away this weekend with my youngest daughter who's fourteen and I was telling her that we were going to be speaking for this interview. I was telling her about the movies and she told me that she would like to see one. I was thinking actually, that *Edge of the Axe* would be the one she would probably enjoy the most.

RA: That's awesome. It's still really good. I mean, that opening in the car wash alone is just terrifying.

PM: Yeah, Wasn't it spooky?

RA: Definitely. What do you remember about that great killer disguise?

PM: That I wished it was me (laughs). Later on, I always got play a lot of bad guys and a lot of shady guys, but I never got play like the murderer. I always thought it would be fun to play that. Like you said, now that I think about it, that car wash scene really was pretty scary!

RA: Yep, ever since then, when I'm in a car wash, it's what I think.

PM: Yeah, that's why I let someone else drive it through, now. (laughs)

Open House

RA: This is another interesting one, in which you play Toby. Talk a bit about your experience on this film.

PM: It's funny, I was just telling my daughter this, that when I got called to go in and audition, I wanted to do something that I hadn't done before and wanted to do something silly and crazy, and I thought it would be interesting if the character was gay. I mean, not just gay, but flamboyantly so. So, I went in wearing a long pink silk shirt that I borrowed from somebody and some way too tight white pants. I just flew into the room and took off and I think that's how I got the job. I just didn't care. Joseph Bottoms and I had already been on *Santa Barbara* together, so we are already knew each other, so it was kind of a coincidence that we got cast in something together again.

RA: Tell me a bit about what went into playing Toby.

PM: Well, from an acting standpoint, it was interesting. I mean it was the eighties and guys were kind of discovering this new side, like wearing earrings and bleaching their hair. It was a lot of people expanding their horizons and trying to find themselves in some interesting ways. You didn't see characters in the movies much like that. I thought that Toby was openly gay and I remember trying to play him that way. I didn't think it would be that important at the time, I just thought that it would be interesting and controversial. Aside from that, working with Joseph was always a treat anyways. He would always pull all kinds of jokes and stunts on the set. If you go back and look, his shirts would always look immaculate in the front and it was because he would take his shirt tails and tuck them through his underwear and pull them out the bottom (laughs). So, they would remain nice and crisp. Yeah, he was a character.

RA: What was it like working with Adrienne Barbeau?

PM: I just remember seeing her on set. I just remember that she was always a pro. She had no ego. She would talk to anybody and she was accessible. Just a nice person. I don't really remember having very many scenes with her.

RA: Looking back, how do you view these movies these days and your involvement in them?

PM: I have to tell you, I can't go to a scary movie and I haven't for years. I don't really like them. My imagination is such that I get scared really easily (laughs). I can still remember *House of Dark Shadows* back in the seventies. I went to see that with a bunch of guys I was growing up with. I remember I had to get up and "go get popcorn" and I stayed out in the lobby. The next group that was going into the movie was standing out in line and they were like "what's a matter man, you scared of the movie?" (laughs). Of course, it meant I had to go back inside. Movies these days I think are so much more intense, with more blood and guts and realism. It used to be more suspense. Now, it's just too much. I'm just not into that stuff.

RA: Yeah, I have to say that I'm more of a fan of the suspenseful ones and the ones that make you think as opposed to the really gory ones. (we discuss current state of movies)

RA: How did you get into your current line of work?

PM: It's interesting, I had done a couple movies of the week with director Martin Donovan, who did *Death Becomes Her* and others. I was lucky enough to get cast in something for him and he liked me enough that he put me in several other things. Martin got a three-picture deal with Warner Brothers and he was going to bring three actors with him. I was lucky enough to be one of them. I did publicity shots and interviews and everything. Unfortunately, Martin had some major drug and alcohol issues. So, I got a call from Warner and they told me that I have to reign him in and that if he can't and doesn't come, then I don't come. I can remember going up to his big house in Hollywood and he was gone. Everything was gone. It was like he just picked up in the night and left. It really affected me. It was supposed to be my big break I had worked so hard for. My neighbor had been doing home loans and got me into it. So, I was doing that while I was acting on the side. I had just finished a stint on *Melrose Place* and I called my agent and told them I was going to take a little break and start a mortgage company. They thought I was crazy. Then, I never went back. It was in 1995. That's how I got out of it. I actually go and take an acting class once in a while with Melissa Scott. I just like to go in a few times a year for two or three hours and work the chops with some people I don't know. It's fun. The business has really changed so much over the years though. I really don't want to be a part of it much anymore. Now, it could change. If you called me tomorrow and said you have two million dollars and want to make a movie, I could say "You know, if you have a part for dead body number two, I'll be there!" (laughs)

RA: Is there anything you would like to say to the fans?

PM: Yes. Keep going to the movies. They're a tremendous source of entertainment. In the past, if there was any joy that I may have brought somebody from seeing me on screen, I really appreciate it.

PAUL KRATKA
(FRIDAY THE 13th PART 111)

RA: How did you get into the acting business?

PK: I was enrolled at Santa Monica City College at the time. There was always some weird thing in the back of my mind that I might like it, so I enrolled in a drama class. I wasn't there to take that, but I just took it for fun. My first day of drama class, they made the announcement that there was auditions later in the week for the spring productions and they said that I was welcome to come out. So, I just thought I would come out and watch, sort of just to observe and see what the audition process is like. I went to the theater and watched and thought that I could do that, so I put my name in. It ended up that I got one of the principal roles in the play and from that point on, I was kind of hooked, doing acting. I just absolutely loved it.

RA: Looking at your IMDB page I see that *Friday the 13th* was your first film. Is this correct?

PK: Correct

RA: Wow, right out of the gate! That's pretty special.

PK: Oh yeah. I mean, I had done some other work, just not any films. Of course, at the time, I didn't realize that it was going to be the big deal that it was. Nobody ever would have thought that it would have the longevity where thirty or forty years later, you would be talking to a guy like me (laughs).

RA: That's awesome. Were you already familiar with the other Friday films before that?

PK: No, not at all. It's a funny story how it all came together, actually. There was a guy that I was studying with named Harris Kal. He had a recurring role on *Happy Days*. He and I were just really good friends, but you really couldn't have been more polar opposite. He was a short, curly haired Jewish guy from Chicago and I was a tall, skinny guy from Southern California. For whatever reason, we were buddies. (laughs) He went on this audition and he came back and told me that I have to go. He told me that they were really nice and that I should go meet them. So, I arranged for an interview and went in. The part that my friend had gone in for was for the role of Andy, so that's what I went in for, as well. The casting director said, "No, you're not right for Andy, but you're absolutely right for the male lead. We would like you to come back and read for the director and the producer". When I was leaving, they added, "When you come back to read for this character, remember that he is not a city guy. He's a country guy, so don't dress in slacks and a nice shirt". I kind of ran with that and came in for the follow-up interview with Steve Miner and Mancuso, wearing work boots and blue jeans and a parka, and I was carrying a skill saw and some 2x4s over my shoulder. They just ate it up and they loved it. I sat down and I read with them. Steve Miner asked me if I had ever seen the first two movies. I told them no, that I don't really like movies like that. They just kind of looked at each other and started laughing. I think that they appreciated the honesty though, that I wasn't trying to kiss up to them or trying to say something that wasn't true. So, that's how it all fell into place for me.

RA: Could you tell me what your experience was like for you being on location at the ranch and on set?

PK: Well, I know that the previous ones were filmed back east and they decided to keep this one local to Hollywood. So, they built an area that included a pond, a cabin, a barn. I'm not exactly sure what was already there on the property before we got there, but they created this area that would be our set. There's actually a documentary that should be in the finishing stages right now called *The Friday the 13th Memoriam Project*. It's dedicated to the memory of Richard Brooker. They included the whole history of the location, including its demise and later neglect, vandalism, and getting burnt down. There's a Facebook page for it. It was really cool because it was really isolated. It was a full set-up where they put us up out there. I was able to commute because I lived close enough that I was able to drive there every day. It was just great. It was like one big, happy family. (laughs) Well, it wasn't always happy, but it was like one big family.

RA: What do you remember about working with the other cast members and who did you really enjoy spending time with on the set?

PK: Obviously, Dana Kimmell because we spent a lot of time together and worked several scenes together. She was an absolute professional, just a sweetheart of a gal. David Katims, Tracie Savage and I hit it off very well. The three of us actually studied at the same acting school in North Hollywood, so we all knew each other a little bit from that, and had the same agent. Then, of course there's Larry Zerner, who is about the most likable guy on the planet. Another person that I really connected with is Catherine Parks. She's extraordinarily beautiful and she's just a very unpretentious person, who didn't try to flaunt her beauty in any shape or form. She was just there to work like anyone else. Her and I had a lot of conversations together and hung out. Everybody was great. Steve Miner and I became friends too. They had been trying to find the leading gal and were having trouble with that. I guess that Amy Steel wasn't available for whatever reason. For about two months, I did numerous screen tests with different actresses. In the process, Steve Miner and I became close. We would play tennis together and things like that. It was just a really cool experience, a lot of it because of the people involved and the relationships that were formed.

RA: What was Richard Brooker like to work with? I know that I have heard that he wasn't what you would expect at all from the character, that he was quite the gentleman.

PK: Yeah, Richard was the definition of a professional British gentleman. I know that he came from a trapeze, circus type background, so he had the experience as an entertainer. He wasn't a real outspoken guy, but he had a great sense of humor and a great personality. He was just a nice guy. It was weird because, I think it was maybe ten years ago, I ran into him at a restaurant in Malibu. I live hours away from there and I just happened to be on a road trip up the coast to Central California. I just happened to go into this cool little Italian restaurant outside of Malibu and he was in there. The cool part is that he treated me like we were long lost buddies. He was just very gracious and open and engaging. I don't think that there was anybody on that set who wasn't nice to be around. Everybody was just very professional. Of course, there were some frustrations on the set. There wasn't a lot of time to do everything and with the 3-D aspect, there was some new technology that was being employed, so there was a lot of technical aspects that required a lot of attention. It was a job, but it was a lot of fun. Everyone was very professional and everyone was treated well. It was fun.

RA: Did having to do the shoot for 3-D require more work than your average film, like having to make sure that things are being thrust at the camera and things like that?

PK: Well, some of that I was unaware of. I wasn't really clued in to a lot of the technical aspects. There was a lot of time spent on getting the focal points and getting the shots set up correctly when there was a scene where they would play up the 3-D effect. That took some more time, for sure. The death scenes were very laborious because they required a lot of set-up and rehearsal to get the technical aspects down. Some of the aspects to the 3-D made it more arduous or cumbersome from a technical standpoint. As an actor, you weren't too aware of it, though. It took a little longer, but everything takes a long time in filmmaking as it is.

RA: I have some character questions here. Now, it wasn't exactly one hundred percent clear what the history was between you and Chris in the movie. I know that there is a lot of talk about the previous summer. Do you have any deeper insights into this?

PK: Well, I think that in the previous year, the two characters had gotten very close to each other. Then, I think that when she got traumatized from the attack from Jason, she had a bit of PTSD that she went through. So, when she shows up again, I'm ready to kick things off again from where we left off and she is definitely struggling. So, that was really the essence of that. Plus, it's of course the classic situation of the guy trying to maneuver into a situation of intimacy with the girl, who's kind of fighting that off a bit.

RA: I've heard a lot and I've seen the still shots of an extra scene that was filmed with you and Dana running into Abel's character again. Can you tell me some information on that lost scene?

PK: You know, I don't have a lot of recollection of that. I have a copy of that still myself. I think it was just to kind of add some depth to Abel's character. Making a finished product for a movie, the most important thing is what you remove. The idea is to tell the story and have it move forward, and remove anything that might interfere with flow and momentum. I think that was the decision there. That's all I really remember about that.

RA: I know you didn't really have any scenes directly with them, but what was your take on the addition of the bikers to the story?

PK: Like you said, most of the scenes that they were in, I was not in. Movie making is very compartmentalized and for money's sake, you don't really have people around if they're not being used. I do remember running into them and again, they were young people like the rest who were very excited to be making a movie. I think that their characters were some of the more richly woven characters in the film. I thought that they really added some uniqueness to the thing. If they weren't in it, I think the movie may not have been as interesting. The storyline that they were involved in was cool. How they came to the cabin to burn the barn down and end up getting killed was a nice extra. I thought it was just great.

RA: Definitely, What I also liked about it was that when I first watched it, I thought that the character of Ali was actually going to save the day and live. Obviously, that changed very quickly. I remember being disappointed that that character died. Speaking of which, I kind of expected the same from your character of Rick.

PK: (laughs) Well, that's the formula. Everybody dies but the girl, usually.

RA: What was it that went into making your death scene happen? I still think that it's one of the more shocking deaths in the series.

PK: It was actually a pretty involved process. A couple of months prior to the start of filming, I went out to Stan Winston's effects lab. This was still in the early days of his career. I went out there to a nondescript industrial park. They made a body cast out of me from about mid-torso up, over the shoulders and over the head. Up until the point where they did the face part, it was fine. Then, they told me that they were going to get to the hard part and that they were going to put this silicone stuff over my face. They said they were going to wrap my head in this cast and I was supposed to breathe through these two straws in my nostrils. They asked if I was claustrophobic and I said that I think I can handle it. They put it on and got the breathing holes established and everything was fine. They told me that after it was dry, I would need to move my face around to free it up from the silicone, so the holes that I was breathing through were going to disappear. They said, "Don't freak out, we'll get that cut off you in no time." Well, that's when it got a little unnerving, for sure. I couldn't breathe and I could hear them running the saw. It was almost like one that they would use in an autopsy, just a small circular saw, to crack the thing open. It was pretty intense. So, now they had a mold of me and they made a mannequin out of that mold. The mannequin was a life-size replica of me that was very exact, from skin tone to hair and everything. They also made the skull in such a way that it had collapsible plates in it, so that they could show the crushing of the skull and if they needed multiple takes, they could keep doing that. The evening that they were shooting my death scene, it was about three in the morning and they wheeled this mannequin out to the cabin and it was really eerie to see something that looked exactly like me. Nobody gets to experience that, where they get to see an exact replica of themself, plus it was three in the morning and you could hear the crickets and everything. It was a surreal experience, for sure. Then, they rigged the eyeball up to a piece of monofilament line and lined it up to the central axis of the camera, so that you couldn't see the line because it was in the direct field of vision. That's how they did that.

RA: Wow, I can imagine that being creepy. After *Friday the 13th*, I noticed that you didn't do any films for quite a while. What was the reason for that?

PK: Well, part of it was kind of a strategic mistake. I changed agents and my agent thought that doing a role like that so early on put me into a league I shouldn't have been in at that point. It was something that they felt I should have worked up to. I also started to have misgivings about the business and wondered if I really wanted to dedicate myself to a career that was so unpredictable. There are just legions of very talented actors that never make it and just languish in poverty. It's not due to a lack of talent, but due to how fickle the business is. I was able to support myself after *Friday the 13th* and did some commercials, but I went back to school and had the idea to get a degree in Marine Biology. Long story short, I ended up going into chiropractic school and that's the path I took. At the same time, I always had this huge void in my heart for working as an actor, so as the years went by, every now and then someone would contact me, usually a young filmmaker who was a *Friday the 13th* fan. I've taken on a few projects here and there since then. I recently did a film called *The Bone Garden* that also stars Tracie Savage. I think it's on Netflix and Amazon. I also made some movies with a guy named Scott Goldberg out in Long Island. He's a real creative guy. I also shot some footage for something called *Twice Rising* with a guy named Ron Atkins.

RA: If you had anything you could say to the *Friday the 13th* fans, what would you say?

PK: My experience with the *Friday the 13th* fanbase has been nothing short of extraordinary. They are the nicest, most generous, kindest people. They're genuinely grateful for the interaction I've had with them and I'm the same way towards them. They're just the coolest. I am very grateful for the fans and thank them all for their dedication. I have nothing but love for them.

PJ SOLES
(HALLOWEEN)

RA: How did you get involved in *Halloween*?

PJ: Well, John Carpenter told me that he had seen *Carrie* and he thought that I would be a perfect fit for Linda. I did have an audition and it was unusual though, because I actually just met with him and read with him. Usually, you meet with a casting agent or you have to go through a few auditions. I guess that they had already looked at a bunch of people, and he told me that in his mind, he had kind of already settled on me. So, I read with John and we did the scene together and he said to me that I was the only girl that said "Totally!" right. I said, "How else would you say it?" and he said, "that's why I want you to do the part." I went, "really?" That was unusual too, for the director to offer you the part on the spot like that. He asked if I was willing to do it and I said it was exciting and that I would love to. I thought he was very cool and I liked his style, so I just said I would do it. It was nice not having to wait for results, like at the doctor, and just getting the part on the spot. He asked me to stay so that I could help pick out the guy who would play my boyfriend in it, and we decided on John Michael Graham for Bob. It was really fun. I was married at the time to Dennis Quaid and there was talk about having him come in, but he was doing a movie of the week at the time, so we had these three guys come in and we chose John and he and I got along great.

RA: Could you describe for me your character of Linda and what set her apart personality wise from your counterparts in *Halloween*?

PJ: Well that's what I think is so different from the Rob Zombie movie because the first thing that really struck me in that is that all of the girls seem to have the same personality. No offense to them. It was a different era, the seventies, and the personalities are a bit more distinct. Linda of course is the one with the boyfriend that actually goes all the way, Annie is the one that is hoping for that, and of course Laurie could probably only dream of having a boyfriend, even just holding hands. She has no idea what that area of life is like. I think they're attracted to Linda because she has guts and is the more wild one. She smokes cigarettes and she's kind of a bad girl. It's exactly like someone I knew in high school. I went to the International School and my dad was working there in Algeria at the time, so I went to school with a lot of embassy brats and military brats. My friend Cindy Clark, whose father worked for Caterpillar from Peoria, IL, was going out with a Belgian guy and smoking cigarettes. I was a straight A student and was editor of the school newspaper, so I kind of fashioned Linda after Cindy Clark. In high school, I was so naive and so young, so it was fun to play a part that was very wild. She was the girl that was so ahead of the others and it's amazing that she was friends with Laurie. But then again, I was Laurie in High School, and was attracted to someone like Linda. So it was nice that the three of us had very distinct personalities. I do believe from my own personal experience, that it was possible for those three to be friends.

RA: What was Jamie Lee Curtis like to work with?

PJ: She was nineteen at the time, it was her first movie and she was very nervous. She thought for the first couple of days that John was going to fire her, but of course it turned out that she was doing a wonderful job. I think she was very insecure. Probably because she told me that she was more like me in high school, she didn't know how to play a good girl that was getting straight A's. She said "You're so lucky. You get to play the fun girl! I was the fun girl in High School. I don't know how to play this girl because I wasn't like her". So that was really funny. She smoked and I didn't. It's not like she taught me, but I was a very bad smoker. I can see in certain scenes that it was embarrassing to me. I barely puffed anything! But even that would be believable since Linda was in High School and maybe she wasn't adept at smoking yet.

RA: What was John Carpenter like to work for. From all I've heard, it sounds like he was pretty laid back.

PJ: He really was. He was totally laid back, not much older than myself. I was already 27 years old. John was very soft spoken and he and Debra Hill would sometimes talk to each other in whispers. It was a very intimate set. You really felt like part of a team and that it was a team effort. We would gather up the leaves after a scene and put them back in the bag together. Everybody really worked together to make this movie happen.

RA: What was your experience with Donald Pleasence? I don't believe that you had any scenes with him.

PJ: Yeah, we didn't have any scenes, but we were there every day and I remember eating with him for lunch and he always sat at the head of the table. He would remain in character pretty much. I think that we all would say "okay, he's from that method school of acting." He was very quiet. Once in a while he would hear us giggling and chit chat among us at lunch and we would see him crack a smile. It was later that we found out that he had a daughter around the same age at the time, which is why he took the film, but he never told us that. He was very quiet and somber. It's not like we left him alone, but he wouldn't really volunteer to engage with us. Plus, we didn't have much time for lunch honestly. It was like a half hour, then brush your teeth, wash up and get back to work.

RA: Tell me about your thoughts on the iconic house from the film. I had the pleasure of actually getting to visit it last night and it was an amazing experience!

PJ: They really changed it a lot, didn't they? I don't think the owners really want people to come around. The guy with the hedge is cool in Pasadena. He loves his hedge, but as far as Orange Grove street, I'm not sure they really want all of the people there. I thought it was a beautiful street with the trees. My daughter and I were in *Horror's Hallowed Grounds*, filming with Sean Clark visiting the sets. I think she was in Junior High. We went to a friend's house and in there was a picture there of that house and there was me and Jamie and Nancy standing in front of the house. She said "How come your parents have a picture of my mother in their house?" They said it's because they used to own that house when they filmed *Halloween* there. So, she came home and told me about that and I thought that was really cute. It's a small world.

RA: Wow! What was it like filming your death scene? It still stands out to this day as one of the quintessential moments in horror history, one of the biggest scares of all time, if you will.

PJ: Well, with John being as considerate as he was, he approached me and asked me if I considered doing the nudity. He said it would just be himself, Debra and Dean Cudney there, and just said to do whatever was comfortable if I was comfortable with it. They kept it very intimate and closed. I came up with the line there. Then there was the death scene with Nick Castle playing Michael. He was grabbing the phone cord and Nick didn't want to hurt me in any way, so he kept asking me "Is it okay? Is it okay?" and I said, "It's okay, it's just tickling me. You're going to have to do it a little harder". Nick would say that he just doesn't want to hurt me. I told him to give me a little bit more. We did about three takes, because he was just doing it so gently. Then, as I was falling out of frame and going (makes choking noise), I thought they were going to say, "That's a wrap on PJ", so I wanted to extend this and just keep going and get as much screen time as possible on that and just kept going and making the noise. (laughs)

RA: What are your thoughts on *Halloween* now, your work on it and the fan base?

PJ: I'm so proud to have been in this movie. I'm so proud when people come up with their kids. I'm a little amazed that they would show it to their five and eight-year-old kids, but okay. It is quite tame today, though. There's very little blood, no actual stabbing. There's the knife and the after effects and the intention of the horror, but you don't get to see very much. Even my scene seemed more playful. I love that it has a life of its own. People just love it and love the characters, and everybody knows every single minute of our scenes, so I'm very impressed by that and totally blessed and honored.

RAY SAGER
("MONTAG THE MAGNIFICENT" in THE WIZARD OF GORE, worked on many genre favorites, such as MY BLOODY VALENTINE, HUMONGOUS, TERROR TRAIN, etc.)

RA: First off, thank you so much for taking the time to talk with me. I was just reading your bio and I must say that I was blown away by the number of movies that you have worked on in the genre.

RS: Well, in this industry you just have to keep going. You either make it or you don't. I was very fortunate to have worked on all of these movies and was able to keep going. It's what you have to do, keep moving from picture to picture to picture. I came to Canada from Chicago years ago with about two hundred bucks in my pocket and not a lot of friends here. I just started rebuilding and enhanced the career that I had in the States. I felt really good about that.

RA: How did you get your start in the film business?

RS: Well, I was an actor first. I went to art school and theater school and found myself drifting around after that. I was in Chicago and went to Movement Theater there and the Art Institute.

Even after I gave up on the idea of being an artist, I kept going over to watch the experimental films that the art school put on. More and more, I started to feel that if I was going to act or direct, I was going to do it in movies. That is what got the ball rolling for me. Then, around that time I got into acting and ended up doing quite a few movies. Unfortunately, one day the thrill was gone for me. I had always wanted to get on the other side of the camera. I had a great mentor in the horror world and I just kept pushing to do things on the other side of the camera, and he eventually let me. That's where it really began. Then, I got my way into PBS and worked my way up into floor manager, before going freelance, in terms of assistant cameraman, soundman, editor. I just kept doing every potential job in the movie business. I think the only job I haven't done is being a mixer, or doing hair.

RA: Wow, that is amazing. You've pretty much had your hands in everything.

RS: Yeah, I thought I would need it if I eventually wanted to produce, which was in my mind when I came to Canada. I always felt that it would be good to know all of these things. When I got to Canada, I went out attempting to produce stuff. We had some really good ideas and I was with a couple other people. I eventually ended up being an assistant director and I think the second project that I did up there was *Terror Train*. I had done a few commercials before that, but there was a certain sophistication involved in how they do it up there for film, so there was a bit of a learning curve for me. The first one was a movie called *Funeral Home*. It was originally called *Cries in the Night*, before it became *Funeral Home*, which I saw one day by accident. After that was *Terror Train*, and then I did *My Bloody Valentine* after that. After I did *Humongous,* which is another horror film, I produced my first feature here called *American Nightmare*, before I went off to produce other features.

RA: I know that at the start of your career, you did quite a lot of work with legendary director Herschell Gordon Lewis. How did you get hooked up with him?

RS: It was a pure accident. I had just completed my last year of theater training at Goodman and I was kind of wandering around, in a sense, not knowing what to do. I ran into a guy that I used to study with, who was from Iran. I ran into him on the street and asked him what he was doing. He told me that he was working on a movie. I asked if there were any parts that I could do and he told me that they just had a guy that quit. It was a small part, but he asked if I could work that night. I said yeah, I could come in tonight. So, I went down there and it was Herschell's show *The Girl, the Body, and the Pill*. I ended up being on set and I did two lines and they liked it. They then kept writing up the part and adding more lines. I ended up becoming one of the feature characters in the show and that's how it started. Then, I did a few other shows with him, with bigger parts. He also let me direct some stuff and it was really great of him to do that. Some scenes, he would give me to direct or he would say "I'm finished for the day. Do you want to direct that scene?" Things like that.

RA: I ran across an early film of yours while doing research for this interview. I had never seen it before, so I had to give it a watch. I wanted to talk about when you played the main character of Montag The Magnificent in *The Wizard of Gore*.

RS: That one came about a bit by accident. I've actually posted a video on YouTube explaining that it was a total fluke. I was on the crew at that time. I was in New York and was supposed to do a show for Harry Elkins. We did the first half of the movie in Chicago. When I got there to New York, they told me that he had gone broke and the show was cancelled. I remember when the guy was telling me this, we were standing in the middle of this three-story Park Avenue mansion with a Rolls Royce parked out front and I'm thinking, "How is he broke?" So, I ended up broke in New York. Thankfully, I met some very good people there, like a designer in Long Island who put me up and was going to put me up for as long as I wanted. So, I called Herschell up and told him I was there and okay, but I could really use the work. I was working behind the camera then, and hadn't acted in a long time. He told me that he needed some people on a crew and that they were starting in a week. So, I hitchhiked back to Chicago and ended up on the crew in the grip department. The guy that was cast as Montag went a little crazy about two or three days into shooting. We were shooting in a high-rise building and he just had a meltdown. He looked perfect and was right for the part, an older actor. He just started having a meltdown. He didn't want to wear the tuxedo to start with, then we find out that he was an outpatient at a mental institute. So, now they were looking around for someone to take the lead. They had to keep shooting and only had the location for a few more days. They were trying to figure out what to do, when Herschell looked at me and asked me if I could do the part. I told him that I don't even know the part, I hadn't even really read the script. I was told that I would make a lot more money working in front of the camera than behind it, plus they already knew that I could act. So, I took the part. I just said that I would only memorize a day ahead for the lines and that's all I'll know, so don't change the schedule or add new lines. So, it worked and we got the movie done and it became a big hit for them. It was one of the bigger shows that he did. I think it may have been about a three-week shoot. I always thought that I wasn't very good in the because, a. I'm learning on the fly, and b. I'm way too young to play it. I was thinking of trying to channel Richard Burton to play it. All of a sudden, it just became this cult classic.

RA: There was one thing about the movie that really confused me. I honestly didn't know what was going on at one point. I couldn't figure out if what Montag was doing on stage was real, or what was really happening and it wasn't explained. Could you help explain it to me?

RS: I thought it was kind of a brain fart that Herschell had and I don't think that it was completely thought out. I think that actually for its time, in terms of dealing with altered reality, I think it was kind of a breakthrough. Nobody was doing that. I thought that aspect was kind of innovative, but it wasn't really thought out to its conclusion. I think that the perception was that if there's enough blood and guts, nobody is really going to ask. There have been many great things filmed since that have dealt with that altered reality, where you think, "Am I in reality? Am I outside of reality?"

The basic concept of *The Wizard of Gore* is that the audience was hypnotized, so that they could not see the killing that was going on, so it was like a trick on the audience. Then, the idea was to take it to a local TV station and do the trick on a bigger audience. One thing that Herschell really excelled at, was that he would grab the headline of the day and make a story out of it and write it up in like two weeks or so. It was a time when drive ins were flourishing and his films worked very well at the drive-ins.

RA: Moving on back to your time as an assistant director, I want to touch on some of those films in the early eighties. The first one is *Funeral Home*. Can you tell me your memories of working on that?

RS: It was the first one that I did in Canada. It was very tough on me. They had a very different method of scheduling shoots up there. The director and I, who is a really nice guy in reality, did not get along. I was really not that confident in the way that they were doing things there and I was on a learning curve. Although I was in the union as a First AD (Assistant Director), I hadn't done it the Canadian way, which is a lot like the British system. It was the director's first movie and he was easily irritated because he had so much riding on that movie. He went on to do other big movies after that, so it worked out well for him. Funny story. I was working a lot with Paul Lynch, who I did a lot of movies with, as a director. We were doing a movie called *Cross Country*, which I was also Assistant Director on. Part of the deal with *Cross Country* was that we started at The Grand Canyon and then we drove all across America to do all of these pick-up shots, like location shots with actors to actually show that we had traversed this distance.

Our last stop was actually Philadelphia. Paul was a big fan boy like myself and was really into the films of Abel Ferrara. Well, *Ms. 45* was playing there in Philadelphia, and he said that we had to see it. I had been driving with him and his wife and they were always fighting. They were fighting in the theater and we were the only white people in the theater. The funny thing was that it was a double bill of *Ms. 45* and *Funeral Home*. I didn't know that *Funeral Home* was actually the movie that I had worked on. They had a big fight and she went to sit somewhere else, so I decided to sit with her to keep her safe. I watched *Ms. 45* with her and I wasn't planning on staying for the next film, but the credits came on and I thought, "This looks familiar". The audience loved it! I was very excited about that. The people there were yelling at the screen at the scary parts and I could tell they were getting a real enjoyment out of it. I had no clue that this movie that was so difficult for me was so well received. That was very gratifying to me.

RA: After *Funeral Home*, you went on to work on one of my all-time favorite slasher films, *Terror Train*, a film that is criminally underrated in my opinion.

RS: I'm not sure why it wasn't bigger and other films are. I don't know if it was a bad release pattern, or maybe at that point Jamie (Lee Curtis) was overexposed. She had just done *Prom Night* with Paul Lynch. I first saw her in *Halloween*. After the difficulties, I had working on *Cries in The Night*, I wasn't really sure about going to Montreal to make this other horror film. When they told me that it's starring Jamie Lee Curtis, I said I was in. I didn't know Lynch at the time, but I just wanted to work with Jamie, mainly because I was so impressed with her in *Halloween*. I thought that she was one of the most talented new actors I had ever seen. She was totally natural. That for me was a big attraction of doing *Terror Train*. I really knew nothing about it until I got there. We did shoot it on a real train. It was a great adventure, in many ways. It worked out really well. We came in on schedule and on budget, which nobody thought we would. We had John Alcott shooting it, who had just come off of *The Shining*. He was perfecting this style that he started on *The Shining* where he put every light on a dimmer. He did that on *Terror Train* too. I went up to and apologized, telling him that I know he is used to doing longer shoots and we were only doing a five week shoot on *Terror Train*. He told me that if it were any longer, he probably wouldn't have done it. He just got done doing a nine month shoot on *The Shining*, and said he would never do that again, because Stanley (Kubrick) would re-shoot everything.

I thought it was a real bonus working with Alcott. They rewired the whole train, which took about three days to do, so that all of the lights on the train, you could dim from outside. It made everything exceptionally easy. It was Roger Spottiswoode's first movie that he ever directed. He was a brilliant editor already. He had done *The Wild Bunch* and a few (Sam) Peckinpah movies. He was an incredible presence. He is a very clever man and came up with the concept of optical blow-ups when he was working on *Hard Times* with James Coburn. He used a lot of that in *Terror Train*, as well, where we needed a close-up and didn't have one, but just made it after the fact by just taking the medium shot and creating a close-up. Roger had two weeks of rehearsals with the actors in his hotel room in Montreal. When we got to the actual, physical train on the platform, the blocking that they did in the hotel room wouldn't work. In the English system, the blocking is done by the operator, not the director. The director really just works with the actors. So, it was normal to say that me and the operator were going to work on the shots and the director would just work with the actors and we would call them when we're ready.

One day, we went a little over the ninth hour and into the tenth hour of filming. All of a sudden, the camera crew started walking out, packing up and leaving. I figured that I must have done or said something unintentionally, to make them walk out. I got a hold of the production manager, who was at the other end of this train, and I was freaking out, trying to figure out what was going on. The deal was, that he never booked them for overtime, so now, he had to renegotiate their deal for overtime hours, just to get them back. Normally, we didn't go overtime though. It was a very efficient shoot and the actors were well prepared. It's not usual in the business, but it was all going well. I also had to go with a second unit to Vermont for a few days, on a real train that was running to shoot the finale, where the villain is pushed out of the train. We were only shooting at nights, because that was the only time that we could get on the train. We would come in at five or six at night and work eight or nine hours. By the time, we were done in the morning, there was really no place to go. All of the bars were closed, so I would open up my suite and turn it into a party room. All of the crew and a few of the actors would show up. Eventually, Jamie showed up and eventually David Copperfield showed up. This went on every night.

David was dating one of the actresses and they used to just go off on their own every night. One night, he came up and said that they would really like to come to my party. I said, "Well, every night I've been inviting you, but you never show up. Now, if you come, you're going to have to bring a magic trick." He ended up bringing a brilliant card trick. It was unlike anything that I'd ever seen. I had done a little magic myself before, so I showed him a card trick and he thought I was very good, which was a very high compliment from him. When he showed up and would do some of the close-up tricks, I noticed that his hands would tremble, and I figured that it's the reason why he works with big illusions, because he gets nervous doing close-up magic, which I can understand. Magicians pick the thing that suits them best. From what I hear, he has gotten much more confident with the close-up magic over the years. That is what I remember best about those times. He ended up showing up a few more times to my parties. Jamie showed up a couple of times. Then, some of the other people started opening up their rooms and the party would just flow between rooms and between floors. I guess we were lucky we weren't thrown out (laughs).

An incredible experience for me was working with Ben Johnson. I was a big fan of *One Eyed Jacks* and he was fantastic in it. Sadly, not many people had heard of it and I wanted more people to know about it. He stayed to himself pretty much. I had a friend of mine who ran a movie theater and we were able to rent the whole place out and have the cast and crew come and we all watched *One Eyed Jacks*. It was an amazing experience to sit there with Ben Johnson, watching this amazing film that he was in. If you were to ask me what my one biggest highlight of the shoot was, that was it. It was one of those magic moments where you're sitting there with a hero of yours and watching their show. I would have liked to have watched *Halloween* there with Jamie Lee, as well, but I don't think we could have gotten that. I think it was still in release in some places at the time. It was one of the last shows that I saw before I left Chicago for Canada. I was just so enamored with her. I think she probably thought that I was stalking her. (laughs) Anywhere that Jamie went, I had to be. As an actor, I just want to know how these people do it. She was extremely professional on the show, she understood the part, asked the right questions, was always on time. She was everything you really want from an actor on a set. She was a real pleasure to work with, as were all of them. I would work with many of the others on other projects later and still keep in touch with some of them. Not all horror films work out that way, like I found out with *My Bloody Valentine*. Sometimes, they can be pretty complex and grueling.

RA: Let's talk about that one a little bit. It's another one of my all-time favorite slasher films. Can you tell me a bit about your experience working on *My Bloody Valentine*?

RS: It was in the middle of Sydney Mines, Nova Scotia. It was on the outskirts of Sydney, maybe about twenty or thirty minutes away from Sydney. It was a town that had closed down. It was like the town without pity. The mine went broke and it was still standing there and we needed to shoot at a mine that was vacant. The resources that we were looking for were not in that town anymore because people had left. It was by the ocean, I remember and you could walk down and see Newfoundland from across the ocean. It was beautiful, but it was almost like a ghost town. The last time anything filmed there was a film years earlier called *Goin' Down the Road* with director Donald Shebib. Nobody had told the town that we were doing a horror film. They would say, "Don't tell the townspeople that we're doing a horror film. They're going to be upset." Finally, I ended up doing some directing on it at the request of the director because we were behind, like a lot of pick-ups, dialogue, special effects and things. I did that for about two and a half weeks or so.

In the first scene that I directed, a guy got hurt, and it was the last guy you would want to get hurt because he was a local supplier of everything in that town. He could get you anything in that town. Out of all the guys, I thought. He got hurt and had to go the hospital. I felt guilty and ended up walking after he got hit by a car. The director convinced me to go back. So, I wasn't driving there, so I took a cab back to the set. Well, the cab driver says, "What kind of movie are you guys making?" This was like three or four weeks into the show. Finally, I was just so sick of all of it and trying to make up stories about what kind of movie it was. I just said, "You know what? I gotta tell ya. We're shooting a horror film." Then, the cab driver said "Oh ... well, that's good because we love horror films. Everyone thought you were doing something like that *Goin' Down the Road*, where we looked like idiots." So, news ended up traveling fast all over town and they were much more receptive to us being there from that day on. It also turns out that the guy in the hospital wasn't really hurt. He was faking it and just wanted the insurance claim.

RA: Can you tell me about your experience like working on the film *Humongous*?

RS: With this one, I was thinking that this was going to be my last film, if it doesn't go well. I didn't want to get on another difficult shoot again. It was the first time that I worked with (director) Paul Lynch. Everyone said that he is a bit temperamental, but I actually worked well with him. We went on to do many shows together after that. In fact, the first show that I produced, he was the executive producer on. I think what he liked about me is that I was persistent and just wouldn't stop. I remember that we shot up in Muskoka, outside of Toronto. I remember that it rained almost every day. Really, there wasn't a day that it didn't rain. We had dogs, the monster makeup, blowing up a boat, and all sorts of things to deal with. When it was raining, everyone would panic and want to go under a covered set. It was ridiculous. I would make sure that we had everything set up and all blocked out and ready to go, so as soon as the rain would stop, we would go and we never lost an hour on the schedule.

We completed the whole schedule on time, on budget and it was actually a relatively easy shoot. It worked out well, so I stayed in the business. It was also the beginning of a great relationship between Paul Lynch and myself. He was responsible for finding me lots of work and setting me up with various people. He got me into Northstar where I was head executive for nine years, where I was producing three movies a year, like *Bullies* and all of the *Prom Night* films. I was producer on them and they were filmed within Northstar. That was all Paul Lynch. He kept pushing to get me in there. He knew Pierre Simpson and got me the interview, and it stuck. Unfortunately, Pierre died about seven years ago. I felt like I could have stayed there forever, but I was there for nine years and felt like life was kind of passing me by, so then I went freelance again and started making a lot more money and building my resume more. It was a good run, though.

RA: I wanted to ask you something. When I saw *Humongous*, I noticed it was very dark and hard to see.

RS: Oh yes, I know. There's a newer version out now where they have corrected that and make it easier to see. I don't know why that decision was made, but it was a bad decision. It was printed dark. It wasn't shot dark. Actually, it was shot quite well. It was something that happened in post. It was printed dark and I'm not sure why everyone let that go. Even Paul Lynch admits that it was way too dark. Maybe they thought our monster wasn't as monstrous as possible, or just thought that having the whole thing dark was the way to go. I don't know. It was just one of those bad decisions. Avco was the one that distributed it and they should have never let it go like that because it hurt the movie. The movie could have been very strong. The acting was very good in it by everybody, which is good because a bad actor can sink a project. All eyes will be on them and how bad they are. If the actors don't believe it, then you won't buy into the show. *Humongous* had some very good actors, though.

How I think that I originally got Lynch's attention though is the part when we had the boat landing on the island. It was supposed to be in a storm, and in the fog. They had so many preparations in mind for it that including going to Niagara Falls where they had a loch, renting the loch, creating a storm above it and it was going to be expensive. I just went to him and said that I know that if they're going to an island in the fog, everything would be dead still. I told him that they didn't need to have this churning water and all the effects. We would have gone over schedule and over budget by doing that in Niagara Falls. I suggested getting a big warehouse, like a boat warehouse, and putting the boat on a cradle. We could fill the warehouse with smoke, the fog, and do all of the scenes in the fog there. That's what happens, they get lost in the fog and they drift to the island. Everybody thought it was genius and it worked out very well. I think that we shot that in the first week. When you do those things, you set an imprint where people trust you. From that day forth, I was trusted by Lynch and that was it, and Lynch was not a guy that had that built in trust readily available. I won my stripes and it went easy from then on. If I had an idea, he would trust me and go with it, and it worked.

RA: Do you have anything you would like to say to the fans out there?

RS: Don't give up. No matter how bad things can get sometimes, don't give up. I can't tell you how many times I had that conversation where I said "Well, this is my last show", or "I'm going to leave if this doesn't work out". If you're truly passionate, you don't get that choice, and if you aren't that passionate, then maybe you shouldn't be doing it.

ROBERT RAY SHAFER
(PSYCHO COP)

RA: First off, I just want to thank you for joining me for this interview.

RS: Thank you for having me. I've been working on my latest movie, *They Want Dick Dickster* lately. It's about a down on his luck director named Dick Dickster, who made a cult movie back in the eighties called *Cult of Doom*. A film school student is making a documentary about him and his bizarre behavior, then a porn producer comes along and wants Dick to make his cult classic into a porn film called *The Cult of Poon.* (laughs) There's some little inside jokes throughout it. His film was released in 1989, and that was when we released *Psycho Cop.* I also do a couple of lines from *Psycho Cop* in it and put a couple of actors from *Psycho Cop Returns* in it, because they're still friends, and also for the reference for the film's fans. We just signed the contracts today to release it, so it's a pretty exciting day for us. It's very funny. We made it in a mockumentary style because after spending eight years on *The Office,* I thought that I could do that format. There's a lot of cameos in it, too. Richard Grieco came in for me and a whole bunch of film directors are in it.

RA: That's awesome. How did you first get into the acting business?

RS: A woman, a girlfriend. She was an actress. I never really had a desire to be an actor. I had no training at it. I was kind of fooling around with male modeling for a bit, which I hated. I was too tall for that. You really need to be around 6'2 and I'm around 6'4 or 6'5. So, she said I should go take some acting classes and I did. The class I went to was with a great teacher named Peggy Furey, and in my class were people like Sean Penn, Michelle Pfeiffer, Meg Tilly, Meg Ryan and Nicholas Cage. So, it was this really competitive place and I worked my butt off and learned the craft. I learned how to be a stage actor. She taught classical American theater. We would go through periods where we were doing playwrights in class like Tennessee Williams, and Harold Pinter. She had been around back in the day with James Dean and Marlon Brando and all of those people, so I was really learning from one of the greatest acting teachers ever in Hollywood. That's how I got started and then the rest of it was just trying to be able to do work that was as good as that work. I think a lot of the younger actors that I run into today really have no formal training, nor do they desire to do it. It's disappointing, really. They really don't want to be in theater or do plays. They just want to be on TV and on films, being famous. Ultimately though, there's a method and a craft to be learned here. At some point you're going to need it. You can think that you're really charming and have charisma and that the camera loves you, but then one day Anthony Hopkins or someone that really knows their stuff will be standing there watching you(laughs). What that means is that unless you're the star of the piece, the editor is going to choose the other guy's take. That's essentially what actors are competing for is making the editor choose your take. If you don't have that inner life going on and know how to create a character, you're going to be in deep trouble.

RA: Ha! That sounds a lot like pro wrestling. There were a lot of guys in the business that thought they would go straight to WWE and didn't have to bust their asses on the indies like the rest of us. I totally get that.

RS: Funny you mention that. My cousin is a prolific B-movie filmmaker, Fred Olen Ray. He was a pro wrestler as well. In fact, he's in *Dick Dickster,* as well. We put these little things under each person's name in the credits, and his is "Producer, Director, Wrestler". (laughs) Because everyone has to be a hyphen down here. You can't just do one thing. A girl once gave me her business card and it said "actress, singer, dancer, producer, writer, director." (laughs) I'll never forget it. I still have it, actually. I remember I said to her, "Why don't you just pick one?" (laughs)

RA: (laughs) That's great. How did you get involved in *Psycho Cop*?

RS: Well, I auditioned for it. Wallace Potts was the director on the picture. In the first audition, they were doing scenes from the Sam Shepherd play *True West*, which I was later able to do the 20th anniversary of in Pasadena, where he wrote the piece. I had been doing it in class and I had just seen John Malkovich and Gary Sinise do it on PBS. It was a real career launcher for them and it's what really made them get noticed. So, I was not only familiar with it, but when I saw that they were using it for the audition, I knew. I could tell midway through the audition that I had made an impact and I got the part. It was meant to be.

RA: What is your take on Officer Vickers and what were your thoughts on the character when you first got the part?

RS: Well, I liked Christopher Lee and Vincent Price, the old-school horror villains that I grew up watching on Chiller Theater. It was on at midnight on Friday nights. I would stay up and watch it. Those guys always had what I call a malevolent glee and that's what I was trying to get into in the role. For me, with the first film, we sort of dubbed most of it. The performance was actually a bit different from what ended up in the vocal track. Wallace wanted it to be scarier, but I always knew that we were making a comedy (laughs), so that was the tradeoff there. I knew I had to give him what he wanted, but I also knew that I was going to be the one who was on screen with it. The other thing that had happened when we did the first one was that I had signed a five-picture deal for that character, so I was feeling pretty confident that I was going to be the next Freddy Krueger. It was a big deal for me to get a five-picture deal. In fact, I was offered a role in *Back to the Future Part II* that I turned down because of the five-picture deal.

RA: No way, really?

RS: Yeah, I remember that Juliette Taylor was the casting director and my agent told her that I didn't want to take the part. She was like, "Are you kidding me? You're turning down a part with Robert Zemeckis?" (laughs). My agent was like, "No, he's got a five-picture deal. He's going to be the next big horror villain." So, even though we didn't make five of them, the picture was still really good to me. I got to go to Cannes for the film festival and I really learned a lot making that picture. (laughs) I learned not to be buddies with the other actors, especially when you've got to kill them. I was nice to them, but I also knew that I had to kill them in the movie. I don't go there to be everybody's set buddy. I go to work and do my thing. (laughs) There was a funny exchange one night. Palmer Lee Todd, who plays Laura, was standing there with me. We shot in Malibu Canyon and it was really cold out there. She was standing up on these apple boxes and she looked me in the face and said, "I'm not scared of you." (laughs) The scene was for me to throw her up against this tree. I had been pretty gentle with her up until she said that and I said "Well, you're about to be." Let's just say that she found that tree with a little more enthusiasm on that particular take (laughs).

RA: (laughs) I bet! Now, you were talking about this a little bit. I noticed that the first one is not as blatantly funny, but the second one sure as hell was. It's like they did a completely different route on the second one, like they just made it all out bonkers, and it was hilarious, with one-liners everywhere.

RS: Well, Dan Povenmire, who wrote that is also the creator of *Phineas and Ferb*. The director, Adam Rifkin is of course, a prolific filmmaker. Everybody in that picture was talented and that's one thing you can never hide. Barbara Niven has a huge career. Everyone from the picture has always continued to work. It was very well cast. Bill Paxton's dad is in the picture. We just had a lot more fun making it, because we just knew that we were just going to camp it up. At the same time, I get comments all the time about it being so scary, which always makes me laugh because I don't see it as scary. But, I guess it is pretty creepy. You know, you're supposed to trust the man with the badge. Actually, we've got another one in the works. Rifkin and I decided that we wanted to do it again. We went to this thing in Hollywood called Horrible Movie Night, and they invited seven or eight of us from it there and they screened *Psycho Cop Returns*. Everyone is supposed to shout out at the film as they're watching it. The great thing was that we had never seen it screened in public. The best thing was that it just totally kicked ass (laughs). It still holds up. It can be anytime, anywhere. That's the beauty of it. When it played, everyone was pretty much silent. There wasn't a whole lot of talking back to the movie because the movie is working. They like to go in there and mock movies and make jokes, but all the jokes were happening up on the screen. So, that was very pleasing to us to see the film work on that level with an audience. They also had a screening at Alamo Drafthouse back in April in Texas. I think the interesting thing for us is that when we made it, it kind of just disappeared because of how Columbia-Tristar handled the distribution. It was part of a multi-picture deal and we were all pretty psyched that they picked it up. So, we never really got much love for it. It played on cable in the nineties quite a bit, but then it disappeared, so after it came out on DVD and with internet, you'd be stunned at how much mail I get about it. It's pleasing to me. I view it like an antique shop, like most actors do with older work. It's pleasing to me that people still like it now, but it's not really something that I think about much now. I'm always looking ahead to the next thing.

RA: Did you do much improvising or your own jokes when you were doing the movies?

RS: There was some. It was pretty tightly scripted though, so there was no reason to improvise. People always ask me that about *The Office*. They ask me if we were improvising a lot and I just say hell no. Nobody was doing improv. That's all on the page because the page gets approved by the network. The only improv that happened on *The Office* was when Steve Carrell or Rainn Wilson were trying to make each other laugh. Even on *Dick Dickster*, the improv that we did on that was very limited. We did a couple scenes like that, but we all had the stated goal of what we were trying to achieve. I think a good improv happens in the moment when something happens that you're not expecting to happen. That's what makes a good improv. Actors just improvising for no reason is not good. (laughs) Nobody wants that. I had one of the actors on *Dickster* that kept asking if we could do this or that and I was just like, "Why don't we just do what's written?" (laughs) It always has to be about what's driving the picture forward, not necessarily about what the character is doing. Everyone wants to be funny, but sometimes it doesn't service the story in any way. There's a lot of jokes that you just have to leave on the cutting room floor because it's slowing down the process of getting to the end. You've got to move the plot forward. It's like I've always liked Christopher Guest and his films, but some of it can be kind of languid and slow. It can be funny, but it can also just be these talking heads just rambling on.

RA: What do you think was your personal favorite line in the *Psycho Cop* movies?

RS: Well, there's so many of them, but I think the one that everyone always quotes is "You have the right to remain dead. Anything that you say will be considered extremely strange because you're dead. You have the right to an attorney, not a lot of good it'll do you because … you're dead",

RA: Another one I like is "Suspect is blonde and considered extremely fucking stupid!"

RS: Yeah, that's another good one too. (laughs) "Here's Johnny!" was an improv line. There were a few little spots where that stuff got stuck in, but most of it was on the page. It's really easier for the director and the writer really doesn't want you changing his stuff anyways. I'm a writer too, so I always respect writers. When I audition, I always try to do it exactly the way that it's written. When we were doing the *True West* play, there was an author's note at the very beginning that says "Do not change a thing." (laughs) To me it always seems lazy when actors start to improvise. It just shows me that they didn't really concentrate much on the script and preparing for it. To me, that's the cardinal sin because it shows that you don't really pay the material the respect that it deserves. If someone is putting up the money to get this made, there's a reason for it. When I was auditioning people for *Dickster,* we had one actress come in to read named Jan Broker who plays Cocoa Heart, a porn producer. I left a full script out in the waiting room for anyone to read and get the tone of the whole piece. When it was her turn to come in, she asked if we could take someone else so she could finish reading the script. I was thinking, "There's my girl right there." That shows to me that she had the interest and wanted to get the tone and get the whole thing right. Sure enough, she got the part and she was terrific in it.

RA: Speaking of some of your favorite parts, what would you say was your favorite kill in the movies?

RS: I think it would have to be in the first one when Zack got the billy club down the throat.

RA: Oh God, that was a brutal one!

RS: Yeah, he was a real pain in the ass, so I particularly enjoyed roughing him up. He's actually a big celebrity fitness trainer now. Cynthia, who played the blonde who is always losing her hair brush, is the model for about eighty percent of all the female romance novels ever done now. I read that a while back. Who knew?

RA: Wow, that's big. (laughs) I probably see her every time I'm at the grocery store then.

RS: That's right, that's her. Then, I guess that the best kill in the second one is … well, that's tough. I know that the toughest one to do was throwing the girl off the roof because that was an extremely dangerous stunt there. We were up on a ten-story building in Burbank shooting that and the first high fall was a stuntman dressed up as the girl. We threw him down about three flights and then they brought in another stuntman. It was towards the end of filming and it was a true high fall. There was one of those big, huge bags down there for him and I remember he hit the bag wrong. All of the stuntmen went running because they were afraid that he was in deep trouble. Fortunately, he came up okay. I don't know, I had so much fun killing all of them (laughs). It's hard to pick just one out. The stunts were reasonably convincing in it. I mean, how often does a guy get to snap Julie Strain's neck? (laughs) That's always fun. It was a good cast and crew. We were shooting nights again. It's kind of a weird deal because your clock just gets so screwed up. Same thing on the first one, it was mostly nights. On Part two, it had to be at night so no one is in the building. By day, that's a Bank of America building and people are working on all ten floors there, so you couldn't shoot in the day. We didn't get to take possession of the building until six or seven at night. We would shoot all night and then come rolling out of there when everyone else would come rolling in for work. It was a lot of fun. We shot on film, so every day we would get to look at the dailies and see what we had done, which is a great thing that people don't get to do much anymore. I remember working on a film out in Utah and they told me they didn't want me to come to the dailies, that it would ruin my performance. Al Pacino goes to the dailies. There's a lot to be learned from your performance and you can see what you're doing and what adjustments you need to make. We had a great cinematographer on that one, Adam Kane, who has gone on to do a lot. In between takes, we had a running gag. He would say it was great and I would say, (in a Bela Lugosi voice) "Yeah, but is it spooky?" (laughs). That was our thing.

RA: That's cool that you got to use so much of the building. I remember the parts that I liked were when you would use the copy machine to send the pictures to everyone.

RS: (laughs) Yeah. You know, another tough one was when we speared Justin Carroll and the porn actress. They had to elevate them and everything. I don't remember what Joe's one-liner was there, but all of the scenes had to have one.

RA: Have you seen the *Maniac Cop* films and how do you compare the two?

RS: You know, I've never seen any of those. I don't really watch a whole lot of horror. I watch some of it. I think lately it's gotten too much into the gore porn with the *Saw* movies. I like things like *Rosemary's Baby* and *The Exorcist* because they contain real evil, as opposed to just a villain chasing and mutilating people. I did this picture a few years back called *Knifepoint* and it's pretty brutal. It's a home invasion movie and the killers are just sadistic bastards. I wasn't the killer, I was a victim and my family is killed in front of me. It was a sick film. My wife and son get killed, my daughters get raped, they cut my fingers off and rape me with a gun …

RA: Holy shit! That sounds messed up!

RS: Yeah, it really was. The guys I think were trying to make something like *Last House on the Left* and they just seemed to be doing it to be shocking. I remember that the script seemed pretty flawed to me. I kept thinking that there were too many holes in it and the script didn't make sense. Another flaw was that they had like seven killers loose at once. It's a gang that takes over this family's apartment. You don't need that many bad guys. They're all trying to outdo each other. It kind of loses its focus. You don't know why they're so crazy or how the hell they're going to get away with it. That's an example of what, sadly, a lot of horror has become lately. When you're making them, you want to try to find a unique villain. I think that's what every horror director is searching for. When I was watching *The Exorcist* or *The Omen*, those got to me. Every hair on the back of my neck stood up because it felt really evil. I think that Satanists and demonic things are more frightening to me, because it deals more with the supernatural and the unknown, as opposed to just some psychopath.

RA: I've always wondered that about Vickers. Is he just off duty at the time or just a satanic, crazy person?

RS: You know, there was a very muddled explanation in the first script. He's really some other character, I forget the name. There's a cop that gives an explanation and then I tear his heart out, and that was a great kill. (laughs) "Have a heart." See, I can still do the voice (laughs). I don't think that they ever really explained it, nor did I really ask anyone. I always just make choices and do them and then if they want me to adjust it, I will. Playing a psychopath is a lot more fun than playing a sociopath. A sociopath is trying to hide that he's crazy and act normal, but a psychopath is just flat out batshit crazy. If you've ever spent any time around someone who is manic depressive, and I have with some family and friends, when they go into an episode, you know it. That's the way that I've always seen him as he was just going through an episode. He had that maniacal energy and really put it to bad use (laughs). That malevolent glee, like with Christopher Lee. I actually got to do an 80s-sex comedy with

Christopher Lee. It had Fran Drescher in it and so many great character actors. I remember just hanging around on set with him and listening to what he had to say. I went and watched a bunch of his performances. He was always sort of above the fray, even though he was all the way in it. He was special forces in World War II and he was a man's man. He was the real deal, so when you get to be around people like that, you're just in awe of their talent. You don't ever want people to question what you're trying to accomplish with it. That's where the reviews come in (laughs). When you're fully committed to it, some people are going to like it and some people aren't, but not all people are going to know the circumstances of what you put into it, so you just try to do your best and hope for the best. It's subjective, really.

RA: Do you still get recognized from it?

RS: (laughs) Yes, I do. More from Bob Vance from *The Office*, obviously. *The Office* is like a cult religion. There's really nothing like *Office* fans. In fact, they had a convention in Scranton for the show. I went there. They had a magazine there for all of the actors there and they had a write up about me that said "How does a cult horror villain make it to a network sitcom?" That doesn't happen very often. It really shows my range.

RA: Yeah, that's really one of a kind

RS: Yeah, it's like Bruce Campbell. He's got a light touch as well. He's had a very good run in horror films, as well. I remember running into Robert Englund a few times here in LA and chatting with him. Recently, there was talk of some people wanting to remake *Psycho Cop*. I had been ambivalent about it, but suddenly I got really possessive of it. I did not want anybody else playing that part. The guy who wanted to do it was named Jay Baruchel.

RA: Oh yeah, the guy from *Tropic Thunder* and *This is the End*, right?

RS: Yeah, the Seth Rogen crowd. He's apparently a big fan of the *Psycho Cop* series. I really did not want him doing it and I was thinking about that with Robert Englund and when they replaced him with Jackie Earl Hailey. They're about the same age, so I don't know why they would do that. Why wouldn't they bring Robert Englund back? It just didn't make any sense to me.

RA: Exactly. And that's the thing. I really liked Jackie on *The Watchmen*, but as Freddy ... eh, not so much.

RS: Well, he's not going to improve on it. It's very hard to improve on something like that. It's still fresh and a huge, popular series. So, then I got with Rifkin and I said that we should make a third one. So, we're about two thirds of the way through writing the first draft of the script. We're calling it *Hip Hop Psycho Cop*. We're bringing it right up to date in 2016. It's still the same format, but I plan on making it a lot scarier, as opposed to campy. I mean, there will still be a one-liner in every scene, but we really want to go for more of a fright.

RA: So, am I right to assume that this will be *Psycho Cop* in the hood, basically?

RS: Bingo! (laughs) We obviously have to tread lightly though, what with Black Lives Matter now. I mean, he can't just kill black kids. I'm sure people would just lose their minds over that. He just kills everybody. He's *Psycho Cop*, he doesn't care! *Psycho Cop Two* was denounced by the fraternal order of police when it was released.

RA: Really?

RS: (laughs) Oh yeah. They said that I was misrepresenting policemen. I mean, it was a horror comedy. We weren't trying to make him a nice guy. It's funny that anyone would take the time to respond to it.

RA: (laughs) Yeah, that's crazy! I really do love the part at the start of the movie where he walks up to the characters in the cafe and he says something like "You boys aren't getting into any trouble, are you?" or something like that.

RS: (laughs- in voice) "You boys stay out of trouble now, you hear?"

RA: Yeah, that one!

RS: Well, that was a great moment for me because it was the only time in my career that I've ever been up on an apple box. I've never had to. I'm six foot four, so they never bring me up, they always try to bring me down (laughs). We tried to get that height perspective and had a real low angle, so we were trying to make him look like he was ten feet tall. Of course, the funny line for me with that is after I walk out and Rob Schweitzer says "Wow, if that's not an example of inbreeding, I don't know what is!" (laughs)

RA: How do you view that now, being a kind of slasher icon, looking back on it?

RS: Well, that's what persistence and survival does. I just kept at it. It's cool to me. I haven't been on any of the horror convention circuits, but I may start doing that. We'll see. I've had people that have been wanting me to do that. I've just always felt like I wanted to keep doing new things. I really would be interested in it now, though.

RA: Yeah, you really should give it a shot. I'd try Texas Frightmare. It's one of the biggest ones in the country.

RS: Do you think Joe Vickers would do well down there?

RA: Oh yeah, definitely.

RS: Well, I still get requests in the mail for Joe Vickers stuff. I know a lot of people that do those shows, so I know that there's a following for it.

RA: If you had anything that you could say to the fans out there, what would you say?

RS: Thank you, thank you very much. Thanks for watching and I'm glad that you appreciate my work. It's not an easy game and to really get any kind of recognition for it is great. I think it's a gift. Lots of people tried, lots of people died (laughs). I feel lucky to be a part of it. I don't take anything for granted. It can all be taken away any time. I'm always very grateful.

RON KOLOGIE
(ICED, CARDS OF DEATH)

RA: First off, I just want to thank you for joining me.

RK: Thanks for having me! *Iced* is actually getting more attention these days. It even had a screening not too long ago here in LA. They invited me to come to the thing and it was quite entertaining. We did a nice Q and A afterward and all the hipsters really like it, it seemed. It was at a place on Melrose. It's called Nerd Meltdown and was at Meltdown Comics. They have what is called "Horrible Movie Nights" and they had *Iced* one night. It turned out really good and was an entertaining evening for everyone.

RA: Cool! I'll have to check that place out sometime.

RK: I'm not really into horror films so much but these are fun to go to. There was another one I did about a year and a half ago for *Cards of Death*. They had a re-release screening for it at a place called The Silent Movie Theater on Fairfax. Again, it was a sellout crowd.

RA: Cool. Tell me a bit about *Cards of Death*

RK: It's an interesting one. It's only available on VHS, I believe. It's through a company that has this little niche thing going for it, primarily for collectors.

RA: How did you first get into the acting business?

RK: Well, I grew up in Buffalo, NY. I was studying at the Studio Arena Theater there and I did my first Equity play at fourteen. I played Balthazar in *Romeo and Juliet*. Then, after High School, I got into Carnegie Mellon. I was there with Holly Hunter and Linda Kozlowski, Michael Reid, Shelly Burke. Those are just a few of the notables in my class. Another one you may be familiar with is Tom Savini.

RA: Yeah, definitely! I've ran into him at a few conventions.

RK: Yeah, Tom Savini was in our class. We were all 18 and 19 years old and he was thirty something. He got in on the G.I. Bill. I really don't know why. I guess he kind of wanted to get a college education, but he had already done several things with George Romero, so it was interesting. For Halloween one year, he even did my makeup for me. It was a couple great years there. Then, I came out to Los Angeles and got on *General Hospital* as a regular. I was always looking for stuff to do and I got an audition for a movie that was called Blizzard of Blood. Of course, Blizzard of Blood was the original title for what would become *Iced*. I don't know why they ever changed it. I thought it was a great title.

RA: I wonder the same thing. That's really an amazing title.

RK: Yeah, much better than *Iced*. (laughs) I guess they must have thought it was too gory sounding. I don't know. They cast it in Los Angeles and then they shot it in Salt Lake City.

RA: Was it at one of the big ski areas outside of Salt Lake?

RK: Yes, it was near Solitude. All of the ski areas are around there, like Snowbird and Brighton. We were staying down in a city called Sandy just outside of Salt Lake City. We would take a van up to the cabin that they rented for the filming. Of course, *Iced* is a movie that's supposed to have a lot of snow, but it was one of those years that was very sparse with snow. So, we kind of had to find it. (laughs)

RA: They didn't have a snow maker for the movie?

RK: No, they didn't have it in the budget. On some of these low budget movies, there were always problems. We were kind of shocked, as the actors, that they would show up with a 16mm camera as opposed to a 35mm. *Cards of Death* was shot on video, as was the other one I did, *Dark Romances*. Those were some of the first shot on video features that were being put out at the time.

RA: One of the people that I wanted to ask you about from Iced is of course Lisa Loring, who played the original Wednesday Addams. What was it like working with her?

RK: Ah, Lisa! We were born on the same day in 1958 I found out. I didn't really get who she was as a kid. I mean, it was cool when we found out, but she was very sweet, but she had been through the business and may have had a little jaded perspective of it. She could be a little rough, but on the movie she was very professional and she really wanted to do a good job on it.

RA: I did some research and found out that she was going through some problems in that period. Did you see any of that?

RK: I think prior to that she was having a lot of problems. I think this was kind of a way in which she was trying to get away from it. But, she was a real team player when it came to doing the film. We heard some stories from her, but nothing was ever seen on the set.

RA: One of the things that always stood out to me about *Iced* is that it does have some cool death scenes and some good effects to it, like the snow plow running a character over and the ski pole through the head.

RK: Yeah, or like when Elizabeth Gorsey gets the icicle through her eye.

RA: Exactly, and then there was your death, of course, with the bear trap.

RK: Yeah, that was a great one. I step into one and then I fall into another one (laughing).

RA: How long were you up there for?

RK: We were there for two weeks for the shoot, so it was like a twelve-day shoot.

RA: Were they long days?

RK: I don't really remember that being the case.

RA: Okay, so was there a lot of down time?

RK: No, not really because if you look at the movie, everyone seemed to be in it quite a few times except for after the deaths. So, there wasn't a lot of time. We all would go up every day together. They didn't leave anyone behind when they would go up there because of the distance to the shoot.

RA: How was director Jeff Kwitney to work for?

RK: He was under a tight schedule, but he had a lot of cooperation from the actors. We knew that it was a low budget film and we did the best we could to move things along. He was under a lot of pressure from the producers to make his days, so consequently we really didn't have more than two or three takes per shot.

RA: Were you given much leeway to incorporate your own ideas into the character or was it more by the book?

RK: It was pretty scripted. It wasn't something in which we really improvised. I guess there was this one scene in which me and Doug are skiing through the trees and then I fall into the snow. Those type of things we improvised a bit. It was supposed to be just skiing through the trees, then the lines. During that scene, I fell and then he fell next to me and we had a laugh and then we said what our lines were.

RA: That's actually one of my favorite scenes, because it gave you more of a feel for the characters.

RK: Yes, it was an important scene that showed Carl not to be so much of a cocaine jerk.

RA: Did you have much of a skiing background before Iced?

RK: Oh yeah, growing up in Buffalo. I was skiing since I was twelve.

RA: By the way, you mentioned Carl being a "cocaine jerk". I wanted to talk about the character. He was really the one that stood out the most in the movie and there was actually a lot of depth to the character. I wanted to ask what it was like playing that part and getting in that mindset. Did you do any observations of people like that to prepare?

RK: Thank you for saying that. I'm glad you liked the performance. As far as observance goes, it was the eighties, so all I had to do was observe some of my friends (laughs). Then, of course every other movie then had some type of cocaine addict in it, it seems. In this movie, Tim Buksell was the production designer on it. Tim still directs commercials in San Francisco. He gave me all of the props and the "paraphernalia" for the shots. Of course, it wasn't real cocaine. I'm not sure what it was. I think it was baking powder that they used. I can't be sure of that, though. Even though it looks like I'm snorting it in there, I never got anything into my nose except around it.

RA: Again, Carl had a lot of depth, beyond the cocaine stuff, like with waving the gun around and the cutting. There was a lot going on with him.

RK: Oh yeah, that's a great scene too. I actually put that scene on my acting reel. They were trying to make it that Carl could possibly be the killer, to try and throw people off who it might be. But, I always thought that he was just a real desperate soul trying to get attention from the girls. Being a pharmaceutical representative, that was how he was trying to make his bid for fame with them. Then, unfortunately he became an addict of it and became controlled by it.

RA: Were there any challenges playing a character with that type of emotional baggage?

RK: In that scene, from the bathroom and then going up the stairs, cutting my finger and looking at the blood and all that. That was a really tough scene and it was real emotional. We relied on all of our acting training to do it. Then, that part with the gun. (recites line) "Life's fragile, Doctor."

RA: What would you say was your favorite memory working on it?

RK: Just doing the film was fun and acting on it. Being Carl was such a blast. I rented a car when I was there, so I would take everybody out to the discos in downtown Salt Lake City on nights that we knew we weren't going to shoot until late the next day and we would just party and dance and had a blast. It was a very close group of people, the actors. It was at a time in Utah where if you went to a bar, you had to join as a member to drink. I think one day I drove everybody up to Snowbird and we had drinks up there. It was fun. Elizabeth Gorsey was a riot, who played Diane. We just had a blast.

RA: How do you view *Iced* now, looking at it now?

RK: Well, back then we had problems with the production because they didn't pay us for the last week. The actors actually had to sue them through SAG. We finally got the money, but it was a long, hard process. During that period, one of the producers was fighting with someone over something in Brentwood in a parking garage and got shot with a bow and arrow. It was all over the rights to the movie and how it was going to get distributed. (My reaction ..." Holy shit!"). There was a lot of drama after the fact. I don't think it had much of a release. I don't think I remember even seeing it the first time around.

RA: What are you up to now? I see that you're still acting.

RK: Now, I own a construction company which I've had since 1993. My main jobs in acting have been in commercials lately. When I was in my forties, I did around 35 national commercials. Bank of America, Bayer, Honda, Lexus Toyota, Sears, Hardy's. If you go to my website you can see some, at Ronkologie.com. Then, I took about eight years off. I got back into it a few years ago. What started it back up was I got a call from Will McMillan, who was the director of *Cards of Death*. He said you won't believe it, but somebody found a copy of it in a video store in Tokyo and they bought the rights to it and they want to show it at The Silent Movie

Theater in LA. He said they want to get the cast and crew together. He was able to contact most everyone and they showed up. It was a blast to see that. I actually brought my two daughters to see that. One of the emcees said to them, "Did you know your dad was so hot" and one of my daughters said, "Yes, he tells us all the time". (laughs)

RA: How did they enjoy it?

RK: They loved it. They were amazed by the response of all the young people who weren't even born yet when these movies were released. So that kicked it all off, then I got a new agent and started submitting myself again. I did a play called Villa Thrilla, and started submitting to Independent projects and in the past year I've done like seven of them. It kick started my career again. I just signed with one of the biggest commercial agents in Los Angeles recently and I'll be getting that started again. It's interesting to get back into the swing of things again.

RA: Do you have anything you would like to say to the fans out there?

RK: I would say look at it as a bit of film history taking place in a time when films were shot that way. I would say enjoy it as a history lesson.

RUSSELL TODD
(Friday the 13th Part 2, Chopping Mall)

Friday the 13th Part 2

RA: How did you get involved in the film? Take us through your audition and what you think won you the role.

RT: I actually saw a poster in Backstage (a publication) in New York for auditions. I'm not sure if it's still around. I answered that and I got on the audition. I think I just had one callback and they booked it. Then, I found out what it was and I thought it was kind of cool, because I enjoyed the first one. So, when I got it, I was really thrilled. You know this was the first big movie that I got. It was with a major studio, so I was excited about that. I was living in New York at the time working as a model and an actor. I had really just started the acting thing.

RA: Describe the character of Scott for the readers. What was your take on him and what went into bringing him to life?

RT: Well, he was a guy that was kind of up to no good. He was a nice guy though, a very nice guy, but I think he liked to be a little mischievous, as he was when he found Teri by the water. I think he was playful and that's what I loved about him. Personally, I'm playful as well, so when I read that in the script, I thought there was a lot of similarity between myself and him. He wasn't really that deeply layered though (laughs). There weren't that many facets of him that made him that complex. He was just a nice guy who was playful and mischievous and I could relate to that. (sharing my own counselor stories) I was never a counselor, but I was a camper for years ever since I was six years old, so I knew a lot about summer camps like that.

RA: Your scenes with Kirsten Baker were great and very memorable. What are your memories of working with her?

RT: We had a lot of fun. I think we gelled very quickly. She was also playful and fun. We would go out socially to a bar in town and some other places. We would also go out together and pretty much hang out together. But, the whole cast got along really well. I think that we were all pretty young. The camaraderie was great because we were all together making this movie and we all wanted it to be fun and terrific. It was like being on the road. It was fun being out of town and in a place you don't know.

RA: (Reading his script) "A hand shoots out and clutches Scott by the hair. The blade slices through his throat..." End of Scott! (Russell asks what page it was on) That was page 83. (Russell says he is surprised he made it that far as he was one of the first killed) How did they go about making your death scene and the part where you're hanging upside down?

RT: First they had to do a prosthetic piece, a foam latex piece on my neck, which was done by one of my dear friends who I grew up with. He created that and it was pre-slit with the blood tube, so when they would start pumping the blood, it would come out. Once they were ready for that scene, they put me upside down with that little appliance in place. It took a number of hours upside down, so people kept holding me up so I wouldn't get dizzy or a blood rush. They said it would take a long time. We only did one actual take of the slice and the blood going, because they didn't have a second appliance. I would say it was a couple hours at least upside down. I was upside down and they had someone above me pumping the blood. As soon as it got into the eyes, they would just yell cut, because it would just roll down. Once it was slit and the blood flows, they cut pretty soon. It was getting in my nose and everywhere.

RA: Did you film anything else after the death scene? I know they don't always shoot in sequence.

RT: That was funny, because it was my last scene. I'm sure you've read what I've said it before in other interviews, that I called my parents up and told them that it's my last day and they're doing my death scene. Then my mom says, "Why did they wait till your last day? Are they going to kill you?" (laughs) She didn't know what all of this was. She just knew I was making some crappy movie off in the woods and she's like "who are these people? Is this a snuff movie?" I said, "Mom, it's Paramount Pictures. I think I'm okay!" The rest of the film wasn't filmed chronological, but funnily enough, that was my last scene.

RA: Were you able to see any of the other kill scenes being filmed? If so, what are your memories of them?

RT: Actually, no, because of the space requirement like for the one with Bill. It was in one of the bedrooms and that was very small. Pretty much, when you were done filming, you were off doing your own thing, either at the campgrounds where we were filming or get a ride into town. What's funny is the campground itself was at this one end of the lake and you had to walk down this long road with these tall bushes on both sides to get to the bunks where we lived during filming. When you would walk down there, you would hear people every night in the bushes messing with you, going "Kill, kill, kill, kill," trying to freak you out and even though you knew Jason wasn't real, it was still scary every time walking back.

RA: A quick word association here. What was your experience like working with:

RA: Steve Miner?

RT: Steve was a cool guy. He cared a lot about his actors. He's very easygoing. I don't remember any difficulty at all with him. I knew that he was on a schedule and these things are usually shot very quickly, especially on a lower budget, but he was nice to everybody and a funny guy.

RA: Bill Randolph?

RT: Bill was very funny. I remember he was also a prankster and a really nice guy.

RA: Stu Charno?

RT: Also funny. Everything was funny with Stu, I think even today. I saw him at one of the signings a while back and we sat next to each other. We had a lot of fun.

RA: Marta Kober

RT: Marta I didn't really know that well. She was very nice, I remember that, but really didn't know much more about her.

RA: Tom McBride?

RT: Tom was very nice, unfortunately not with us anymore. He was a very sweet guy and very kind.

RA: Amy Steel?

RT: Amy I liked a lot. At the conventions I've attended, it was always great to see her. Just a really sweet lady, fun and down to earth. Really dedicated. She always really worked hard to do a great job.

RA: John Furey?

RT: I also like John very much. Good actor, very dedicated, fun and we hit it off very well.

Chopping Mall

RA: What made you get on board with this project and how did you get involved? You were already known for *Friday the 13th*. Did they pick you because of it?

RT: I don't remember how I connected with Jim Wynorski on that, but I'm really glad I did. We're still friends today, which is great. He's a great guy. I really don't know. It must have been my agent just submitting me for that one. It was after I did *Where the Boys Are*, and I think he liked me from that and that's how I got that role. They actually just screened that one at The Egyptian Theater in Hollywood a few months ago. A lot of the cast showed up and the entire house was packed.

RA: What was your experience working with director Jim Wynorski? I also interviewed him previously.

RT: Jim was great. He has a great sense of humor and knows so much. He's done so many films. I just think he loves what he does and I think it shows.

RA: The Mall Itself. What are your memories of filming on location at the mall?

RT: That's the Sherman Oaks Galleria. It was just a mall at one point. Now it's a gym, movie theaters, offices and no longer your typical mall. But, I remember we would usually come in around 8 or 9 at night, when everything would shut down and we would work all night until six in the morning and then get out of there. I was very thrilled because we were a bunch of people running through a mall with uzis and with robots trying to kill us. It was one of my favorite movies. I loved how in one scene, they put in a fake glass door for the sporting goods store and I was able to throw a crowbar through it and they start playing that western music. It was like a fantasy. I felt like a little kid doing that kind of a scene. We had a lot of fun. I shot there many years prior, but to be able to destroy it was great.

RA: What was your experience with the robots like? I really want one honestly!

RT: I do too! (laughs) It was really cool. I mean, obviously, they didn't speak at that point, but they were cool looking and the whole idea was fun. I don't know where they are now.

RA: Which title do you prefer, *Chopping Mall* or *Killbots?* I'm just curious. I myself prefer *Killbots*

RT: I do too. In fact, I think I have a poster somewhere that says *Killbots*. People would send these from all over the world. Yeah, *Killbots* was a great name, but I also love *Chopping Mall* and the tagline "Where shopping will cost you an arm and a leg". It was just perfect.

RA: Could tell me what you are doing now and about your Steadicam school. How did you get involved in that side of the business?

RT: I was doing a soap opera in New York from 1990 to 1992, *Another World*. I was working like 50 hours a week and as an actor, it's an amazing job. I mean, how many people can say they were on a soap opera. At the time, not many. It was a great gig, but it was exhausting and when I was done with it I kind of said I'm done with acting. I loved acting, but found it boring being the same person for three years. So, I went back to LA afterward and still did some commercials, because it was fantastic money and you get to do some fun things. I went on a commercial audition and my good friend Kirk was working there behind the camera and leaving there and he told me he was going to work at an agency that reps some of the biggest photographers in the business, as well as production designers, costumers, editors, etc. He said they were looking for an assistant in the TV department. I went and spoke with them and the woman who owned the agency was really dynamic and she liked me and wanted me to work there and I said I'd give it a shot. Literally the first few weeks I was there, a guy walks in, Bruce Greene, and he asked if we represent Steadicam operators and I didn't know what it was about, so I researched it and I started the first Steadicam operation of any major agency. It grew to about ten people I had and became a big money maker for the agency. Then they made me the head of the TV department as well there, so I was doing both. Then, after a few years I said why am I working for them, I should be working for myself, so I took the division and opened up my own company about fifteen years ago. It's going great. We do all of the major movies like *Transformers, The Conjuring*, many of the big TV shows. My guys work all over the country. We have about fifty clients. I still get a kick out of putting them on these big shows. I love going to the movies and seeing the trailers and most of them are my clients. It's nice.

RA: Is there anything you would like to personally say to the fans out there?

RT: I'm really appreciative of them following not just my film, but all of them and being so devoted to the franchise. For me, when I go out, people don't really recognize me from that anymore, but they still recognize me from other projects like *Another World*. But the horror fans are some of the most devoted fans of any. I just hope that they continue to love the genre and that the genre continues to put out great things that they can enjoy.

SHELLEY BRUCE
(THE BURNING)

RA: How did you first get involved in the acting business?

SB: My dancing school teacher, the one who ran the dancing school got me started in it. Their kids were into it. As a matter of fact, their daughter is Robbi Morgan from *Friday the 13th.* Her mom and dad had a dancing school that was very well known, that I went to when I was little. When I was six, they told me I should be in acting and that's how it happened.

RA: Cool. I heard that you did a lot of Broadway too back in the day.

SB: Yep, I was in Annie on Broadway.

RA: Were you the lead in that?

SB: When the show first opened, I was one of the orphans. I was the orphan Kate and then when Andrea McCardell left, I took over the lead role from her.

RA: Right on! How did your role as Tiger in *The Burning* come about?

SC: It was just another audition. It was one of the ones that came up after I was done with

Annie. It was pretty standard, just reading a script, nothing special.

RA: I've always wondered this. You looked very young in the movie, younger than the rest of the cast. How old were you at the time?

SB: I was fourteen at the time.

RA: That brings up another thing. I always wondered about the ratio at the camp. I knew that you, Fisher Stevens, Ned Eisenberg and several others were campers, but some seemed older, like Jason Alexander. Who all were campers and who wasn't?

SB: Well, we were all campers except for Leah Ayres and Brian Matthews, they were supposed to be the counselors and we were the campers. Todd and Michelle (their characters) were the ones in charge of us.

RA: Speaking of him, a lot of people forget that he was even in *The Burning*. What was Jason Alexander like to work with on set?

SB: Oh, he was great. All of us had such a great time. Holly Hunter is also in it and that's when Holly was just new to the business and it was one of her first roles, as far as I remember. It was great. We all got along really well. We were pretty much never separated on set or off. Everybody hung out together, had a good time and it was just a great cast to work with, all around.

RA: Where did they film *The Burning*?

SB: We filmed at a campsite up in North Tonawanda, outside of Buffalo. We stayed in a little hotel outside of there in between shooting times.

RA: Growing up in New York, I know that the whole Cropsy legend is a big deal for young campers as an urban legend. Were you familiar with it before?

SB: No, I wasn't. I'm from New Jersey and even though we had camp there, I had never been to summer camp because I was in acting, so it was really fun and new to me, the whole experience. To be that far out in the middle of nowhere was really fun and just a neat experience.

RA: Did you get to do many fun things in between shooting in the area?

SB: We didn't really have a whole lot of downtime because we had to get the shots done in the daylight hours, so really our downtime was spent back at the hotel. They had this little bar and restaurant that we all would go to. We would pretty much go to the hotel, take showers, hang out together, get food and then we would have to be up the next morning to start shooting again.

RA: Tom Savini did the effects for the movie. How was your experience with him?

SB: Tom was great. When we first got there, we started in Buffalo doing pre-production stuff and he had a whole hotel suite with his whole workshop all set up in there. We would play basketball with Betsy Palmer's head from *Friday The 13th*, because he always traveled with it, so that was really cool!

RA: No way!

SB: Oh yeah, we had a lot of fun with him. He's great to work with.

RA: That's amazing. Did you get a chance to see some of his effects happen for the film?

SB: Oh yeah. You could pretty much be involved and watch anything. I was always into stuff like that. When I was younger, when I was eight, I did an off-Broadway show in the village in New York and there was blood used in the show. I used to help mix the blood. I just thought it was so cool. I was always into the kind of stuff.

RA: What was your experience like with Lou David (as Cropsy) when he was in full make-up?

SB: We never really saw him. I didn't even know that I came close to being killed until post production when I saw it. All of that stuff was done afterwards. I never knew that he was behind me and the shears were up. I never saw any of that because it was all done later. I didn't know I was that close to dying and nobody told me! I don't think we even met him. He wasn't really doing scenes with many of us. A lot of his were in the woods or in shadows, so we never interacted with him. The one thing I do remember being impressed with is when we were in Buffalo, Tom had just books and books of burn victims and there was so much research he did to get that look right for what a burn victim and the skin would look like.

RA: I'm actually glad that Tiger didn't get killed. She's one of the more likable ones in the movie. I would have been sad.

SB: Well, thank you, that's good to know! (laughs) We just had a lot of fun all around, like on the lake scene out on the dock and the food fight scene. I can only imagine if someone had the outtakes from that because it was just insane. We were so out of control. It was a blast. We had fun playing baseball in that scene. That, and the raft scene. None of that part with the sinking of the canoe was planned. We were just laughing so much and splashing so much that we ended up sinking the canoe and they put it in the movie. It was great. It was a lot of fun. You couldn't have picked a better group of people for it because we all genuinely liked each other.

RA: How would you compare *The Burning* to other camp slashers like *Friday the 13th*?

SB: I don't know. It's its own entity, but I think we really pushed the envelope on it. Tom did such a great job and our rating was high because of the gory effects, not because of anything else. I didn't realize what a cult fan following it has until they were re-releasing it on DVD. It was so cool to realize that.

RA: It was even banned in the UK for a while as one of the "Video Nasties"

SB: I know, I had heard that. It was really crazy. If I remember correctly, we had to actually cut down the raft scene because they wanted to give us an X rating rather than an R rating because it was so gory and graphic. That whole scene was just crazy, with Fisher getting his fingers cut off and everything. Again, it was one of those scenes that was kind of cut together, where not everybody is all there together in that one spot. It really looks seamless once it's edited together. It's crazy when you see the craft of editing at work.

RA: What have you been doing since *The Burning*?

SB: After that I did some smaller stuff for a few years. Then, when I was sixteen, I had Leukemia, so I had to take a step back to deal with that. Then, I came back later and did some things like an off-Broadway cabaret show, *The Wizard of Oz* and then I worked with a couple of different bands for a while. The one I was with the longest was called One Track Mind. I was the singer in the band.

RA: What are you up to now?

SB: Right now, I have a couple of book keeping jobs and I have a crochet business that I started. I give ten percent of all of my proceeds back to the Pediatric Cancer Research. My Grandmother taught me how to croquet when I was little and it's something that I love doing. I make a lot of handmade stuff. People can go to my website (amethystsoteria.com) and check things out. I also do custom work.

RA: Is there anything special you would like to say to the fans out there?

SB: Thank you for supporting this movie all these years. It's gone from one generation to the next, so it's not one of those movies that's been watched and forgotten. It's got a great fan base and I am so thrilled for that. I find new fans all the time. I have a convention coming up in Tampa and did my first convention a few years ago. I was floored by how many fans there were. So, just a huge shout out to all the fans of horror and the fans of *The Burning* who have kept it going all these years.

SUMMER BROWN
(THE PREY)

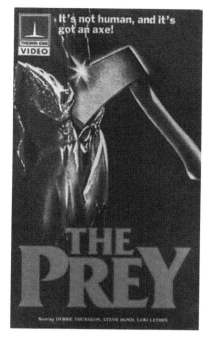

RA: How did you first get involved in the film business?

SB: Eddie (Brown- her husband and partner on *The Prey*) was wringing out a serious novel ("Handsome Harry Klein And The Woman's Liberation Front") and I was a waitress at the Trident in Sausalito. That's where we met Alex DeRenzy, the future king of porn in America, who had just returned from abroad with hundreds of hours of footage of a sex fair in Denmark. Eddie got hired to watch it all and organize it into a movie, a job way more fun than writing at home alone. The more we hung out at Alex's and watched the steps to making a film, we thought it didn't look all that hard, and that we could do that. Eddie had a fertile imagination and I was an excellent organizer. At that point, all we needed was a script and some cash. Eddie and I wrote *China Girl* (the adult film, not the David Bowie song) together, found investors and we were in the movie business. *China Girl* was a huge nationwide success (#7 one week on Variety's Top Fifty chart) and we had no trouble financing future films.

RA: I know that before the film, you were predominately known for making adult films. What made you want to make a slasher film?

SB: In 1978, *Halloween* had just struck it big. We thought we could do that, too. Actually, we thought sex films were more fun than horror, which we found to be truly pornographic, but we wrote a script, were given the money by a distributor and given the chance to explore another genre.

RA: Where did the idea for *The Prey* come from?

SB: We were hikers and spent lots of time in Yosemite, Mineral Springs, Yellowstone, Maroon Bells, and the Grand Tetons. Sometimes, when you're out there, just the two of you in your sleeping bags, and you hear a rustle, your imagination goes crazy. It was, in fact, thankfully, always just a bear or squirrel, or raccoon, but if you let your imagination run…. So when we got the chance to make a scary film, we thought about what had scared us and what could have been out there.

RA: I've always loved the location. Where was it filmed, how was the location picked and what are your memories of filming amongst such beautiful scenery in Utah?

SB: The film was shot in the Southern California mountains. I don't know why it says Utah on Wikipedia. We scouted Big Bear first, and couldn't find a location without a telephone pole or TV antenna in the shot, and the lake, which was in the first draft, was full of noisy speedboats. Remember, these kids were supposed to be lost in the wilderness. So, we moved on to a beautiful mountain village where we shot the film and two years later bought a tiny cabin where we have lived ever since. I'm not sharing the name at this time- we like it quiet —let's just say it is a stop off for the Pacific Crest Trail, though. It's a hikers and rock climber's paradise.

RA: Jackie Coogan is well known for his role as the original Uncle Fester. How did you get him on board for the film? What are your memories of working with him?

SB: We knew Jackie Coogan through a mutual friend. His scenes always brought the film to a different level. Nobody else could ever chew a cucumber and cream cheese sandwich with such conviction. I remember when Eddie was telling him how he wanted the scene played, Jackie rolled his eyes said, "Ya know, I got ties older than you." He ad-libbed a lot and most of his throw-aways made the final cut.

RA: Another famous *Addams Family* alum plays the monster in the film, Carel Struycken. What was it like working with him and how did you get him on board?

SB: Carel Struycken was a pussycat. Very quiet, very old world charming, very tall and very handsome. We did not capitalize on that, although you can see his beautiful eyes in the last shot. He was patient with us and generous with his time when it came to making his effects. It involved lots of rubber and glue. This was an early film in his career. He has gone on, and made his mark on the industry.

RA: There are some amazing effects in the film. Can you tell me about making them happen and working with legendary John Carl Buechler?

SB: John Carl Buechler was then the apprentice to Rick Baker and was a great score for us. We knew nothing about how these things were done, and we all got a first-rate education on this film. He could do no wrong. I think perhaps several shots did not dwell on the gore as much as they could have, but that is my perspective today, 35 years after the film was made. Today the camera slowly goes bruise by bruise. Our film seems a bit reticent in that way.

RA: I know that the film was not released for several years after filming. Could you go into detail on what happened?

SB: I didn't know the film was not released immediately after completion. We thought it was sold to New World Pictures and that it was released, although I have no proof of that either. Then, I heard it was sold to Thorn EMI.

RA: Several minutes of the film were cut from the final version. Do you know what happened there?

SB: Yesterday I decided to screen a very rough DVD copy of the picture sent to me by a colleague from the UK. (I have no idea where he got this DVD which appears to be printed off a VHS -or who made the VHS he used.) The film business is pretty slippery. Anyway, I had not seen this film for 35 years and wanted to refresh my memory for this interview.
Yes, it appears some footage was removed. I remember a very charming scene with the Forest Ranger. No, I didn't know it had been removed or what else was cut. Much more horrifying was the inserted 25 minutes of supposed flashback, featuring near-porno footage of a gypsy camp and its racist neighbors to explain the fire at the opening scene and the creation of the monster in the woods. It looks for all the world to be someone else's movie that was accidentally cut into ours. The color timing is completely off and at 25 minutes … wow, that's not a flashback … it's another movie.

RA: There's an abundance of stock nature footage in the film. Could you tell me why that is?

SB: Returning to talk about the film that Eddie and I made before others touched it, we thought the abundance of stock nature footage was quite wonderful as it showed the glory of nature in the wilderness, and yet how everything is prey: eat or be eaten.

RA: Why did you not continue making slasher films after *The Prey*?

SB: We did not continue making slasher films as we never really liked the killing part.

RA: This is one of the rare films that is still not yet on Blu-Ray or DVD. Are there any plans for a re-release in the near future?

SB: Why is it not yet on DVD? I don't know. Perhaps it was too short, not gory enough, and not enough nudity. That must be the reason for the twenty-five minutes of unmatched film inserted by the US distributor. He died some years ago, so we will never know.

371

RA: How do you look back at the film and your time on it these days?

SB: It was a wonderful, magical time. We were young, ambitious, and full of hope. We housed cast and crew in all the motels within a two-mile radius during the week, and they all went back to LA for the weekends to see family and do laundry. We hired the local mountain climbers to be sherpas and haul the equipment up to the peak. We shot it in Panavision and had one dedicated crew member who drove five hours back and forth to LA every day to deliver film to lab. All meals were catered by the very hippie restaurants in town, so all the bread was home-made. We shot the film in three weeks. It was October, and it was blazing hot during the day, but down-vests at night. The budget was miniscule, the sunsets were glorious. Hey, we were all together in the wilderness making a movie. How could that not be great?

RA: If you could say anything to the fans of the film, what would you say?

SB: To our fans I say thanks for staying through to the end. And wasn't the ending a surprise? 35 years later, I still get a shiver on that one. There's definitely a sequel there....

TED VERNON
(SCARECROWS)

TV: Thanks for talking to me about *Scarecrows*. I wanted to let you know that I just did a movie called *Zombie Infection* and it was filmed over in Russia and it was all because of *Scarecrows*. The director is a big fan and he called me up and invited me to come over to Russia. I told everybody! I hate being a good guy. I killed everybody in it. (laughs)

RA: That's awesome! Good for you, man. The first question I wanted to touch on was, could you tell me about your Pro Boxing career in the eighties?

TV: (laughs) Oh boy. It's funny you should mention that. I had a forgettable career. I was a good puncher, but I wasn't a good boxer. I knocked a lot of guys out and had fun with it. I always wanted to fight and I met a lawyer buddy of mine, unfortunately due to a traffic situation, and he used to fight. I asked him where he went to and I went there. Two weeks later I had my first fight. My first fight was actually against a guy named Rocky and I knocked him out and broke his jaw. Then, I just fell into it. You see, you can teach a guy how to box, but you can't teach a guy how to punch. I could always punch, but I'm not a good boxer, I'm not a good dancer. I had lots of fun with it though and I did it and I'm proud that I did it. It was very interesting and it was a great learning experience, but I did get my hands busted up pretty good. I did well though and I had a lot of fun with it.

RA: How did you make the transition into acting?

TV: You know, I've always liked it. I had a band and I played rock and roll music. You know, that's acting too. I also did a lot of plays and a lot of things. I've always like acting. Actually, with *Scarecrows,* William Westley approached me and he liked me and he thought I could be the character that I played in it. He came to me and talked to me about it and I was really interested in doing it. I liked my character. He was a tough guy with a big heart. There was a lot of heart to him. It wasn't really such a stretch for me because that's who I am.

RA: Cool, so tell me, how did the involvement in *Scarecrows* happen? You said earlier there was a good story behind it.

TV: That's interesting. William Westley was a car dealer/auto trader. We got to talking. He was also a frustrated film maker, and he said he was trying to make this movie and said I would be perfect for the film. I asked him what it was about and he told me, and I told him it sounds interesting and that I'm interested. We talked and talked about it, and he said he's ready to go. He said he had the script, but he didn't have the money. So, I asked him how much it was going to cost and he told me, and I said "Okay, you've got it". Then I said, "Okay, now you've got the money, let's go make a movie", and that's how it happened. Then, about halfway into the movie, he ran out of money. I supported this guy. I had his rent, his apartment, I had everything and I really took care of the guy. I wanted to be treating this thing the right way. When he ran out of the money, it became a situation where he tried to lean on me a little bit and said, "Well, if you want to make this movie, then we need this". I don't like to be pushed around. At that point, he had this girl working with him, that he wound up marrying I believe, and she and her family had money. I said, "Well, fuck it, I'm done. I'm not going to give you any more." Then, he went and got her father to give him the rest of the money. I'm the only guy that ended up getting paid by the way, as far as investment and getting money back. It's one of those things, you just don't screw with people. I'm in the classic car business and have been doing it a long time. I know how to do business. I also know the film business. I helped make *Village of the Damned* with Christopher Reeve too. That one was mine. It was his last movie before he got hurt, but if you look up the movie, you'll see I'm the executive producer. It was fun, but I wasn't there for it. John Carpenter asked me if I wanted to come out, but I said no. I didn't need to rub elbows with all the stars. It wasn't bad, but it wasn't as good as the original. The original was very good. I'm proud of it, though. I actually made money on that one too, but I digress.

RA: So, once that *Scarecrows* got into production, tell me a bit about where it was filmed and your experience on the set. It's a very unique movie and has an incredibly dark feel to it and is still a good scary movie to this day.

TV: People still love the movie. There's no question about it. We filmed it at an abandoned house in Dayton, Florida. It was an old farm house, a real mess of a place, but it was perfect. You gotta give Westley credit, he picked the right place. It was really an eerie place. I was working six days a week at the time, 9-5 on my regular job and then would shoot at night, so it was tough on me. We only had one TV and the only tape that we had to play was *Scarface*. I learned that movie like the back of my hand. We had one port-o-potty, that didn't get emptied very often, so I blew it up with dynamite, so they would get us a new one. I really did. That shit went everywhere. BOOM! (Ronnie: laughs. I'm amazed by this and laughing, in disbelief) Yeah, the guy wouldn't come get it, so I blew it up. It was hysterical, you should have seen it. It's funny, that movie I did in Russia, the director calls himself Wesley after the director of *Scarecrows*.

RA: Did you have to do any kind of special training preparing for the role?

TV: No, I was in shape already, so I didn't need to prepare. It was a strenuous role, no question. I didn't have any stunt people. I really don't like using stunt people and I like doing my own stuff. I did a movie called *Hammerhead Jones*, about Pro Wrestling, and I pretty much got the dog shit kicked out of myself. Oh boy, did I get beat up wrestling.

RA: (NOTE: we talk wrestling, about my own career and about his days in the business)

TV: I actually got to manage Rocky Johnson, the Rock's father. Steve Keirn (also known as Skinner and Doink The Clown) actually trained me. I'm still friendly with Steve. He's a good man. He treated me real well and we've been friends a long time. He was running NXT for WWE for a while. I love the wrestling business. I just love wrestling. I think I'm going to watch it tonight.

(NOTE: more wrestling conversation. It happens. I can talk wrestling all day long with people. We eventually get back to the film talk)

RA: One of the things that I spotlighted in *Scarecrows* was some of the effects. They were amazing! What went into them?

TV: That was actually a sixteen-year-old kid. His name was Norman Cabrera. He worked with Rick Baker and was in high school at the time he did the movie. He was terrific.

RA: Yeah, the scarecrows looked great in the movie and surprisingly, it was quite a gory movie, too.

TV: You know, it's amazing to me how many times I have been contacted about the movie.

Right now, it's even being re-released for the third time in the UK. It's amazing to me. When I was in Russia, this cat made me sit and watch the whole movie with his family. It was really nice the way they treated me there. It was amazing.

RA: One thing that I always noticed about *Scarecrows* is that they never really explain where exactly the scarecrows come from. Did you know much about that, like their background in the story?

TV: Well, all I know is that we parachuted down there and were wiped out. I think the whole mission was cursed. It was like it was meant to be, and they said it in the show. How did we fall into the place? How come nobody got hit by a bullet in the raid? One of the guys said it, "We kept shooting, they kept falling, but they never shot us." It was almost like a setup, like we supposed to not die there, and we were supposed to die where we died. It was one big set up. We got fucked. I think that only one that lived through it was the dog (laughs). That was my dog. That was his last film. I had that dog for sixteen years. He was a bulldog that I got in Florida. He was in two or three movies. He was like my kid, before I had a kid. That was just a great, great dog. He was trained and he would bark on command. He was standing by the plane barking and I was proud of him.

RA: What are your thoughts on the movie now, looking back on it?

TV: I think it was a great experience doing it. I'm honored by the fact that I have so many people that talk to me about it. I'm proud of it. It went from nothing to something that people are still talking about thirty years later. It's still huge and liked by a lot of people.

RA: What do you have going on these days?

TV: With my TV show now, *South Beach Customs*, I'm very busy. People pay me to make appearances all over the world. It's truly very nice. I'm very happy about it. It's good for business.

RA: If you could say something to the fans out there, what would you say?

TV: I would say that I appreciate the fact that they watch the movie and I hope that they like it. I'm honored by the fact that the movie is still popular. It makes me feel good that I was able to do what I did. I'm a pretty humble guy when it comes to things like that. It's a great honor that it's still thought of years later. I would do a *Scarecrows Two* if I was approached (laughs).

TIFFANY HELM
(FRIDAY THE 13th PART 5)

RA: How did you get into the acting business?

TH: My parents were already pretty established in the industry. It was just kind of a natural transition. I really didn't want to do it initially. I first started modeling because I knew that it was a shorter career, like it would only last a few years and then you move on and do something else with your life. I knew that acting is something that you could get sucked into and that you could be waiting for that role into your sixties and I thought I didn't want to get into that trap. However, when I got into modeling, I was told by my agency that I have a great commercial look. So, the agency started sending me out on commercials and that led into theatrical, and then I was there. Working my first few jobs, particularly the Robert Altman job absolutely got me hooked. It was every actor's dream to work with someone like that. So, I quit school and pursued it 100%.

RA: That's something that's pretty significant too, that you and your mother (Brooke Bundy) were both in slasher films. Do you ever both kind of recognize that and have a laugh about it?

TH: Oh, I think it's great! In fact, one of the nicest things about doing one horror con a while back in Texas is that it was arranged for her to surprise me. When I got off the plane, she was there and I had no idea she was going to be there. Unfortunately, the show was a wash, but it was really cool having my mom there and we got to set up our tables right next to each other and sell our bloody pictures (laughs). It was awesome. It's very cool to have that connection with my mom.

RA: How did you land the part of Violet on *Friday the 13th Part 5*?

TH: At the time, my look really was not popular and not the norm. I think now that if I were to start again at that age, it would be a very different situation. I remember that my agent was always wanting me to color my hair a normal color and to dress normal and all that. But, I went in for this and they were calling it *Repetition*. It wasn't being billed as a *Friday the 13th* movie because actors would know that it's this great franchise and ask for more money, so they just called it that. Initially, they were looking for a Pat Benatar type, because for Hollywood, that was the alternative look. Hollywood had a very narrow view of what the alternative scene was. What can I say? You either make an impression with the director and producers or you don't and I stood out and that was it.

RA: That's what I always thought was really cool about Violet and I even wrote about in my first book, that she was unique and so unlike your usual character at the time. What of yourself did you put into that which really stood out, aside from the character?

TH: It was pretty much all me. I was who I was for that and I didn't have to change my appearance in any way. The wardrobe people really didn't outfit me. They wanted my opinion and took me out shopping and just said "What do you want?" I just thought, "Excellent!" If you've heard some things about my death scene, it was supposed to be this hard-body Pat Benatar like new wave girl doing aerobics in her bedroom, and they re-wrote it because it wasn't natural for me. It was not my thing. We tried it that way, but it just didn't fly. They were very open to my input on it, which was very nice. Any director or producer that gives you the room to define your character makes a good environment to work in. They trusted me with the character and it worked. Just looking at some of the feedback I've had from so many fans and how much they relate to my character has really made it bigger than I could have ever thought. I just came in as me at the time, because that's who I was and that's what was going on in the alternative world at the time.

RA: You mentioned your original death scene. I remember seeing a picture of that somewhere before, showing you in the make-up and everything. Is that something that the censorship board wasn't too keen on, as well? Is that why it was cut?

TH: Oh yeah, that's what was said. That was a Polaroid from when they did me up in the make-up, which they use to match for continuity before shooting. They had it so that I was going to be in my room laying down scissoring and he was going to come up and machete me down through my crotch (laughs). When I walked in to the producers and the director, they were like, "Yeah, that's not gonna get passed by the ratings board". I don't understand what their criteria is because there is some pretty horrific stuff, but I think they were concerned that it would not get past the ratings board, so they decided to re-do it. That's when we brainstormed on what we could do and the end result is what you see in the movie.

RA: Another thing that I really highlighted in my book is the dance that you do in the film. It's one of the classic scenes of the entire series. It's just so unique. Where did that come from?

TH: That actually came from an iconic club that I used to go to in West Hollywood called The Odyssey. It burned down, but it was a great club. There was a boy there that used to dance to "Send Me an Angel" up on this podium and I was absolutely mesmerized by him and his dancing. There were a couple other people there that did it similarly and they had their specific songs, but when I saw him do that, I just thought "Oh my God, I need to do that." So, I just worked at doing it. I had a couple of my signature songs at this club that I would get up and dance to and that was the dance. I was able to bring that. So, it was really cool that I was able to bring that to the movie because at first, they wanted me to dance whatever 80s style was going on at the time. I was just like "I'm not comfortable doing that. Here's what I'm comfortable doing." They thought it was cool and said to go with it.

RA: Cool, did you ever see the spoof video of it on YouTube?

TH: Yeah, the one with the woman dancing and Jason starts tapping his toes. I love it. I absolutely love it. I actually posted that on my Facebook page. You know the saying, you know that you have arrived when someone is spoofing you. I think it's awesome.

RA: What would you say are your favorite memories of making the movie? Any stories you'd like to share from the set?

TH: Where we were shooting and going through those orange groves at night, there were a few times that Tom Morga would spook us, walking through there. Ninety percent of the time, it's a great experience working on a film set. You develop relationships with the actors and the crew and you really become like a family. Danny Steinmann was awesome to work for. Any director that gives you that freedom to put yourself into the role or change up the lines is a great director. It's really nice to work under that kind of energy. Juliette (Cummins) and I were very good friends on the set and used to get into all kind of trouble on the set (laughs). It was just a really great crew. I have nothing but fond memories of working on it.

RA: How do you now view the notoriety of the series, and of your role as well in the horror community?

TH: It's a little bit of a mind blower, honestly. A friend of mine that I met at a horror convention a few years started ago started my fan page on Facebook. Just seeing the response that I get is pretty mind blowing. I have one for my photography business and it just pales in comparison to how many people are on board for that, and specifically Violet. *Reform School Girls* gets some attention too, but *Friday the 13th* is really the one that just trumps all. It's always interesting to me to hear from the people who really related to Violet when they were young and who grew up watching the movies. I've pretty much just recently let the secret out, but I usually don't talk about what I used to do. But, now that the people around here (her hometown) know, they think it's really cool!

RA: You mentioned another movie that you did and I wanted to ask you about your work on *Reform School Girls* and your memories of making that.

TH: (laughs) It wasn't that great, actually. That was the one project that I actually got fired from. There was the obligatory shower scene and I was told that I had to pretty much saunter by the camera nude. I thought when I signed on that I could do it. At the time, I really wasn't completely confident with my body. I was working with people like Darcy Demoss, who was like one of those hot bod girls. I felt like I was conspicuous and overweight and like I was going to stand out among all of the girls there that were like Playboy models. So, I called the union to find out what I could do about the nudity issue because it wasn't like I was refusing to do nudity, I just didn't want to pretty much saunter by so blatantly. I mean, I had done nudity before in Altman's film, so that wasn't the issue. The director was very angry with me. So, I talked with the union and they said that I could back out of the nudity clause at any time, except after it had already been shot. I felt terrible for doing it, but I just felt like I wasn't comfortable with my body. I see it now and think, well so what, what was the big deal? At the time, I was super self-conscious and they wouldn't work with me. I even offered a solution. My best friend was on set and working as an extra and she was just a tiny little thing. She was very comfortable with her body. She was happy to step in for me, so they used her. They were not happy with me and it was towards the end and they just canned me. There were a couple more scenes that I supposed to be in that I wasn't in. So, it didn't end well.

RA: Can you tell me a bit about getting to work on *Freddy's Nightmares*? I don't think I've ever seen that, actually.

TH: It was a great show. It was a lot of fun, plus I got to have Freddy's baby! It was just a short show and I play a very pregnant southern waitress. This writer comes in and he's trying to make these stories and I end up going into labor. It's one of those things like in the movies where you wonder if what you're seeing is really going on or just in someone's head. So, I have the Freddy baby that was used in one of the movies. I have a nice picture somewhere of me smiling and holding my beautiful baby (laughs). It was a fun show to do. You might be able to find it online. *Heartbreak Hotel* is the name of the episode.

RA: Okay, I'll have to look for it. Why did you end up leaving the acting business?

TH: Well, we had moved to Seattle from Los Angeles. I just wasn't cut out for Los Angeles. I don't like the heat, the crowds, the noise, the pace. In Seattle, there is very little going on in the film industry. A lot of the people in Seattle aren't open to filming there and don't seem to understand the amount of revenue that these things bring in. A lot of the things that are supposed to be set there end up being filmed in Vancouver because they are more willing to work with the industry. Well, that and the exchange rate. The people in Vancouver are like, sure come here and work, while it's more challenging in Seattle. So, there weren't many opportunities for me there. I did a couple of small things, but not much. That was when I started exploring the other side of the camera, and started my portrait business. We ended up living in Seattle for about eighteen years before coming back to my homeland in Canada. I'm coming up on five years now living up here.

RA: Looking back on it now, how do you view your time in the industry and your work on some of these projects?

TH: I think that being as young as I was, I definitely didn't appreciate it as much as I should have. I'm very appreciative for it, though. It was a very different, unique time in my life. Not everybody can say that they did that. It shaped me for who I am today.

RA: If you had anything you could say to the fans out there, what would you say?

TH: I say really embrace who you are. I look at what made me different then and how I can use that for my creative self today. Those are the things that shaped me. Really find those things that make you different within and embrace those.

TOM DESIMONE
(DIRECTOR OF HELL NIGHT)

RA: You've had quite the career in film. How did you get started?

TD: Well, it was one of those things I had always wanted to do, even as a kid. I started when I was around ten years old with 8mm movies. I had an uncle who was an amateur photographer and he also shot a lot of 8mm stuff. He kind of took me under his wing once he realized that I was interested in it and it became a hobby of mine growing up. All through my formative years and my teen years, I just shot more and more. I knew that was what I wanted and my parents encouraged it, because they figured I had a talent. I went to Emerson College in Boston to get my degree in directing. There weren't many film schools back in those days. Then, after I got my BA, I came to California and got my Masters at UCLA in Motion Picture Production. Then, the rest is history.

RA: Did you have any difficulty finding work after this?

TD: Well, yeah. What happened was, when I got out of UCLA, work wasn't just waiting. Back in those days, you had to do all kinds of apprenticeship work and you had to know people. So, I worked for a while for a small company that made educational films for schools. I did pretty much everything. I was like a one-man band. It was a very small company. While I was there, I asked them if I could shoot something, so they let me shoot a live action short film. While

I was there, struggling to get work, somebody suggested that I go into the X-Rated business and that I could make some money there. I thought it was worth a try, so I did it. I borrowed a camera from where I was working and went out and shot some test footage and brought it to a company that was releasing adult pictures and they told me to come work for them. So, that started me on the road to filmmaking and then I started doing feature films. We would grind them out quickly on 16mm, showing them in theaters and whatnot. So, I did that for a little while and then I left there and went into business for myself. While I was doing it, I had a friend who was a fan of mine and liked my work. He was a fairly successful writer in the television industry. He was having a New Year's Eve party once and he introduced me to a producer there. So, we talked and he asked if I had any ideas and I told him that I do. That became a picture originally called Lips, which became *Chatterbox*. It was my first crossover film from X-Rated to R-Rated. It was originally a script that I had wrote about a girl with a talking vagina. It was originally going to be X-Rated, but he said we could clean it up and make it cute and funny. So, it became a totally different picture. It was never a great picture, but it's a cult favorite now. People always talk about it and it was my gateway into the legit business. About a year later, he called me and he said that he had this picture that he wanted to do with Linda Blair called *Hell Night*. So, I did that and just continued working and making pictures and ended up in television.

RA: Now, *Hell Night* is one of my all-time favorite horror films. Tell me a bit about working on that.

TD: I liked *Hell Night*. We had a good cinematographer for it, from Sweden. We had a great relationship. We both had the same vision in mind, which doesn't often happen. We wanted it to look artsy and not cheap. It was my idea to put them in those period costumes because I thought that if we're going to have a haunted house picture and have these people wandering around an old mansion, they should look period. I couldn't envision them in t-shirts and jeans like most of these college kid pictures are. They liked the idea and that's why we decided to have them at a Halloween party and to have them up there in those costumes. I was happy with the way that it looked.

RA: Where was the house itself that you filmed at? It had an interesting look.

TD: Well, the house itself was in Redlands, California. It's a museum now, but it was a private residence at the time. I saw pictures of it from the location manager and I said we have to have this house. It was a big house and had big grounds. It sat way back from the road, which caused a lot of problems shooting, with them going in and out of the gate. The gate was like a half mile from the house, so we had to do a lot of cutting to make it look like the gate was outside the mansion. We actually built that gate for the driveway because we had to wreck it later. They wouldn't allow us in the house. They only allowed us to shoot on the grounds, so the interiors were done at a home in Pasadena. We went in and stripped it out and dressed it down, putting cobwebs in and making it look haunted. Then, with the scenes in the tunnels under the house, those were sets. We also had to build the roof because they wouldn't even let us on the roof at the house. We could only shoot on the grounds, so we had to construct that on a soundstage and make it dark and use wind machines. When it's cut though, it all comes together. I really like the way they did that. It was a difficult shoot because it was just supposed to be two weeks on the exterior of the house and then two weeks on the stages. We got out to Redlands and the weather was bad. It was cold at night, which is when we did all of our shooting. We would shoot until the sun came up and then go back to the hotel to supposedly sleep. I never got any sleep because I was always working the next day's pages. The logistics of the house and running cables everywhere because of the distance was difficult. We ended up doing four weeks there instead of two, so we went over budget and over time, but everyone was happy with the footage. It ended up going six weeks total.

RA: What went into the casting and what were they like to work with?

TD: It was originally conceived with Linda Blair in mind. The producer had worked with Linda previously on a TV movie called *Born Innocent*. It caused a bit of an uproar due to a rape scene in it and people said it was too graphic for TV. She was starting to take off at the time, but she ran into some personal problems with drugs. It really hurt her career, but this producer had worked with her and wanted her to do *Hell Night*. She was pretty much pre-cast, but everyone else we had to audition. We liked Peter Barton, but he was kind of depressed. He was up for a big picture, *Romeo and Juliet*, and he thought he had the part, but lost it, so we hired him. The other actor was Vincent Van Patten and he was a handful. He was a bit of a problem and one of those actors who never wanted to do what you ask them to do and always had a better idea of what to do. I would have to redirect him a lot. The fellow that played the head of the fraternity, Kevin Brophy, had worked with the producer before on another picture. He was a child actor and had a good career before that.

There's an interesting story here, as well. A few years ago, some guy died who was kind of a loner and a movie buff, and he left in his will a million dollars to be shared between Kevin Brophy and Peter Barton. He had seen them in the movie and was fascinated with them. So, out of the blue, they get a call from the guy's lawyer and he left each a half a million dollars. I saw it on the news one night and thought holy shit, that's my picture! (laughs) I knew where Kevin was and called him. He was going to use the money to refinance his career. I know after *Hell Night,* he kind of fell on hard times and had a wife and kids. It's one thing to struggle in acting when you're single, but a real struggle when you have a family. We've stayed friends for a long time.

RA: Another thing that I really liked about the film is the look of the killers and their story.

TD: Oh yes, the Garth family. That was the thing is that everyone thought it was just one killer until the very end. We did several make-up tests. The first scene that we shot with the monsters was at the gate where Kevin Brophy gets attacked. After we saw the dailies, the producer wasn't happy with the way he looked, so we went back and re-did that. Unfortunately, that actor died right after filming in a car crash. He never saw the finished picture.

RA: That's too bad. I have to say that my favorite part is where the killer comes up through the floor, under the rug.

TD: Oh yeah, everybody loves that part. That one we did on the stage, because there was no way that we could cut a hole in the floor in the real house. I think the writer came up with that. That was something that was added later. We were trying to figure out a scary way to get into the room. Every time we see that, people scream at that part because they don't want them to turn around. That was a fun thing to do. Then, Peter really injured himself when he was going down the stairs. He actually sprained his ankle and all that limping around that he did was real. He had to not work for one day and we had to shoot around him. Then, the scene that I always regret is the scene where the girl gets her head cut off. He picks her up and holds her against the wall, then he swings the axe and cuts her head off. The way I envisioned it, she was supposed to be up against the wall and when he cut her, I wanted her body to fall away and her head to still be in his hand screaming. We constructed this very elaborate set where she laid down behind the wall and put her head through a hole in the wall. Then, we had the body of a dummy. We connected her head to the dummy using mortician's wax, so it looked real. It was difficult for her because she was lying on her stomach with her head back, so we had to do it fairly quickly once we got it all set. Then, we of course had to make sure that he didn't hit her with the blade. So, we had it all set up and it went beautifully. After we did it, they said it was too gruesome and we could get an X-Rating for it and I didn't want that, so now after it hits her, it just cuts away. It took us hours to set that up and it's never in the film.

RA: What were some of the other effects that went into the movie?

TD: Well, I really liked that thing at the end with the gate. I also like when he twists the kid's head on the roof and cracks his neck. We tried to stay away from a lot of the gore because a lot of that was being done then and we were hoping that we could rely more on shock than actual gore. I think we did a good job of that, especially with the end scene. That was a nightmare to shoot. We had the guy strapped to the top of the car and we had a stunt woman in the car driving, and we went back and forth between the real actors and the stunt people. Alot of it was done on the stage, like the close-ups of her behind the wheel with the glass breaking and him reaching in. Then, of course, getting it rigged to look like the gate was going through his body was very time consuming. It was just very slow when you're working in the dark and the cold. After that, I went on to do the show *Freddy's Nightmares*, and we had a lot of blood and gore on that. We were always rigging blood bags and tubes going up actor's sleeves.

RA: I had heard some stories about this one. What was it exactly that happened with *Savage Streets* and your involvement in it?

TD: Well, after *Hell Night*, I had done a "women behind bars" picture called *Concrete Jungle* with Jill St. John. The producer was kind of an idiot. He was a guy that just pulled money together and stuck his name on things. It was a nightmare working for him. After *Concrete Jungle,* he called me with another script that he wanted to do called *Savage Streets*. I took it and brought Linda Blair on because I had worked with her on *Hell Night*. The problem with that script was that it was really base and below what I what wanted to put my name on. It just kept getting worse. He had these money people in New York that I thought were mafia people. I never met them, though. He would just keep submitting pages and making changes. It was some stuff I really didn't want to be associated with. We had some actors come in to read and one I liked very much. He had some good credits to his name. We told him we would give him the lead and we gave him the script. That night he called me at home and told me that he just read the script and didn't want to be associated with anything like that. He even said that he was surprised that I am. So, I mulled it over all night and then decided that the guy was right. I didn't want to be associated with it. By then we had cast already and my brother and Linda were in it already. So, they got Danny Steinmann to do that. They were really low budget exploitation pictures and after doing *Concrete Jungle* and things like that, I didn't want to go backward. To me, it was just too distasteful and there were things there that I really didn't want to put my name on, like raping a girl who was handicapped and things like that. There were things that I thought I couldn't even film there. But on the plus side, Bob did well in it and everybody remembers his character and it led to the *Friday the 13th* picture with him.

RA: I wanted to ask too, about your experience working with Wendy O. Williams

TD: Oh yes, that was an adventure. After I had done *Concrete Jungle*, I was trying to come up with something to do. I thought I would spoof women behind bars pictures, because I had two of them early on. Another one I did was Prison Girls, which was really low budget and in 3-D. I wish my name wasn't on it. So, I wrote R*eform School Girls*. It was pitched to New World and they said they wanted to do it. So, during casting we were trying to figure out who would play this tough lesbian and we had a music coordinator who suggested Wendy O.

He told me that she was doing a nude laying for Playboy, nude skydiving and I thought that she sounded daring, so we called her people and she came in and took the job. But, it was an odd working relationship. Not that she was a problem, it was just unusual. Her manager was also her lover and he was kind of like a Svengali over her. She couldn't move or say or do anything without his approval. He would be on the set every day watching her. She had her own trailer and she wouldn't hang out with anybody. As soon as I said cut, she would go back to her trailer with him and they would eat alone. She had a lot of strange rules and didn't want to do certain things, so I kind of gave her a black brush. I wanted a performance out of her. I didn't want to get into a battle with her on set. It worked out okay, but unfortunately, she had a bad ending. She ended up marrying him later. He was the one who discovered her on Times Square working as a dominatrix. Somebody actually found a porno of her and snuck it onto the set and the guys were watching it. It was pretty graphic stuff. I said, "Jesus guys, don't let her find out we have that. Turn it off." This manager of hers pretty much created her and gave her that name and started the band around her and her image and everything. Eventually, he got a scholarship and ended up working at a University in New England and she sort of became a faculty wife. That wasn't the life that she wanted and she just went out in the woods one day and shot herself, which is tragic.

RA: That is truly fascinating. It makes me wonder, who was who you would say is the most interesting person that you had a chance to direct?

TD: Well, a lot of them were a pain in the ass and a lot of them were easy to work with, as well. Linda Blair was always a lot of fun. I liked her and we got along well. Jill St. John was a bit difficult. She never wanted to wear what we wanted or wear her hair how we needed. She would tell us that her fans expected more from her. Every actor has their own things that they bring to the set, like Pat Ast on *Reform School Girls* was a challenge because she was primarily not an actress, but a personality. I met her in New York years before. I was at a club one night in Greenwich Village in the seventies, and they had an upstairs lounge where people would hang out and get high. I went up there and she was just sprawled out on the floor on a bunch of pillows smoking pot. She was kind of holding court. At the time, she was hanging out with Andy Warhol and people like that. She was just fascinating and I agreed to use her down the road. So, when I was making this picture, I remembered her and wanted her to play the part of Edna. They were hesitant, but I told them that I wrote it with her in mind. They really wanted Sybil Danning and wanted her on the box cover. So, I agonized over this and when I wrote it, the warden was a man, so I said why don't we make the warden a woman and give the part to Sybil. That way, I could have Pat as Edna and they could have their way, too. They agreed to that. She was a real challenge on the set though because she could never remember her lines. We would have to shoot in bits and pieces and tape cards all over the set with her lines. Then, her health was an issue. She was diabetic and either sick or not sick. She couldn't walk. We had to carry her from the trailer to where we were shooting at a few times and that kind of thing. It was a real challenge, but it turned out okay, because in the long run, you're happy with the end result and forget that stuff.

Originally on *Concrete Jungle*, Shelly Winters was supposed to play the part of the social worker and I was thrilled about that. There was a line in the script where she was arguing with the warden and the warden called her a fat bitch. Shelly objected to the line and asked the producer to change it and he said no. So, she got pissed and quit the picture, so we got someone else. The woman was not fat, so they took the line out and I said, "If you took it out for her, why couldn't you take it out for Shelly?" I was so disappointed that we lost her. I really did like the other woman we got for the part though, Nita Talbott and she turned out good.

RA: What are you up to now?

TD: I'm retired now. I'm just writing a book, but not about any of this. The last thing I did was *She Spies* for MGM, a show that was kind of like *Charlie's Angels*. After I did the films, I got tired of doing the same old bad girls pictures. I told my agent that I was tired of doing these schlocky pictures with naked women, so he told me he would get me some TV stuff. The first show I did was *Freddy's Nightmares* and I really enjoyed that. I did some things at Universal in Florida like *Swamp Thing*, and from then I just did more television. I enjoyed television a lot. The work was fast and the money was very good. It was a lot quicker than making pictures. Plus, I got to travel a lot. I was in Barcelona for six months doing a series there called *Dark Justice*. It was wonderful. Then, I did a year in Mexico City doing a soap opera down there. We shot about 120 episodes. It was a good life. I traveled around and met a lot of people. It was much less stressful than making the pictures. It was much quicker too.

RA: If you could say anything to the fans, what would you say?

TD: I hope that I entertained you and you got your money's worth. Whenever I did a show, that was the first thing on my mind, if they're going to like it. I remember when *Hell Night* came out I went to several different screenings to see if it worked and it always did. You always knew when the screams were going to come. Whenever I see fans and they tell me they liked my stuff, I tell them that I'm glad that they did and that I did it for them. I'm glad they liked them.

TOM WRIGHT
(CREEPSHOW 2, TALES FROM THE HOOD)

RA: How did you get into the acting business?

TW: Originally, I went to school outside of Philadelphia, PA. I lived in a small town called Westchester. A friend of mine was a director and I used to do some things with him, like play a lot of voices and such, just for fun. He would always tell me that I'm an actor, I just didn't know it, and he proved it to me. He said that he would prove it to me by putting me on stage. He got me in a play and put me on stage and it went great. That was in 1974 and I haven't turned around since.

RA: How did you make the step from stage to film?

TW: It's sort of a natural transition. I did probably fifty or sixty plays in New York, but you always have an eye on trying to make the best living you can. I moved to New York in 1976 and occasionally there would be different films or TV shows that would come there. You just hope that you can audition for them and find your way into a hiring corral of talent and that's what happened for me.

RA: How did you get involved with doing *Creepshow 2*?

TW: I actually got my SAG card through doing stunt work. I was always an actor, but I was an athlete as well in college. I got asked to play football in the film *The Wanderers*. They needed guys to play football and I jumped in. There was a big fight scene in the middle of the film and I really got interested in the way that the choreography was handled and performed. A guy named Dick McDonaugh took me under his wing, and I trained for a few years as a stuntman. When *Creepshow 2* came along, it was the perfect job because it required both an actor and a stuntman. So, they got a two for one when they hired me.

RA: Very cool. So, you did all of your own stunts for the Hitchhiker segment?

TW: Oh yeah. I did five car hits from different angles, I rode on top of the car, we crashed through guardrails, we went down in the gravel pits while I'm strapped in the front hanging on. I did all of my own stunts on it.

RA: That's amazing. I wasn't aware of that. Were any of them kind of sketchy?

TW: The sketchiest one to me was crashing through the guard rail and when the car goes down into a gravel pit. That was pretty intense, but I had a lot of trust in my fellow stuntman and thankfully it came off without a hitch.

RA: What was some of the direction you were given to playing the part of The Hitchhiker? You had some interesting mannerisms and ways of moving.

TW: The director, Michael Gornick, gave me a lot of freedom. Basically, we just had to consistently remind ourselves of where the character was in his deterioration. Like, every time she would run over him, a different bone would break or things along those lines, so we just had to keep a consistency of his injuries. I love horror movies and as a kid, I would watch tons of scary movies and I was subscribed to Famous Monsters. So, for me, it would always sort of take me out of the film if there was a bit of logic that wasn't handled correctly, so we were very self-conscious to keep it consistent. We really tried to keep track of his demise.

RA: I noticed that, how as it went on, the effects just keep getting gorier and the character gets more messed up. Then, by the end, there's almost nothing left of him!

TW: Exactly. It was all very intentional and we were very aware of it.

RA: I also noticed that it has a very good morality tale to the story. Really, Lois's character

was not a very good person. There was definitely an underlying message there.

TW: Yes, there definitely is. There is very much of a karmic message in there, as with all of the stories really on the movie.

RA: What was Lois Chiles like to work with anyways? She did a great job on it.

TW: Lois was cool, she was very good. We were in Bangor, Maine in November filming, when it was like ten degrees outside when we shot at night. We would shoot all night, so it was a pretty brutal shoot. You had to be a bit of a trooper to hang in there and she was a trooper. She would never complain or anything.

RA: Movie logic time. If she just would have stopped after hitting you, none of this would have happened, right?

TW: No, I don't think any of it would have ever happened. I think that's what it's all about. It's really a good ghost story, and really a classic ghost story, in a sense. I think the way that they structured it was exactly right.

RA: Another good ghost story that you were in was your role in *Tales from The Hood* as Martin Moorhouse

TW: Oh yeah, that was a good one (gives an evil laugh). That was a really great job. It was made by Rusty Cundieff and Darin Scott. They had a really good, solid understanding of what makes a good horror film. They paid homage to the genre and they really paid close attention to some of the turns that had to be made. Some of the ways in which a horror movie is structured, they just really understood that and knew what they were doing. They knew what the impact of each story was about and how to visually manifest those ideas. I really have a lot of respect for those guys.

RA: Did they have you on board for the movie because of your role in *Creepshow?*

TW: They sort of did. They remembered me from my role as the hitchhiker and they wanted me to play Moorhouse because of that association. So, that was a pretty cool honor, really.

RA: How did they do the effects and make-up, making you into Moorhouse?

TW: They used KNB with Howard Berger and Greg Nicotero. They were the same ones that they used for *Creepshow*. So, it was like a reunion with them. We had a lot of fun. I also remember that working with Wings Hauser was great and I was charmed by that fact. I've always been proud of that movie.

RA: How do you look back on those films now?

TW: Pretty fondly, really. They were movies of a certain time and of a real particular genre. They really don't make horror movies like that anymore. It was a different time. They certainly don't make many creature movies anymore. We really haven't seen a good creature movie in quite some time. I think the good old fashioned horror flick that you or I would remember from our youth has slowly faded away. For now, anyways, I know there is always someone to come along to try and resurrect it. I have always liked horror films. They're fun. I have lost touch a bit with the genre lately, I'll admit. I just didn't really see many innovations being made.

RA: Another one that I want to ask you about is one I always tell people is my favorite zombie movie (laughs), and that's *Weekend at Bernie's 2*.

TW: (laughs) Oh yeah, that one was a hoot. It was a lot of fun, a total send-up type of film. It was a lot fun because I got to spend about seven weeks in St. Thomas with my family and my good friend Steve James. It was a good job.

RA: What are your favorite memories of making that one?

TW: Clowning around with Steve, for sure. We had a load of fun. We had known each other forever from New York. It was fun to be in a creative environment with him because he and I would kid around a lot, and a lot of things that we did together, we would put into the film.

RA: What was it like getting to work with Terry Kiser in that Bernie role?

TW: Terry is a very talented guy. He had so much experience from doing things like the Carol Burnett show. He was a lot of fun to work with.

RA: Another movie that you did has me noticing a bit of a trend here. That's four movies with a supernatural tinge to them that you did, and that's the Steven Seagal film *Marked for Death*.

TW: You're really hitting all of the good ones. That was a fun, but grueling shoot. We had to go down to Jamaica several times to film. It was ... culturally challenging. There hadn't been too many films shot in Jamaica by that time. I think sometimes when an American crew steps into a third world country, they expect things to operate in a certain way, but they just don't. So, it makes it a bit more difficult tom accomplish things that would have been much easier when you were in The States. It was still pleasurable, but it was also difficult.

RA: What were some of the problems that you ran into while filming that?

TW: Well, let's say that you go to Las Vegas to shoot a film. Las Vegas is used to crews coming to shoot films there. They have a police force that can lock up the streets when you need it. If you need a camera part or you need an extra light, you can just run over to one of the equipment shops and rent one. If you need to fly actors in and out, it's really simple. When you're in a third world country, you don't know what you're going to walk into, to a certain extent, so it's a bit of adventure. If you need a spare part, where do you get one? If you're shooting in downtown Kingston, how do you lock up a neighborhood so you can use the side streets. It can become really difficult. I wouldn't say that there were problems per se, but there were some logistical problems.

RA: What was Steven Seagal like to work with?

TW: I won't touch that one. Better left unsaid (laughs)

RA: Fair enough. Another one I want to ask about is Basil Wallace. I put his role as Screwface on this on a list I did for a website and ranked him very high on the list of top underrated villains.

TW: We become good friends while working on this. Basil is a really good guy and a very solid working actor. He really loves the craft and he brings his best A game to every single day. It had a good twist too. I think it really threw everyone for a surprise.

RA: There's another role of yours that didn't really dawn on me until I was doing research for this. It was an "Oh yeah!" moment to realize that you played Mr. Morgan on *Seinfeld*.

TW: That was the easiest job I've ever had. It was a real pleasure to work with those folks and Larry David is a genius. The way that he ran that show just made it extremely easy for actors to do what they do and put on their best and that's what you want. You want someone to allow you to your best. Larry was demanding and very specific with what he wanted, but if you're a theater actor, you're used to that. For me, it was an easy job and a lot of fun.

RA: What would you say has been your favorite project?

TW: That's tough to say. All of them have been very special and distinct and I love them for one reason or another. I would say, in general, that when I was on Broadway in *A Taste of Honey* with Amanda Plummer has to be up there. Then, I did a movie called *Matewan* with John Sayles, which is where I met my wife thirty years ago. It was a great cast and a great crew, the perfect blend actually. A lot of times, I really think that my favorite job is going to be my next job, whatever that may be.

RA: What are you currently working on?

TW: Right now, I'm doing a three-show arc on Ray Donovan. I'm also doing a few shows on a show called *Murder in The First*. I'm still keeping busy.

RA: If you could say anything to the fans out there, what would you say?

TW: I would say two things. Number one, support your local artist. Support your local film maker. Get involved and find out where they screen and be supportive of them. It's become a lot easier to make a film these days, but there aren't nearly as many places to show it as there used to be. Local artists need a lot of support. The other thing I want to say is go out and get to the movies. Don't allow the viewing experience to get smaller, which would be just sitting alone at home. Movies are meant to be a public spectacle, so get out and rub elbows with people and go to the movies.

TOMMY LEE WALLACE
(Legendary horror director)

RA: First things first. What got you involved in the film business? How did you meet John Carpenter and begin working with him?

TLW: John Carpenter and I grew up in the same small town in southern Kentucky, Bowling Green. We went to the same school, a K-8 teacher's training facility on the campus of what is now Western Kentucky University. Though we were aware of each other throughout childhood, being a year apart in age kept us from being close friends until our teenage years, when our lives got caught up in rock 'n' roll, especially Beatlemania and the British Invasion, and in making our own music as well, first in the school orchestra (John violin, me trombone) then as guitar-totin' troubadours in the local coffee house scene, and finally in a rock 'n' roll cover band, playing frat gigs for actual money, our first real encounter with show business. John was a creative dynamo, drawing comic books, writing stories, even a novel, writing songs, and making his own movies with his dad's tourist camera. He opened my eyes to the possibilities inherent in a creative life, not as a hobby, but as a career. He knew he wanted to be a film director before I even knew just what a film director was. I'm proud to say I helped steer him to the college library, where there was this thick blue book about colleges. It was there that John picked University of Southern California, to which he then transferred as a college Junior. I went off to art school in Ohio and, after graduation, gave up notions of glory as a graphic designer in New York, and instead followed John to Los Angeles. As I was entering USC Cinema, John was more or less on his way out the door with what you might call his thesis film, *Dark Star*, in close collaboration with Dan O'Bannon. They found a movie deal that allowed them to expand their student film into a full-length feature. Given my art background, I was welcomed onto the crew of this endeavor, mostly helping Dan with sets and various art department functions. While I worked my way through the USC film program, I logged numerous experiences earning tuition money in the "real" film world, as an animation cameraman, a commercial editor, background extra, storyboard artist and lots of other things, so when John's second feature, *Assault on Precinct 13* came along, he invited me to be the Art Director. He and Dan had had a falling out yet he loved working with friends, so I was the logical choice, especially since I would work dirt cheap. From there, things proceeded pretty logically, through *Halloween* and *The Fog*, with me playing an ever-expanding role on those films, until I struck out on my own as a writer looking to become a director, with John's blessing. We have collaborated numerous times since then, most often as co-writers.

RA: In *Halloween*, you have the distinction of getting to play the boogeyman himself in one of the scenes. How did this come about? What was it like getting to play Michael in that intense scene?

TLW: The phrase "getting to play the boogeyman" paints the wrong picture. First and foremost, no one, at the time, had any inkling of the enduring phenomenon The Shape would turn into. (The script didn't call him Michael.) Had we known, there would probably have been a long line of volunteers to play the part in a given scene, but it just wasn't like that. *Halloween* put us in a fight for our lives, and while some of it was fun, you must remember we were making a movie on a shoestring, on a grueling schedule. All that mattered was us making our shooting day, getting everything we were supposed to get on film, and maintaining a standard far above and beyond what anyone might have expected going in. Nick Castle was a mutual friend from film school, who had, on a whim, done a funny turn as the moody, playful FEET of the "beachball alien" in *Dark Star*. After a few close encounters with some fairly clumsy extras on *Assault on Precinct 13*, I'm pretty sure John picked Nick as a lucky charm, a close friend, and somebody reliable who would be easy and fun on the set -- most of all a person who could move really well. Nick's father had enjoyed a successful career as a dance choreographer in the movies, so you could say it was in Nick's blood. It's funny how the original Shape was just a regular-sized person -- Nick, and occasionally myself -- but in the sequels, he got steadily bulkier and taller, and sometimes more lumbering, as subsequent directors seemed to remember the original as bigger and taller than we really were, and felt the need to cast accordingly. As movie after movie popped up, the inflation of size (not to mention violence) just blew up out of control. Virtually all the other Shapes (and all the Jasons too, for that matter) were pretty beefy stunt men. Some moved better than others. I created the Shape mask from an off-the-shelf Captain Kirk mask, with some modifications, including stripping off the sideburns and painting the whole thing fish-belly white. With Nancy's input (Nancy Loomis, actress, costumer, ex-wife), I gave the character a nondescript set of coveralls and some n.d. boots, and we were good to go. Because I was also the Production Designer, it was my department's responsibility to design and build any and all set inserts, that is, breakaway doors and windows – and louvered closets, of course. So, during those scenes which involved the breaking of a door, or a window, or the like, I was the person most likely to successfully execute it on Take 1 (important on a low budget!) -- the one on set with a similar build to Nick, the one with the most proprietary interest in all things pertaining to the Shape, and, traditionally, the jack of all trades on John's sets, up to that point. Also, it wouldn't have been right to ask Nick to risk injury busting through a trick set. I ripped up my hand a little, going through the wooden door in the kitchen scene. Couldn't have that happening to one of our actual cast members. The closet scene was the most extended passage for me as the Shape, and I like to think I upheld Nick's high standard of grooved, steady movement. It's fun to think back and remember performing the scene, but I can't say it was particularly fun at the time. We really were crammed in that tiny little closet-not-a-set, me, Jamie, and of course the camera operator, and possibly an assistant as well, with our own louvered doors in place; what I remember, most of all, was it was hot as hell, and doubly so underneath that mask. We were all on short sleep, and under really enormous pressure. The real fun came after I cut that scene together and we knew we had a winner. Ditto for the rest of the movie.

RA: You also got to play one of the ghosts in the classic *The Fog*. What was your experience like working on that film?

TLW: Again, "got to play" doesn't really capture what was going on, and it wasn't just one ghost I "played", but many. *The Fog* was a surprising challenge for us. We were well under way before we realized that, although we had more than three times the *Halloween* budget, the movie we were trying to make was far more than three times more ambitious and complicated. So, thank God we had more time to shoot, but the shoot itself was tougher by far, than "Halloween". I was referring before to the care one must take, in a scary movie, with the physical movements of anyone the audience is supposed to be frightened of. During principle photography, we were relying mostly on crew members as extras, especially because so many of the ghost-players in the fog were actually carrying lights! Unfortunately, the job description for good grips and gaffers and electricians does not require that you be able to move gracefully, or in scary fashion. Most attempts to do so were clumsy-looking, even comedic, which required cutting around some otherwise-effective stuff, so we realized we had to be very careful with movement. I became the "utility ghost" throughout, used primarily when movement was crucial, or when a hand or an arm had to do something very specific, like grabbing the guy at the Weather Station, or punching through the stained glass, or reaching into the Pastor's study to grab Jamie Lee.

Then came post-production, and a brave realization, on John's part, that the movie we first put together was simply inadequate. Not terrible, just flat; not special enough. And not scary enough. This brought about some additional scene work, a whole new prologue, a more complete climax atop the roof of the lighthouse, and the punching up of virtually all the ghost scenes by additional closeups of a given ghost, or ghost hands, rushing in toward camera. This all took place in something like a three-week period in post-production, an insane, frantic scramble to shoehorn such a thing into our already-tight post schedule. I saved that page from the editing room calendar; it's really something to see. So, to finally answer your question: If you notice the closeups of individual ghosts looming up in the fog, those would be me. Again, we were on a very low budget, especially with this additional stuff, on what you might call borrowed time, so the reshoots were by no means full-crew, or anything like it -- John called it the Mystic Unit. One late night, after Dean (Cundey, DP) set the lights, gave us a meter reading and went on home for the night, it was finally just John behind the camera, and me in front of it, doing ghostwork, and unconsciously harkening back to our earliest days as friends, when it was John's back yard, his Dad's camera, and I was his subject for the day, cavorting around with a bass guitar while John directed and operated, preparing for the day he'd go off to Hollywood and make good. That is one of my fondest memories of the Fog days—late night, misty sound stage, nobody around but me and J.C.; we really did get back to the basics there, for a little while.

RA: Halloween III: This is truly one of the most underrated films in horror history and a personal favorite. How did this one come about?

TLW: I guess the stage first got set for "H3" when "Halloween 2" came along. I was invited to direct "H2", kind of a logical choice, since John didn't intend to do it himself. Remember that sequels were not then the everyday thing they are now. Neither John, Debra nor I were very excited about the prospect, to be honest. Our group mindset was kind of "hey, 'Halloween' turned out great horror movie, what's left to say?" Naive of us, but true. Still, that train was leaving the station no matter what, John and Debra stood to make some good money, and of course, I was getting the chance to direct. That could've been that, but when John and Debra turned in their script, much to my dismay I hated it! A lot of time had gone by since the original, and in the meantime, a kind of arms race of gore had taken place in the slasher-movie world. As a result, "H2" on paper was pretty grisly, especially when compared to the original. I felt it was kind of betrayal of what made "Halloween" so good, where the scares and suspense were created mostly by getting inside the viewer's head -- not much blood and gore at all. It was a terrible predicament for me, because that gig was my big directing shot! A cardinal rule of making a successful movie is you've got to go out with a great team, and the head of that team needs to be a Director who is gung ho about the show, and wild about the script. It would've been unfair to John and Debra for me to pretend, so I had to pluck up my courage and withdraw from the project. I went off and did some writing assignments, including "Amityville: The Possession" for Dino DeLaurentiis. That worked out OK, and I was in the process of tackling a 2nd gig for Dino in New York (adapting "The 5th Horseman", a novel) when the phone rang and it was Debra, asking me if I'd be interested in directing "Halloween 3" which, she assured me, was going to be completely original, a fresh start, no knife, no Laurie, no Shape. It was doubly gratifying to be invited back into the fold, with old friends. That doesn't always happen in Hollywood, once you've said "no". I took a deep breath, this time I said "Yes", and we were on our way. As to "H3" being underrated: Thanks for the compliment, but these days I tell loyal "H3" fans to relax. Over time it's steadily risen in the eyes of the public, so that these days, it enjoys an awesome fan base, and continues to find new and enthusiastic support year in and year out. It is, after all, a film that's really about "Halloween" itself, its rituals, practices and history, so it does tend to pop up each October. It's been gratifying to see it find some measure of respect.

RA: How did you pick the location for Santa Mira?

TLW: We scouted northern California for Santa Mira. We'd had good luck on "The Fog", finding our ideal spot in and around Point Reyes, so we scouted there, and many points north, finally finding the hamlet of Lolita, a little ways south of Eureka. In much the same fashion as our experience on "The Fog", we just sort of rounded a corner and there it was, the eerie little town square, the factory, the motel, and so on. It's great when you have the scale right, several parts laid out in front of you so you can literally do action shots running through the entire place, and not have to piece things together, as is so often necessary. Picking the right location has a lot to do with the basic feel of a place; if it's got the right vibe, it makes the telling of the story a lot easier. Lolita was, and still is, a strange little place off to itself, on a hill a couple of miles from the ocean. It's lonely and a little odd, in some intangible way, and it set a great tone for the story.

RA: Tom Atkins is always the man! What's it like working with him? He was perfect as Dr. Challis by the way.

TLW: I agree. Tommy was just right as Dr. Challis, kind of a tortured soul in many ways, amoral, alcoholic, but heroic when the chips are down, just the right kind of character for the early 80s, when it was becoming evident that our country and our world were absurdly screwed up, we had a second-rate actor in the White House, and there was no reason to be very optimistic about the future. *Halloween 3* helped seal the deal on Tommy as a cult superhero — it makes me smile when I attend one of these weekend "Horrorthons" and see people walking around with a T-shirt that features his face, and "ATKINS" underneath. Isn't that great? Working with him was a treat. He was always well-prepared, always upbeat, reliable as hell, just what you'd hope for, especially for my first time out.

RA: What exactly was supposed to be happening during the commercial? Were their heads melting? Where did the bugs and snakes come from?

TLW: self-explanatory, really. You've got a mask with an embedded electronic chip, which is triggered by a stroboscopic signal from the television set. The chip ZAPS the victim, which releases the horrors of hell from within the victim's head -- bugs and spiders and snakes, destroying the victim and, presumably negatively affecting others within reach. Well, it was the mask doing the melting, but you could also imagine the heads melting as well. It was partially black magic, remember, so dark awful unexplainable things were going on, simultaneously, to a ton of kids out there.

RA: What do you suppose happened at the end? Did Challis save the day, or all we all screwed?

TLW: Well, the movie itself tells us he was partially successful in stopping at least some of the broadcast, so things couldn't have turned out as bad as they might've been. Cochran's fiendish plot, remember, was to make a sacrifice of innocent children -- not to destroy every child in the land, but simply to have a proper bloodletting, because "it's time again." So, it was a twisted "win-win", if you want to look at it that way. I imagine a massive tragedy occurred, with horrendous casualties nationwide, but the rest of the country, and the world, survived -- at least until next time.

RA: Conal Cochran is truly one of the greatest villains of all time and seems like a James Bond villain all the way. Talk a bit about the character, his creation, intentions and what it was like directing Dan in the role.

TLW: Conal Cochran was invented by the writer of the original screenplay for *Halloween 3* Nigel Kneale, who was commissioned by John and Debra before I came on board. Nigel, a legend in English sci-fi/horror circles, was an old favorite of John's. His screenplay was wonderfully inventive, a dark vision of an evil man with a vicious sense of humor. Its tone was a little too relentlessly dour and bitter, and its ending was far more downbeat than the one we eventually came up with. Nigel was pretty cranky about anyone messing with his stuff, yet virtually everyone involved agreed that the work needed punching up for an American audience primed for pop up scares, roller coaster action, and cranked-up suspense. Nigel refused to do this work, and finally removed his name from the credits. John did an anonymous rewrite, and then I did a rewrite as well, which accounts for the inaccurate credit. I would guess that about 60% of Nigel's work stayed in, including the essence of Cochran's villainy. Directing Dan in the part was, as you might expect, a pleasure and a privilege. Like Tom Atkins, Dan was a complete professional, always well prepared, always easy on set and ready to go. As a first-time director, I really had it good, with a cast and crew (mostly people I had worked side-by-side with on previous Carpenter shows) and producers who really gave support and let me do my job without interference. I couldn't have been luckier.

RA: *Fright Night Part II*: How did this one come about?

TLW: I was getting around town as a writer-for-hire, making a modest name for myself. I hooked up with a writer named Miguel Tejada-Flores, to co-write a screenplay, *Trapdoor* for a boutique studio, Vista Pictures where he worked as their development executive. *Trapdoor* came out OK, but didn't get made. Miguel then put my name in to write and direct the sequel to *Fright Night*, a "go" project at Vista. It was a great company, run by a couple of veterans, Herb Jaffe and Mort Engelberg, and peopled mostly by a bunch of young, energetic go-getters. The budget wasn't huge, but it was generous by my standards, with enough time and money to do the script well and thoroughly.

RA: What was Roddy McDowall like to work with?

TLW: Roddy was a champ, happy to be working, and not taking this gig for granted in any way. Like the other professionals, I've described in this interview, Roddy was always well-prepared, hard-working, taking his work seriously, never afraid to argue a point if he saw a better way to interpret a scene, but always respectful and good-humored. He was full of stories of course; he knew everyone in Hollywood, including the biggest stars from the 40s onward, and he enjoyed telling stories, without making a big deal out of it.

RA: Why did Amanda Bearse not return?

TLW: The decision not to put Amanda in the sequel came about before I was brought on board, ditto the decision not to bring back Stephen Geoffreys. As a screenwriter, I was grateful for the change. Both characters had made powerful impressions on the audience -- leaving them out of the ongoing narrative made it easier for us to forge a new story about a character who had supposedly moved past the Jerry Dandridge days. We weren't about to leave Peter Vincent behind, since Roddy had shown willingness to be in the sequel, but it was very helpful to have a little space and running room for some new characters, to help set our new story apart from the old one.

RA: What went into some of the amazing effects in the film?

TLW: *Fright Night Part 2* had a decent Special Effects budget, so we were able to carry on the standard set by Tom Holland in the original, especially as to creature effects and rubber. We used a small company, Fantasy 2, run by Gene and Leslie Warren, and staffed by Brett and Bart Mixon.

Sculptures, molds, models, miniatures, animation, live-action inserts and opticals were all done essentially under one roof. This was pre-CGI; everything in the movie was analog. I believe CGI is the perfect tool to make a good effect that much better, but sometimes not so good when you're working from scratch. The problem with animation, old or new, is weight. It's very, very hard to create the illusion of huge, living objects, a dragon, say, or a flying monster, actually having any real weight, whereas cruder, analog solutions, tend to be a little more believable than the slickest CGI. Perhaps part of the reason is that they're generally not perfect, and that, ironically, makes them a little more lifelike, in some mysterious way. In some cases, on "FN2" simpler turned out to be better. There's a brief scene in a stairwell where Regine confronts Peter Vincent, intimidates him, then WHOOSHES downward into darkness, presumably as a bat, or a wraith of some kind. We'll never know for sure, because in fact, the actual thing was merely a piece of black cloth I tore and tied until it was shaped like an avian body, a crow or raven, on the wing, in a dive. We put it on monofilament and reeled it into the shadows with a power winch. It looked splendid, precisely because you couldn't quite make out just what it was, but it ignited the imagination and created an impression more evil and scary than any designed creature could've been -- all with a dumb piece of cloth. Things like Regine burning up and Boz's belly getting slashed used time-honored tricks, traditional methods starting usually with a sculpture of one kind or another, molded and reproduced in latex, painted up and then manipulated, puppet-style, or mounted on an armature and animated. Burning Regine was an impossibly skinny body suit, worn by an impossibly skinny actor, with flames added optically later. Boz's belly was a sculpture of a midsection fixed to the floor. There was a hole underneath, giving Brian Thompson room to slip into place and more or less wear the thing, allowing the costume to bind the two elements together. The belly was loaded up with live wormy critters from underneath, pushed upward and ultimately outward through pre-cut slits.

RA: Merritt Buttrick unfortunately passed away shortly after this. What are your memories of working with him?

SLASHED DREAMS PART 2

TLW: Merritt Butrick's part wasn't a very big one, so we didn't spend a lot of time together. Nice guy, professional, one of those actors you think you'll probably get another chance to work with later on, on something of greater depth, but then you turn around and he's gone, one of many taken by the AIDS epidemic that raged during that time.

RA: What exactly were Belle and Louie supposed to be?

TLW: We were following the blueprint of the original *Fright Night*, which took all kinds of liberties with the old vampire rules, kind of upping the ante on what vampires could do, what they could be, how they could survive, how they could be killed. I thought that was one of the most appealing features of the original -- it felt like they were making it up as they went along. We decided to uphold that tradition, and go it one better: Hence Regine, who followed the Jerry Dandridge pattern, a conventional vampire, more or less, but accompanied by her three-person posse, who were all over the map, breaking new ground, you might say. We felt comfortable working in that magical realm where it seems only natural that beasts of different stripes might well band together against a hostile world, to satisfy their darkest appetites. Belle seems pretty much your garden-variety vampire, but with very exotic features. He (or was it She?) had the usual taste for blood, as well as for roller-skating and for maintaining total androgyny. But still a vampire, pretty much. Boz is a ghoul of an indeterminate sort, almost completely normal, except for a surreal appetite for bugs and other creatures which magically inhabit his insides, rendering him, finally, something super-human. Then there's Louie, a funny sort of werewolf, give or take. It seemed logical to me that this somewhat decadent gang would find each other, regardless of the details of their differences. In the end, you either went along, suspended disbelief, or you didn't. I love this character. He embodies the philosophy of the first bully I ever encountered in grade school, who said, with a smile: "I like ya but I kill ya." Remember too, that we made a sequel to the most difficult of all sub-genres, a genuinely scary horror movie which might also be called a comedy, or at least a movie with a powerful undercurrent of humor. That affects everything. It's hard to pull off, a real balancing act, and you can count the times it's been achieved on one hand.

RA: Let's talk about *IT:* This one scarred me for years as a kid. It's an enormous project to take on and you pulled it off great! Talk about your involvement in the project.

TLW: My involvement with *It* came through the front door, as it were. The producers contacted my agent, I indicated interest, they sent over the two scripts (it was originally presented as a two-night miniseries on ABC) I read Night One, got very excited and said Yes immediately. I had not read the novel at this point, so the human story behind all the horror just hit me like a ton of bricks. I met with Larry Cohen a time or two in Los Angeles. I had virtually no problems at all with Night 1, in fact I found it nearly perfect, a brilliant piece of adaptation, basically ready to take out and start shooting. Night 2, on the other hand, deviated drastically from the book, to the point that I felt, in trying to simplify a very challenging 1000-page novel, Larry's script had gone off the rails, and would disappoint *It* fans, if I made no attempt to capture more of the book on film. Larry was resistant, ultimately refusing to come to Vancouver to help me try some of my ideas. In pre-production, on a tight schedule, and having no money for another writer, the rewrite task fell to the only person I knew who would work fast and work for free, namely me. It all worked out in the end. I'm very proud of both nights -- wouldn't have minded a little more time and money for a few of the special effects, but hey, the most important things were there, the entire cast was stupendous, especially the child/adult matchups, and, though the condensing of the book was a brutal process, leaving out gobs and gobs of cool and interesting stuff, I think we captured its essence in a meaningful and respectful way.

RA: The casting of Tim Curry as Pennywise was pure genius. He was very creepy in the role. What was he like on set in that character?

TLW: Tim was another true professional, always there, always prepared and ready to work. He was very quiet and self-contained on set, not a lot of small talk, stayed aloof without disappearing. You could engage him in conversation, and he would occasionally drop a wry little line or joke. Mostly it was evident that his favorite approach to working was keeping to himself, but in a friendly way.

RA: All of the kids were phenomenal in the movie and those were my favorite parts. What
are your memories of working with them?

TLW: My experience with the kids was a surprising one. Here were all these adult stars, gathering to be in the show, and I was a little intimidated, to be honest, not just by their stature, but by the sheer numbers of them in a given scene. I needn't have worried. They were all gracious and generous, working together and showing respect for me, making my job much easier than I imagined it would be on set. On the other hand, here were these kids, mostly unknowns, doing these star turns, arguing about the size of their trailers, killing a lot of time in petty, behind-the-scenes stuff -- and on set, things could so easily break into chaos, they were a handful. I lost my temper a few times, that's for sure. In truth, it wasn't as bad as all that, and the overall picture was pretty positive. They really were kids, after all, and they were mostly just being kids, and all that energy -- I think we did a good job of capturing that on film. The thing about kid actors in general, and these kids in particular: There are directors out there, especially back in the bad old days, who would do anything to a kid, tell em their dog just died to get them to cry or whatever. I had kids of my own, and knew that the best thing was just to treat them with respect, be honest with them, and tell them what the story needed them to do. Kids are natural actors; they love to pretend, and they know innately how to make stuff seem real. But put seven, or eight or ten of them on set at once, plus a classroom or cafeteria full of kid extras, and you've got a challenging day in front of you. One key to our success: Since the story was two-tiered, a kid story and a story of their adult counterparts, it seemed only right that the kid and adult actors should spend some time together, even though they don't appear in the same scenes. We arranged to have the adult actors fly in and hang with the kids for a couple days before we started shooting, and the results paid off handsomely. They worked out body language and personal tics (Stan tugging his ear, Bill's hand on the side of his face) and other specifics, but most of all they formed this intangible but significant bond, a mystic link, if you will, between their childhood selves, and the adults they became. Like you, I thought they were all, to a man (and woman) simply phenomenal, and truly the thing which made the movie special.

RA: Were there any other parts from the book you wanted to film, but couldn't due to time, etc?

TLW: You start by understanding that a true adaptation of this novel would have to be a mini-series stretching over many episodes. If I were to custom-build this project from the ground up, I'd insist on no less than six full hours, maybe eight. There's just so much material. And, although it would be an epic challenge, I think there must surely be some way of dealing with King's ultimate conflict of good vs. evil, played out in -- what was it, a sort of cosmic battle in inner/outer space with the great turtle, or whatever the hell that was all about? Gimme enough time and money, I'd love to tinker with that, tease it into a film sequence. There must be a way. The point is, we had two back-to-back MOWs in which to tell the story, so the best we could hope for was a sort of Reader's Digest high-point rendition, and I believe we accomplished that. Fans of the book will all have their favorite moments which didn't make the cut. Mine was the scene where this bully kept an old refrigerator in the woods, and these horrifying leech-like things flew out and ... well, it was complicated. And it wasn't even something happening to the main bully, Henry Bowers. So, cut, cut, cut.

RA: What are your thoughts on the upcoming remake?

TLW: What remake would that be? "They" have been talking about a remake since *It* aired in 1990. I'll believe it when I see it. Mind you, I really would love to see it, if they get it right, if they have enough time and money, if their writers and director have a clue, if they cast cleverly, especially "Pennywise", if they get extremely lucky, if they catch lightning in a bottle -- they should probably just call it "If".

RA: How do you view your films these days?

(Author's Note: The question was asked before filming was started on the remake)

TLW: There was a time when I didn't think much of my own films. After all, *Halloween 3* was perceived as a flop, *Fright Night 2* didn't really get a proper release -- in a way, "It" was my only certifiable success -- oh, I had plenty of other bright spots, *And the Sea Will Tell, Final Justice* and *El Diablo* to name a few not in the horror genre, but by and large, I felt an overall sense of failure until I started going to these weekend horror conventions. There I met fans of all stripes and all ages, who were so kind and full of praise for the work I have done. It means so much, and gives me a chance to take a closer look at my own stuff. Some of it's pretty damn good!

RA: Are you a fan of any current horror films in the last few decades?

TLW: Not many. Writers and directors have fallen into a lot of what I call "torture porn", like *Saw*. I respect the originality, but hate the end result. Then there seems to be terrible confusion about what "scary" is, and what it is not. Gore is not scary. Torture is not scary. Spectacular CGI is not scary. Making a scary movie involves, first and foremost, telling a good story. You set up an expectation, or a series of expectations, and then you toy with these expectations in clever and interesting ways. You employ simple tricks, ways of maintaining suspense, of ratcheting up nervousness, you drop in comic relief as a way of rebooting -- you use a whole raft of tricks playing on the audience's simple enjoyment of being made nervous and frightened. I am amazed and appalled at how infrequently the basics are being used today, replaced mostly by bombast, violence and gore. And explosions. We are living in the time of American empire, which means a time of perpetual world war, and the militarism and violence that goes with it, right down to our movies, our commercials, and our lives on the streets, awash in guns and police behavior reflective of a racist heritage we have not yet begun to face up to. Right now, the empty lameness of our action and horror movies are throwing all that back at us. How long can we ignore it? I would call "Insidious" a notable exception to the trend. I was sucked in and intrigued from the start. It delivered the goods, big-time. I haven't seen the sequels, but look forward to them. I was also impressed with *Cloverfield*. Not scared, for the most part, but fascinated. Well, the sequence in the dark subway tunnel did manage to scare me. Impressive. Rare. Can't comment on most of the recent batch. I'd like to be optimistic, but I don't expect the movies to grow up much until our culture, and our country, turns a significant corner. I'm hopeful, but not holding my breath.

RA: Do you have anything you would like to say to the fans out there?

TLW: To the fans, I say "thank you" from the bottom of my heart. I may not be done yet, thanks in no small part to the help and encouragement of my son Win. Together we're working on several new projects: Watch for *The Gate* and *Scaryland*, both in the horror vein, and a TV series, *Midnight Motel*, a tale of what happens to Los Angeles after "The Disaster". Stay tuned.

TONY MORAN
(HALLOWEEN)

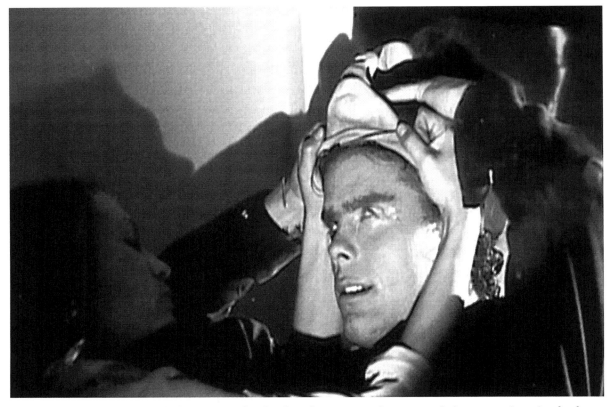

RA: Tony, you are one of the men who had a chance to play one of the most iconic slashers of all time in one of the biggest slasher films of all time. How did you get involved, working on *Halloween*?

TM: My agent called me in for an interview. I went in for the interview and I chatted with Irwin Yablans and John Carpenter for about ten minutes. It was at about 830 in the morning on a Friday and later that afternoon I found out I got the job.

RA: Wow, that's quick. It's usually not that quick of a turn around, is it?

TM: No, it really isn't usually.

RA: How much time did you get to spend on the set?

TM: Only one day, just for the unmasking sequence.

RA: How was that experience, getting to play that part? It's small, but very notable.

TM: It was great. Anytime you do an independent movie with a crew, usually, almost ninety eight percent of the time anyways, it's like one big family. It's people with common goals helping each other and having a good time.

RA: What was the experience working with Donald Pleasence like?

TM: He was a nice guy. He wasn't unfriendly, just after his scenes he would go to his trailer. He wasn't a snob or anything. He just seemed like a good guy. He was one of my favorite actors. He was a classic British actor.

RA: What was John Carpenter like to work for? I've heard he was pretty laid back and easy to work with.

TM: Down home, just a good guy in general. It was only his second film and he was easygoing and very easy to work with.

RA: How about Jamie Lee Curtis, what was it like to work with her?

TM: Party chick, she was pretty wild at the time. Really nice though. She has a great sense of humor. (I tell Tony she doesn't seem much like the party type) Oh yeah, she has changed a lot over the years.

RA: What are your thoughts on *Halloween* now, your role and the massive fanbase that is out there?

TM: Really, the only word I can use is blessed. I can't use lucky, fortunate or grateful. Actually, I could definitely use the word grateful. I think the most accurate word is blessed. It's unbelievable that this thing from 1978 can still be as strong as it's always been. It hasn't finished yet, either. It's like a speeding train that won't slow down.

RA: Do you have a final message on here that you would like to say to the fans out there?

TM: With all honesty, I would like to say thank you very, very much for making me basically who I am today. Without the fans, I'm nobody. My one dream is that one day I can meet every single fan of *Halloween* that there is in the world.

TRAY LOREN
(ROCKTOBER BLOOD)

RA: Tell me about what it was like growing up in the Sebastian household, with your parents in the movie business. How did you get started in that business with them?

TL: It was great. They were doing a lot of productions. They're independent producers and they did a lot of B-movies, that were done for Paramount mostly. I got to act in probably 90% of those. It was about '74 or '75 when I first started doing theatrical movies. It was a lot fun and a great experience. We did that as a family, doing those productions for Paramount. Then, I found this movie, AC/DC's *Let There Be There Rock* at a film festival and did a distribution deal with them and Warner Brothers. I worked with them for a few years on that. I was married to a woman for twenty-five years who hated the movie business, so I got out of it and I started doing commercial fishing. I had a Captain's license and a Pilot's license and I sort of semi-retired. Growing up in the business was a great experience and a lot of fun and I wish that I never got out of it. I just faded out because of the situation at home, but now I'm fading back in a little bit.

RA: That's great to hear. So, tell me about *Rocktober Blood*

TL: *Rocktober Blood* was a film that I did in the late seventies- early eighties. It was a little before it's time, I think. It was sold to a company called Vestron. A little while after they bought the film, they went out of business, so it never really got released. It was released for maybe three or four weeks I think, in a very limited release. After that, everything kind of got stuck. They owned the rights, then Lion's Gate bought them out and everything that they owned went to Lion's Gate. At that time, it just sat forever on the shelf. I got a call from a friend of mine about six months ago or so and he was looking on eBay and saw that one of the soundtracks sold for like $700. I said, "You've gotta be kidding me. I have a case of those things", so I found out that there was a whole cult of people that had been watching this movie. My son and I did some research and went on YouTube and found that there was like 700,000 views of the movie and it had a huge cult following. Anyways, I got into some of the distribution and production aspect of it for a re-release and it all worked out very well. Right now, I'm even working on a sequel to it. It's sort of had a rebirth lately, or maybe it could be considered a first birth, because it never really had a proper push when it was originally released.

RA: That's too bad that it took so long. It's a really great movie and it's got some amazing music to it, as well.

TL: Yeah, it's great that it's picking up notice. As far as horror and slasher films go, it really holds its own with everybody. Like I said, we're working on a second one and I'm working on a production deal now.

RA: Were your parents supportive of your part in it or did they try dissuading you from it?

TL: Well, everything I had to do, I had to read for. It would have been easier if it wasn't my parents, so I had to jump through all sorts of hoops and do all kinds of stuff. When this movie came about, Rocktober was a big thing back in LA. There was a station called KNP and Jim Ladd was the host of it. He did a movie that I did also, called *Captain Midnight*. He had a thing that he called Rocktober that came every October. So, I started thinking about this. I'm sort of the one who came up with the movie. I said we should do a movie called *Rocktober Blood*, and my mom kind of took off with it from there. I was always sort of going to be in this movie. With the rest of the movies, I had to find out if there was a part open and I had to read for it. With this particular movie, I was in it the whole way. I was in on the writing and everything.

RA: What went into your part of playing the lead, Billy?

TL: When it comes down to it, I only got to play the rockstar Billy only for a short while. It was pretty much just the opening scene where he was making the album. Everything after that was Billy's twin brother, who was the psychopathic killer, so it was pretty much getting to play a killer most of the time. I loved playing that and can't wait to play the second one. It was pretty much just one role, as much as it looks like it was two roles. I did very little of the actual good guy. It was a lot of fun. When you're playing something like that you can pretty much let loose and do what you want and be as crazy as he is.

RA: How did they go about doing the live show part at the end?

TL: We probably had about five hundred people there crammed into a sound stage, then we went ahead and did the live performance. We would do one shot and go through a whole song, then they would go in and do the close-ups. The crowd was just there for the duration. It would take about a day or two for each song, I think.

RA: So, was that Sorcery (the band) up there playing then?

TL: Yes, that was Sorcery up there with me.

RA: That's one of the things that always stood out to me about the film was the music. That was one of the best soundtracks I have ever heard and they were just an amazing band.

TL: Yeah, definitely. They were a great band. The singer, Nigel, was pretty fantastic. He was just really, really good. All the guys were. I still talk with Terry Morris all the time, who was the drummer. They were really nice to work with and really good guys. They're all doing good still today. In fact, when we do Part Two, they're going to be involved again. Basically, Billy is still out for revenge on the people that stole his songs and he's going to kill everybody in the band. So, all of those guys are going to get to do a scene of getting killed off.

RA: You know, I always wondered about that with the end scene, like if he died or what happened, because it was kind of open ended.

TL: Alright, well what's going to happen is that the last thing that he says is "I'm back!", while he's getting electrocuted. Then, it's going to go into the new movie and he's been in prison for the last thirty-two years. It's going to have him walking out of the prison gates, all tattooed up. It's going to be modern. Next, he'll be going on Facebook and starting a new band and getting together new members. Then, he's going to be getting a tour going across the country which culminates in Los Angeles, where he'll have something in store for all of the old band members that have been using his music. That's the quick version of what it's going to be like. People can always go to my website for the project and for the first film and check it out. We're always posting more news on it and fans can get a chance to pick up *Rocktober Blood* merchandise from there, like Blu-Rays, T-shirts, soundtracks and other things. The website is www.rocktoberblood2.com.

RA: I like it. So, have you already started shooting it?

TL: No, I just have the story together and I'm getting bands together. There's two or three groups that I'm looking at out there for the band members for the new band. There's going to be a whole new soundtrack for it and the music is going to be more updated for today's music.

RA: That is very cool. I was thinking that I honestly would have liked to see a prequel too. I mean, there's the whole thing how you supposedly killed over twenty-five people before the events of the first film, but you only get to see a few of them. I always thought that would make an interesting story.

TL: Well, you know what? Maybe we'll do that one next. (laughs). That would be an interesting story. I had never even thought about that.

RA: How do you view the legacy of it and it being an underground hit?

TL: It's not so much surprising to me as it is very flattering to me. After all of these years, that it's still managed to hold its own. It's pretty amazing that after that length of time, that people can pull out this movie that hasn't really aged that much and that it's still so popular right now. That's exciting to me. It's just a fun, fun movie.

RA: If you could have anything to say to the fans out there of *Rocktober Blood*, what would you say?

TL: Well, I want to thank you for supporting the movie for all these years. It's great that people are enjoying the movie. I've got like 3,000 fans on my Facebook page. It's just very flattering that people are still into it. So, because of the response from the fans, we're going to get that Part Two going and I can't wait.

INDEX OF SLASHER FILM REVIEWS: